THE CONCLAVE
OF
LIGHT BEINGS

The Affair of the Millennium

THE CONCLAVE OF
LIGHT BEINGS

The Affair of the Millennium

By
Ruth E. Norman & Vaughn Spaegel

UNARIUS ACADEMY OF SCIENCE
EL Cajon, California

The Conclave of Light Beings
The Affair of the Millennium
Copyright © 1973 - Reprinted 1999

Library of Congress Catalog-in-Publication Data

Norman, Ruth E., & Vaughn Spaegel
The Conclave of Light Beings
The Affair of the Millennium
ISBN 0-935097-35-X

1. The Higher Worlds of Spirit
2. Archangels - Light Beings
3. Reincarnation
4. Continuity of Consciousness

Title I

Library of Congress Catalog Number 94-61990

Printed in the United States of America

Ruth E. Norman - URIEL
Cosmic Visionary
Co-founder, Unarius Academy of Science

Vaughn Spaegel
Subchannel to Ioshanna

CONTENTS

Foreword

This is the true story of two, or more correctly, four Higher Beings or Super-Celestial God Forces who have, in the eons of time, now arrived at the state of complete unified oneness, after having successfully completed their countless thousands-of-years trek in service to the numerous earth planets, the two biocentrics never meeting or contacting each other in a physical way due to the vow they had pledged in this long ago past.

It was realized by the Super-Celestial Beings, the thirty-three hundred that came first from the Spiritual Planet Aries more than one million years ago, that the earth worlds were rapidly deteriorating. They knew something had to be done to save these countless millions of souls from total destruction, to save them from themselves! Thus the vast plan, the plan of a million years into the future, was so set in motion.

Countless and various were the manners and ways these great Beings set up, on this seemingly endless "worlds-saving" project, to help bring man back into a more proper relationship with his infinite nature and with the higher Spiritual Beings who serve the lower worlds in this great rescue mission. Their efforts have been continuous and never-ending throughout this entire million-year period of time -- a personal expression to aid mankind where e'er he may be found on these countless thousands, yes, millions of planets, physical and astral, as well as spiritual worlds.

One-half of the biocentric polarity unit would be residing on some one earth plane while the other functioned from the Inner, expressing their countless and various duties or services to help man in his evolutionary climb. In their compassion and dedication to spirit, they gave up, completely, during this lengthy duration, the pleasure of each other's companionship and extended themselves purely in their service to mankind.

Each one took on the embodiment of either a male or female and, at various times, expressed as an artist, a musician, an astronomer or scientist, or even as the ruler of some civilization such as Lemuria, Atlantis, Egypt, Greece, or Rome. The largest of civilizations and countries have been blessed by the Presence and leadership of either one or the other of these developed Spiritual Beings. To even begin to enumerate or relate of the vast accomplishments achieved, of the infinite number of planets and peoples so aided and saved, would be completely impossible.

We could, however, mention a few of the lives expressed by the masculine polarity in his missions on physical planes. He was the great Being Amon Ra in Lemuria, 165,000 years ago, and even before this, he was the greatly loved and admired ruler and leader of the ancient civilization of Yu, in China, 500,000 years past. So advanced was this great soul in his evolutionary climb that during this era the people actually worshipped him as a God, known as Yada. So great were his powers, even then, that he transcended entire populations through his spiritual teachings. You will remember him as Leonardo da Vinci, who lived but five hundred years ago. Then again, in this century, he became the giant of all times, the genius Nikola Tesla.

Still further on into the present, on the higher Spiritual Worlds, he is known by all advanced Super Beings as the great Serapis Bey, who appears as a great, scintillating golden Flame atop some lake of blue, there to give his mental lecture and then to disappear -- surely he is the most Advanced Being ever to grace any planet's floor, other than the Unarius Moderator Himself.

The feminine part of this biocentric polarity has expressed likewise in many ways and expressions. She too has served as the leader of various countries or civilizations, as in the long ago Lemuria. One point of expression known of by eartheans was her lifetime of Isis, head Priestess of the great temple of Isis, in Egypt, 10,000 B.C.

The Being, known in the present 20th Century as the Moderator, Ernest L. Norman, was at that time the great Osiris. At a later period, he became the first and greatest of all scientists -- the one Anaxagoras -- and she, at this time, again served as his wife, Nada. Later on, in Egypt, he became the magnificent one -- Akhenaton, Pharaoh of Egypt; she, Ioshanna was then his mother, Queen Tiy. Previously she had expressed as the one, Queen Hatshepsut, whose history as the great and only woman pharaoh is well known. Also well-known are her lives lived as Bathsheba; as Kadijah, wife of Mohammed; and again as the mother of Cleopatra. She was also with the great Zoroaster, Ernest Norman, in Persia about 750 B.C.

In Atlantis she ruled in several incarnations as King of Poseid. At another time, she was the wife of King Darius of Persia. Vaughn lived the life of Darius in that past civilization. Ioshanna served and functioned as the noted astronomer and mathematician, Johannes Kepler, as an artisan, a goldsmith, and as an opera singer. She has served as the ruler of Russia, Peter the Great, a position which benefited man greatly, as with all the others. She has served as a leader, as governor, yes, and even as a slave girl -- all of these experiences and expressions to learn of life and to pass on to man the spiritual powers and energies they each wielded.

Best known and of greatest service to the great Golden Age of Egypt, Ioshanna was then known as the Pharaoh Hatshepsut, who built many magnificent structures in Egypt. Also, her lifetime as the Queen Maria Theresa in Germany is well known because of her great wisdom expressed. She was the only woman in the history of Europe who has wielded such power and influence on the leaders, not for her own purposes or for self-interest, but to reform the institutions and provide the leaders with a higher understanding of their true purpose as the leaders of their nations.

It has previously been related that she was the beloved and betrothed of Jesus of Nazareth, their marriage being postponed due to the early conclusion of his mission and life. Almost 2000 years later, in 1956, they were married in California, U.S.A., when he, as Ernest L. Norman, was the Unarius Moderator. The times that these two highly spiritually developed Beings have come and gone on earth planes have been countless -- this earth plane being but one of many planes which they have visited and served, for a cycle or span of time, to give of themselves in this million-year trek.

Thus it is now, after all the coming and going, that the long worked-for conclusion to this great cycle of the millennium has been reached; cycles have swung and the great Golden Age is now in progress. The closing months of 1973 see the victorious bringing together of these two great Spiritual Beings -- the first meeting of the million-year endeavor. They have now properly polarized the many other worlds, preparing the people in their individual climbs.

Now it is the scientist-leader of great spiritual dimensions, Nikola Tesla, who comes to her in her closing years on the world of planet Earth. And just as Ioshanna used to come to him as the gray-tipped winged dove, radiating her love to him from the Spiritual Worlds when he was expressing as the one Tesla, he now comes to her psychically and in a third-dimensional way, with his love radiations, helping to make her stay thus more Light-filled. From time to time he inspires the subchannel to bring to her one beautiful red, red rose, always with a message -- words of love.

Although no word has been proclaimed, it is felt by these two that, at proper cycles in the very near future, wondrous happenings and phenomena shall occur. She, on the earth, rather expects that her Twin Ray shall descend from his heavenly abode, and like the silver knight on his steed, come flying to her in his great silver craft, along with his many space dwellers, to snatch away his beloved, taking her to their heavenly home among the stars!

We of the higher worlds are quite aware of how happy shall be the other Stars to have our own two brilliant Stars back home again -- the Great One, the Moderator, and his biune having already so ascended in time past. It has been surmised by even they too, that the very heavens shall reverberate in the cele- bration which shall exist on the countless planets -- those who have been aided during this century -- no, the million-year past endeavor!

But we shall not give too large a peek into our greatest love story ever lived. We shall permit you, the reader, to live with them through these wondrous pages of Light. And so, if you see in your semi-sleep state some great, golden spiraling galaxy within your mind, projecting golden rays of Love and Light to you, you can know that one or both of these Archangels have touched you, for now they can function as one. Or, when you see some beautiful whitened dove to which you feel attracted, know too, they are there. No, there is no place where they are not for these Beings are of the Infinite.

The Hierarchy of the Unarius Brotherhood

Preface

The first pages of this book were written by the Unarius Moderator on June 19, 1956, at which time he stated that it was a first chapter of a very important book for mankind. Now here, twenty years later, is received psychically, after being re-lived on the inner plane, the continuation and conclusion of this vast epic, an epic which has been carried on, yea, for five hundred thousand years!

Could the Moderator have known twenty years ago, as he attuned psychically, that he would not complete the book started – that he was, in essence, writing this first chapter for the great love story which Ioshanna would complete nineteen years later -- with the avid help of Vaughn? I'm sure this was all part of the great plan; without a doubt, he did know!

Throughout the pages of this book the epic unfolds. It was not written verbatim, from the beginning to the end, as is customary, but it was lived and conceived, then put together in a most unusual and unique way. Surely, there has never been a book written in this manner -- thousands of pieces of a jig-saw puzzle being fitted together. It was only after Vaughn and myself, Ioshanna, had begun to experience the inner realizations and revelations that the hours turned into days of living on the inner world; bits of the information would then infiltrate down into conscious mind where they would be jotted down or spoken into a tape recorder -- sometimes but one piece of information, maybe one sentence or a paragraph; then Vaughn would add his very informative visions. After we had a multiplicity of pieces and little bits of memory and realization, then came the chore of putting them together -- and what goes where.

Thus, it became an intense and exciting work of life. Interestingly, too, no one seemed to become tired, even after the hard pushing for fourteen to seventeen hours per day! There was so much power present that no one became sleepy or tired -- again proving principle!

We are aware that this book shall, in time, replace that of the Bible, for it does carry the very Light of Heaven, and the Truth unto man; it shall long be remembered through the eons of time. It can and shall be used in instances for healing many persons; they need but to tune into these celestial mansions described, and of which it was long ago foretold.

You too can walk, mentally, up the seven golden steps and take one of the seven golden keys, and pass ye through one of the seven golden gates into the golden, crystal temples wherein lies the wisdom of the ages. These are the ages of not only your civilization and time, but ages past -- back many hundreds of thousands of years, two, three, five hundred thousand years ago, and this too seems but as a yesteryear in the eye of the Infinite.

Yes, dear ones, ours is the Infinite way, and we would like it, also, to become your way. The gates to this great inner Temple are ever ajar. May the doorway to your mind, likewise, be ever opened to new truths, to new concepts of understanding that will bring full illumination. The Light of Heaven is truly shown within this book. Countless have been the years and many have been the spiritual persons who have striven to help bring it about.

As you read the truth of the Light, then you are lifted, and transcended and made whole. Be ever wise and walk this true pathway to the stars. If it were not so, I would not have told ye.

The Kingdom of Heaven is within, and the Father who ruleth the Kingdom is ever in attendance and watches over his fold. So it has been said, and so it shall be. The Kingdom of Heaven shall come into the hearts of man, and love shall abide where now no love exists.

He who seeth not shall see, and those who heareth not shall hear; the halt shall walk; those who have been unilluminated shall see the light of pure understanding, for the very Angels of Heaven hath, to thee, spoke.

Archangel Uriel

A Word from Ernest L. Norman

Triumph over time is the story of reincarnation. Throughout the countless ages of man's history upon the world, man has sought the answer to life, yet in the dread of death he sought ever ways and means to prove unto himself the continuity of life.

It is in this story that the author and his wife, living quietly as they do in the California hills, have found the answer, through clairvoyance, back through the pages of history. It was through these clairvoyant revelations that she was seen to be, formerly, one of the great queens of Egypt and he was her son, a Pharaoh, reigning as they did over Egypt more than 1000 years before Cleopatra's time.*

These revelations were further corroborated by outside clairvoyant sources, and were further verified by historical manifestations from the sacred writings, as they were written in the history books.

There are also a number of other persons who are reincarnated in this time and place, who have had an active part in the drama of this story. It is to the best of our knowledge and belief, that this story in its entirety is true. May it prove to be a message of life and its continuity to those who

* Ioshanna, herself, ruled the double kingdom – Egypt – at one time, as King (or Pharaoh Hatshepsut, the only woman ever to rule as Pharaoh).

xv

are fearful and know not of the divine purpose of the Infinite Creative Intelligence.

The material of this book proves conclusively the reality of life as a continuity lived both on the astral and celestial dimensions, as well as on material, third-dimensional worlds of the atomic form. Therefore the rich pageantry of the history of the Earth world contains an image or reflection of life as it is lived from the imprint of a fourth-dimensional design, the creative format engaged in by countless higher and more advanced intelligent individuals.

This is the story of the visitations of higher beings on Earth who, as wayshowers for humanity, have provided a treasure chest of knowledge about man's spiritual design.

Ernest L. Norman, Moderator
June 19, 1956

Ernest L. Norman - RAPHIEL
Scientist, Philosopher, Poet
Co-founder, Unarius Academy of Science

Triumph Over Time

It is midmorning in the ancient city of Ramasetison, the year 16,020 B.C. Ramasetison, the City of Eternal Light, rested quietly in the warm morning sunshine on the planes of ancient Atlantis. There was nothing present in the warm spring air which would denote anything unusual or which would forecast the coming events which would completely revolutionize the way of life to the many millions of dwellers in this great and wondrous city.

Looking about us as we are standing upon one of the many sloping hilltops which dot the landscape, we at first seem to be impressed or to feel that there is some strange familiarity as though we had been here before, or that perhaps we had seen cities somewhat similar to this particular panorama which is spread before us, yet there are many differences. We are immediately impressed first with a huge and beautiful tower which rises several miles to the north of us and situated as it is in the center of a large flat plane. The tower seems to rise into the very heavens and indeed it is that we find it is over 2000 feet high, and its base is wide enough to encompass a small city. Immediately to the rear of this great tower of gleaming white marble-like substance is another structure which bears some strange familiarity with the scenes of our modern times in Egypt. Here is situated a huge white four-sided pyramid which towers in a perfectly formed geometrical pattern to the height of about 600 feet and would surpass in beauty and size many of the structures of the more modern times. While these two buildings do, in themselves, portray a distinct and awed appearance to this vista, yet a closer scrutiny seems to also bear out many differences in the city which is immediately before us. We are aware of wide paved thoroughfares and many smaller bisecting streets which are the familiar patterns of everyday cities, yet there are no vehicles like the modern automobiles or the tramcars with which we are so familiar, save with one difference. Overhead and running at regular intervals are silently gliding, long monorail cars hanging suspended in their lamplight standards, which are curved at the top to support the rail.

We are also impressed with the fact that we can see moving sidewalks whereon the people seem to stand or to bring small collapsible seats and are thus transported from one place to another easily and without effort.

We see also that within every inch of available space which is not used for structures, there is an intense and profuse vegetable growth which surpasses anything we have seen in our modern times; yet all the vegetation seems to assume a particular brilliant hue, and it all seems to be very well cared for. The luxuriant growth of trees and shrubbery, plants and flowers, defy description; it could very easily be a horticulturist's paradise, yet it seems to fit and blend perfectly with the scene which we are seeing before us.

Surrounding the various blocks and on the elevations of sloping hills between this vegetation and profuse growth, we see the various homes or structures wherein the inhabitants of this great City of Ramasetison live. Here again there is a vague sense of familiarity; yet on a closer scrutiny the resemblance is strikingly apparent. Many of these dwellings are cubistic or square-shaped, others seem to be round or oval. Their exteriors are done in very brilliant pastel hues, such as pinks, corals, tans, yellows, blues, greens, orchids and golds. Here too is one striking difference. With hardly any exceptions there are no windows apparent in these exterior surfaces. There do not seem to be any roofs, but rather, the buildings come to an abrupt halt, without any apparent slopes or tiled surfaces.

Going into many of these buildings, as we shall later on, we shall see that they are all built in the same familiar pattern. The rooms are built either around a quadrangle or in a circle around a great central patio wherein is a beautiful dancing fountain of water which plays up and down in a thousand different kinds of streams which rise and fall in curtains of water of various patterns that seem to dance and play about the many and variegated forms of aqueous plants which are growing in various niches or receptacles placed in vantage points about this great fountain. The pool of beautiful clear blue water at the base of the fountain is literally populated with many thousands of birds and various types of rainbow-hued fish which resemble the ocean gardens in the tropics of our modern times.

Around this central patio is a veritable paradise of lush vegetation, beautiful and strange blooming plants and flowers whose scent makes the very air heady and warm with a luxurious perfume. Under a portico which surrounds the entire interior of the dwellings, we see open windows and doorways which lead into the various rooms of the building. The dwellers or owners in these buildings live in a sort of Utopian state and are surrounded with the easiest and best of the luxuries of life. True -- they are not the luxuries of our own machine or electronic age, but they are luxuries, nevertheless. Let us examine the way of life of a typical dweller in one of these beautiful homes, but first we must examine the populace.

There are three different races of people dwelling in this great city, as in all other cities of Atlantis. The original inhabitants, as they were found many countless thousands of years ago by the migrants from Lemuria, were a rather pale and insipid race of people with very white skins, albino complexions and hair, their eyes pale milky-white. They were dubbed, for want of a better name, the moon people. After many thousands of years, another migrant race appeared, after the original settlers from Lemuria. They were the dark ones who came from the East and were displaced by the Aryan race which had descended from Shamballa. These dark ones served in a capacity of gardeners or horticulturists, people who worked in a capacity on the outside of the dwellings or in various places of this city, while the albino, moon people were the interior servants and slipped silently like pale shadows from room to room doing the bidding of their golden-haired masters.

The rooms themselves are very large airy places which are designed primarily for comfort and relaxation rather than as a place to accumulate a lot of unnecessary accouterments, which do nothing for the peace of mind of the dweller. There are numerous lounges or places to stretch out, which are upholstered artistically in some strange type of synthetic fabric, over which are draped carefully tanned skins of beautiful wild animals which come from the surface of the earth. The floors are sometimes of a beautiful parquet hardwood, and sometimes with a mosaic style, covered with an assortment of soft wool rugs, or animal skins.

The bedrooms usually are associated with a sunken pool which is used in place of our modern bathtub. The owner of this house does not turn faucets when he wishes a bath; he speaks a certain word and the pool will fill silently with tepid water just the right temperature and delicately scented with his favorite perfume. After his morning ablution, the water will quietly melt away.

There are no kitchens in these homes, in the generally accepted sense of the word. Diet to the inhabitants consists mainly of a wonderful assortment of fruit and vegetables, which are grown mostly in their own gardens that surround the building, and they are usually consumed in their raw state, just as they are plucked from the tree or ground.

There are other strange devices with which the owner of such a dwelling can amuse himself; and while they are very electronic in nature, yet it has been many hundreds of years since these appurtenances were constructed, and the present owners at this time know little or nothing about them, save that by pressing a certain key or using a certain vocal intonation such apparatus can be brought into effect. The golden ones or the descendants of these Lemurians know, through history, that the original builders of this great city were electronic engineers and physicists of the highest nature, and their knowledge surpassed anything which our present-day scientists know about; yet little of this knowledge remains with the dwellers of Atlantis at this time.

Underneath this great city are great catacombs and chambers wherein there are huge machines which run silently and perpetually, night and day, unattended, save by robots. They generate the huge amounts of power which are necessary to furnish the nerve force which pulses and courses through this magnificent city. The sustaining force of these great machines is some strange atomic force which was conceived by those ancient-day scientists.

Yes, we might even say that in the present-day, in the year 6000 B.C., the golden race of people in Atlantis was a decadent race, and they were slowly passing from the face of the earth. However, this fact was well-known by the sinister dark ones whose black eyes darted constantly about, and yet whose minds kept the innermost secrets of their conniving mechanisms for that future day when they would take over this great city, and this great civilization.

Yet it is not so, that all of the golden ones remained untrained or unacquainted with the ways of their forefathers, for indeed, in the great tower, in the gardens, in the buildings about the tower, and in the great pyramid, reside many hundreds of men, and their families, who are the priests or the governing element of this vast city; and within the archives of these great buildings are the secrets of this past atomic age. Many of these priests are highly trained, almost as much as their forefathers; yet it is that the prophecies of those forefathers had so warned them that they had contrived to keep all these things secret, and the great massive steel doors remained closed to the dark ones. They could not gain access to either the temples or to the subterranean cavern.

Yes it was, that the secrets of Atlantis were well guarded at this time and at this place, yet there was a note of uneasiness, for had it not been that prophecies also contained mention of a great advent which was to have happened, perhaps even long before now, an advent which would mean the liberation and the restoration of all the old Atlantean glory, as it had faded and passed. This advent was the coming of the son of Ra! It was foretold that he, indeed, could resurrect in the great pyramid, through the flame of life, and that he could again give to the people that past glory.

Perhaps this was the topic of conversation with two men who stood on a parapet atop the tower as they were preparing their charts and scrolls for the midday advent of checking the great central sundial in the astrological calendar, which was the great disc of stone over the central dome above them.

Sharamute and Sharazar* stood and gazed out over the city; their eyes were filled with a faraway dreamy look. Perhaps they were thinking of past reincarnations and tuned to their akashic records and had seen some of these past days of glory long before the cataclysm when Lemuria, in all its splendor, sank beneath the Pacific in a roaring cataclysm.

Sharamute and Sharazar were inseparable as they were twins, born at the same time from the same womb, and their mother, Hatalock, was now accompanying them from the spirit dimensions. Slowly the words were spoken by Sharazar, "Yes, brother, it should have happened before now, and indeed, the people are wasted and weak, and we have great fear of the dark ones. Perhaps it is not too late, if it comes before we two shall see the end of flesh and the vision of the inner light."

* Sharazar later became, in the 21st Century, the Unarius Moderator Ernest L. Norman - Sharamute, his biune, was Erza.

"That it may well be," spoke Sharamute, "That all these things shall come to naught, for indeed, if we should see the secrets pass from us to the dark ones, our days would bear much misery and pain, yes, even death."

At that moment they broke their reverie to turn again to the great sundial which was approaching the parallax in the slot of the great calendar in the dome. In their right hand they posed their writing stick, which was a strange electronic device which could write some sort of a syllable or cypher in the hard metallic surface of the thin bronze plate which they were holding in their left hands, and clasped against their breast. These records and charts were thus always kept the same and filed away each day against the time and place wherein some future generation would have need of this knowledge.

As they watched the thin strip of light move slowly toward the small dot in the center, and as it passed to this point, the writing stick descended up the plate and there were a series of small white sparks, as they bit into the hard surface of the metal. No, Sharamute and Sharazar could not tell you how these instruments worked, for they had been handed down to them through the many thousands of years of the past, yet there has been nothing added or taken away from the way they left the strange cyphers upon the surface of the metal.

Their task completed, both stepped slowly into a small car which fitted snugly inside a tube directly in the center of this great tower. There was a slight hissing noise; the door closed, and the car dropped silently down through the hundreds of feet of many levels, until finally it rested upon the ground floor. Again the door opened and the two stepped forward. Slowly, their purple and yellow robes making a slight rustling sound, they moved down three steps from the car and moved along the great central corridor which let out into the courtyard and into the rear of the tower. Emerging into the bright sunlight, they parted, as each one found his respective pathway to his own quarters, where they would partake of the midday meal.

Yet, they were destined not to reach their doors at that particular moment, nor would it be for several hours that they would be again enabled to seek the sanctuary of their homes and loved ones. For suddenly the earth beneath them quivered with strange trembling, rumbling sounds, and momentarily the sun was blotted out as if a great hand had ripped away the sunshine from the earth. A jagged streak of lightning split the sky, and there was a deafening crash!

Sharamute and Sharazar paused, frozen in their tracks, their faces ashen with fear -- what was this strange thing that had happened? Almost immediately there were screams of fear from the various houses in the courtyard about them. People began rushing forth, women and children, all with the same terror depicted upon their faces. Outside the temple grounds and down into the city proper, the scene was being enacted with even more riotous proportions.

Suddenly the spell was broken and life again flowed into the frozen muscles of the two men. Turning, they picked up their long flowing robes and rushed madly for the interior of the great temple. This they did instinctively, not knowing what else to do. Arriving back near the platform of the car, all seemed serene and quiet as before. No, nothing was amiss here. Turning, they raced back down the corridor avoiding and dodging the various people who had likewise seemed inclined, in some unreasonable panic, to seek the inner recesses of the great tower. Going back up the central corridor and out into the main thoroughfare through the quarters, they covered the intervening distance to the great pyramid in breathless gasps of haste. Speaking the secret and sacred word, the great portal door swung swiftly open. Going inside they seemed to be momentarily transported into the coolness and quietness of the days before this great fear had assailed them. They stood there, looking foolishly at each other, wondering what this panic was all about. Going over to a nearby bench they sat down quietly to rest a moment to gather their scattered wits, and to discuss this strange phenomenon which had just happened. Yet they were not to remain alone for long.

Stretched out before them for many hundreds of feet was the great flat tiled surface of this interior room of the great pyramid. From the walls the interior was dimly lit by strange torches which hung at regular intervals from the walls. There were no flames in these torches, but each one gave forth its own ghostly light from a round crystal, ball-shaped dome from the top of the stem. Hanging down from the center of this great room was a huge chandelier of literally thousands of these tiny, wonderfully self-illuminated, faintly glowing or luminous balls. The floor itself was flat, save for a great triangular-shaped block of red granite, which measured thirty feet each way, and was raised just one foot above the surrounding floor. Up near the far end of this great room was a huge altar, and back against the end of this altar was the depiction of Ra, the Sun God, done in many gleaming and luminous painted bands of some strange glowing metal around a circumference of some ten feet in diameter of the purest glowing crystal.

As Sharamute and Sharazar began breathing more easily in the restful quiet of this great sanctuary, there began a procession of the various priests, entering into the temple in this great room, for indeed, was not this an occasion wherein Ra must be reminded of the safety and comfort of his people, and did they not indeed demand an explanation for this strange happening which had interrupted the serenity of their lives!

As the many hundreds of priests and other people filed within the great room, so that all seats around the walls were soon occupied and many persons were still left to stand, the great door slid silently shut. For a moment all was quiet. Slowly, there began a certain rhythmic chant as the great Mantrum began to be sung by these hundreds of voices. Hardly had it begun, however, when it stopped; the faint luminous glow cast by the multitude of small globes was suddenly eclipsed by a bright, blinding luminosity which filled the entire room. Slowly this light began to fade and, as the many hundreds of eyes became more accustomed to its softened tones, they saw that there had been a strange miraculous phenomenon happen. Standing squarely in the center of the raised red granite dais in the center of the room stood the luminous figure of a man! As the many eyes focused upon him, they could see that he was of noble means and that his countenance was serene and untroubled by the many curious gazes which were focused upon him.

His robes were of the softest white color. His eyes were large and luminous. His hair, a dark reddish brown color, cascaded in beautiful waves about his shoulders. A closely kept pointed beard upon his chin and just the mere outline of his mustache proclaimed him to be attired in the ways and the times of the day -- yet strangely enough, he did not seem to be like any of them in this room; for indeed, he was not.

As the silence intensified, all waited for him to speak. None dared to ask, not even Sharamute and Sharazar who were standing closely to the head counselor or priest, for indeed his face was whitened or ashened with fear and superstition, much more so than any of the others. When, as the room seemed to reverberate with sound, yet the voice was soft, mellow, and well-spoken. The lips moved, and he uttered this simple statement, "I am Amon Ra, Son of God."

The Conclave of Light Beings

The following verse was inspired from the Moderator, Ernest L. Norman to Ioshanna during the time of the Conclave of Light, March 23, 1973 when she was being honored, while she was in the spiritual dimensions undergoing her most high initiation due to the successful mission of Unarius.

Go ye forth unto the four corners
   of the world
And speak ye the Truth
   as it hath been told to ye.

Let no man thirsteth for this
   knowledge who asketh
For it may be the one so refused
   couldst well be the one who hath
   to thee taught in eons ago.

Let no man hunger for Light
   that ye may shed unto him
Lest it be that he may,
   in some future time
The Light Bearer be.

Thou hast learned well,
   that which thou seekest.
Let no man be deprived of that
   which he seekest
Which ye may share with him.

Guardeth ye well, that which
   ye hath attained,
That the thieves in the night,
   stealeth not thy wealth of wisdom
For the wolves cryeth loudly
   and their teeth - long and sharp
Would render the flesh
   from thy very bones.

Thy Brother hath prepareth ye well,
   dear sister.
Be wise and careth ye always
   of that which hath been
   placed in thy care.

For many there shall be, in the future,
   with great offers of gold
Wouldst thou their coffers fill.

For there is no thing to which man
   wouldst not stoop
In his worldly worship of gold -
   in his lust for power and dominion!

Fear not, and tread lightly -
   even the fiercest of winds
   passeth on.
Thou hast chosen well thy way
   and the lessons thou hast learned.
Chooseth ye wisely, thy friends
   but calleth all men friend.

Be it so!

Chapter 1

A word from the Higher Ones: Thus it is that these two God Forces, either one of which has been in the past worshipped as God himself, are now in this great once-in-a-millennium affair being so honored. The meeting and the joining of, yes, the marriage of these two advanced God Forces has, as was taught, formed a unified duality called a biocentric or a polarity. It was these two, amongst others, who, in that long-ago, five hundred thousand years, so set this vast plan in motion; also at this particular time bringing into action the great and cumulative efforts of these countless thousands of Beings, whose efforts have been carried on for eons in the past.

Thus, in this present pinnacle of our expression, in our relating to you information regarding these activities, we have removed all stops or limitation; we have gone to all possible efforts and extents to create for this unified duality of God expression, a rightly earned honor and acclaim.

It can be said of these two God Forces, Uriel and Michiel, that they have not spent any life together on the earth plane, but that either one or the other was in the spiritual planes during the time the other has been upon some physical, third-dimensional earth world, endeavoring to help lift the consciousness of that particular world. Thus it is, that at this time of the celebration, there is much more than has been related, for this celebration will carry on for the entire year, in our projection program, to pay honor to these two who have worked through the many eons to arrive at this point, the last position on the Logoi expression, and they will now occupy the position of Archangel, of which there are but four in this entire Spiritual Unarius Brotherhood.

The biune polarity of Ioshanna, as you know, is Michiel (the other two, the Moderator and Orda, or Raphiel and Muriel). Thus when Ioshanna, now existing (in part) on the earth plane, completes her great and important mission on earth, she shall need not return to these third-dimensional earth planets. The plan, which she herself helped set up in these many eons ago, is now a realization of completion – thus, the celebration.

We of the Hierarchy feel there are no limits to which we could go to emphasize the praise these two Beings so rightfully deserve. Thus, when she has completed her little span upon earth, they shall, for the first time in the history of their countless thousands of years of expression, be wholly together in this unified expression and will need go out no more. They shall continue to serve in the spiritual worlds as they so choose and reign as the Supreme Rulers of the entire Unarius system, formerly called Shamballa.

Little wonder that our sister was so overwhelmed, as she experienced in 1964, in her great revelation, much of that which is taking place here on these inner dimensions, and that she returned to earth consciousness and described that which

4

she had remembered of this great and wondrous crystal plateau – the beautiful clouds of energy creation that billowed and collected in the areas above with which she had become so familiar on these inner worlds of Light. It remained in her consciousness so vividly that she wrote to many friends there in the earth world that she was going to lead the way to build this great City of Light on the earth; she felt it was in that immediate future. Still she was not so wrong, for thus it shall be, and all shall be made manifest.

All that which was expressed in the great cycles of the past, in your so seemingly luxuriant time of the great Renaissance when you experienced, such an abundance of art, of sculpture, of dance – all these expressions of former times, which you have termed some pinnacle of spiritual expression, shall truly be dwarfed in the future to be known as the New Age of Spiritual Renaissance! For the plan has been well made and shall be well kept. We share your joy that we are thus able to bring to people of the earth worlds the true Light whereby you too can lift yourself up from out this negative maelstrom into which you have become so deeply mired.

The long-awaited millennium is at hand! Everywhere about you are the signs of the quickening of Spirit, the Light that shall henceforth be directed and shone into your world.

Accept this, then, earth people, with open arms, with greetings of joy and thanksgiving. For were this not so, before many years would have expired, your little earth and many others about it would have become but a shambles, and naught sufficient would remain to pick up the scraps, as it were, so far has man reverted in his downfall from what otherwise should have become his progressive climb into great spiritual awareness.

Dear ones, share with us the love and honor, the unified homage which we are paying to Uriel, a God Force, who is being joined with her polarity, Michiel, her biocentric, here on the celestial dimension during this never-to-be-compared celebration! Although the feminine unit or part of this biocentric unification still exists on the earth plane, they can even now function as one, for it has not been previously known by the one who lived upon the earth, of the other. Thus now, the relationship of the oscillation of the two, which are in essence one, can actually function as one unit in the present.

Heretofore, Ioshanna has been merely satisfied to have in her consciousness a glimpse or a contact of what she has termed the golden galaxy. Yet now, the relationship and oscillation, between the two parts of this unified concept we have termed biune, or biocentric, can more correctly and totally function as one unit, as one great generating and projection system, disbursing their Light upon your world.

Treat not lightly this great blessing you have in your midst, for it is your pipeline from Heaven, your very extension from that which you have called Paradise Itself – that which you call Heaven or Paradise, or any one of the many names that have remained within your minds as some myth. We assure you, dear children, it is anything but a myth; we here work with and draw from the great God Power – the source of all – that which you call the Central Fountainhead, for ours is a service based upon Love – a Love which the earth man has not yet tasted.

Rise up from your knees, those who feel they must so worship. Know that you, each and every one, have within you the spark, that which you call the Father Within, and you need but to look within. For we of the Inner and higher worlds, who know of these things and are so endeavoring to bring all these treasures to the unilluminated mind. We ask only your acceptance and cooperation, for that which you have so long awaited, that which you term your millennium is at hand!

Earth people, rejoice with us! An even greater concept than is this biocentric polarity, which has been achieved, is also the quadrocentric situation that now exists! – thus, a double cause for this great celebration.

Now that she, Ioshanna, has made her great step up, this situation is the very first of such dual polarities that have ever been developed. It is an all-time first! Thus, we do indeed have double cause for our full year of celebration. And even of greater importance is that we celebrate the successful deliverance by the Unarius Moderator of the entire Unarius Library - an attempt which has been made but stifled many times in epochs of the past. Now, here in the present, the destructive forces were outsmarted and overcome. Had it not been that Ioshanna had won her six-week battle against the negative forces, the earth world would not now be experiencing its new Golden Age! But successful she was, and glad that we are; our praise and appreciation does run high!

Chapter 2

Throughout the many years during which time the Unariun Moderator was voicing the Unariun texts and bringing the Mission to the earth world, I would often see the Illumined Brothers in consciousness. In the first formative years, they would appear as tiny sparks of golden Light. These would appear into consciousness quite often. Then as time rolled by, and as I gained awareness or a step-up in frequency, these Beings would appear as larger Lights – sometimes the size of a tennis ball. Then in later years, and while he was still in the physical, this luminosity that I knew to be he, appeared on certain occasions as a great golden Light. It would usually come into my focus just before I would go to sleep, and there this great Light, seemingly a galaxy whirling and spinning off golden and yellow radiations, would oscillate into my consciousness for several moments and, from its outermost rim, would shoot out from its very self, bright, starlight configurations! The best possible description of these offshoots would be similar to that which the children use on the Fourth of July – the sparklers, but far larger in size.

This great oscillating Light that would come to me was most beautiful to behold. I was always most joyous when I would see it hover, then disappear, again to reappear in another direction.

Always, it seemed, after such a visitation, some-thing important would take place very quickly. It was as if this energy or power was being built up for whatever it was that was to happen later. I often would lie to look, wait, and wonder if I were going to experience this visitation on the various evenings. This was always a unique and rare occasion.

"There were many such visitations, but they were very widely spaced. I would usually relate it to the Moderator the next day, and he was always happy to hear that we had made the inner contact, that I was able to view his true Spiritual Self in the way in which he truly exists. Thus it has been through the years that he, in his Spiritual Self, has visited me on the Inner, and I have come to know him more as a Spiritual Being due, too, to the great work which he was doing, rather than to place importance on the physical man which was visible.

This visitation has continued during the last two years, ever since he left the physical. Then on one occasion, March 22, 1973, came into my vision an entirely different configuration! This visitor, al-though very brilliant and very large, seemed to be like a very large V-shape – almost like two comets meeting together – very difficult to describe. The coloration there was the yellow-gold, the same as was the Moderator's Spiritual Self. I wondered about this seemingly different Being. Then I real-ized that the Moderator had told me, before he left his physical body, that he felt he would, due to his Mission which he had brought on earth, move on to another galaxy in another part of the Spiritual Worlds. He felt as though this was something he had earned, and I am sure it is true.

Thus another great Being came on the evening of the 22nd of March, 12:00 a.m., and I wondered about it. He seemed to dart right down much more quickly, not pausing in the ceiling over my bed as before. This being just came right down close to me, and the next moment I went out with him, and knew no more!

Then again on March 25th it happened – the appearance of the great golden bird. Of course this was just the way my consciousness saw it – two great curved arms of electrical energy meeting at one point. This looked similar to the way a comet would appear, but the two were joined. It is absolutely impossible to adequately describe, but I feel at least to try. However, there, I felt, was a new spiritual contact and Brother – and which later was found to be so.

Vaughn has recently developed the ability to "see" inwardly (he has been giving akashic readings). Lately, if I ask some question, he is able to "tune in" and receive the answer! His new ability has been of great help and service.

This next morning, when I so related about my seemingly different Visitor who literally "took me out," he asked: Where did you go last night? My reply was, "Why don't you look within and see? Perhaps you can tell me!"

This truly set some things in motion and really

11

started things popping! From that moment on all Heaven broke loose, and there has been so much power here, such interest, excitement, joy and love! There has been a great Conclave of Light Beings on the inner worlds, and I was taken there as honored guest! Little by little, and bit by bit, did it infiltrate down into my conscious mind, along with the added help from Vaughn, who would describe the scenes.

Doubtless, if I had been instantly aware of the entire situation, it would have been much too much to conceive, and possibly a very dangerous situation. But the all-wise Infinite permitted me to become aware of this great infinite happening, little by little. Vaughn and I have had ten days of truly "living in the spirit," so great has been the power, transcendencies and inspiration!

Effort was made to jot down some of these realizations which came into my consciousness – a memory or a flash, sometimes with a tear. Vaughn would also add what he saw of the great Conclave. He related that this was a great Spiritual celebration. He said, "Mainly it is in your honor, Ioshanna, as you are receiving a very high degree – great honors are being bestowed on you due to the great work which the Moderator and you have completed." However, it was much, much more, as we learned later.

At first I felt it to be a mastership degree being bestowed. Then, later, it was shown that the initiation was of a far greater advancement than Mastership, even of the highest level, for this work to be expressed on earth is just the most stupendous of all time. More power than ever is to be projected!

Now the main purpose for this great gathering, this great conclave in the Higher Spiritual Dimensions which began to take place this very night. is, we understand, especially for a specific energy projection program in which these hundreds of thousands of Spiritual Beings are taking part; each one of whom could be called a Master, Archangel, Logos, etc. These people have all been formulating instrumentation of an electronic nature, created from the mind energies, to be used in projection for healing and help to the earth worlds, including the spiritual worlds.

This earth-shaking information is of such a magnitude that it will bear repeating in various ways before one could possibly conceive even a small measure of the vastness, of the importance, of the tremendous force fields and energies that were created and set in motion at this Conclave this very evening, and is still going on!

First, we learned there were more than a hundred thousand persons taking part, and that the work had been going on more than one hundred thousand years in preparation! It was known by these great, wise, and learned ones; for they could foresee, in that long ago, what the earth people would do with their planet. In order to save many of these earth and astral worlds from total destruction, something must be done to change the off-balance. This is what all the talk about the New

Age is. It is not simply that man will eventually change, for something has to happen to cause him to change.

Dear ones, we do have the complete, beautiful and most glorious truth and realization of it all. This information will give you, each and every one, a new sense of peace and new hope! The only and great difficulty is, and will be, in finding words to even attempt to define or describe these things to you. Still this cannot be done by a simple reading or thinking about it, but, as you do ponder these things, you will be attuned to we and those in these higher dimensions, and into all these energy configurations and projections that have been set into motion. You will be so attuned to them that your consciousness will expand. You will begin to change, as have these three dear people working with me – Helen, Dotty and Vaughn.

I might say that Vaughn, this very afternoon, has been so taken up, so practically "knocked out" with the powers that he is scarcely able to walk across the room, and it is so wonderful, for there was much healing work necessary to be done. Dotty, too, almost every time I look at her, will tear or jump with the shock of the waves that now come through! Helen had some very beautiful experiences and transcendencies, and a little shedding of her psychic negations. It has been a most wonderful week and, I am sure, a more productive one indeed for me than I have ever encountered in my entire evolution!

It was five hundred thousand years ago that I

came with eleven advanced Masters from the planet Lemuria to Earth, in a dematerialized state, to seed the earth. However, we are getting ahead of the story.

There are various electronics that were created by the very mind energies of these great Spiritual Beings, which we shall endeavor to describe and relate to you. The very first thing that I became aware of was a few nights previous to this date when the great Crystal Lens was impressed in my consciousness; it appeared as though I were actually viewing a great glistening glass construction; it appeared enormous. I couldn't estimate the size, for it more than filled the room.

This Crystal Lens, I knew inwardly, would be used for great healing purposes. All my life I had been rather aware of crystal configurations; they had always meant much to me. Now it is all plain to see why.

The design of this great Crystal Lens was made in diamond shapes, and the light it emitted was tremendous. The singular diamond shapes were about two feet in diameter, and there were countless thousands of these shapes, all formed in one great configuration and emitting beautiful diamond-like shafts of Light!

Every time I would think upon this Lens, it would seem larger in size! This kept building and building within me. As I relayed it to Vaughn, he said, "Do you know, it is actually an asteroid, practically as large as a planet!" So it is a tremendous, tremendous thing! Countless thousands of

Spiritual Beings have worked and built this with their mind energies, over many thousands of years. Using their psychokinetic energies, they have created this Lens, for this particular purpose and need for the earth worlds! They do not wish, in fact, they will not permit these earth worlds to be destroyed. This, now, is going to be their one great purpose, mission and objective – to save man from himself. And this is what it amounts to!

Upon my first viewing of this Lens, and it seemed to maintain its position in my consciousness for several minutes, I contemplated it and tried to estimate just how big it was. Each time I would place consciousness upon it, the size would seem to expand! And such was the way it was, for it is actually a dimension! As I would discuss this with Vaughn, he was amazed and as confounded as was I; he went right along with me in these realizations, adding his words of concept as well as his viewing and transcendencies. It was a tremendous experience for both of us.

Between the two of us, we learned and relearned that the very mental and psychic structures of each Being involved in the building of the Crystal Lens had been impinged within its construction; the very consciousness of each individual had been impregnated in the crystal of the huge lens structure!

So it is that this scientific, integrated, and harmonious creation can generate and regenerate the great power of energy from the Infinite Minds. Yes, it is the development of these hundreds of thousands of Higher Beings who have arrived at this higher junction of Consciousness throughout the period of five hundred thousand years time, that has gone into this magnificent, scientific creation, an infinite creation!

This crystal Lens has a dimension of its own and can be directed to any solar system, to any terrestrial or astral planet. The lens is, in essence, a gigantic computer, and it automatically calculates the specific frequency necessary to treat the individual desirous of healing. The lens is seen as a spheroid. It is made of the mind energies of the countless participants who so created it. Vaughn relates, "When the Consciousness of Ioshanna is brought into focus, the energies are then projected from the Lens, then demodulated through the electronic wand, (which is an adjutant to the Lens) into lower frequencies more compatible to the psychic anatomy of the earth person to be healed!"

Never before in the history of the worlds has such a gigantic projection of psychokinetic energies been attempted by the consolidated minds, the accumulated minds of thousands of Advanced Intellects residing in the causal worlds. Never has such a gigantic undertaking ever been attempted! It is a super-colossal endeavor, but as they inferred, the need at this time is so great, so dangerously close to oblivion have the earth worlds come in their degenerative state. Other worlds and dimensions are likewise affected in this negative degeneration, hence, the great plan for this Spiritual

Renaissance, the Golden Age, was initiated, to put into effect this great energy projection program. It was started, as was said, in these countless thousands of years ago with the knowledge that in the sixth cycle of the Recessional, there would be a great need for a spiritual rebirth of all earth worlds and astral worlds as well.

They tell us that Love will be known in the hearts of man where before it was a stranger! Disease will be unknown! This will be the first time in the history of this earth, and all other earth planes, that such a Light has shone as the representation of this Higher Consciousness now being formulated – this great Light – the apex of the Lens. The Light, when called to action, bursts from the apex of the great crystal Lens from which the powers of the inner planes of Unarius shine and are projected. From the wand are projected and channeled the energies through the inner consciousness of the present Unariun Channel, Ioshanna.

A very important factor was shown in my inner vision, just a day or two after I first started to view the great crystal Lens. When it was first brought into my consciousness, this great, magnificent crystal Lens was formed of various diamond-shaped crystals. Two days following, the Lens was projected into my consciousness a second day, to make sure I got a good look at it. More correctly, I was out there taking a good look at it! That is more likely the fact.

The second day as I lay down to sleep, the

room was filled with the most exquisite blue-green color, almost a fog. That is the nearest appearance I could describe. It was of scintillating, oscillating energies in their very, very highest form. It seemed as though it was a great cushion, yet it appeared everywhere I could see. No matter where I looked, I was confronted with this tremendous and almost shocking elegant color of blue-green. It was beautiful to behold! There is no earth color that could begin to compare.

Then, a few days later as I was thinking upon this color, it came into consciousness that this was an accumulation of particular frequencies that had been accumulated for the earth's purpose; that was all projected down upon the surface of the Earth itself to serve sort of a positive pole or polarity for the other numerous frequencies which would, in time, likewise be projected. In other words, they would sort of serve as a magnet. The more I thought upon this, the more I realized, "Well, yes, that would be very logical!"

Now, in contemplation, I rather view the entire globe, and many surrounding globes, all covered with this magnificent blue-green energy field – the force field that has actually been projected down to cover this entire area, which will be using other frequencies to follow.

Vaughn: "It just came to me that this force field is the means by which a neutralization was made of the negative force fields which surround this area, and which have accumulated for the many thousands of years – the force fields being the amassment of the negative thoughts of the people."

Ioshanna: "And yes, if man could actually see the great layer of crud, of psychic force – viruses that surround the earth – he would be very fearful, because it is a terrible, negative amassment in which the world is engulfed. This great blue-green energy field is to polarize and help change the great negation that exists throughout planet Earth. In other words, we have already started in our war against the destructive forces!"

Chapter 3

It was upon this very first morning after my visitation in the Spiritual Worlds that Vaughn questioned and remarked thusly:"My, you seem so different this morning. You seem so much more ethereal and I can't get over how complete-ly different you are! You seem as though you lack any physical consciousness at all!"

Individually, the scenes began to flash with-in, and the more he talked, the more visions came into each of our consciousness. With me, it was a factual reliving!

As we discussed this great plateau which was on the Spiritual Planet Eros, on the seventh plane − the great scientific city and plane − other views would come into Vaughn's con-sciousness, and he would see. First in his view came a great and wonderful scene − an inner chamber of a glorious temple − and as he continued to look upon it, it built up and he was able to see more and greater details. It seemed, as he started the description, the en-tire situation opened up within me and I sud-denly became aware of the whole procedure, the entire conclave, which I was psychically attending. But not all the details of the build-ing, inside and out, were at once made apparent; this had to build slowly in conscious mind.

As the area to this great enclosure was ap-proached in astral flight, the huge temple ap-peared to be conical in shape. The outside of the top portion or dome seemed almost transparent, yet the top of the dome was covered in gold. Gold, it is known, contains properties peculiar to it alone, which are invaluable in healing work. One could almost see through it as it was of the crystaline appearance that was reflecting, radiating and streaming out a brilliant light in all directions. The light appeared as diamonds! Atop the topmost part of the dome were thirty-three large, white, strong searchlight beams, the purpose being for healing influences in the lower dimensions. The light was reflected from so many facets, it was like watching thousands of brilliant stars at night as they reflect the soft light of the moon.

Attention was attracted to the surrounding, beautifully sculptured, formal gardens. Centermost in this surrounding area in front of the great temple, is a large, oblong reflection pool, crystaline in appearance, upon whose surface floated many white and rose-tinted lotus blossoms, two feet in diameter, large enough to serve as a lovely boat amongst which swam many beauteous and graceful swans; each wore a wreath of flowers about its neck. They, too, somehow seemed expectant of something unusual, what with all the glitter and commotion about. The pool was so crystal clear, even the coloring in the energy force fields above were reflected — most exquisite. Plants, flowers and shrubs surrounding this delightful setting were all grown with love and psychokinetical energies. The foliage was in countless shades of green, many new shades beheld; all formed and created of the crystaline substance from which all things in this Higher World are formed.

It now is observed these so-called reflection pools were, in actuality, large crystal lakes. The entire surrounding area of the great building consisted of vast gardens. One could easily spend an entire day walking about any one of the lakes. They were of a clarity never before viewed, and shimmered in the reflection of all the light about them. And today, 'tis the Springtime, and the beautiful trees are all blossomed and gay, and yet we here need not await for a Spring season for trees to flower — for ours is an eternal Spring!

With the first psychic viewing, in the approach to the grounds surrounding the large temple area, the large oblong-shaped, crystal-clear pool was seen in the formal gardens. Upon closer scanning, it is now evident that there was not only one of these great areas of beauty, but rather they completely surrounded the entire temple periodically, and which (the temple), in itself, was thirty three thousand feet in circumference and seven thousand feet high. These same reflection pools — more correctly, crystal lakes — were repeated seven times seven about the great temple. One was oval, one square, one round, one triangular in shape, and so on, each surrounded with different trees, various shrubs and glorious, scintillating flowers.

Even the giant redwoods were represented as were the eucalyptus, in their countless varieties. These great gardens were a paradise not to be compared! There exists no flower on this spiritual planet that is not therein represented and expressed in the number seven or its multiple. One could spend many days drinking in the great beauty expressed here in the vast gardens – all formed from the crystaline structures, the mind forces of the Light Beings. One is soon made aware he is indeed in paradise!

The entire area, temple, etc., within and without, was one great amassment of transcending luminosity, uplifting even to the psychic view. But one gets lost in a maze in any attempt at proper descriptive adjectives to so define. We could add of the garden, of the tremendous Tree of Life: Upon this tree was every conceivable fruit that has ever existed. Yet, this is not the factual or the true Tree of Life, for the Tree of Life is obtained in understanding from the Book of Life, of its message.

Among the lovely trees were viewed many magnificently hued butterflies, all iridescent, the size of which was astounding, for the wingspread of the average exquisite creature was at least one and a half feet wide! They glowed as the light reflected upon the soft, textured wings, similar to that glow of the hummingbirds on earth when seen in the sunlight. The colorful birds also observed, were beautiful beyond description and seemed to actually dip into the area of the temple occasionally, as if to add their measure of love. Many of these species have never been seen on earth. There were none of the drab brown or gray birds, each winged creature was a magnificent, colorful, radiant creation — an example of the advanced way of life and living in these beautiful, higher spiritual worlds. And each living thing, all expressed this same crystaline radiance — beauty beyond compare. They emitted their intelligence unto all other living things. Yes, they too, were emitting their projections to add to all others. Everything on this great plateau expressed thusly, for they were so created.

Foremost in the garden, surrounding the great conical temple stood an enormous and most beautiful, solid gold bell. This great golden bell is encased in a large pyramid-shaped, clear crystal encasement; an enclosure for protection from influencing energies. As such, nothing can come in contact. Any mind forces contacting it would be instantly repelled. This magnificent bell must have been easily one hundred feet high and half as wide. It should be told, of the exquisite golden bell of the temple, when it is rung, (by means of a specific sound frequency), the tremendous vibrations so set in motion, regenerate all the collective, positive frequencies that have ever been expressed through the surrounding and the distant planets, so intense and concentrated are the mind frequencies impinged there, in the gold crystal formation! It is at the precise moment that a concerted effort of all the many thousands of persons living in this great city, instantly, psychokinetically extend themselves in consciousness to aid in the tremendous, infinite projection project! Thus it is, in part, the unique and rare properties of the gold crystal itself, along with the Infinite Mind frequencies, plus the cosmic energies, create a continuous regeneration of the frequencies so set in motion, frequencies far, far beyond the scope of man to conceive! Yet, were one to tune in with the inner ear, he could sense this indefinable and exquisite intonation – vibrations that factually transcend one. To merely tune into the thought of the intonation – the continuous generation is regenerated!

The lighting (we shall term it) of this temple was most unique. Over each great doorway (or archway) appears a light or ray of a certain color. Each huge archway of the thirty-three have a certain color frequency, brilliancy and dimensional influence. There are thirty-three lights or rays, each color denoting the particular frequency of the dimension or development from which came the individual or group entering this particular archway.

There are thirty-three great, sparkling, crystal chandeliers in a huge semicircle, poised in air about the museum. Each chandelier has seven crystal tiers or rows of sparkling diamond-like prisms. There are thirty-three large drops in a circle on each top layer of the seven, then, each layer graduating in size. Moreover, along the concourse upon which the Logos-Queen will walk, there is also another great group of thirty-three huge, dazzling, crystal (electronic) chandeliers hanging in mid-air, spaced at intervals. Specific frequencies have been there impinged in the mind creations within these elegant radiating chandeliers, and which are actually all a part of this vast regenerating system of Inner Light for man upon the earth. The great crystal lens, the crown, the throne and the wand, the large crystal balls we've called chandeliers, all play a great part in this projection program, the bombarding of Light frequencies unto the earth; directed first through the Mind of the Logos (the one on your earth, to now be initiated), who lives on the Light Frequency Beam.

Chapter 4

The entrance to the golden temple is made through the thirty-three vast and tall great entrance ways (or doors) which are, in themselves, covered with solid gold and extend up about five stories tall; yet with the great size, they are so exactly balanced that a touch of the small finger would slide them back into the walls. The heavy carvings and deep embossings covering the golden entrance way doors, portray in picturization, many important historical events which have taken place upon this great spiritual plateau, called Parhelion.

Information about these beautiful archways must be related — and I wish, too, there was a better word to call them — where one passes from the exterior to the interior. Overhead in the arch are impinged and implanted specific energies which quicken the individuals passing through, and which is a help in their own particular need, their own particular frequency; for those coming from that particular dimension must, and they always do, enter through that particular passageway. They can't do otherwise because they wouldn't feel harmonious; it would be similar if we had to live in a cold, cold room or a hot room. This is not actually temperature, but it is what we need to keep our body comfortable there. These energies are to keep the psychic body in good psychic frequency relationship with the people — the people within the area. In other words, they breathe these radiations or energies. Instead of what we use as air, this is what they intake to support their psychic structures. They breathe in the radiated energy, you might say. Of course, they have no lungs. This is what flows through their psychic structures to keep them vital and radiant, and in tune with the all-creative Infinite. So isn't it very wonderful? The more you think about it, the more expanding it becomes within you. Each archway has its own color tone, its own frequency, and if one would sense carefully, there would be a different fragrance from those various people, everything is all so harmonious. These people who walk through this particular archway, move on directly to the specific area where they will form their great individual triangle for the occasion. We could say there were at least thirty-three hundred personages in each triangle, and there are thirty-three patterns of triangles. The triangles separate at either end, forming an opening for the pageant to traverse, leaving a huge semicircle.

To further relate of the great entrance ways: Over each of the great archways there was an insignia which seemed to be embedded in a tapestry of great beauty. The insignia denoted the particular position or ray from which the person would come, as he moved through the archway. The insignia had an astrological significance, not based on the symbols known to the present day astrologers, but which was a science formulated at the beginning, even before the Lemurian civilization, by the Ancient pre-Lemurian Masters more than one hundred thousand years ago! All of these persons who came to this temple for their own initiation, came from different planes, dimensions, or worlds.

Chapter 5

Vaughn: Approaching the outside of the huge cathedral temple and the seven golden steps, coming closer to the walls, I see the beautiful replica of the lovely statuary that has been left to posterity on the earth worlds from the Grecian eras. Here depicted on the walls are the beautiful figures of the Grecian Gods, Apollo, Athena, Dionesius, and many others. Interwoven and seemingly a part of the crystaline structure are many symbolisms, seeming astrophysical or astrological designs such as two fishes intertwined. There are circular designs with finer and finer renditions of the circle, and as it grows smaller and smaller towards the center, interlaced amongst these circular vortexes are very fine cross lines, indicating the forces of the cosmos. As I see into the structure, I am aware of colors. The statuary or the sculpture work has a luminescence which is of such great beauty that one wonders where the lighting comes from! The very material from which the designs are formed have, seemingly, their colors in the substance of the design. It is almost similar to viewing an oil painting or having a light shine from the back, yet these works of art are living art, they take on motion!

Walking along between one arch entrance and the next one, I see that the sculpture work has changed in design and that now it is of an India design. I see replicas of the Buddha and other renditions of the culture of India. There are Egyptian designs of the great golden era of Akhenaton. Then comes into view as my consciousness becomes more attuned (and there are no bare areas on the walls), in between the art work sculptures are many portrayals of many hundreds of kinds of flowers, plants and leaves, and these are in color, as is everything here colorful. It is very beautiful and so over-powering. We sense no cluttered feeling one would expect if he saw a wall adorned with many different designs. The designs do not conflict with one another. They have a separa-tion to them so that if we view the beautiful sculpture of Adonis, there would be no conflict with anything that would take our consciousness away from it, yet the surrounding areas, the flowers, the shrubbery, and the leaf pattern-work add to the sculpture. It seems to be in the background, although it is all portrayed seemingly on a flat basis, yet, nothing is flat. We see everything as if it were in a fourth or fifth dimension, because we see depth, height, width, and we see all around! This is very in-teresting to see, for what I'm looking at, is this beautiful sculpture of Adonis and I can see it as if it were in a park land. I can see the beautiful patterned shrubbery behind it, the trees beside it, and seemingly, the flowers blooming from trees.

So when one gazes at any individual work of art, here on the outside of the museum, one seems to be in a park land or in the midst of the natural habitat of wherever this work of art was made. The scenes change as one continues his walk around the building, and one is taken into the various cultures of the earth worlds and other worlds. Much of it is not in rapport with my earth consciousness; there are designs which are very strange to me. I see pyramids of many different shapes – the pyramids of the Incas, the Mayans, the Aztecs, the Egyptians. Here is seemingly a pyramid which is a representation, or rather, it is the original pyramid that was built in Atlantis! This scene shows a procession walking into a huge doorway – priests. They all have a metal cap over their heads and wear long flowing robes. One sees the pyramid as a whole, as well as the coloration. This temple-pyramid seems to be of a pearloid quality, as if there were many millions of pearls glued to the top of the pyramid. It looks like pearl, or alabaster. The top has a tall shaft made of gold, from which there are thirty-three rods extending in a horizontal position.

Then the next scene shows the interior of the temple, of the pyramid. Inside there are many elegant columns. The columns are easily a good hundred feet tall. It is very difficult to see anything on top, because it is so high. One sees the living flame on the inside of the temple, resting upon a very large rectangle of crystal clear quartz. The flame is a whitish yellow. It is white but has some kind of a yellowish cast to it.

Ioshanna: How far back in history would you say these epics or these revelations relate? Vaughn: This depiction of the temple of Amon Ra, I believe, is sixteen thousand years in past earth history. The carvings and the sculptures of India go back to at least ten thousand years. Ioshanna: I am sure if we could look far enough and stayed in this particular consciousness fairly long and could view the entire area, which would doubtless take years to do, one would, without a doubt, find there, replicas of the Aryans, who first set all this great plan in motion five hundred thousand or more years ago, think you not so? Vaughn: Yes, these are the picturizations I see on the walls! There are so many that I'm only selecting those which are relevant or which would have a meaning to me in this state.

I see a picture of a huge airship. It seems to be cigar-shaped. It is hovering over the ground and a procession of people are emerging. They seem to be in a dazed condition, as if they were sleep walking. They are beautiful looking in appearance. There is not a blemish in their features, and as they walk out, they are in pairs, two by two. They have young children as well as young adults. Ioshanna: Where would you sense these people have come from? Vaughn: They have come from another solar system, closer to the center of the galaxy. Ioshanna: These persons, you would feel to be the Aryans? Vaughn: Yes, these are the original Aryans who have come down through history as those people who have been in the northern latitudes, such as the Swedes, the Norwegians, and their appearance is most beauteous. Their hair is reddish-blond, their eyes are blue. Ioshanna: What would be their purpose in coming to this planet when they had, from what I sense, an ideal way of life in their own distant galaxy. What would their object be to come into a degenerated planet such as the earth? Vaughn: Well, these people have reached a very high state of development. This development, such as it is, is used in service to all those who have been created from the same substance, the Father, from the Infinite Creative Intelligence. Ioshanna: Vaughn, could we say these people came, in a way, to seed the earth plane? Vaughn: Yes, they came to do a service, to help those peoples who have reached such a low level of understanding. If they were not helped by those of a higher development they would then be absorbed back into the Infinite and lose their individual consciousness. Therefore, they took it upon themselves – a great humanitarian project – to come and voluntarily interject their consciousness in a lower plane: and in so doing, hopefully, give the necessary trajectory to these Aborigines who were so separated from their higher selves and had thereby lost contact with the higher beings in the spiritual worlds, and so they were found thus mired in their pits of clay and at

35

that time, living in their abject state of consciousness; almost like stone age or savage persons, without a concept of their alignment with the Godhead within. They had no sense of any relationship to a higher consciousness. Ioshanna: They had degenerated to that point! Is that what you are inferring? Vaughn: Yes, one can accept the fact that they had degenerated to such an extent. Ioshanna: Now what you are saying, in essence, is that these great Super Beings, we could call them such, who had ascended to such a state of awareness of spiritual development that they actually reverted consciously, in full consciousness of what they were doing, and took on, in a sense, a dematerialized form to enter into the earth world through their spacecraft, and then come down into the earth plane to mingle with these eartheans, to teach them a higher way. They actually gave up, in a way or sense, their own personal development? Vaughn: Yes, this is the only way it could be done. They actually gave some of themselves; they gave themselves and, of course, there was a great intermingling. This meant there was absolutely no sense of "self" in these great Spiritual Beings, which they were. It is fantastic! It was very hard for the Aborigines to appreciate. This is the reason they degenerated, because of the very fact they only considered their own selfish needs and therefore, lost contact with the great reservoir which is the Infinite Creative Source. They, themselves, thought they were the deities; that it was within their own abilities to plan and to take full responsibility for their own lives. Ioshanna: Are you speaking of these Higher Beings? Vaughn: I am speaking of these lower beings because that was their attitude before the Higher Beings came. They had become so aggressive in what little attainment they had that they were overpowered with their own ego consciousness and digressed!

Ioshanna: It was impressed with me a time back when I was in special attunement, that this Being who operates this so-called mechanical robot here (myself) in the physical, was one such Being and came to help seed and to actually set in motion this particular plan, which is, at the present, being culminated in this great conclave, and which we have termed the Conclave of the Light Beings. Would you see anything to that effect or enlarge upon it? Vaughn: Yes, the scenes on the exterior walls of the temple enlarge upon this, as this temple is the culmination of this great effort which was started about five hundred thousand years ago. It was planned in every detail; the various persons who would take the various parts, the many peoples they would help, who, themselves, would take part in the plan and help to raise the consciousness of this earth plane. But it was more than one earth plane that this plan encompassed. It was a plan of many dimensions and the reason the earth plane here has been given such a great deal of attention is because of the central fact of its degeneracy! Therefore, those individuals in this plane needed that much more help, and therefore, the earth plane itself needed a great deal more attention and power given to it. So these great personages that we see depicted along the exterior of the temple are those Higher Beings who had planned the seeding of the earth plane five hundred thousand years ago – all of the great Avatars and philosophical individuals who were known in earth history. We could go back to the time of Osiris, Isis, and the great Queen Hatshepsut; the Pharaoh who brought in the Science of Life, Akhenaton, the great philosophers of Greece, headed by Anaxagoras and his students, Socrates, Plato, Aristotle, Archimedes, Hippocrates. It is all depicted here in living action! Yes!

It is an incredible scene, as are the other descriptions. One has to attune himself to a different consciousness because viewing the walls of this temple, which are so extensive – a perimeter of at least twenty-five miles, and the height of the wall is at least a hundred feet – so interspersed with the great epic upon which all history is based – the great eulogies of the great poets Tennyson, Homer, Keats, Shelley, are all derived from much of man's groping for the lost paradise. A great deal of the history of the earth world, now in legend form, describes much of what they hope to aspire to, from the very Gods that lived amongst the men of earth in the Grecian legends. It has always been taken as a fact that the Gods lived amongst them and thereby were the peoples that much more imbibed with the very essence of the Higher Realms. It has been stated in much of the legends of these Gods, they were handsome, tall in height, such as ten to twelve feet, and that their very breath would be similar to the power of thunder — as the God, Thor, is described. This is only symbology because the power of these great Beings who have come from the planet Aries was such, they had the inner contact with the Infinite Creative Source, and in that sense, they, themselves, were Gods or infinitely minded or, in another sense, an abstraction of the very Infinite Itself in a finite way.

So the vast depictions here show the cities in which the Aborigines first lived, some of the interior of their households. It shows a vignette or a depiction of the way they lived, the barbarous manner in which they fought each other. Their daily lives were all shown. In essence, it was like a time capsule envisioned! For instance, one could look at these scenes and one could feel he was right back in that era, living there; it seemed they came into action. It is very exciting! Ioshanna: So these so-called Gods, as the earth men or Aborigines at that time viewed these people, in essence then, they actually, before they came, were not living in a physical body. They were true spiritual beings and needed no physical body. Is this what you feel, they took on this physical body for this particular purpose? It must have been so if they were so advanced! Vaughn: The bodies they lived in were so ethereal they had an entirely different appearance than the people who lived on earth, the Aborigines; they seemed transparent! These bodies were not earth bodies, because first, they had no need for food. It was not a physical body; there were no arteries, no blood, lungs, heart, etc. It was purely a materialization and yet it moved, spoke, expressed great intelligence etc., so that to the earth people, they were, to all intents and purposes, physical. That was the only way these Higher Beings could converse with them on their own level. Ioshanna: And remarkable too that they weren't frightened of them, but I suppose the Higher Ones had frequencies set up within the eartheans' minds that they were so transcended at the time, they weren't fearful of them. Vaughn: Yes, true. It is also the same pattern; now five hundred thousand years seems like a great length of time to the earth peoples, yet, for instance, five hundred thousand years ago compared to the present time, the state of consciousness of the earth people is very similar to what it was then, in that long ago. They had advanced and progressed, but had then sunk back again, and regressed during the same period of time, (five hundred thousand years ago) and now again, there has been a great deal of preconditioning for the arrival of the Gods from outer space! Ioshanna: so, like you say, it has come full cycle! Vaughn: That's right. We have come full cycle again, and here at this time we have amongst us some of the original Spiritual Beings from the higher planes, the Aryans, in our midst in many ways – invisible as well as visible – to again interject the power from their consciousness to the earth minds. Ioshanna: We could say, fertilize the earth minds with the spiritual understanding! Vaughn: That's really what it is.

Ioshanna: One thing more, and I am sure all the readers of this book would be vitally interested. Approximately what length of time would you say that these Spirit Beings stayed on earth before they returned again to their spiritual abode – which I assume they did? Vaughn: It took a great deal of work in terms of accomplishment for these Higher Beings to interject into these people the knowledge that they had a need to uplift themselves. They therefore remained a very great length of time – at least a thousand years – and in that period of time, they changed their form not one whit! They remained in the same appearance; and again, this gave the earth people the right to call these higher Beings Gods. That's why they were called Gods. They did not die. They maintained contact with the Source and had eternal life. Ioshanna: So then their physical bodies were more or less in a materialized state.

When the Moderator lived his little earth span in the 20th Century, he was aware of, and told me that he (along with myself) was one of the Aryans, so he was aware of this situation. Most often situations of this nature are not related in conscious mind but he was aware that we were of the original Aryans who came from this distant galaxy, as he termed it, to seed the earth with spiritual understanding or awareness, light and power, in order that the world at that time, not be destroyed. So evidently it has been one continuous evolving and progressive endeavor up to this point, would you say? Vaughn: Yes, and it's of interest that you say the greatest Intellects who have, themselves, arrived at a point where their lives lived were in a consciousness so far removed from this low plane, and did so return to live amongst the savages, the people who know of only one thing — hostility and reaction. The Higher Ones returned time after time, epoch after epoch, which should be good proof to any of us, of the great love that is evident in the celestial realms, which apparently was sadly lacking for these many hundreds of thousands of years. Ioshanna: Well, Vaughn, you have added a great deal regarding scenes portrayed on the outside of the temple which, up to this point, have been lacking and we are all most grateful for this wonderful and excellent addition. Vaughn: May I add too, that there are scenes showing the Aryans and the various other points of transition as they reappeared on the earth plane, and other scenes from the times that they lived upon the earth. I see a scene of Zoroaster in the garden, as he was considered to have been a nature lover and taught amongst a garden of flowers, to his students in the land of Persia. We see the scene of a beautiful garden of many trees and varieties of flowers, particularly roses and gardenias. Then we have a scene of a temple in the time of Osiris and Isis and we see the rendition of Osiris, Isis and Horus, as it has been known on the earth plane.

Another scene is shown of the time that Jesus lived. He is shown atop a small hill with many surrounding, sitting and standing, to listen to him give a sermon on truth. We see depictions again, as you may call them such, of other visitations at other times – of Krishna, of Buddha – and in each we see the particular rendition of that particular country; the vegetation and the buildings, as such, all in lifelike reenactments! One can continue this way for many years to take it all in.

Ioshanna: In other words, the outside of the building itself is a great historical pageant, an education that any individual could spend many, many months or possibly years and gain a great understanding of all the important historical events that have happened on the lower earth planes due to these incredible and wonderful impressive renditions, or as you so aptly termed it, reenactments. That is a very good word for them, for it is very plain to see how they actually seem to come to life, into action, into motion and color, and one feels that which is being depicted! Vaughn: It has also come to me very strongly that what we see in the temple of the Conclave of Light Beings is actually a synthesis, an integration or combination of all of the temples that have been described in the Pulse of Creation Series books. Here we see in essence, the story of the degeneracy of the earth plane and other planes, and how the great Advanced Beings from the Planet Aries came down and reseeded the plane, and having failed, returned again and again and again. The scenes so depict their returns, and so as we enter the inner portion of the temple, we see the present victory that has finally been attained after five hundred thousand years!

Inside is portrayed the ceremony which is the crowning achievement of the Light Beings who have thus striven and worked for these hundreds of thousands of years; they have finally become victorious over these great denizons of the lower worlds, the lower astral realms – who live in the dark. In so achieving, they have strengthened the very Infinite Itself, with the addition of many thousands of souls who will regenerate in an Infinite way, their own new consciousness! Ioshanna: What a beautiful and wonderful concept. These persons, as they so attain, as you say, actually strengthen the Infinite due to their attainment! Isn't that thought an expanding experience! It is to me. Vaughn: Yes, it is a glorious picture of what has been achieved and what lies ahead. One can almost see the face of the Infinite in this way – if it had a face. Ioshanna: I know what you mean. It makes one feel really close to God. It makes one feel very godlike – as a part of this great Infinite Oneness. This is what I personally was so impressed with during the entire two weeks. There was a feeling present of a complete oneness with all the glorious radiance and love of all these many countless thousands of Advanced Perfected Beings that was truly heaven. Vaughn: Yes, this is a wonderful opportunity for one of those people who thus was contacted and who represented the abject state of the earth world five hundred thousand years ago! I have no doubt that I lived in that state of consciousness and have had the experience of having been touched by many of the great souls – the Avatars and the Logoi. Ioshanna: I am sure what you say is true and due to this fact, that far back, that you made the contact with these higher Spiritual Ones – it was the motivating impetus that served to move you forward through the years, even though sometimes there was a detour. But we can certainly look back and say, always did you get up from the tumble. The proof of the pudding is that you are here at this point where you are now, and that you are expressing in a completely opposite position and point where all actions now being related are of a completely opposite and positive nature.

Although the greater portion of the walls, both inside and out, were covered with the (previously mentioned) creations, we can't call them reproductions, for they were created even before the events took place! The remaining portions of the walls, themselves, were of a most exquisite composition and structure. Although they were all of gold, yet there were no smooth or even surfaces. The complete area was entirely uneven in texture, giving great depth and a third, fourth and fifth dimensional appearance. The nearest way it could be described would be to say it appeared as if one may have used sort of a véry thick golden dough, then kneaded and squeezed it, forming ridges and valleys within it. Some differences in the thickness of this peculiar but exquisite finish appears as much as three to four inches. It is all so magnificent. The vast size of all things truly takes one back, yet in this state of consciousness, it's all conceivable and seems normal.

Chapter 6

Vaughn: Attuning my consciousness toward the assemblage, I couldn't help but be over-awed by the height of each individual. The average height is in excess of ten feet and there were those who seemed taller. It seems that the Logoi and Archangels had a stature higher than those who were on a lower level or frequency. Fifteen feet would be more reasonable, and still with the great height and stature, all was still dwarfed by the immensity of the structure! It still seemed as if each person was only a midget. The greater the psychic development, the larger one becomes. One must be encompassed in some field, so the height of each person indicates his own spiritual development. Now it can easily be understood why the throne itself (which we'll describe later) was of such a great size; because it had to encompass the great development of the Overlord, the Unariun Moderator. It could easily be seen that he could easily fill a five hundred foot area, if we could really see the psychic anatomy. The aura, or psychic self is what gives the immense feeling of size.

The largest mountains on earth are considered to be the Himalayas – thirty thousand feet high – and yet it is quite believable that a "Prince" could have attained such size in his development. But does it all mean that he has all of the intelligence which is representative of the numbers of frequencies? Ioshanna: Indeed so! Vaughn: Like a computer — the more one adds to the cells, so each cell signifies intelligence — so that's what the universe means, or the Infinite? Ioshanna: One can get lost in a maze of words with any effort to describe. That is the feeling I had the other day when suddenly I was psychically, astrally, spiritually and soulically and in every other way, taken out there and as I stood here on the floor and viewed the entire situation, all I could do was stand and cry, for lack of the ability to describe or define the great Infinity! I felt so perfectly helpless or futile to even attempt to put any of the great glory of the Infinite into earth words; everything so immense — so dazzling in color! Vaughn: The size of the people being dependent on their spiritual progression is just beginning to develop in my own mind. Moreover, the reason the cities are so large is not only because of the numbers of people who live there but of the size of the individuals themselves. The dwellings they live in, we understand, are of huge proportions. The mansion of the White House would represent the average household of anyone living on this plane! Ioshanna: Yes. I always rather felt that the average person, after he has developed to, at least, a mastership degree would be at least nine to ten feet; and of course, the greater the awareness and spiritual development, the greater would be the psychic abilities, or aura, whatever you choose to call it.

Yes, that is all very interesting, and as you say, each cell would indicate the amassment of intelligence that has been developed or earned.

Vaughn: So, if we go back and consider the pyramid which was built by Amon Ra in Atlantis which necessitated ninety-eight acres of ground, which was necessary to put together the pyramid, consisting of the hundreds of millions of cells which collected the energies from the Infinite, then one could consider that a person of the highest degree of attainment would comprise something of this nature. A Prince could be of the configuration of a pyramid as was described by the Moderator. Ioshanna: Like the Moderator said, one time when he was in a Unity Church in Los Angeles, the entire roof of the building seemed to disappear and the head and shoulders of Elijah was seen by him. He said it more than filled the building, which was a large cathedral! Vaughn: If any mortal man had seen that, he would hide his head in fear for man always fears the unknown.

As we approach through the exquisite gardens which surround the entire golden temple and come into view of the seven golden circular steps, we note on the landing, seven beautiful golden angels, each with a huge golden key! Up to this point the great doors of the magnificent structure were symbolically closed, until all was in readiness. Now is the time when the seven golden keys can be inserted in the golden locks and the many entrance ways shall swing open wide!

This city is the heavenly abode of the saints, the philosophers of old; of all who have progressed to at least the point of mastership, to so live. This knowledge should create within you, the reader, the cause and the reason to so evolve yourself from out the mundane material worlds and consciousness; to strive that you may likewise attain illumination and entrance into this great golden city so indescribable, called by the eartheans Heaven. The floor is created of the crystaline structures; embossed and embedded there is the great pageantry of the spiritual dimensions, and seemingly sprinkled with gold — thus the energizing power. (Vaughn joins me with this attunement.) We both see it thusly:

All activities of this gigantic city were brought to a temporary halt in order that every person might attend the historical conclave! For, indeed, each one of these Spiritual Souls had taken part in the creation of the monumental structure and all that both surrounded and filled it! Most important is the great lens which permanently exists in these inner planes. This defies description. Suffice to say, it shall serve to help change this earth world (and others) back onto a more progressive evolution. Doubtless, no earthean could conceive a project requiring such as one hundred thousand years to complete, involving as many (or more) persons taking part; yet, such it was.

Moreover, it was the very life-force, the intelligence, the creative and psychic energies, combined with cosmic energies (God force) which actually formed the substance called crystal, of which all things in these higher Spiritual Worlds are created — beyond human conception, no doubt, yet it must be told. Possibly in some distant future, man shall evolve to the point where he can conceive such truths.

Vaughn relates: The size of the great projection room, if it can be called such, (museum, a better word), is comparable in size to a large city and is the main hall in which this ceremony is to take place. This event is heralding the completion of the great crystal lens, as well as signaling the completion of a certain elevated frequency development of our Channel, Ioshanna! Of interest was the delightful fragrance that filled the temple. Lovely flowery scents were emitted from the Beings of the Ascended Ones. The particular scent our Channel carries or emits is similar to a gardenia. In the center of this huge area, there were three wide levels or crystal tiers. Each translucent tier was colored a different hue; the first tier blue, the second gold, and the third rose, the embedded frequencies actually changing the psychic of the individual who thereon steps! Upon each one of these three plateaus of crystal glows a large, oscillating, scintillating, yellowish flame of living energy!

It seems almost incongruous to speak of this great gathering place used for energy projections, as a temple for it compares in no way to earth temples — other than being of a conical shape. However, there exists no thing on earth by which it can be compared in size; for even — what with the more than one hundred thousand persons present, it could easily accommodate several times that number.

The interior is in no way cluttered with furnishings, rugs, wall-hangings, artifacts, etc., for it is most beautiful in its serene simplicity and was created for the one purpose of Light projections to the lower worlds.

Chapter 7

The golden walls of the temple were all deeply carved and most exquisite to behold. All were covered with enactments of an entire past history of spiritual importance. There are no earth colors like it, to describe the so-called atmosphere or to so factually compare. A combination of colors seemed to weave in and out together over and above the great wall areas. The ceiling, at the moment it appeared, was a glittering mass of pulsating bluish-white luminescence! But this, too, took on different hues as the psychokinetics came into play. There was no sense of measurable height, as it seemed to be like the open sky. Certain areas of the floor of the temple were transparent; it was smooth as marble and translucent, these too, portrayed the vast historical pageant of ages past in living color and action!

Lest you may wonder about the lighting, one of our hosts states: No, we here do not use, nor do we need, electric lights! We are using the auric radiations from all present which are more than adequate to illuminate any city, regardless of size. Moreover, we are not bound nor limited with the repetitious rotation of some earth about a sun, that permits daylight for a time, then removes it, leaving all in darkness; for ours is an eternal day. Yet, even if this were not so, in our particular advanced state of consciousness, one would but need be conscious of greater light, and thus it would be!

No one was seated in this great conclave celebration. All were to participate in the ceremony and need be too alert to be seated. Some of those present were of the personalities who gave dissertations in the Unarius texts; that is, the Pulse of Creation books, etc.

Standing all about within the great expansion, were an incalculable number of personages gathered about in a large semicircle on either side. These Spiritual Beings were all Angels of the higher orders, and any one of them could be considered at least a Master, an Archangel or Logos; their faces so perfect and beautiful to behold − waxenlike − each one emanating a radiance!

A little detail may be needed to clarify the positioning of these many great souls, the assemblage, for it is of importance. There was a large semicircle, in which the assemblage was gathered. This was divisioned off into thirty-three large triangles, the Being of highest attainment in frequency would be the one in the front and forming the corner position; then those behind him of a slightly lesser degree in spiritual stature and so on. It was the arrangement carried out with the entire thirty-three sections or groups of triangles of Light Beings and as Vaughn, too, has viewed it all so accurately says, each first person was positioned directly beneath the great overhanging crystal arrangement. These hanging configurations were not simply an ornament but were likewise another part of the great electronic network. These crystal hangings were attached to nothing, but rather, hung suspended in mid-air. just above the head of the first person in line in the pyramid or triangle shapes.

These brilliant crystal balls appear similar to a huge, inverted crystal chandelier; that is, the topmost circles of the configurations are the largest, then the subsequent rows are graduated with fewer circlets of crystal drops on down each round, until the last row had become but one large, brilliant, diamond-shaped ball of about twelve inches in diameter.

The number of rows or circles of crystal balls concerned in these great crystal hangings is of importance, but far too detailed and lengthy to describe here. You can rest assured, however, the number thirty-three, representing all the various planes and dimensions and logoi, and the number seven, (the seven planes), play important parts in all these various appurtenances, and are expressed in the creations.

It must be said that the size of these great crystal balls was incomprehensible. They would have to be, to make any showing in this enormous and inestimably-sized building we have called a temple — and which is, in effect, far more than a temple, but it must be called something, and we lack proper words to thoroughly define such a structure as this vast museum on these great spiritual planes.

The colorful array emitted from these exquisite pyramids of crystal is most beautiful to behold for each facet is a prism and reflects back the color which it has caught! It is as if the walls were lined with thousands of mirrors and as many floodlights, projected upon these great pyramidal crystal configurations! The colors were tossed back and forth in a re-generative expression. Yes, they even reflected back the great colorful energy clouds that had assembled toward the roof area. Each, in turn, the crystal-clear lakes in the fountain bases be-low, reflected beautiful iridescent rainbow-hued emanations. Vaughn now tunes into the scenes of this great temple. He recalls the immense chandeliers and says: There were thirty-three giant crystal hangings, each one having seven tiers. These tiers were beautiful, radiant prisms of crystal. The topmost tier was the largest, then they graduated in size, and in circular patterns, on down until the last tier was but one huge prismatic, triangular ball! (The top rung is thirty three hundred feet in circumfer-ence.) These great prismatic chandeliers were regularly positioned above or over the assem-blage. The last (or lower) rung of the seven tiers, which was the singular ball, hung di-rectly over the head of the being (or person) standing on the front point of the great triangu-lar formation of the vast assemblage: the front or foremost personage signifying the topmost rank spiritually. Thus – the thirty-three indi-viduals who defined the thirty-three Logos, so formed a great semicircle. This formation was spaced, or positioned, on either side of the great concourse, along where the Logos being honored traversed toward the dais, the great Crystal Island, whereon is the great Golden Throne.

Due to the vastness of the entire temple and area, the almost inconceivable size of all things involved, it was felt necessary to reiterate or recall, to again bring into the mind of the reader, added descriptions, in order that he, too, shall better be able to tune in, and as the pictures build within consciousness, be able to view these glorious and gigantic settings and proceedings. Because all things there existent are Infinite Mind Creations, they, as well as the Personages, the Light Beings present, continue to regenerate the occasion as one reattunes into the scenes. So, dear reader, if you may, for instance, feel you have heretofore read, in this book, some certain mention, it is due to the fact that we here, in putting these revelations and experiences into word forms, are endeavoring to turn for you, the gem of Truth, that you may view the various facets, and in so viewing, that you, each one, can likewise share in this glorious, never-to-be-forgotten inner experience!

Being Infinite in nature, it all lives today in energy creations exactly as it was then all occurring – all that which took place on March 26, 1973, and can again be viewed as taking place in the present! It lives in the now for whomsoever will! This will be continued eternally! Moreover, as the attunement is made one is transcended and lifted in consciousness and a stepping up will occur — a spiritual quickening!

* * *

It should be related here too, and possibly earlier, that it was in 1954, just a few days after having been brought into the consciousness of the Moderator that I was transported temporarily to this city of Parhelion, and brought back in conscious mind after the attunement, vivid memory of the great alabaster or pearloid appearing walls that surround the entire plateau or city. I was most impressed that the wall was quite thick; say, perhaps two feet, and was very high, like, for instance, twenty feet or more.

The top was not straight or flat but was artistically designed in a scalloped pattern. Now I realize it was of a sine wave pattern. I was most impressed with the unusual feeling that came from this great structure, sort of a welcome warmth or well-being. I felt I was emerging from within the great wall but remembered not, that which was within, but soon related to the Moderator I had just seen the great wall surrounding the city of Shamballa. Of course, he was pleased, but this was the last and only "conscious" contact with that high dimension until the year 1965, when I experienced the visitation related in my Bridge to Heaven book.

Chapter 8

Of the entire interior enclosure – other than the great historical depictions or reenactments throughout the great walls and upon the floors – the central focal point or interest is the great crystal, circular throne island, upon the topmost of which stands the great golden throne. Surrounding this great crystal island are the seven (previously described) crystal lakes, within which stand the seven flowing, seven-tiered fountains, (one fountain within each lake).

Now at the very base of this great crystal mountain or island, (it is much more than a platform because it is at least seventy-five feet tall), around the base are the three circular crystal tiers. They are actually three platforms of a different color. They are crystal and luminous and each one emits a different color – the lower one blue, the middle one gold and the topmost tier or platform is rose crystal. Now these plateaus are not simply three steps, but each tier is at least ten feet wide; then one must take another two steps in between, before he arrives at the second plateau or tier, and likewise on two steps in between the next tier to the top platform (making seven steps in all). Then, after the individual passes over these cleansing auric tiers, he has been thoroughly cleansed and purified and is then projected farther ahead in his spiritual evolution. In other words, this is the initiation which brings about the, shall we say, mastership degree from one who has previously been an adept.

Now these crystal plateaus or circular tiers are most magnificent. The whole structure is most elegant and exquisite to behold. It is all luminous; the light colorations emanate from out the large semicircular tiers. These tiers are plateaus or platforms upon which the initiate steps or passes over; and exquisite to watch their various colors ascend up through the crystal. Upon each of these three tiers or plateaus rests a great golden flame, sometimes called the Pillars of Fire. These the Logoi walk through in the ceremony as they pass over the colorful tiers. A topmost platform holds the great golden throne.

At one side of this throne platform there is a small circular table which holds the crown and the scepter. Then on the other side is a circular, clear glass table upon which rests the great Book of Life. Surrounding the entire island are the great fountains (as were described) which emerge out of the seven lakes or bases of these fountains. So if you can, try to picture the entire setting. It is all most magnificent indeed — the large seven lakes or bases from which the fountains emerge, then the spurting, bubbling, beautiful patterns of the dancing waters, never quiet, streaming out in all their intricate designs with the various colors, each one portraying the different patterns, infinite in design!

Surrounding the entire area and covering the greater portion of this great temple – and which, remember, extends about five or six miles – thus, hang the great configurations of crystal (we have termed) chandeliers. They are actually great crystal pyramids and positioned in the, we shall term it, atmosphere between the floor and the ceiling (but of course, no atmosphere exists on this plane) these thirty-three great crystal pyramidal balls are all a part of the great electronic function and plan. They are exquisite to behold, each one shaped like an inverted pyramid. Surely all persons are quite familiar with the way crystals look.

Now these crystals are not atomic substances but are especially made. Each individual crystal, in itself, is formed from seven prisms. So the dazzling effect, the intense coloration that these great balls of crystal create is near incomparable and inconceivable. As was stated, these thirty-three great balls are hanging in mid air; now the lower one of which (single ball) drops above the lead man of the group of each triangle. As was told, besides these thirty-three great chandeliers positioned over the assemblage are also thirty-three more identical chandeliers positioned directly over the great thoroughfare or esplanade, through which the procession will pass. So this indeed does make an exquisite sight!

Now the crystal platforms or tiers that are positioned, encircling the bottom of the throne island, serve a very important function. These are the platforms upon which the initiate steps, which will change the individual from one frequency unto the next. Ordinarily one passes over one tier and into one golden flame. In this instance, the individual taking this initiating is jumping over the next position, initiation, or her position in line, and passes through the entire three tiers. Thus will be viewed the three different colors as she passes through. The Spiritual Being can be seen as she encounters this experience. One can actually see the Being take on the color of the crystal tier upon which she has stepped. It is very beautiful to watch – most impressive, most meaningful, most purposeful, and indeed, almost a sacred experience – yet nothing in the infinite is sacred – rather, is scientific.

Now, atop each of these three tiers or plateaus, rests a great golden flame, the lower or first flame being the smaller of the three, although it is in no way small. This great scintillating, golden, oscillating energy configuration, more correctly called a Pillar of Light, or pillar of fire – sometimes called a flame is at least twelve to fifteen feet tall and three or four feet in diameter, the next being larger, and the next even larger in size – the size, of course, denoting the frequency thereof.

Thus, in this glorious procession about to take place, we will see this Being, along with her biune, step into the three pillars of fire – unscorched! She is known on the earth plane.

At the termination of this initiation, and we could term it a marriage ceremony, for that is truly what it amounts to, as well, she now comes full circle with her biocentric and they will henceforth function as one. They can function as one or separately (or as an individual). Henceforth, thereafter the flame emergence, she will be known as the Archangel Uriel!

It should be said, too, that this is the first time in history that any individual has been known to jump over or to skip a step, a level or a degree — yes, or we could call it a relationship to the Infinite — yes, a thousand-year step. The Moderator has so factually related in the Pulse of Creation books how each step alone requires normally one thousand years, and in each degree there are at least thirty-three planes to ascend, the degrees of Mastership, degrees of Logoi, etc. And so this is a very involved, very lengthy, and time-consuming expression or endeavor; more correctly — evolution; when we really conceive and think upon it, it is little wonder there was such a great celebration! This was a momentous achievement for all Unariuns on the inner worlds of Light.

Chapter 9

The joy, beauty and love that filled this great auditorium when occupied was something to behold — and one quickly becomes caught up in the excitement and the transcendency. All faces were radiant and joyful, for each one had taken a part, not only in the construction of this great crystal lens to be used for energy projections to the earth worlds, but also in the very creation of this magnificent building itself, and which was, we learn, constructed for this very purpose — for this, the new spiritual cycle; the cycle of rebirth for the earth worlds! A very tremendous and wonderful occasion! No earth words exist to thoroughly describe these wonders!

During this awe-struck observation (in viewing psychically), was a feeling to look to the extreme right as most unusual musical sounds were heard; a most peculiar tone and melody, seemingly coming from behind. The sound seemed not as voices, yet, when turning to more directly view, there stood a large group of radiant young boys, all seemingly between the ages of twelve and say, sixteen years — surely several hundred of them — all gowned in the most exquisite shade of soft radiant blue satin. The full sleeves came below the wrists and the satiny robes fell below the knees; their faces almost like alabaster. They were humming, and yet it sounded almost like a stringed instrument. They had been taught this very peculiar way of emitting sound, with special frequencies and vibrations from the mind, that would lend itself in particular healing needs. This delightful and transcending expression, they seemed to carry on during the much of the time celebration!

They too wore the familiar conical hats relative to this spiritual realm. These young men were, of course, being prepared for their next life, soon-to-be, upon the planet Earth, for they have been trained well in the arts of psychokinetics, mind transference and spiritual healing. They will, in a few years time, be projected into the earth aura, into the body of a newly conceived fetus, there to take on an incarnation to help in this great movement of the spiritual evolution of the earth worlds.

It may be helpful to again mention that within the center of the large auditorium, stands a magnificent, huge, crystal island. In the lower areas are three crystal tiers. Upon each of these three crystal tiers glows a great golden, scintillating flame, graduating in size, the lower tier the lesser in height, the second next taller in height and the topmost tier the largest and tallest of the three. However, let it be said, these great golden energy fountains, termed flames, are very vast in size, the width of even the small flame being at least ten feet in diameter, rising seven times as tall. There are many of these cleansing flames on this plateau of a far less intensity in frequency and degree, yet these three magnificent, glowing, living golden flames upon this great crystal platform (atop which sits the great golden throne) are, by far, the largest of all, the frequencies of a much higher intensity.

Upon the crystal island stands a great golden throne. This throne was created as are all things in these spiritual worlds via the psychokinetical and cosmic powers. This structure is at least fifty feet tall and within the crystaline structures were implanted special and specific frequencies which make possible that only such a greatly Advanced Being – as the Avatar Unariun Moderator – could so sit upon it. When he will do so, thusly connected with his own great force field, (especially the palms of the hands touching the arm rests) a most brilliant light will burst forth like a gigantic explosion, too intense to look upon!

This action (his sitting) would be a great blinding flash! This action would mark the beginning of the New Age of Spiritual Ascendency that was coming to this earth plane! This, the great Light which shall be descending and projected from the inner worlds and from the highest planes of Shamballa – now Unarius.

Chapter 10

To further help create the picture of this great museum within the mind of the reader, for it is a most tremendous view and gathering, we shall reiterate some: Now, there is, in the centermost area of this great museum, a huge crystal platform or island, upon which stood the great golden throne platform – and which, in itself, is an enormous structure, reaching easily fifty to sixty feet high and about half as wide – in the centermost area of the great temple (as we have so limitedly termed the building) and which too, seems more vast with each viewing. To complete this magnificent setting, all about or around the base of the crystal platform, (atop of which stood the gigantic throne of gold reaching high in the area) are seven gigantic and magnificent glowing, flowing crystal fountains.

These fountains and crystal pools are not the common garden variety, as boasts the city of Rome, but rather, each one forms a beautiful display of color, beauty and symmetry, circulating countless thousands of gallons of crystal-clear water, which catches the colorings of the radiations existent everywhere. These exquisite structures are created, as are all things in this city, of the crystallized mind energies, and carry the diamond sparkle and beauty of all else about.

The great bases which themselves formed

a small crystal lake, held the seven-tiered crystal bowls, which were filled with the sparkling crystal water. The topmost bowl was about four or five yards in diameter; then graduating on down, each one becoming larger in size to the base. Within the crystal formations has been implanted certain coloring, each of a different hue, yet the overall appearance was crystallized gold, but in these spiritual dimensions, all things radiate much color. Crystal acts as a prism; thus, we here in Parhelion never lack for beautiful color in all things.

The spraying turbulance of clear foaming water was ever in rapid motion, the moving water in each fountain creating beauteous patterns, quite similar to your "dancing waters" on your earth plane; yet even these are dwarfed by the magnificence here; in fact, your dancing waters were copied from these very fountains! The built-in electronic mechanism is all synchronized and harmonized with that of the great gold and crystal organ, and the fine streams of water, which shoot high into the ceiling of the enclosure, form an infinite variety of beautiful patterns – all timed to the music – a heavenly display of beauty.

No colored lights are projected upon the waters, yet they appear as such. The color emulated is exquisite beyond description and emits, as do all creations here, the radiance of the spiritual selves of those who have so formed these elegant structures and of the seven planes of those who have so created them.

These seven great fountains that surround the huge throne have been artistically placed in regular areas all about the base of the throne so that it almost appears as one great crystal lake. The countless tons of (crystal) water forming and playing the infinite number of patterns and designs stagger all imagination, but above all other beauty is the transcending effect one senses as he contemplates all this beauty. Uplifting energy is continually emitted, and one is literally carried away with it all.

At one time an individual fountain will perform — the others all quiet, as if to watch the performance. Then another will join, when suddenly all seven of the great central sources will burst forth in unison, ejecting their force in full measure and color, the patterns of water rise and fall as if in a dance, the music of the organ swells and one is lifted beyond compare. This all, indeed, is a breath-taking and glorious sight — the water in constant motion, the illumination and colors ever changing, the music all blended in harmony! Surely, there could never be a more exquisite experience.

Perhaps a little further description of the beautiful fountains that surrounded the great golden throne may help portray the picture to the reader. Now each of the seven fountains were bedecked with various and completely different statuary. For instance, one would be adorned with the lovable cupids, another the Grecian ladies at the bath, another the beautiful and loved by many, Grecian pillars. Each of the various fountains was an individual creation and unique entirely in design. Some were of the baroque configurations, others with the figurines of the beautiful nudes expressed the French motif, and so on. But they each were individual and exquisite in their work of art, each one having been created by and from one particular dimension and level of this great Unarius Center. One of a well-loved design is the Ionic motif.

Each of the fountains with columns, the columns graduated being much smaller at the top than the bottom caused them to appear graceful. Although these were all seemingly of marble, yet as all things in this great city and plateau, were formed of crystaline mind energies.

The elegant crystal statues, it must be said, were illuminated from within, and even though the lighting surrounding the entire area was most brilliant and luminous, still there was a peculiar radiance from this statuary that shone as if all else surrounding it was in darkness. Within each crystal pool at the base of the fountain, swam gracefully about, lovely snow-white swans, thirty-three in each lake, and beautifully colored fish, some speckled, some golden. These colorful fishes were of an infinite variety. Some of the lovely fantailed fishes were easily eighteen to twenty-four inches in length; for it must be known, that all things in this dimension express no limitation of size or volume, for it is indeed a gigantic city, and all things within and without are relative in size. All such artifacts and expressions upon the earth are greatly dwarfed by all things in these dimensions.

To complete the ne'er to be forgotten picture, many colorful male peacocks strutted about, their iridescent colors brilliantly being displayed. One is aware that he can be in no earth world dimension, for this is truly Heaven. All this and much, much more I have seen and experienced and felt and lived and loved.

Very quickly, after entrance was made into this great museum, we were confronted with the beautiful sing-song chant of the energies, which seemed to come from the minds of the collected personages who filled the temple and the great hallways. The auric emanation from these chants seemed to rise and billow in great clouds of colorful radiance above the heads of all those present. In the distance there was soft and beautiful music playing. The instruments being used were difficult to define, for the sound was entirely different than anything existent on the earth plane. It seemed to be a combination of instruments the Chinese use, mingled with the sing-song chant of the energies, which created a most beautiful vibration and seemed to transcend one beyond any normal existence. There would billow a great cloud of accumulated mist of the golden energies, and then, as the crescendo of the music would rise, the frequencies toward the ceiling would take on a different hue and become deep purple. Then a blue would rise and intermingle, along with a beautiful ultra-violet, and finally a ruby-red would rise to the ceiling, joining the great vastness of colorful display. It was the most glorious sight that one could imagine — this great intermingling of all these radiant colors. Colorful, luminous infusions and cloudlike formations were created by the collected masses of mind energies from these many thousands of persons who had so gathered together in this great cathedral for this large celebration and coronation.

Soon, it was realized from whence came all this motion of all the variegated color that seemed to be billowing, forming and collecting into the vast ceiling of this great area. On one side of the auditorium, we will call it, stood an enormous (and it is almost sacrilege to call it), crystal pipe organ, for it is the most magnificent structure anyone could imagine. To begin to describe the size, one feels lost for words and yet, some means of measure must be indicated. It could be compared to a good sized mountain. The entire structure was curved in front and constructed of thirty-three very large and long crystal pipes. These vast crystal pipes were at least three feet in diameter; that is, this first row, and possibly two hundred feet tall.

There were thirty-three rows of these pipes, or crystal tubes, (if you will), each row diminishing in size until the lower ones were but a foot or two in height. It was an electronic organ, operated by the mind forces. Any one person attending or visiting on this planet or plateau could operate this exquisite mechanism, merely by thinking of certain melodies or tunes. Due to the particular and peculiar frequencies with which it was constructed, any individual need but think of the melody as he approached the organ and it would immediately begin to play whatever the individual was conscious of! No one ever repeats a composition. Other than the crystal, it was composed of solid gold. The entire front was heavily encrusted with vari-colored precious gems. None of the mechanisms or works were visible — only the beautiful, deeply carved, golden front along with the great amassment of the beautiful crystal tubes which, in themselves, sparkled and radiated like so many diamonds. Then as the notes were played, the various colors would rise and fall in the beautiful tubes, each note having its own specific coloration or shade. Thus, when several notes in one particular area were played, one could see several colors rise in that particular crystal tube, so if many notes were played at once, and it was a complicated composition, all of the tubes would be filled to different degrees with the glorious color movements, creations or energy force fields that would be moving up and down this glorious crystal display. It was indeed a most exquisite creation of color and motion most difficult to conceive if one were not familiar with these energies and of their infinite expressions. However, suffice to say that they appeared like beautiful thick clouds or colored mists in their interplaying and interweaving of the various frequencies which did, indeed, portray a most beautiful exhibition. When notes of a lower nature were expressed, the colorations in the pipes would drop to lower levels with the louder tempo or crescendo, all this activity would rise higher in the vast tubes. At such point, as an extreme allegro and crescendo was reached, all colorations would shoot from out the top of these beautiful crystal tubes and arise into the ceiling, there, to join the other great amassments of coloration and energy fields; a most exquisite sight!

It must be said that this glorious and magnificent mechanism, especially created for energy projection purposes, which, too, has been at least one hundred thousand years in the making, is a beautiful sight. This is indeed an understatement, but we have no earth words to even begin to define or describe such beauty, and it is beyond any earth world description.

Vaughn: As I again reattune consciousness to the great Conclave of Light, I now view the inside of the great golden temple, I see completely around the inside of the entire circumference, a huge balcony. It extends one hundred feet from the floor of the temple, and there are thirty-three levels or tiers. There is a partition which protects the people sitting in the balcony from the intense and higher frequencies that build up in the temple. There are the frequencies that have been created from the build-up of the mind energies from the ceremony, as well as the actual temple's crystaline energy form. The partition is actually an energy shield and it is completely protecting these viewers from any danger that would be incurred to them, as they reside in a less compatible frequency than those higher Beings taking part in the ceremony itself, and of which number numerous thousands. These viewers, or spectators, are the peoples from the earth and astral planes, and they have been given this privilege in so being present in their sleep state to help them in their future lives in the earth worlds in which they reside, or in other worlds. It is a vast balcony, containing many millions of individuals from the earth and astral planes for this great (so-called) balcony can accommodate an almost infinite number of astral souls. As has been mentioned previously, the circumference of the temple is twenty six miles, so one can see how a balcony stretching around a circumference of twenty six miles, and having thirty-three levels could indeed accommodate millions of persons. If need be, more room could easily be made and the walls expanded to seat as many more millions of persons as would be the need.

The balconies have been divided into sections, to keep or to separate the people from different earth and astral worlds, for their frequencies are not compatible to one another, as they are of a different nature, one to the other.

So a partition or energy shield separates the balconies into a sectionalized manner. In each of these sections, the persons so seated are in an order denoting their status, or degree. The persons sitting toward the front are those who will take an immediate part in the Unariun Mission, for which they have been preconditioned for many lifetimes to so lend their help. Those persons towards the rear, are ones who have not yet made their physical contact with the Unarius teachings, but who shall in the near future, do so. They will also carry on in various manners, all according to their training on the inner worlds of Light. In this way they will make their mark on the world in which they live.

These people are of many persuasions, artists, musicians, politicians, teachers, scientists, etc. They are the ones who will be the leaders in their particular group and will help carry on the Unariun Mission. In this manner they will condition the minds of their fellow man in this new age of spiritual recovery. It is known that the only way any one person can progress into the inner worlds, is through his own positive acts and deeds. Hence, it will take the combined efforts of these people to inculcate, to reach out to their brothers and sisters on their earth planes and with their own volition, so raise their own consciousness. In this manner the total consciousness of the entire earth plane can be raised in frequency! All this is being done with the great assistance of the entire Shamballas. (I must remember the new name Unarius.) The present assemblage of the Conclave may be called the 'kick-off point' from where the Light will pour eternally onto these lower earth worlds as well as astral worlds.

The sections of the balcony have different colors indicating the planes from which these people have originated. There are many hundreds of frequencies and the coloration is of a many hued beautiful glow; red, blue and yellow are the basic colors and these seem to stem from the sides of the temple. As a closer view is focused, it can be seen that these colors are coming from huge prisms which are positioned around the inside of the walls above the balcony, so that the light shines down upon the people sitting in their apportioned places in the balcony sections. This projection from the prisms, is an initiation for these individuals as they are having their frequency stepped up; they are being spiritually quickened for their own mission on the earth and astral planes.

Although these balconies stretch a vast distance from, and all around the center of the ceremony, the great crystal island, upon which is the great golden throne itself, the person has no difficulty in viewing the procession as it nears the crystal island. Their view is telescoped according to their need. All of the millions of these earth peoples as well as the astral, are going through an initiation, because of their presence in this ''once-in-a-millennium celebration". In the future years and epochs of time, the tremendous in-pouring of the powers which were created from the combined intelligence of all those higher Beings in attendance, will be the earth person's catalyst for their own personal progression. This power will serve to motivate them in their mission to lift the consciousness of their fellow man upon their own earth worlds. So this is perpetual motion; it is regenerative and ever upward in the manner in which this power so acts upon each one.

Although the great assemblage hall had been empty of persons, within a few moments after it was first viewed, and quickly after the sharp blast from the unmuted trumpets was heard, in started streaming great lines of the beautiful people – each one dressed in soft colored robes, each the color relative to his (or her) own particular dimension or frequency, all wearing the pyramidal-shaped golden head covering.

As was previously mentioned, the assemblage was all separated according to spiritual rank and divided off into various groups of huge triangles – those foremost, being of the higher order such as the Logoi, Avatars and Archangels. Then came the Masters of the first degree and so on, down to and including the Adepts; any one of whom could perform the miracles as expressed by the man Jesus.

Foremost and tallest of this great assemblage is the Logos called on the earth, Leonardo da Vinci. Now the highest frequency and color in the spiritual realms is white – the whitest of white, for it is the blending of all colors, when blended in perfect harmony and balance. When the earth man or artist mixes his entire paintbox, he comes up with black. The reason is, the colors are not perfectly blended or harmonized. In the Spiritual worlds, pure white light is the highest of all frequencies. It is, in effect, a yellowish-white, and when the clairvoyant person or seer views the lights (or Beings) of yellowish-white or whitish-yellow, one knows that it is of the highly scientific plane, or dimension, or Being.

And so it was, the polarity or biocentric of the leader or number one Logos, formed the front or lead Being, as he was the highest of that dimensional triangle. His entire assemblage, which he headed, was of the whitest of white and shone with a brilliance most bright. The aura about the group which he headed, was of an enormous size and brillance. The auras or rays of these most Advanced Ones extended out many yards above them and contained all the colors existent, in the outermost radiations of the aura – a most magnificent sight! Thus it was, this Logos who is to take the initiation with his biune (on earth), was gowned in a most exquisite robe of white pearly satin. He wore the gown (or robe) of that level and which was relative to that dimension, frequency and realm. The robe which he wore was exceedingly full. It hung in great ripples about him, and we would not dare estimate the dozens of yards that hung full in this beautiful garb. Foremost, we could see a huge scarf, like a toga, was started and attached from the right front of the neck, his arm therein loosely encased in the drape. Then the entire full length tossed over the shoulder, fell in a drape, loosely hanging in a large U-shape over the back; the folds all dropping in place, forming a most graceful semicircular pattern over his entire robe. Then the continuation of this drape lifted over the left shoulder and dropped down in the front into long graceful folds to the floor. This material is not of the common earth-plane variety – of a simple satin. It is an especial crystaline substance made, as are all things in this dimension, of mind energies. Interwoven in this beautiful cloth, are many exquisitely mind-created, golden roses, each one of a different design. Even though the material hung in folds, each flower shown in its particular form, for this was the way it had been so meticulously designed. These elegant flowers, embroidered in gold, were centered, each one, with a precious gem – that of the deep red ruby heart. The Logos had created this elegant creation to wear when he met his biune from the earth, with whom he would enter the flame pillars in their new initiation.

His long, golden-red hair hung in waves over the shoulders. His head was encircled with a huge aura of white, the radiating emanations extending our a great distance, fringed in gold; most beautiful to see, brought for the time, all eyes to eagerly drink in his beauty. Upon his head had been placed the elegant, pyramidal hat, all bejeweled. He was the tallest of all!

Within his hand, he held what the earth man would call a lovely staff, and yet this was, in effect, a relative adjutant to the vast and intricate electronic works which we have called a generating plant. This wand was bedecked on the outermost sides with most brilliant diamonds. Yet the end was a function in this electronic scheme in conjunction with the wand carried by his biocentric. He wore upon the left lapel the favorite red rose, which had become a love symbol to all those of this higher center and city. In order to keep all records or concepts in order, let it be said that this tallness of size of which we speak has to do likewise with one's spiritual progression. But remember, dear reader, these sizes of the Beings have nothing to do with size in the physical world which is but of atomic structures. As he stood, shining forth midst the great circle of radiating aura about him – which was of the beautiful, purest white radiations – he appeared as a great radiant white mountainous diamond – the aura forming a great arc over and about his head, emitting the colors of the entire rainbow! No, a rainbow does not begin to describe it, for the rainbow shows but three colorations. There are an infinite number of colorings here; when they are properly defined and separated, we here on Parhelion use them in our prismatic effects. As has been told, all things are created thusly — via mind energy. The crystals, themselves, are radiating prisms, spiritual crystalized energies.

Of interest too, each group so designated, radiates its own specific auric emanations and colorations; i.e., the higher the spiritual advancement, the nearer the pure white radiance, etc. (This segregation placement due to frequency relationship.)

Each person, male or female, wore upon the shoulder, scarves draped and folded upon which were colorful flowers, all crystaline in structure. Both sexes wore the hair long, most often in waves which was a golden red hue. Sex was not in evidence as is common on earth. They all have long since evolved beyond such expressions. The flowing garments were of exquisite texture, each worn with pride. The men's robes were of a different design; they, too, wore and enjoyed the great full scarves that draped so gracefully about their shoulders and arms; then swung over the back, similar to the lovely robes of the Grecians. Each great triangular group wore one color, but graduating in density according to rank or position. The most advanced Being who occupied the front and corner position, wore the deepest of the tone, then each succeeding row behind him, the colors became less vivid (or lighter in shade) according to his rank or dimension. Placed over the flowing golden hair of each one of this vast assemblage was his all-important golden pyramidal hat, each set in accord, in gems. At the peak of the cap was the important round golden ball. These were especially formed to regenerate their mind energies and were a close companion to each one on this plane or city. Here all things were crystal and radiant.

Above all things noted, were their happy faces, expressing the Infinite Love – and it was sensed by all! When all were positioned, it created a magnificent sight. It was all too immense and tremendous for the mind to absorb – for my limited earth conscious mind to take in when I'd return to Earth; yet here, in this state, I was one with all things. Nothing seemed too much to conceive; it was all one great wave of love.

Now all persons had suddenly moved into position for the greatest of great events ever seen by mortal mind, and yet in this state, is it mortal? Rather difficult to define. Although normally, gatherings on this plateau were most quiet in nature, for this especial and important gathering, trumpeteers were used. As was told how the main assemblage was positioned in large pyramidal groups and at each group – one, the leader – stood foremost at the corner point of the formation, and here it was that a gaily clad uniformed trumpeteer would step out and stand, statue=like, with trumpet poised at his side. The costumes, of satin, were shiny gold, draped with a cerise (red) colored sash. The trumpeteers, each wearing long, wavy gold= en hair which fell on their shoulders and which was covered, in part, by the vivid blue, conical helmets – all shiny; each helmet bedecked with large colorful plumes of the ostrich, stood at attention.

The pretty red plumes from their helmets, seeming to waft as if in a breeze, were slightly in motion – most graceful. The vivid blue scarves, which swung from their shoulders onto the floor, dropped in huge billowing folds, then fell over the frock coats of gold. These coats were belted tightly in the middle, with a wide elegant belt, in the front of which was a large golden insignia denoting the dimension and grade from which they came. Their breeches of gold were shiny and fitted their forms in a more masculine way. At the knees were the buckles, similar in design to that of the waist. Upon their hands were white, glistening gloves, seemingly of the same materials as were the high, white boots.

Yes, we are extending great efforts to portray to you, the reader, a more detailed and exact picture of this beautiful sight, for they especially are an outstanding point and moment in this exquisite array. Surely the affair of the millennium!

Chapter 11

Directly in front of the throne and on the floor, had been placed a large soft golden cushion. Standing in front of the magnificent golden throne was the Unariun Moderator. Although he could scarcely be seen, due to the great and intense Light he emitted, he was recognized by his intense luminosity. The Light was of such brilliance that no human form was visible, rather, there was a great golden-white radiance or flame which was he (and his biune). One could discern this Avatar by his great high powers expressed.

The crown which the Moderator would place upon the queen's head was much more than a mere symbol, for it is, in essence, actually a demodulator, demodulating the frequencies projected from the high realms and dimensions and, from the lens onto the crown. It was quite similar in principle to the great throne itself, so far as actual involvement and function. It was made especially for her (the biocentric to the Logos), in this particular position and no other individual would be compatible with it; in fact, certain electronic shocks would be experienced. Thus it too, is playing a vital role and is a factor in the function of these combined psychic electronics in aiding in this vast spiritual healing projection program.

The magnificent crown is a formation of thirty-three golden prongs, each one is a component in the combined electronics. They are formed in a circlet and standing upright. On the point of each gold prong is positioned a large, beautiful glittering diamond star. Around the sides of the crown are thirty-three large, heart-shaped red rubies. Standing upright, and in the front of the crown is a large, golden, seven-pointed star. This star is formed completely of beautiful diamonds. To formulate the top, there are seven golden sections, denoting the seven sections of Shamballa*; the thirty-three prongs to signify the thirty-three dimensions, the thirty-three Logoi, etc., the center sections denoting the Archangels; the red ruby hearts denoting love, upon which all Unarius and expressions are based. Love is the symbol of Unarius. This great golden crown is magnificent to see.

Further attention was attracted to the beautiful golden wand which emitted a great, almost blinding brilliance; it shone and vibrated with a peculiar, vibrant, white light projecting from out one end! The wand was made of golden crystal; the ray beams projected from one end appeared as a solid mass of intense white light – a very high frequency, oscillating in the many millions of megacycles per second! This electronic mechanism emits a (seemingly) solid square ray of intense white light when called into action! When the beam is directed to any one individual or group, the piercing light penetrates the psychic structures and cancels out the particular negative vortex needing correc-

(*The former name of Unarius)

86

tion and healing. This electronic marvel need not be used by hands but is operated by the mind consciousness calling it into action.

Directly in front and to the right of the great throne, stands a lovely but small round table of gold crystal. This was designed especially to hold the crown and the scepter, the wand standing upright in a golden brace made for the purpose. Directly atop the table had been placed a soft, deep red velvet pillow which held the diamond crown in all its radiating splendor, which is the center of attraction.

The round table which held the crown and wand was the only artifact on this great crystal island (which holds the throne) other than one square red quartz crystal table. Upon this table had been placed the great "Book of Life" upon which were the seven seals of gold. The book was covered in purest gold satin, the leaves were finest thin gold, edged in flecks of purest of gold. This book is treasured by all who live in this great city, for it contains all the words of all the great Masters who have, in the eons past, been sent from this city upon a mission into the earth worlds.

The book was about five times the size of your larger earth books; it is unusually large, but this not necessarily need be, for this was symbolic of the great importance within. The messages so held are impinged in energy forms, and in deeply embedded letters upon the cover, in the most solid gold letters, it read: "The Book of Life." The Messengers of the past had heard from their Overlords: Take ye not, nor addeth thereto, not one word from this, "The Book of Life".

Although it was related of the large group of beautiful boy singers, of the great chorus, of the wonderful opera singers, of the magnificent crystal organ, yet there was one small but important group of musicians who were not overlooked, but they were in a rather obscure position that took a little observing to be able to focus upon their particular area and ray beam. Now, as we zoom in, in consciousness, we see much more clearly, and the reason they were not observed before, is that there is so much luminosity, so much color, brilliance and energy in action everywhere, our attention had been focused more on the lower or floor area within the great temple.

Positioned in mid air, near the throne, poised in space, was a group of the littlest Angels, standing atop a tiny pink cloud. They wore long sheer nighties, their red hair cropped, short-curled, in ringlets — with the bluest of eyes. They emitted such gentleness and love. The chubby little darlings appeared in a semicircle, playing their musical instruments — a violin, a triangle, the flute; another her tiny harp. The one with the baton had, perched on her shoulder, a tiny bluebird who added his note. A pink soft radiance shone from within them.

Now it must be said, of the seven little groups of seven, the Littlest Angels, they appeared to be upon a small pink cloud, projected as it were, in the air, and it was strangely noted that they did not have individual auras, but each little group formed one group aura! They all had a beautiful radiation, almost exact circular in form. Emanating from the little group was one instead of seven auras and encircled in an almost precise golden band. Most interesting! These adorable little, it seems almost proper to call them cherubs, were so darling, all dimpled and gay in their song and music. It was they too, who did not remain for the entire procedure, but they simply made their appearance and gave out with their music and song, then disappeared. They seemed to be especially close to nature in all things, such as the birds and flowers. Surely our Logos Queen will especially appreciate this angelic group! It could be said of the Moderator that he often did buy his Love, Ioshanna, these dainty "littlest Angel" figurines upon special occasions, as they both loved the little cherubs.

* * *

From all persons present was the noticed feeling of a deep, beautiful love between each other. This love was projected out and everyone present so shared.

An added note regarding the assemblage itself: All persons present, being of the more exalted positions, were, in themselves, most beautiful. Their inner light shone bright and all faces seemed to radiate such peace and serenity. Happily missing were the taut faces, scowls and tensions so common with eartheans, for all were inwardly serenely at peace and sensing the inner love of the Father, which was most evident, as they each maintain contact with the Infinite Source — the Fountainhead.

Their bodies tall and erect, all emitted the radiance common to all things in this wondrous city. No one was a stranger to another. All shared and expressed the Infinite Oneness which portrayed inner beauty. I saw no blemishes nor evidence of worry. They were at peace within themselves, loving the work they each shared — that of serving the Creative Father. This was so because they each lived close to the Source. Their interests were only of the most high natures — that of serving; of teaching the eartheans this higher way of life. Thus, they had rightfully earned their present state of illumination and function in oneness with the Father Within, and they too have become creators!

But proper and sufficient descriptions of these persons and their way of life have all been well written in the Pulse of Creation books of Unarius by the great leader of the Shamballas himself, the one whom we call the Moderator.

Amongst all these magnificent surroundings, foremost which held all persons spellbound, are the three great, golden pillars of fire, which seemed to grow from out the three crystal plateaus or tiers which are at the lower portion of the great crystal island holding the throne. They seemed alive. These golden energy fountains scintillated, oscillated and shot out from the central core of the flame, even more brilliant golden sparks, darting out into the surrounding atmosphere — when set in motion by the One through his directed Mind Energies. This was done when the individuals or Logoi were to make their ascension — ascension both over the three colored tiers and through the three golden flames, the pillars of fire, and then into the higher dimensions.

It should be realized these three great golden flames are not in any way harmful, nor would they burn one; that is, one who is compatible in frequencies. Any other person would experience a strong electric shock. But only those ready for this forward movement within himself would thus so appear here, for all things are expressed in proper frequencies and in their relationship patterns. The da Vinci biocentrics have prepared themselves well and long for this, their step-up in position from the former Logoi to the soon-to-be Archangel degree.

It has never been in the history of the spiritual worlds before, that these personal positions or progressions were made known to the earthean, except perhaps as in some vague innuendo. However, all the stops have been pulled for this, the new Golden Age! All formerly-held secrets shall henceforth be made known to those who attain and shall clairvoyantly "see" into these spiritual worlds.

Chapter 12

Ioshanna: When you, Vaughn, were relating these beautiful living scenes from the walls, both exterior and interior, of the historic pageantry that actually appeared to come to life, you felt that you could relate many more. Do you want to look further, Vaughn? Vaughn: Yes, as the scenes are shown of the temple in Atlantis, which is shaped as a huge pyramid, and I recall this was the temple that was used as the generator for the whole continent of Atlantis! The whole continent was larger than the size of all North America, and this was the central generating station for Atlantis. It was also used as the scene of annual ceremonies, and the great ceremony that took place in this huge temple pyramid was in commemoration of the departure of their God Amon Ra, who came purposely to bring the Book of Life to the people of Atlantis. As a warning he told that this was the only means by which their civilization could continue, and if they did not heed the information given in the thousand pages of this Book of Life, which was placed under the Flame of Life on the huge crystal dais, they would be lost. Ioshanna: Wasn't that a red quartz crystal, and are you aware of any name this temple may have been called? Vaughn: Yes, the block was of red quartz crystal, and the name of the temple was Amon Ra.

The ceremony that commemorated his sojourn with the people of Atlantis, which lasted approximately a little more than a year, was highlighted by a gift which He (Amon Ra) left for the High Priestess, whose name was Ioshanna, (and who is now the present Channel of Unarius), the name that she took upon herself when she and the Moderator initiated the Unarius Mission on planet Earth.

The love that the High Priestess (Ioshanna) had for Amon Ra, who was considered to be a God, since he materialized upon this crystal quartz during a ceremony that had been taking place, was so great that upon hearing he would shortly be leaving for the higher realms, she swooned and lost consciousness. Upon awakening, she found an absolutely magnificent creation, in the form of a dazzling white Bird of Paradise which the earthman calls peacock! It had the vortexes all about it, which seemed to be the eye of the feather, which was a depiction or a symbology of the Infinite, the power that stemmed from the inner dimensions. So, this ceremony was reminiscent of her great love which she shared with the whole Atlantean culture and race. The yearly ceremonies meant much to these people; the priestesses usually played important parts. For that ceremony in Atlantis, special costumes were made for the priestesses. They were taught in a special manner, a dance which emulated the fan-tailed birds. The costumes, which were of a pure chiffon, had the peacock eye somehow woven in the cloth.

The size of the temple was immense, and with many columns. The priestesses, the fairest of all, would dance out from many portions of the temple and would converge toward the center where the Flame of Life was positioned. They seemingly walked on air, and seemed to be on their toes as ballet dancers. The wide chiffon would drape over them and they would have the symbolic appearance of the Birds of Heaven. They would raise and lower their arms in graceful motion like the birds. They would have a particular way of approaching in a dance formation that had been practiced for many months; this way, it would be a yearly commemoration of the importance of the visit of the beloved Amon Ra.

The Head Priestess, Ioshanna, had a costume of the purest of white; in addition, there was a beautiful blue cape made of the eye of the feathers that covered her. Ioshanna: Actually the head of the bird was formed in the headpiece. The exquisite cape which covered her entire body glittered like thousands of diamonds. It was made of the eyes of the feathers of the beautiful great blue and green bird. The long arms were encased with a tight-fitting material of the same color, and from the arms hung the long, beautiful feathers of the heavenly birds themselves, and which hung to the floor. I am conscious of that from the description that was given before by the Moderator but it is just as real today as it was then. My memory is vivid of that beloved occasion, and I am sure there are many other scenes on the wall that you could relate. Vaughn: Many additional reenactments or scenes can be seen on the deeply embossed golden walls of the golden temple. One shows a wide plane with a huge structure. It is all white, reaching almost ten thousand feet high! This is a portrayal of the first civilization that the Lemurians created when they brought their intelligence to the planet Earth, and in the continent of the Pacific they began to develop the new cities and the various power stations. This gigantic, white superstructure, taller than any known skyscraper was actually a landing place for their space-ships as they commuted regularly from the planet Lemuria to the Earth.

One views the scene as if one were right there at that time, and is taken to the base of this great superstructure, which is shown with huge doorways around the periphery! It is also shaped as a pyramid, but the top has a special superstructure erected so that the spaceships can land. There is a special, one can call it, elevator, which transports the arriving persons from the other planetary systems down to the base of the temple.

This gigantic structure has many purposes. It is a scientific building and has an astro-physical purpose in determining the various changes occurring in the seasons. It is a place for observing the vast sky and for determining the relative size of the solar system. It is an observatory and one can see instruments which are far above and beyond anything that has been seen on earth. The telescope is of an immense size. There are other intricate instruments which are not familiar to me.

On the numerous floors of this vast building, there are laboratories. There are at least five hundred stories here! This is all portrayed on the walls and the floors of the museum.

The great reenactments or depictions that cover the walls, inside and out, plus the floor areas in the large museum of the huge crystal temple on the great plateau of Eros are all depictions of historical portrayals of civilizations and epochs pertaining to souls sent on a mission from this very crystal plateau, called Parhelion. The different scenes show depictions of the laboratories, the observatories, they show the sizes. There is biochemical research of all natures and every aspect of science is given over to research in this great temple, which serves purely as a research laboratory. The Lemurian Masters also live in this temple, which is their home. Ioshanna: In other words, their lives are devoted wholly to science. Of course, we know all such things as you are describing are first created on the inner planes and brought down on the physical as a result of and most often, an exact duplicate. Could it be that this great configuration or enclosure, which we have termed temple and museum, was first on the inner planes, and the temple you are describing is a replica or duplicate, or patterned after? Vaughn: Yes, that is very true, and this is why the scenes shown on the temple walls are very familiar because they are the replicas which have been created by the Advanced Intellects who have come from these planets of a higher frequency, down to the lower planes and there they have built a replica of that which has already existed in the plane such as Parhelion, and other sections of Unarius, the higher Spiritual Worlds.

The great golden temple, in which the "Conclave of the Light Beings" is taking place, has this exception; in that this is the epitome of all the temples that have ever been built! It embraces, in a sense, the history of the individual temple buildings that have appeared in other dimensions, and it is a pageant of what has been achieved in the five hundred thousand years by the Archangels, the many, many Beings who worked along side. As a result, all of these planes have, in their history, a degenerate form of the knowledge that was initially brought to them, but over which their own selfish desires, took precedence. The true knowledge of life as lived as an oscillation with the Infinite was lost by the earth beings, and now it is as a myth or as a fragment of a faith or truth forgotten, that the earth people reminisce, in their literature and their arts. But all of the myths have a basis in fact, and now the great golden walls depict all this historical pageantry that has occurred through the many ages past.

We continue along in the viewing of the great walls and we see the pageantry of Egypt and the

Egyptian history. There are only two eras that are free of pestilence, war, or any form of hostility, and these took place in the time of the reign of Queen Hatshepsut and when Akhenaton was Pharaoh. During this period of time, the exquisite wall scenes on the golden temple depict a great building program that she inaugurated. We see the great temple of Tel Amarna, seemingly to come out of a mountain. It is shown as a beautiful pearl as the whitest of white. A special marble was chosen and mined, and this is the basis of the temple which is built literally, right into the mountain. It is very modern in terms of 20th Century earth. It was one of the most elegant of all structures of that time. It is, itself, a depiction of the inner as brought down through the mind of Queen Hatshepsut. Ioshanna: Did you know you helped me and were close by at that time? Vaughn: I know from my own awareness of the past, lived with Hatshepsut as a personal bodyguard, an aide. Yes, I was very proud to have been with Queen Hatshepsut and to have observed all the great works. In this way, I incepted much positive awareness of what was dominating her consciousness and her determination to bring beauty in the form of architecture, in the form of great formal gardens, and in the growing of many, many new varieties of shrubbery, flowers, and trees, which were brought from various parts of the world. Ioshanna: When you carried me on this palanquin and would go through the great and lengthy tunnel that extended from the front palace to the rear one, on through the mountain, and about which no one at the time, knew, you got a little rough with the palanquin at times and my shoulder would get jarred against the tunnel walls! This, I remember to this day!

Vaughn: It was shown that the great Aton, as was depicted on the walls of all the buildings Akhenaton attempted to introduce at the time, was to show the people that the force or the power of life from the sun was, itself, a small portion of the Infinite; that the power came not from the sun, but the sun helped disburse the power. As I tune in again, it is shown on the walls of the temple, the scenes of the building of the new city of Amarna, the great boulevards and gardens, which were bursting with the greatest profusion of flowers that has ever existed. Roses were very predominant and all of the flowers that we presently see, plus many now unknown, that emitted fragrance never equalled.

Perusing farther along this great wall, the interior and exterior as well, for they both are completely covered with the great, vast and infinite depiction (or reenactments) of this historical portrayal, we could say, almost a millennium of the earth's history is hereon related. It is portrayed, not only of this one earth but of many more which these higher dimensions overshadow. As stated by the Moderator, they serve as mother, father, doctor, nurse, teacher relationship. It could be said, too, these walls portray the great renaissance of wonderful poets, of artists, of doctors, of the great musicians, of opera singers. Expressionists of all types and natures are here on these walls likewise depicting the great influx of the spiritual artwork expressed during the renaissance of the arts. We can now prophesy in this 1973 year that all the great glory, intelligence and wisdom which was so very wonderfully expressed and related in the past will be dwarfed by all that shall be brought into your earth world in this, your new Golden Age, and which it is just entering, in the present! Yes, this is true! There are, on the walls other than scenes, languages also and the poems so treasured by these various earth planes are shown, also the way and the manner they were brought through into the earth planes. It is related how these artisans were overshadowed always by the great Overlords themselves.

Ioshanna: You were saying you saw scenes depicting even beyond the time of Atlantis? Vaughn: Yes, many depictions are shown as existing long before this time. On the earth planes in Atlantis, the pyramid temple of Amon Ra and the great Lemurian temple have their basis from the planet Lemuria which exists in a far distant galaxy, much closer to the center of this galaxy and which is of a very greatly stepped up frequency. The people lived harmoniously, as one great family. The buildings on the planet Lemuria are of such vast heights, they would make any earthman gasp. The highest building on an earth plane is, maybe a thousand feet, where on Lemuria these buildings were complete cities! The people who lived in the many-storied levels have in proportion to each level, a particular purpose, whether it is for the study of aborigine peoples on various planes or the various cultures, or whether it is every aspect relating to physics, astronomy, chemistry, biology; all the sciences are researched here. This is interesting in that some years ago, the Moderator described to me how the eleven scientists first landed on the planet Earth and that their destination was not the Earth but was Venus; but because of the deflection from a giant sun, their course was diverted and they crashed on this plane! Since they were in a dematerialized, or suspended state of animation, there was no fatality; but the aircraft or the spaceship, itself, was damaged; however, with their great knowledge, they repaired it and it was later directed toward a continent lying on the Pacific Ocean — a continent as large as North America and portions of South America. This is the center upon which the eleven scientists based their research on the earth plane and proceeded to gather together all of the races of men, indoctrinating and teaching them in the arts of living.

Ioshanna: This is all portrayed on those walls too? Vaughn: Yes, this is all portrayed on the walls; how they arrived. This portrayal shows scenes from the original planet from which the Lemurian masters came. It shows their dress — they wore one-piece, tight-fitting garb all red. They were, individually or as a group, from ten to twelve feet in height and possessed reddish-blonde hair and blue eyes; were slightly brownish in complexion and very statuesque; in a sense very thin – the calcium men. Ioshanna: I personally haven't traveled that far around the walls to see all that you have there but I certainly intend to, because it all sounds most intriguing. Vaughn: Well, so far, we have traveled a distance of one mile in describing that which has been related. There are twenty-four miles left and this is but one building of many! Ioshanna: So you have great expectations and wonderful experiences to encounter in the future. That was most interesting about the entire cities being in one building and rings a bell, but I don't believe I have ever read that any place before. Vaughn: It has been told to me by the Moderator that the reason the buildings could be built to such a height was that there was no element of friction from the atmosphere. Because of their knowledge of the materials they used, which were of course, of an entirely different frequency and did not contain the atomic constituents of the one hundred and one elements, the atoms of which made for weight; in a sense they were not affected by the magnetic belts of earth. They floated, we might say!

These cities themselves were self-contained; there was no need for the problems in buildings of today such as airconditioning, refuse removal, warming and cooling apparatus, or all of the various heavy mechanisms to obtain the necessary utilities, etc. And the most marvelous aspect of it is, everything was so well-ordered that one arrived at his destination by the use of airships either individually piloted or as a group; or one could travel by means of one's own levitation. One did not have to use any form of travel by mechanized means. The Moderator said to me also, that at one time, when the eleven scientists arrived on the continent of Lemuria, they proceeded to build this huge temple. The natives, at that time, thought that he and his associates were attempting to reach heaven! They were quite confounded by all they saw. Ioshanna: Now comes to mind a very interesting memory; for, after having seen this beautiful crystaline city of Parhelion, (in which I had spent the greater part of these past two weeks), many concepts have been greatly enlarged upon. Now, as you were speaking, Vaughn, of Lemuria, it reminded me of when the Moderator told how it was that the crystal city was brought in a dematerialized state from the spiritual planes and there remained, for quite some time. Later on, after the aborigines depreciated so in their particular evolutionary decline, the Higher Ones then removed the crystalline city and projected it back into the higher worlds (known at that time as Shamballa and of which our city of Parhelion here is all a part). When I first learned of this almost incredible truth, it seemed rather fantastic and difficult to believe. However, now — not so!

It is all conceivable and it seems this total awareness of the moving, the materializing and dematerializing of this city has become a part of my inner knowing and consciousness. Thus, doubtless, these scenes were likewise portrayed upon these incredible and exquisite, educational depictions. These walls are, indeed, a seemingly never-ending, historical education. Yes, it could be said that this mention you made has, in fact, psychokinetically aligned me into that depiction on the great walls of that vast museum.

Vaughn: Here is another scene that is shown to me now, the great Spiritual City of Shamballa, which is only a myth to most earth people today. It is shown on a huge plateau in the area which is today called the Gobi desert. At that long ago time, the area was beautifully and completely full of vegetation. It was not a desert. It shows the city of Shamballa, very similar to the present description of the city of Parhelion — since it is one and the same, in a sense. The beautiful and fertile area around the crystal city of Shamballa is shown in all its various hues and colorations of crystal, the minarets and the other varied shapes of buildings, triangular, circular, rectangular and many manners of futuristic buildings. Again is shown a vignette portion of what occurs in the buildings. I see a group of beings in purple robes gathered around in a circle and they are all eagerly gazing toward the center. The center of the circle contains a crystal quartz cube and it shows a flame being built up! Ioshanna: Tell us more about that. Just how is that done? Purely by the psychokinetical energies and the cosmic energies involved? Vaughn: Not entirely so. It is expressed in collaboration with their mental energies. They are building up an energy body with the help of the individual who is to appear and who will then become part of the energy body whose consciousness will be lent to it! Thereby, this individual who is appearing, has made a progression or is transferring from another solar system. In a sense the flame creates a frequency which is a means of travel or by which this soul was able to come from a higher planet. Ioshanna: Of course, that would necessarily need be so because the higher one on the inner planes had direct contact with the source for this great energy creation, for the reservoir from which they would draw to build it. So isn't it wonderful? We are now really getting down to the fine points! Vaughn: It is fabulous. Now we begin to see the actual means by which the beings have actually become a part of the Infinite Supply and thereby can live in a much more creative way! They have no limitations whatsoever; it is all very vivid. Ioshanna: What you are seeing is marvelous. If you can attune to further description or details about it, please do so. It is a wonderful opportunity for the readers later. Vaughn: The room in which the gathering has come together is not a mere room; it is more of a dimension. It's as large as the great park land we see in Central Park in New York or the Balboa Park in San Diego. It is not a room but seems to be all open. As in all of the creations from the inner, these rooms are a part of their natural habitat. They are not four bare walls with a ceiling and certain types of furnishings, but they are actually part of nature! It's alive! It isn't static. Everything pulses and breathes, and is replete with waterfalls, fountains, with wildlife, with beautiful birds, exquisite flowers, lovely trees and shrubs; it's quite ecstatic and abundant. It is the Infinite!

Yet, now I see an opposite picture – not pretty. I see another picture represented on the walls, showing the base of this great crystal plateau, the opposite form of life. This is the life which existed after the removal of the great crystal city of Shamballa. It shows a complete bareness. The vegetation is gone; this is now a desert land. One sees the coloration has changed. It is not green and lush, but is now a yellowish and depressing brown. It is desolate and the people have changed in their appearance. They now show faces of cruelty, despair and anger. There is none of the beauty that had preceded this time. This is a depiction indicating again how, when left to their own, the native peoples here had declined. They would rather decline than progress, it is the easier way. It seems even more of an emphatic statement – that one sees the state of man in the lower planes and sees how he has been constantly given all of the resources that are at hand, the Infinite Supply, by the persons who have progressed and come down to help. In spite of the help, within a few hundred or thousand years after the help has been extended and, left to themselves, they seemingly degenerated at a far more rapid rate than they had progressed! Ioshanna: And which must have caused the higher ones a pang in their souls after all their great efforts! Yet, we know they wouldn't become emotional because they have long passed that emotional state. But it is a very sad state when individuals do, as these wonderfully progressed, perfected, beautiful spiritual ones, give up their life in these beautiful realms of what the earthman calls Heaven, and voluntarily come down to help the aborigines; then to see that they not only do not take what they have suggested, or take their teachings and heed, but even more than that, regress farther backwards than they were in the beginning! It is a very sad thing. Ioshanna: Yes, I, myself, do have a slight but not a fond memory of such sorrow. Vaughn: Which is an indication of how great your assistance has been because of this memory and the great love that one who is infinitely minded could have, and which exceeds any understanding we eartheans have.

Ioshanna: So now this new great, golden epoch and era is going to be different! Man is going to be helped against his own will! It must be done! It must be, for if it isn't, many of the surrounding earth worlds and astral worlds will also be destroyed − and we shall not stand by and see it happen! We shall extend all the effort, and this is what this great accumulation of the vast and infinite number of Perfected Beings and Minds have so set in motion all this marvelous electronic equipment that is more or less a generating system and reservoir to collect all the great, the strong and positive Infinite Mind Energies from the very Source, Itself, to be (and is being) projected upon the earth plane for this, the great Golden Age! It is of this vast and never before attempted conclave in which celebration of this pinnacle in the evolution of the entire earth world is now being reached, in the present — Spring of 1973. So be it.

Chapter 13

Upon our first observation, there seemed to be seven trumpeteers; however, our vision at that time wasn't sufficiently clear or long enough for a more pointed observation or focus. It is now plain to see, there are many times seven! Thus, when they quickly snapped into position in the many rows each way, allowing sufficient room in between the rows for the great trumpets to extend, it was indeed quite an exciting moment.

The dashing, colorful trumpeteers made a dramatic appearance as they stepped in unison from out their assembled positions, held in the triangle ranks and, as one, they silently, suddenly appeared, forming a straight line diagonally across the thoroughfare, facing the arched area from which was to come the one being honored — the Queen. Their costumes so brilliant, outshone by far, the pastels worn by most. Their shimmering white boots that reached high over the knees, were glistening in the radiance as they stood statue-like at attention! The mental applause was tremendous.

They made a most striking appearance, for these personages had all been carefully picked, of the thousands who have volunteered — those with especially fine musical abilities. It should be said, these slender golden horns were several times larger than the great trumpets of old, of the earthman. The golden horns glistened in the intense Light that was everywhere. When all was in readiness and their mental signal received, in unison snapped to attention, standing completely erect, they slipped from their sides, their long trumpets of gold, and, as if all being raised by one arm, they were lifted in unison to the lips. A long, high-pitched, earth-shaking, ear-splitting blast was heard! Then, as one, all of the many trumpeteers instantly ceased. All was still. Again came the resounding blasts of the great golden horns. The silence had been broken! The trumpets' blast blared out like shots in the stillness of night, through the great corridors; this continued seven times. The pronouncement had been made! The long awaited time – the great work extending through the thousands of years – was now at hand and the proclamation of the arrival of the great new Golden Age is proclaimed. It's in the now!

From each of the elaborately-decorated thirty-three large openings or archways in this great temple, began to march two by two, beautifully clad in glorious chiffon robes and gowns, thirty-three rows of lovely young ladies. One row of two would be gowned in a very delicate shell-pink color; the rows of two in the next archway would be of a very faint and pastel buttercup; the next archway was filled with ladies in a beautiful orchid shade, and so on through the long thirty-three rows. Each of the girls in the two rows were dressed in the same colored chiffon gowns, varying in shade according to rank. In unison, all the double rows of ladies began moving forward in rhythmic, swaying, ballet motion. As they moved slowly toward the center of this great auditorium, it appeared as one great living rainbow, most exquisite to behold! Their arms were motioning gracefully, the butterfly gowns billowed and fluttered; their own brilliant, psychic aura adding to the colorful spectacle. The music, itself, created much color and was swelling and cascading in these glorious shades, modulating and interweaving, rolling toward the ceiling. The chant of the energies became more and more intense, the pastel color and cloudlike formations finally ascending and building to a very high pitch. When the music-chant had reached the most high peak, at this point the misty, colorful formation would be directed and dissipated out through the ceiling and suddenly, in one great burst, be directed out to all lower planes to be used for healing benefits.

At this particular point, the great golden bell in the courtyard was suddenly heard! It had been struck! A great and almost ear-splitting tone filled the entire temple and city. It grew more intense with the passing of moments as the sound was projected out into (so-called) space and the frequencies gained a regenerative momentum. This was, to all present, a breath-taking moment, for it was known of the great benefits so destined therefrom. As the heavenly intonations were slowly lessening in strength, intensity and tone, all present seemed to be even more filled with the infinite glow. The magnificent maelstrom of energy which the frequencies of the golden bell set in motion, resounded through space and could be heard hours later. The saintly ones now knew their great and concerted efforts were materialising in benefits to all eartheans, their excitement high!

All of the young ladies who'd entered the arches of gold before, had gracefully danced together in a radial effect. As the first couple of each line of thirty-three lines of two met, they came to a halt. The music became slowly softer and the chant of the energies gradually subsided, until they died away, then a complete silence was reached. The thirty-three lines of ladies of two, all paused. They then raised their right hands to touch the two forefingers to their forehead, then they touched their heart, then the lips; then they raised their outturned palms just over and in front of the head, then dropped them to the side. This little symbolic gesture was a sign of gratitude to the Infinite, a significance of rededication to their own progression and to the cause for all mankind. (This salute was later repeated just before they started their march back, to return again through the archways.) Each one of the many thousands of persons joined in this simple but significant gesture in rededication to the great Infinite Intelligence! The love that was generated at this moment was tremendous.

Immediately after the great gates were symbolically opened (these doors are never really shut), in flew countless numbers of beautiful, colorful songbirds, who continued to fly in and out, before and during the entire proceedings, singing their bird songs of cheer, adding their glorious notes of love. Only the song of a meadowlark could compare, and this too, an inadequate comparison. Suffice to say, the gay colors of these beautiful song birds run the gamut. However, all of the birds made an exit before the doves entered.

At the precise moment, just as the flower girls made entrance, a great flock of radiant, blue-eyed doves of the whitest of white came flying out over the esplanade, about midway between ceiling and floor. They were flying in a pattern. The rows crossways, were seven in number; then came the thirty-three lines of seven. The lovely birds seemed whiter than usual, perhaps due in part to the bedecked colored ribbons about their necks, which seemed to join them all in a beautiful pattern; the ribbon which the doves held in their bills drooped softly in each direction so that an almost basket-weave formation existed over the heads of the spectators.

Each lovely white dove wore a different shaded ribbon about its neck. The formation was a large V-shape as the beautiful birds flew slowly o'er the runway. They continued on over the heads of the many Maids of Honor and the one to be crowned. They ushered her up to the throne. The impression was, the lovely birds were Aryans too, thus, the blue eyes! This was a magnificent spectacle for just below the snow-white doves, were seen the beautiful Ladies in Waiting — lines of seven, thirty-three times; each graceful form wore her own particular dimensional shade; the colorful bouffant gowns each carried its own lacy train. Some pastel shades present had not been previously seen, but consisted of all the softest of radiant pastels. The gossamer of the gowns seems to have been sprinkled with glittery gold dust, so sparkling were they all. Each wore a different hair coloring (of gold or red) each a different shade in her gown — no two were alike. The gowns were similarly made of high princess style, the shades diminishing in tone according to rank. Upon their lovely loose-flowing hair was placed a lovely tiara, each with one sparkling bright star to honor their Star Queen Angel. (Normally they too, wore the golden cone-shaped hat.)

Each lovely girl gracefully carried upon the slender arm — the one opposite the hand holding the beautiful veil of the bride — an elegant spray of freshly picked flowers — a different shade than that of her gown; all tied with great ribbons and bows that fell to the floor in colorful harmony. These saintly ladies, themselves, were each one especially chosen and were beauteous of both face and form; seven each, from the thirty-three different dimensions. Each one of these charming young bridesmaids, framed in her wide aura of gold, made a most pleasing picture as they moved slowly up the wide, crystal concourse, carrying either side of the lengthy veil which nearly filled the wide esplanade and extended on at least three city blocks! This was indeed a spectacle of spectacles and no thing was overlooked, all care having been taken to make this the most exquisite affair of the millennium! And indeed, it is all that and much, much more!

Each one of these heavenly ladies, plus the many flower tots and all others participating, were persons who have, at some one time in her many past lifetimes, been in contact in some one way or another — a student, a handmaiden or friend of the queenly one — but each one has had her personal contact, this in order to keep all things thoroughly compatible, frequency-wise. There were no strangers to the queen; some have been her princesses in former incarnations, others helpers, etc., thus, it was all a most joyous and compatible affair, not one blemish was there to mar the exquisite beauty and perfect harmony everywhere about. Yes, even the glorious bird of iridescent color — her favorite friend of the past — the Bird of Paradise, was remembered! Seven shimmering rows of thirty-three of the radiant, beautiful birds were seen in a proud strut, forming a line o'er the wide thoroughfare, just before the time the flower girls entered. The heavenly birds (Peacocks) all had their fantails erect, they were shaking their feathers in their glorious way; the radiance of the Light that shone upon these feathered friends was a breathtaking experience!

Doubtless, other spiritual worlds shall, in the future, be repeating this heavenly sight — far too uplifting and exquisite to attempt, as we are, to put into word forms. It is almost sacrilege to try! Yet, try we must.

The greatly honored guest will soon make her regal appearance through the great golden central archway, the gigantic crystal organ will begin to peal the most heavenly music. This will bring into action the many glorious variations of most exquisite color that shall rise up through the great crystal pipes, creating a most magnificent display! When the tempo is soft and slow, the cloudlike, colorful formation drops lower into the clear tubes, as if in a graceful ballet. Thus when the music builds in tempo, the color rises nearer the top of the crystal pipes. Not until the heavenly tones reach an almost ear-splitting crescendo, but still harmonious — do the colored energy clouds rise to and spill out over the top of the pipes. They are then joined to the great formations of energy that rise to the ceiling above and then accumulate. All stood aghast, awaiting to view this most glorious spectacle, most magnificent to see!

Vaughn: Just before the great procession began flowing in through the great archway, my attention was suddenly attracted to many great white clouds overhead. Then the clouds began to appear, to swiftly move toward the center of this great gathering place. Soon it was discernible that what seemed as the ceiling, filled with billowing clouds, were actually countless hundreds of Music Angels! They moved in unison, coming closer, to and over the area over which will pass the honored queen and her heavenly entourage. The tall Angels hovered above in the higher areas of the great enclosure when my psychic vision realized it was indeed a great host of Angels! Angels who were humming in unison for the incoming Queen, the Logos!

This was truly a sight to behold! I now had to pinch me to make sure I was fully awake – and indeed, no dream ever had it so good! It was all for real! The great chorus of heavenly ones filled the entire upper areas, and instead of seeing what was formerly the semblance of a conical crystal covering, there were countless hundreds, it seemed, of the beautiful Angels – all draped in lovely loose flowing gowns of various shades of pastels. These Beings too, were all divided in color according to dimension and degree. Those toward the front, the shades would be most vivid, then they became paler as one viewed those in the distance. Although they formed one great ceiling covering, hovering together, yet the colors all blended harmoniously – a most magnificent sight to behold!

Those in the distance seemed smaller, this doubtless due to my perspective to which I'd been accustomed. Each beautiful Angel was seen, her hair flowing loosely all about her; the sheer billowy gowns they wore seemed little more than the sheerest gossamer and were draped loosely and softly about the shoulders, flowing out seemingly in the breeze so gracefully. The pink, slender bare arms and tiny feet seemed so graceful as they all gathered, poised in midair; gold cords were draped about the waist, the ties hanging long and loose. Most noted was the exquisite fragrance emitted by the great heavenly gathering.

The angelic appearance upon their radiant faces penetrated the very depths of my very being, as I stood aghast. I had in the past, rather felt such things were fables or tall tales, yet here I was in reality, face to face with a host of the saintly ones! The great beauty and love expressed by this spiritual host, was beyond any means of description and far superseded any view I had hoped to imagine!

At four precise and evenly spaced points there appeared, seemingly in front of all others, nearer the crystal floor upon which the observers stood, hovered four tall, slender Angels, each holding poised to her lips, a very slender trumpet of gold. The graceful instrument was exceedingly long and I caught me wondering how it was balanced, just being so used to the atom formed structures. These four, positioned at the quarter points, divided the entire area in four sections, seemingly leaned at a slanting position — half between sitting and lying. In unison, and at a precise moment, all four sounded the golden trumpets which brought forth most heavenly golden tones. It was a brief announcement made, which was repeated periodically, seven times – the angelic salute to the Logos queen.

The radiating tones seemed to stir the angel gathering to expel and direct an even greater and more pronounced wave of love to the countless thousands gathered below!

The auric emanations extending from this heavenly group and surrounding them all was of the whitest of white and extended in such great distances about each one, they indeed appeared to be wearing large wings. It was a glistening white, the aura that these blessed ones projected, for they were far advanced above these even high dimensions, and only visited other worlds and galaxies at especial times and need, or celebration. This, doubtless the reason artists have painted, in the past, angels with wings – due to the great white radiations or auras.

This host of many thousands, and when it was questioned as to the number present, it is sensed there were thirty-three hundred, called the Heavenly Angels. Their individual service is healing of group consciousness and to project their intonations of love into lower worlds. Theirs is a selfless service of love. It was impressed that the love emitted by this great gathering is of such intensity that all who are touched by their musical tones are healed! The (silent) sounds emitted by the hum of their voices carry healing energies! These adoring healing angels wore no adornments whatsoever on or about them; instead, within the hand of each is seen one long-stemmed, elegant deep red rose bud of beauty beyond compare.

Now, just before the ring bearer appears, are seen thirty-three young candle bearers, each carrying a single candle, purely a representation of the eternal flame. They moved up the esplanade in a V-formation, dressed as choir children with full smock gowns falling near to the knees. These were caught at the neck with a large colorful bow that dropped near the floor corresponding with the color of their particular smocks, each of which was relative to his particular ray. This was a mixed group of both boys and girls some of whom were in training for vocal groups on the earth planes. They sang not the earthy popular tunes but all carried a continuity relative to some spirituality. These groups were of the ages of ten or twelve, but most sincere in their musical expression. They bore the single candle with pride as if it were their gift to the Queen.

Then, just as the flower tots were scattering their colorful petals below, the angelic hosts were seen, all in unison, to toss to the approaching queen below, beauteous roses. A magnificent spectacle it was – their gift of love to their "Archangel, to be". For she is to pass from the degree of Logos to that of Archangel – with the crowning.

Such was this beautiful and heavenly assemblage! This sight was near more than could be borne even in our ascended state of consciousness. What a joy and blessing to have experienced this great gathering! They reminded me of pictures we've seen of the heavenly hosts — but this was more than a picture and I'm most humble and thankful that I've been so blessed as to have been present, especially for the entrance of this great assemblage of the most heavenly ones! — a never to be forgotten moment; for the tone that poured forth from them in unison was tumultuous!

As all anxious eyes were directed to the great central archway awaiting for whomever it was to emerge, the great organ softly began to emit most exquisite tones. The music caused one to feel love.

Heading the tiny ones was one single golden-haired tot, surely not more than three. She was dressed in the sheerest of cloth, pale pink for this is her frequency in color and ray. She stepped proudly on through the long thoroughfare, realizing that which she carried so high, to be of great import to this gala affair, measuring each tiny step in tempo with the great organ, which was pouring forth exquisite melody, one tiny foot was bended up to the knee of the other leg in a graceful prancing attitude.

Then a host of tiny young children, mostly girls, came tripping out, down the thoroughfare in a graceful Spring dance. They were all dressed in dainty flower colors. They carried gold, woven baskets, all filled with their own particular shade of petals, corresponding with the precious costumes they wore. These wee tots were all scholars of the dance, preparing for a life and a time when they would again live upon some such earth plane when they'd ballet dancers become. They were brought in for this one particular purpose, to serve as lovely flower girls for the honored guest. They were dancing about in gayful glee (for they loved the particular expression they chose) tossing petals about over the thoroughfare for the One o'er to tread, making sure every inch of the floor was covered with their colorful array. Each one was bedecked in an especially-made costume that appeared as some one particular flower! No two were garmented alike. There was the tiny, pale buttercup whose petals, so dainty and fragrant, stood erect about the wee one's body; tiny stamens extending from atop her small head. The colorful petals she scattered were the pale buttercup flower. Then the fragrant sweet pea children made a beautiful sight; for there were many of the various shades, all decked in the profusion of color, unique alone to the lovely sweet peas, who scattered about their own flower tops. Of especial interest were the wee daisy tots. The shades and patterns of these happy flowers which so profusely grow in these heavenly realms, emit their own spicy, gay moods and the many colored petals stood erect, as the freshest of flowers from the midriff of the pretty young things. The colors of daisies ran the gamut of the entire paintbox, so varied do the daisies grow, in these realms. These loveable tots seemed especially proud as they twirled about causing the tiny dresses looking as flowers, to literally spin in delight! Yes — spinning, dancing flowers it seemed!

Unique above all, seemed the colorful pansies whose beautiful faces formed the large headwear in order that their beauty be not hidden. Then came the delicate poppies; the more brilliantly colorful field poppies so gay in their sun color. Next were the shirley poppies in their infinite number of shades, again each shade was represented. The tiny ones wearing these poppy frocks were especially happy as their sheer tiny skirts would flutter, bounce and billow as they gracefully danced about. Each girl seemed to take on the very mood of the flower she represented! These colorful tiny ones who appeared tripping their dainty ballet, seven abreast and in thirty-three rows. Each flower that existed upon this plane was hereby represented in these colorful costumes so gay! This was indeed, a living garden long to be remembered!

As was mentioned, the little dancing flower tots scattered petals to cover thoroughly every inch of the thoroughfare. Still when the much honored guest came forth and thereover walked, not one petal was disturbed! She literally floated slightly above the great crystal floor.

As the procession began to make appearance at the far end of the beautiful esplanade, several long city blocks away, the countless beautiful voices – mixed male and female – broke into glorious song. These were all personages of the opera who had, at one time or another, achieved great earth fame. This great assemblage was all garmented in the roles they had especially expressed on earth.

The one leading and directing these vocalists held within his hand a most beautiful baton, with all of the gems of the rainbow. As it slashed the air in his graceful motions, the sparkle from these stones glittered and reflected throughout the walls of the temple. They completed seven beautiful vocalizings. The first was her favorite and in her honor – the beautiful Mona Lisa song. Ava Maria having special significance to them both, was rendered next; then the heavenly San Sans – the Swan – which is loved, not only by them but by most great spiritual souls; and so on, through the seven heavenly renditions. All really fine music was first written in these higher worlds and inspired to an earthean. The harmony was breathtaking and uplifting. Within this vocalizing was created especially built-in energy, compatible to all other such harmony. There can be no blemished frequency present, no disharmony can exist.

Those great operas for which they were best known and here now were all costumed as the particular notes they played, or of which were most familiar to eartheans; such operas as the famous Rigoletto by Verdi. The gala costumes of those elegant portrayals in these earlier years were very elaborate, and heavenly laden with ornaments and heavy and beautiful jewelry. Such representations as the opera Carmen by Bizet, the popular Mefistofele, by Boito, a Midsummer Night's Dream by Britten, the great Faust by Gounod and Handel's Alcina; the ever loved opera Pagliacci by Leonacello was, here in the great assemblage of operatic voices, all represented in full regalia and costumes: Mozart's Don Giovanni, Puccini's Madame Butterfly, his great number Tosca, the well-known and beloved J. Strauss' Die Fledermaus Gala, as well as his Electra were all represented here in this great chorus of opera singers, not only they, but the composers as well were present to add their powers and light!

Verdi was well represented in the many writings such as Aida, Don Carlo, Falstaff, Macbeth, Otello and, of course perhaps greatest of all, his Rigoletto; La Traviata taking no second to best; the popular Flying Dutchman by Wagner as well as his ever-popular Tannhauser, his Tristan and Isolde, were all represented — these but a few of the greats of old, so joined here in this temple of gold to do honor to our Queen! There represented were many more: Rossini, Strauss, Tchaikovsky, Victor Hugo and many more, far too numerous to relate herein, but we can assure the reader that any of the operas or operettas of the past that have remained in your history were first created here in these higher dimensions, and as a result, were brought to earth through the pen of some one or more of these composers and artists. The gala array, the form in these elegant and extravagant costumes of some, in countless yards of voluminous, sheer chiffons, velvet, metals, the high styled coifs and powdered wigs, are all here now re-enacted in the present for our Queen by these very authors, composers and singers! Thus it was that Ioshanna was so warmly attracted, for at one time she, herself, had likewise so expressed in these opera performances, for she had been one of the quite famous sopranos of the past. So it was that these personages were all most familiar and in good rapport. Enrico Caruso, himself, gave a special solo rendition for the Queen, in an after-gathering of the entourage, which literally shook the chandeliers in the ceiling, and some were noted to peer upwards to make sure he'd not shatter the great electronic works! Yet, they were of radiant crystal — not glass. This, too, was one of her many delights. *

It should be related here, Raphael, one of the Queen's favorite artists, painted for her a most magnificent creation, that of the Angelic Chorus that appeared for a brief time. This, he had created and presented to her for her home, as she had always loved especially, the paintings of Angelic Beings. This painting is curved or dome-shaped and shall be placed over her bed in her new home here on Parhelion,

*It may be related that one may obtain, even in this present day, the recorded voices of many of these 'greats' of the past on (pseudo) stereo records.

for it fills an entire circular ceiling and is done as a living art expression, with the background of beautiful, snowy, billowing clouds over a backdrop of heavenly blue sky. This magnificent work of art by Raphael, shall await our Archangel until her earth mission is fulfilled; meanwhile, she slips to this plateau in her astral and sleep state.

It should be observed by the reader, that these great opera singers of the past, carry particular psychokinetical energy; that it is projected through their voices, for all these personages have lived and have been schooled in these higher dimensions, learning and attaining the vital principles of psychokinetics by which they project these healing frequencies through their voices. Any recording you may hear, of the voice of Caruso, carries these healing frequencies due to his contact with these higher dimensions.

Soon after the renditions of these glorious voices, were heard the harmonious and exquisite tones from thirty-three huge and golden (Italian) harps that stood near the throne area. These most elegant instruments, the strings of which were being touched by the long, graceful fingers of the same number of beautiful girls – each one a queenly beauty, now advanced or spiritually progressed to the degree of an Angel. Long golden hair flowed o'er their shoulders in soft waves, covering them down over their torsos. Each was gowned in the exquisite shades of coral, pink, orchid, yellow, blue and so on; the lovely robes flowing in great ripples, billowing out over the floor, almost covering the tiny golden sandals worn by these angelic forms. From the eyes of these Beings were projected two brilliant ray-beams, healing energies which melded and mixed with the energies from the tones of the strings on their harps.

Upon the shoulders of each of these lovely harpists had been artistically placed a huge, most elegant orchid! It had been all glittered with gold dust — this the only decoration upon their exquisite gowns of pastels. These flowers were each some eighteen inches in diameter, created as are all things in these dimensions of crystaline substance. A more beautiful or lovely group of girls just could never have existed. They are exquisite in both face and form; most important of all, their auric emanations are extremely large, and the beauty of their faces was met only by the grace of their long slender hands. The touch of their long, dainty fingers, as they repeatedly drew their hands high in the air, the motions were as graceful as any beautiful swan. As they created artistic designs in the air, the colored energy pattern remained poised overhead. Their arms and hands seemed to have no stiffness of finger, for it was with a most beautiful symmetry as they lightly touched the golden strings. As these golden harps were lovingly touched by these beautiful ones, the note emanations were seen to dart out from the strings in living color. We could actually 'see' the notes float from the strings, most beautiful to see; they appeared as in a dance. Soon the harps faded into a quietness.

Suddenly, there seemed to take over, a new dead silence; a quietude that was noticeable to the senses as if something vital was about to happen. A great hush descended over the luminous heads of all; all eyes turned to gaze toward the great central archway in excited expectancy as if to get a first glimpse of the so honored guest, and to welcome whomever it was, who would enter through this great elaborate facade. In unison, as the great organ struck out it pealed forth in an allegro tempo, the great chorus of singers joined in. The thirty-three harpists too, all joined in this welcome, as their dainty hands rose high into motion, touching upon the exquisite golden harp strings. The sing-song chants of all rose to a new height and the happy boys' choir burst forth — just after the trumpeteers blasted forth in their high-pitched sounds of proclamation. In unison, and instantaneously, the great halls were filled with magnificent sound and color, for each note carries its peculiar shade and adds to the cascading, cloudlike, color formations. All this is welcoming the procession.

Chapter 14

Then she appeared! From out the distant golden corridor, through the central arch, slowly moved forward the lovely young female form. She was gowned in an exquisite, sheer, diaphanous chiffon of the finest shimmering gossamer! The robe billowed out and seemed to float about her for several blocks behind, as she slowly moved; each step so measured in a harmonious tempo that she seemed to glide, rather than to walk, up the center of this great cathedral thoroughfare. The translucent material of her gown, which was of the whitest of white, radiated the crystaline energies of which all things are formed in these colorful dimensions. The lovely golden hair cascaded in graceful waves far over her shoulders, from the top of her lovely head to below her tiny waist. It seemed to glisten as though made of the finest of webs of the material in the chiffon. The strands of hair seemed to be of a fine, spun glass crystal. Her eyes were luminous and of deepest blue. The Light which shone from them was like twin searchlights! There was an intense beam! Her face was very transparent — as alabaster and most ethereal. The tall lovely figure does indeed present a beautiful picture as she glides slowly down this wide, crystal runway in her shimmering gown, framed as she is in the great, glowing white aura (or halo), which is the scientific significance. This aura extends out great distances and in all directions about her. Yes, we said, a lovely young figure, for she does appear to be about thirty-three; for there is no age for a Spiritual Being who does not believe in age. She appears to be in her thirties, for this is the age she has chosen to remain.

The tension builds! It is she! It is now realized by all, that the lovely Being who is in the center of focus, is the (present) Unarius Channel Ioshanna! What a joyous surprise! Following the many tiny ones, her flower tots, she proceeds to take the long trek over the crystal thoroughfare that all may share in the beauty and joy. It takes some time to traverse the many miles, yet no tiredness is experienced in these realms. Soon the near circle comes full, for she now moves slowly toward the center of the temple, on toward the great golden throne – and arrives there far too soon for the onlookers! As she passed slowly by and in front of the great assemblage, all extended their mind energies in love. Many were the gasps that could be sensed of all the beauty that befronted them. They wanted it to last forever! Soon she arrived at her destination, the golden throne platform, and stopped just before the great throne and the three colorful tiers of crystal upon which she will quickly emerge.

As Ioshanna reached the place of the throne platform and just as she came to the point of making the ascension, there stood her biocentric, Leonardo da Vinci. She beamed joyfully!

He had stepped out of his rank or position (the front or corner person in his particular triangular section) to meet her. He seems so proud of his beloved one. She took the arm he offered, and together paused before they started to ascend to the seven steps of recharging, revitalizing, crystal rays within the three crystal tiers that would, after their passing over them, enable the two, as biune, to step on into a higher degree in their spiritual ascendency − a new and higher dimension.

Thus it was, the two paused and, for a few brief seconds, each gazed into the eyes of the other, in love. As the couple met, the tiniest tot, carrying the wee cushion of gold, stepped up to their side, as the tall one (Logos da Vinci) reached down and removed the tiny golden circlet which the pillow had borne, and slipped it upon the waiting hand of Ioshanna. Then she picked up the second larger circlet of gold and it was placed upon his finger, in love. The golden circlets were significant of the oneness they share − of the oneness of each with all infinity, the circle a symbol of completeness or the whole. All things are complete in the abstract. (In fact, it was in these inner dimensions where the marriage ceremony was first initiated! However, the earthman has even deteriorated this beautiful symbolic gesture which had implied a oneness with the Infinite.)

Then the first radiating blue crystal tier was ascended, and the two stepped directly into the huge pillar of fire. There they remained for some few seconds. The aura and Light of both expanded and grew as they stood quietly still. Thus it was, the two paused for a brief span, the energies subsiding; then the second gold crystal tier was ascended and the two stepped fearlessly, directly into the huge, flaming pillar. Great concentrations were necessary at this time. They remained again, a brief time. The combined radiations and aura of the two made a magnificent sight, in gold or gold-white Light. The aura and white Light of the two continued to expand outwardly and grew as they stood. They then stepped up two steps onto the third tier, which was of rose crystal and there remained. Again out shot great radiations of the already vastly expanded aura and Light into an even greater brilliance, as the third and even larger pillar of fire was entered. Here they remained. They had together, stood tall and erect, glowing radiantly. The now (seemingly) singular Light took on the coloration of this ray. As the great golden flame on this level was larger, they now shone with the three shades as an overshadowing, over and above the former color tones of themselves, which was goldish white.

With the arrival upon this top crystal tier, the glorious great ball of Light which was now the two, was extremely bright! Upon the next golden plateau stood the great and tall (overlord) Moderator. It is impossible to guess his height, but surely, the size of a several storied building. He gave his blessing to both. Then Ioshanna stood erect and quiet; her recharging and ascension complete, she had now been prepared for her well-earned degree. Here, such degrees and honors are, in no sense, bestowed promiscuously, for each being so involved must earn what he becomes; he so becomes, due to great and lengthy endeavor, striving and application. Mastership means mastery over self and the lower worlds.

It should be realized that in such important changes, spiritual initiations or steps up in one's evolution, many kinds of energy are involved in helping to create this new person — and that is about what it all amounts to, a new Being. Required are the psychokinetical mind energies of the Spiritual Beings present, plus the strong positive mental energies of the one passing into the higher state, combined with frequencies within the crystal tiers over which the initiate walks — plus energies directed from colored lenses above and about the cathedral — and perhaps most important of all, the energies absorbed from the pillar of fire. Equally important in such an initiation are the combined energies or the psychokinetics of the entire assemblage: It is these combined and accumulated frequencies that help bring about the change and new state with the individual.

Ioshanna then knelt upon an awaiting seven-sided pillow of gold, just before the huge throne of gold, in front of which stood the Moderator (and his biocentric). At the moment of extreme tension and high-pitched excitement, all eyes and minds were eagerly focused upon the two beings in front of the throne, adding their powers. The illumined ones all, the entire assemblage, stood alert with bated breath, and in unison, everyone present, including the Moderator, dimmed their Lights! They dimmed their Lights! As we telescoped our vision toward the beautiful Queen, tears were seen to fall. It was just too great for her to bear, all this love, of the countless thousands present pouring forth in that great pinnacled crisis, all energy had reached a new high – a moment never to be repeated, nor forgotten!

The intense brilliance that now shone (the two biocentrics) as all other personal Lights were dimmed, was something to behold! The appearance was as ten great radiating suns amongst the darkness of night! The brilliance was more than eyes could take, even in astral state. The two (now Archangels) appeared as one great tall skyscraper, brilliantly illumined! – breathtaking, uplifting and transcending to behold.

This act of humbleness and homage expressed – (the dimming of the personal Lights of all the spiritual beings) by the countless thousands present, as one grand gesture in salute, is an expression of love and commendation toward the newly ascended pair. This act of dimming of the personal Lights o the assemblage was expressed in order that the Lights of the Queen (and her biune) appear the more bright! Surely, no greater respect could ever be paid to any personage! The great infinite love expressed by all, seemed a bit too much for even these Archangels themselves!

The great overlord (the Unariun Moderator) then slowly removed from the nearby rose crystal table, the elegant electronic crown and lovingly placed it upon her head! He pronounced her "The Archangel Uriel" (Leonardo da Vinci being the biune Michiel)! Then as he stood, this great Avatar very carefully removed from its resting place and held within his hands, the most beautiful golden wand! This wand was then touched to the tall shoulder of Ioshanna, then it was placed upon the soft palms of her two upturned white hands. This was his great gift to her! The symbology here was that the Light had been placed in her keeping or possession. He was seen to slowly bend to place upon the cheek of the Queen, his personal expression of love, a loving kiss; yet all others (later) simply pressed the tip of the Queen's fingers to their lips. Most of the eyes of all present were moist, his, perhaps even more than all others. His love for Ioshanna has long endured for countless thousands of years as they and their two biunes, Erza and Michiel (or Esther and Leonardo) have, through countless ages past, walked very closely together as a unit of four (and there are many more) even though they may have been worlds apart! Thus it is a vital and pinnacled time for especially these four great God Forces who now can function as one, or two polarities, and which (two) is the more common manner.

The climactic pinnacle was at hand! An even greater high pitched moment of tension arrived. At the precise moment when they had been mentally prompted, suddenly swooped down two great and beautiful angelic beings! They did not remain for the procession to pass, but swiftly they poised, high in the air, one on each side of the throne, holding highly aloft, each a golden candlestick! Within each were seven golden candles, brightly aglow. The beautiful beings had come from a high, distant galaxy, their adorations and love to add. The long, flowing hair of these two beautiful ones was exceedingly red, the aura surrounding them, filled a great distance about, causing them to appear as though they wore huge feathered wings! The golden circlet over each of their heads shone most saintly, denoting the great heights to which they had ascended. A large, brilliant star shone from their forehead, for they were the Star-Angels. Poised there above in midair for one quick span of time, then they, together, as one, dipped down in front of the throne and touched with their long golden wands, the forehead of the two in await! This act was performed in unison, as great darting beams shone forth from their eyes, adding their blessings of Light. The touch on the forehead was made with the wands; there flashed seven great streaks of lightning, seemingly to reach across the entire Heavens above! Instantly they had vanished, but not before it was noted, of the many lovely white doves (with blue eyes) who were holding within their bills, the trailing sheer gowns of the Angels. A most heavenly sight has ne'er been viewed as they strew their fragrance so rare – the elixir of the very gods, upon the honored ones! Soft, dainty tinkling bells were heard in the distance, as if to call home our visiting ones.

No view was possible of the two – our newly formed biune pair, for the Light was most too brilliant.

Ascended in development far above and beyond any position on this high plateau is one Being called Serapis. This great and advanced soul very seldom enters or returns to this plane of consciousness, for he has long progressed from out these (even high) planes. Serapis never takes on a physical form but his radiant appearance is that of a great golden flame. His preference is to alight atop a crystal lake or water. He then mentally gives his psychic lecture or teaching, then suddenly disappears! Thus it was! At the precise appearance of the two great Angels, did the great golden scintillating flame, Serapis alight upon the lake nearest the throne. He remained but a brief span – sufficiently long to project and deliver his vibrant mental message to the already overwhelming beauty existent.

His Mind was directed especially to the two now being promoted in their new spiritual ascendency of progress, yet all were mentally attuned. His message was pointed and beautiful and carried most high frequencies of Infinite Love.

Ioshanna has long felt an affinity toward this advanced soul and was most surprised and delighted to see that He, too, had projected himself into this (lower to him) sphere! A greater love welled within her already overwhelmed soul – her transcending state as he poured forth his love, his blessings and rays most Infinite! Then he was gone.

Instantly after the appearance of the two great Angels and that of Serapis and the Moderator (an Avatar of the highest degree) had placed upon Ioshanna's head, the crown and laid within her palms the wand, he then seated himself on the great golden throne! As he placed his hands upon the arm rests, this act set in motion, great cosmic force-fields, generative in nature. Such were the tremendous forces and powers existent that all beings present became super-charged – even in their exhalted state of frequency! Thus, an indefinable and indescribable power was so directed in motion, to henceforth regenerate itself eternally! In other words, the crown is likewise, as is the throne, a tremendous generator, channeling Cosmic power out into the lower worlds. Suddenly, was one great, blinding flash of pure white Light! It was a brilliance of a thousand suns, as he, with his great powers, made contact with the powerful generator – the throne! As this happened, it was with his great blessing to the loving couple – an added thrust or forward motion in their progression was made. For a brief period of time, after this great burst of Light, which was like an explosion – yes, it could easily be said – as an A-bomb explosion, multiplied, our vision was blacked out.

Upon regaining our inner vision although nothing was discernible for another brief time, when this Light (which is the great Leader Lord of Unarius), was again able to be viewed, it (or he) was seen to contain all the multiplicities of color in a great radiance, in the outermost areas of the vastly expanded and expansive aura of the luminosity. He appeared as ten thousand lightning bolts!

Ioshanna's version of the intense, climactic moment (which was previously by Vaughn, described): I should like to relate my version of the great flash.

At this precise moment, as the great overlord of all and his biune, took their seat upon the great, golden throne, and all electronics of this vast projection system had been made in readiness; i.e., the vast crystal lens, the numerous crystal balls (we've termed chandeliers), the crown and wand, the entire assemblage who are connected via their conical caps and mind energies – the crystal organ and, most of all the great golden throne. The overlord was now seen being seated! The main contact of all combined electronic components was mentally made! An outburst of energy explosion – a blinding white flash, the likes of which has never been activated, was, in that ear splitting electronics burst – released. The power here, then channeled out to the lower dimensions would dwarf by far, the flash of the atom bomb, plus your booster send-off of your moon ship flights – for we tap the source of all power!

The long-awaited, hard-worked-for moment had arrived! – the millennium of labor of love by as many persons of Light. This, the climax the pinnacle and crowning achievement of near a millennium fulfilled!

Had there been anyone present who had attained less than a mastership degree, it could well have been fatal, yet these persons have been well conditioned and are able to receive this great power. Now, this is the purpose of the crown and Ioshanna's wand – to demodulate and to disburse this vast, never-ending and Infinite Source unto mankind on earth. This great exploding white Light was, by far the most brilliant, ever before viewed on this great crystal plateau in the Spiritual city called Parhelion.

* * *

Vaughn says: Iona, I do not believe I heard, in listening to the replay of your tapes that you included the lovely relating of the ceremony which took place at the base of the throne platform on Parhelion. Did you intentionally omit this?

And Ioshanna replied, "Oh, I just didn't think

141

it would be quite appropriate to include, but if you so believe, I will relate it here now, for I, too, cherish the words that were so inspired from the Heirarchy. It was as follows:

In one of the triangular patterns of personages that formed much of the assemblage, stood one tall being at a corner or peak position. He was exceptionally tall, and his tall cone or conical hat caused him to appear even much taller. He is known as one or the guardian, of "Love" angels. Upon his long white robe is embroidered a double heart of red. There appears at one side of his insignia, a tiny cupid with his bow taut and arrow drawn, as if to let fly an arrow, and as a symbol of his position — that of scattering love into the hearts of couples who were preparing to wed.

Here on Parhelion it is he who performs the ceremony when two biocentrics have earned their unification and so join forces. This is the expression he shall perform this day, for the Queen and polarity (Leonardo da Vinci), just before they ascend the throne platform, and pass through the flames.

Upon his large hands lays open, the Book of Life (The Unarius Lessons textbook). His face was that of an angel; they say he is "An Angel of the Night", and as he smiled, it caused a quiver to run up the spine. We love this Love Angel!

The tall one who chose to be called "Love", stepped into position where the lovely Queen and her escort stood silently (before him). He spoke in soft, warm, muted tones, these words: "Beloved Ones, we are gathered here today to join together these two God Forces as one, in the Light of the Infinite and the Father Within. Do you, Ioshanna, take this soul, Leonardo da Vinci, as your biocentric polarity, to cherish and love, to help in all ways possible in all good he may so express? Do you rededicate yourself in this, your mission to the earth worlds, and to honor above all else, your position as Light Bearer throughout eternity?" And she replied, "Oh, I do, I do!" These words were repeated, using the masculine name in the questing, and the ceremony continued.

"Then, Ioshanna, I rename you (Queen) Uriel, Queen of Archangels, and Leonardo da Vinci, I rename you (Archangel) Michiel. Michiel, you may salute your biocentric, Queen of the Archangels, Uriel." They gently embraced. "May your reign be lengthy and happy in eternity and beyond. May your watchword be love, as ye walk in the Light, and that ye liveth forever, as the rose within My heart, within the chalice of My soul in God's pure Light. More power to you! Be it so. May I have the rings, please?" It was at this point the two exchanged the golden circlets as each one placed upon the finger of the other the gold circles — signifying unity — oneness with the Infinite.

After the exchange of circlets was made, "Love" is seen to bless this couple with the Unarius salute — the two forefingers touch the forehead, the lips, then the heart. Then he

143

bowed gently and with the thin, tiny wand, he slipped from his robe, he touched the two atop the head. As he did so, tiny stars were seen to dart from out the end of his wand. He then assumed his former position, well pleased. Instantly Lohengrin's Wedding March was heard loud and melodiously, sung by the great Chorus!

You will learn from this and other relatings of Unarius, what is meant by celestial marriage, the unification of two God Forces in a united and concerted effort. For here again is the infinite nature of God expressing Himself in another way and in another form.

This crowning of the Queen and her marriage ceremony was reenacted in symbology and/or proxy in the physical or third dimension to bring full cycle, (Ioshanna and Vaughn Spaegel, on May 28, 1973), followed by a magnificent reception held in the most elegant queenly hotel, the Westgate Plaza, which was so appropriate, with the many great crystal chandeliers, gleaming floors — all so fitted for a queen.

Chapter 15

Preparation for the couple's departure, the newly crowned queen and king, is equally as lovely as was her enthralling entrance. As the two, now shone as one, moved from the throne and descended three crystal steps adjacent to the first tiers, there stood in await and at attention, the straight, long line of the colorful trumpeteers who again quickly sent out the trumpet blasts that broke the now existing silence. As the radiant couple stepped from the lower step of the crystal platform, there stood in await, an elegant, golden queen's coach, in front of which stood the thirty-three perfectly matched stallions! They were all of the whitest of white. All were formed, as are all things here in this dimension, of the radiant crystal. The necks of these elegant horses were slender and graceful. The legs, especially trim, stepped high and proud.

The coach appeared all golden and it was, in effect, an amber crystal, flecked in pure gold. As the wheels turned, the clear crystal spokes appeared as one solid, round, gleaming disc similar to the great sun. This exquisite queen's coach was rather circular in form, the doors breaking not the graceful symmetrical line. The coach was bedecked in gems of rubies, emeralds and pearls, as were the reins and the harnesses of the horses − all patterned in one harmonious accord. The golden coach was of exquisite symmetry and glittered and shone with the radiance existent everywhere here. Over the rounded arch of the dainty crystal doors was the symbol of their dimension and ray, the scientific plane, all set with diamonds.

The hooves of these exquisite horses were all of gold, and upon their heads they so proudly wore great plumes of brilliant red and blue, which made a stark contrast against their very white coats. The tails of these thirty-three horses had been especially groomed, and all were quite wavy and hung near to the floor, their silky long manes had been waved, it appeared.

The first single horse that led the parade was bedecked in a great, golden blanket, all glittery with gems, upon which rode a very tall lead man, especially costumed for this elegant occasion. His was the brightest of costumes, the tight-fitting breeches of gold were topped with the long frock of bright blue. Upon the shoulder was a large scarf of cerise that swung low. Over his back was dropped the great cape of gold which was tossed over the entire rear of the lovely white horse, melding the two together. His stirrups and bridle of the brightest of gold, set in emeralds – the Queen's choice. His helmet was conical shaped, matching the temple itself; upon it hung two very huge plumes – one red and one blue. He sat so erect and motionless in his saddle, as he so proudly led the queenly parade, reins taut within the whitely-gloved hand.

To help the queenly picture, rather than the usual coach dog that accompanies a queen's coach, strides proudly before the first single horse, a very tall person. The gold reins in his hands tightly held two beautiful white Afghan wolf hounds, their manes and tails exceptionally long and added to the beauty of the procession. They too, have the baby blue eyes. Although the leads need not be taut, they would not run, given the chance; for like all other things here, they love the part which they play. The master of these mascots is giant in size; he's dressed in the gold and white uniform, in accord with all else in the Queen's entourage. And the tall, golden, conical hat which he wore, caused him to appear even taller.

Upon the front of the coach sat two stately coachmen and two footmen upon the rear. They looked very elegant in their uniforms gay, their costumes very similar to the ones riding in front, all with gold boots high over the knee. The two footmen had alighted and stood at attention, one on either side of the heavenly coach.

The interior of this beautiful carriage was bedecked with soft, satiny cushions, all in her favorite color of gold. The oval crystal windows, trimmed in the sheerest of lace, formed a frame for her happy face so radiant, as she peered out to her subjects fair. Never had any person ever been the recipient of so much love!

The handmaidens had crept shyly up and removed from her the so lengthy and most beautiful veil; a veil which extended nearly four city blocks, which the countless lovely handmaidens each carried in love. Now they had laid it aside carefully in an especially prepared place. They stood in a great semicircle awaiting Her Grace. Meanwhile, the tiny tots, the colorful dancing flower girls, then made their appearance and stood abreast of these young ladies-in-waiting, as they all stood at attention, forming a beautiful sight. When all was in readiness and just before the head coachman gave a mental signal, in unison, the four coachmen, the bridesmaids, the tiny tots, and the entire assemblage − of which there were countless thousands − and all the chorus and choir, in unison and as if to show the way, all of the white horses, made a deep curtsy simultaneously. The horses, in unison, all placed one graceful gilt hoof behind the other, bent the knee, bobbing their heads in courtesy along with everyone present!

The ladies present made a deep curtsy bending low from one knee; the men simply bowed from the waist and leaned forward in unison. These many thousands of people, through their mental attunement, all curtsied to their great Queen simultaneously, and she returned to them, her bow. She smiled sweetly, turning slowly her head from one side of the great hall to the other, nodding to all again and again receiving the great love and adoration they were all projecting unto her, as they continued in mental applause!

It was almost too much for her to bear, receiving their love radiations as it were, she returned it to all. Then the two footmen, each stepped to the door, and kneeling one knee upon the ground, made a step of the other knee for the two to step upon and pass into their carriage, which they did; first she, then he following closely by, they were then seated within. The only ornament within the coach other than a small golden vase which held one exquisite single red rose; most magnificent it was, poised overhead midway to the top of the coach – a beautiful crystal chandelier !

Although the great Archangel Leonardo needed not to visibly signal, he nodded to the coachmen ahead. All was in readiness now for their departure. The horses of white received the psychic nudge and were on their beautiful way. As the lovely golden princess coach, all bedecked in jewels, carrying the Beautiful People, started moving out from the throne area to make its long trip over the esplanade, she to greet her many subjects, the organ again sent out its most melodious music and the great chorus of heavenly vocalists joined in. The songbirds returned, flitting about, to add their own notes of cheer.

And now it was, the great and beautiful golden bell was again heard to have been rung, this time with a more muted tone. The two bell boys were standing one on each side of the great energy bell in their costumes to match; costumes identical with the bell. Yes, even the gold helmets they wore appeared as a bell, and were topped in plumes of blue. Now the procession was in motion. The horses started slowly to move in unison. Their graceful thin necks arched proudly, they lifted their gilded hooves especially high, as if they knew the one they drew was someone special! The mental applause that existed as the golden coach moved through the assemblage, was tremendous.

Because within her hands she carried the golden magic wand, the usual bouquet was not carried. However, lovely flowers were everywhere about. Instead, after the elegant coach of gold and crystal moved slowly up the flower strewn way with the Beautiful People, the crystal glass door was then seen to be slightly ajar, and a tiny glass-slippered foot popped out. With a quick flip of the toe, the slipper flew high into the assemblage! As it arced o'er the subjects, all saw a tiny rainbow encircle the slipper.

Now it had been that each personage in the great assemblage had brought with him, secreted within his garment, a compact packet of beautiful, scented, colored flower petals. As the beautiful, thirty-three snow white stallions and the great golden coach moved slowly through the esplanade, the many subjects each tossed their petals to them and it literally rained flowers! A beauteous sight !

The colorings in the crystal pipe of the organ again were set in motion and the beautiful display of color was seen again, as the music now swelled to even greater heights! A new and beautiful aroma was suddenly sensed throughout the entire auditorium. This, we knew to be the love of the even higher Angels from the dimensions far distant who had not been seen in attendance, but here they sent their love and homage through this exquisite fragrance, seemingly a flower perfume, yet it was an emission from the very beings – these beautiful Angelic Ones!

As the carriage continued to pass slowly down the beautiful, flower-decked way midst the heavenly music, the white doves were again seen to enter to escort the procession. All the assemblage paid the newly crowned Queen and her love good wishes as they in unison called out: "Homage to the da Vincis; homage to the da Vincis!" This sound was heard as long as the coach could be seen. It was a most joyous occasion for all. The joy and exultation had reached a tremendous height. As they slowly moved from view, many of the ladies were seen with a tear on their cheek in joy for the Beautiful Ones.

One of the bridesmaids had caught sight of a lovely wrapped package upon the silk pillow where her dainty feet, clad in crystal glass slippers would rest. It held a huge bow of gold, 'tho the box was small in itself. It had been whispered about, that his (her biune's) gift to her was a great diamond star, centered with a heart ruby of love. This gem could be worn on her hair or upon her gown. It was his own love creation! It is said, the brilliance from this giant star dwarfs the many suns all in one. He claims this is a representation of her, his guiding star!

The Master Leonardo then took his beloved one to the glorious home he had been preparing for her during these many long years he had been awaiting her there. Of course, she, in her astral state, and during her sleep, had likewise been helping to create this beautiful crystaline-structured home. It was just as they both chose it to be, and all formed by their minds. He shall await the time when she can, after her earth mission has been completed, return again to her Love — to part no more, to part no more!

It was heard by the many attending that none had ever witnessed such an exquisite and elaborate celebration; nor had they ever felt or seen such love expressed to them all by other of these Highly Ascended Ones. Surely, it shall ever be remembered by all who were there! And perhaps even more important it is, that those on the earth planes below can likewise attune to this beautiful spiritual Conclave of Light Beings; for as these words will be read and placed into consciousness, because these creations are of an infinite nature, they can thus become reality within the mind of each one. This is a living event, not something that took place and ended, for in the Inner Consciousness in Inner Dimensions there is no starting nor ending, for all things are of a continuous and permanent nature. All things are eternal. All things are Infinite. So share with us, dear ones, these beautiful and exquisite moments as we again attune and become transcended in this heavenly Love expressed by this great Conclave of the Most High and Exalted Beings ever to be concentrated in one area. Yet, there were many, many thousands who had come from the many planets around. And so we trust that you too, dear reader, shall, in your times of attunement, slip psychically into these beautiful worlds and dimensions of spirit and partake of this spiritual joy, the love of the Father Within.

Chapter 16

Now during these past near three weeks of living more on the inner than in the physical, each day brings its wondrous surprises, its transcendencies and stepping up – yes, the progress is being made exceedingly fast. Changes within me are much more than slight; I feel very little the physical person any more – and welcome! welcome!

The past two days, there has been a feeling that someone was endeavoring to make me aware of some great gift that had been bestowed upon me – yes, in addition to all the great honors, the wondrous gala affair held in my honor – even to the beautiful golden coach and the many elegant white horses! Most beloved is the beautiful rose that will endure eternally, and all that is needed is but to attune to it, the beloved of all gifts created by, and we could easily well say, the Father, for all these collected Mind Forces are indeed a great part of the God Force and Source Itself.

After I had been made aware of the magnificent Star of Diamonds which the beloved one, (the Logos Lenoardo) had presented to me in the lovely golden coach, still I was sensitive that someone was impressing, that I had not yet brought down into conscious mind that which his gift beheld. So I stopped myself short for a moment from out the busy, busy day and gave a quick look within. Then it was that I was made aware, and "saw" this exquisite gift of love from the great Being, one who had long ago, been Overlord of all the Shamballas (now called Unarius), and who now has moved to another galaxy – known (by few) as Serapis.

As I reattuned myself into that most exquisite of all ever-imagined experiences, there I did see a magnificent artifact – a replica all covered in emeralds of blue and green – a symbol of the beautiful birds I have so loved – called the Birds of Paradise, the Birds of Heaven, those earthman calls the Peacock. The reason they have meant so much to me is because their feathers reflect all the colors of the inner worlds. They are not just the colors of the earthman's concept but the iridescence and radiance reflected is similar to the colorings of all things on the inner planes and higher Spiritual Dimensions. So I have, through the various lifetimes, set up a contact with these birds, and as the story has also been told in one of the Pulse of Creation books, of how the great Amon Ra left behind – after his ascension from Lemuria where he had stayed with us (Lemurians) for three hundred and sixty-five days – his gift, one beautiful, pure-white Paradise bird, his expression of love to me.

And so, through the eons of time, these birds have been a beautiful symbol of love, and I still carry it deep within my heart for he who had first set it in motion. Thus, the beloved one there, Serapis, had taken up this great significance and presented to me this magnificent bird – an artifact as an everlasting memento from him – all formed of the beautiful green and blue, brilliant, glistening emerald stones. In each eye of the peacock, a diamond shone golden blue. The stones are nonexistent on the earth plane, for they are created of the mind energies and of the Cosmic Forces themselves.

This very unique and wonderful gift of love seemed to take on a lifelike appearance. When my mind energies were focused upon it, the bird would raise its exquisite, feathered tail, showing the colorful fan. Then all the various feathers would appear to quiver and shimmer and show the glorious radiance, the reflection of the radiant energies they represent, the magnificent colors that are expressed in the beautiful inner worlds. The graceful, beautiful front of the neck is formed of the deeper blue stones and graduated over the back and the breast, the two colors an exact replica in color, as are the great birds themselves. And just now as I am relating it, I experienced the most beautiful fragrance – a fragrance of one whom I had never before identified. It has come to me several times during the past six months; I love the delightful fragrance. It is a heavenly scent, but I never knew before who sent his love in this particular wave of his fragrance. Now I know it is the beloved and beautiful – no, he's much more than an Archangel or Overlord – he has long traversed the position of the Overlord of all the Shamballas! He has passed through all the mastership degrees, passed the Logoi initiations, all of the Archangel's ascensions and dimensions, and now occupies some position far beyond even the scope of this high spiritual plane and dimension (which is the Overseer of the entire system of all earth worlds, as well as the astral worlds, in this, our particular solar system. However, many of these worlds are invisible to the physical eye). Serapis, who appears as a flame, a great, golden, living flame, was, at the time of Lemuria, the being, Amon Ra. It was he at that long ago time who created for me (then as Ioshanna) the lovely white Bird of Paradise. Thus again, comes another full cycle and he repeats his heavenly gift in the exquisite artifact, the glittery bird of the gems.

So as I glimpsed from within and saw and conceived this gift of which Serapis was making me conscious in the physical mind, I was overpowered, I was overwhelmed. My cup runneth over. I was almost taken out of my body, transcended, the love was so tremendous, as he came directly into my aura and I saw this most exquisite gift of love!

The lovely, bejeweled Bird of Paradise shall indeed remain forever one of my most treasured possessions, and yet possession is not the word nor the way I feel with these spiritual gifts, for they are glorious creations of the Infinite to be shared by all. I wish not to possess anything, either here or on the Inner — only share in love.

To the great One, the blessed, beloved Serapis, my heartfelt appreciation and love; his love fills my heart. His overwhelming Presence in this, the third dimension, has brought such tears, no words will come. The magnitude of this great Being is quite beyond earthman's conception, at present.

The following information was not realized during the first days of Ioshanna's astral visit, and during the first few chapters, at the time this book was written, for the writing was being done during the time of the actual ascendency! This information was revealed only after the two weeks of Ioshanna's experience of living on the Inner in this glorious Conclave of Light, that the great Moderator and his biune were present at this great celebration! Then suddenly she became aware that the Moderator, himself (the great Overlord over all, and his biocentric), met her at the position very near to the throne, after she had made the lengthy trek in the procession. He took her by the arm and led her to where stood the one who was her spiritual biune, the Archangel Leonardo. He stood in his appointed position at the head of his triangle in the great assemblage.

Now the Moderator, being one step, level or degree higher in this great organization, is thus her Overseer, and presented to Leonardo, his Queen. It was here at this point there was a meeting, a unified quadrocentric assemblage – one of such development that has seldom, if ever before, been evolved!

158

The all-wise Infinite Spiritual Brotherhood kept well their great surprise! The biocentric of the beloved Moderator has been called Erza, in the Pulse of Creation Books (and when she was on the earth plane, was Esther, a sister of Ioshanna). Ioshanna had not realized up to this point and far beyond it, in the writing of this book, that the Moderator and his polarity had returned to this particular universe for this celebration – and she, in her conscious mind, found it indeed a most pleasant surprise, that they were there to await her – for the Moder-ator, himself, to actually present her to her biocentric, Leonardo da Vinci!

After proper presentations were completed, the Moderator and his beloved polarity then moved toward the throne; and thus began their ascent up the three crystal tiers and through the three pillars of fire. They too were being initiated into another step higher in their own progression and position. He (the Moderator) and his polarity could have taken this initiation upon his arrival there as he left the physical in 1971; yet he preferred to wait for the one who had so helped in his mission on earth (as well as in previous missions). Thus, now all four, or the two polarities (biocentrics) experi-enced this transition, this initiation ceremony, at one time; another all-time "first" – a five-hundred-thousand-year endeavor!

Then the Moderator and his biune stood be-fore the throne awaiting the ascent and arrival of the two logos awaiting below. Thus it was, the other two (the Channel Ioshanna and her biune, Leonardo) then moved up the three crystal plateaus and through the three great golden flames, to then await her crown. And from this point you have already read.

It had all been so wisely and purposely blocked from her conscious mind, in order that she may experience the full measure and benefit of all honor and homage paid to her at this glorious advent. Now it has come to her as a complete and total surprise in her physical mind. However, her true self had been a part of it all, right along. Yes, even in helping to create the very throne!

She had laughingly remarked in this third dimensional consciousness, Cinderella never had it so good! Yet, Cinderella was a fairy tale, but you can be assured this is no fairy tale; rather, it is a factual, actual love story that has been carried on through the millennium of time and brought to a most successful conclusion for all, and especially that the earth worlds can now begin to live in Light, due – and in great part – to the complete dedication of these four great God Forces – a unification of a quadrocentric polarity.

Vaughn: The reader may wonder just how the activities, which were of such importance, in fact almost earth-shaking events, were seen by all when the enclosure was so great in size. How could all properly view? And to this, we reply: Our vision in this higher state can be telescoped, as it were. If we need to see at a closer range, we simply become conscious of same, and so it happens. Remember, ours is the Infinite way and we express all things in an infinite nature, totally unlimited and un-bounded!

We have gone to great and extreme lengths over many years to make this event the most glorious in all histories, in all worlds, for we here not only love beauty but so express it in all things. It should be remembered too that we use the Cosmic Powers, and they are not de-pleted in the using. Rather, the countless per-sons viewing this tremendous display of beauty, color, power and love, shall often recall within their minds this pageant, this historical event, and each time it is remembered, the thought processes again regenerate power to those in this exalted state which is all added in a most positive and creative manner!

It was indicated that this great celebration is, in a sense, significant for each individual present. It is, in essence, a stepping up in some measure, for all those present for they had in-deed earned their promotion and progression into states of higher awareness and into higher dimensions and levels. Likewise, in great honor and significance, this celebration pays homage to the Avatar (the Unariun Moderator) and Io-shanna due to their great achievement in this accomplished mission on earth — so recently expressed.

Many have been the efforts of the Avatars of the past five hundred thousand years, striving toward such an endeavor and goal and countless have been the times the forces of evil have overtaken these efforts. The Powers of Light shall, in the present, overcome and victorious be. Thus, the great infinite significance toward this gigantic movement!

Notes:

So spoke Ioshanna: Nowhere, amongst these countless thousands of personages in this great gathering, at which one would almost expect to see various groups in prayer or worship did such exist. No one can be seen in worship attitude. Was this true in your sightings, brother Vaughn? Yes, quite so. No one that I saw was in any such attitude. There was an attunement of oneness, and at-one-ment with the Infinite. However, no worshipfulness of any deity was ever expressed in my many sightings and viewing of this incredible and never to be forgotten Conclave. It appears that they have learned the better way, the higher way of life and expression. They simply realized and appreciated their oneness with the source of all things. They have in essence, become creators and this was the message they taught, that man likewise can so aspire and attain. This was the message that the Unariun Moderator taught as well as the great man Jesus; that the Father and I are one and the same. I, meaning the Higher Self, the inner one that lives on the inner dimensions, when he becomes a developed spiritual Infinite Being, and which he is always a part and can never become separated, regardless of his actions or deeds. This is a very important factor in any individual's attainment.

Chapter 17

That which Queen Iona treasured most dearly was one red rosebud. This rose was a very special one. It had been grown by the Mind of the Moderator especially for her and emitted the delicate scent of one thousand fair flowers. He built within this precious single bud, all the love from within his heart, and it sparkled and glistened like a hundred red diamonds. This rose would never die, but even more, as it was created from his Inner Mind Energies, it was imbued with peculiar energies that emitted the love that he shared with her. The reason this single rose was so meaningful is due to the fact the Moderator's love frequency has been so generously impinged, that when e'er she will glance (or think upon) her rose, or even smell of its perfumed fragrance, it will automatically attune her unto him or him to her. It is as a telephone, not only between two worlds but rather, two universes! So no wonder she treasures this most glorious of gifts — a constant reminder of his great love and admiration for the one, Ioshanna — now Iona — for it was she in the several incarnations on earth who had helped in the mission he brought. Even though they (he and she) were not biocentric and he never had the company of his biune on Earth, she labored with him in all his endeavors for man. Thus, that which he brought could rightfully be said, was an unequalled thing!

And here it might be related too, of the perfect proof Ioshanna experienced after the Moderator left his prison of flesh, of the continuity of life. It was during the very last moments as he remained within the physical (on earth), and in a whisper, as the soul was struggling to escape the flesh. He was trying to give her his last verse of love, but lacked sufficient energy and voice to make the sounds. All she could make out were the three words: rose, heart, chalice!

As it would be assumed, Ioshanna loved deeply the Moderator's many elegant verse — especially those he so often wrote devotedly to her — but here in his last, almost gasping breath, he continued to express to her his love, his true inner spiritual love and oneness with Creation, but the words would form no sound. Thus, for a time, it remained with her a frustration, not to know what he was attempting to tell her in these last few moments on earth — the last earth life he would ever experience in that way. Little wonder it was then, after he had made full ascension, and freed completely of the physical and all its limitations in what earthman calls death, and after the very few days of inner adjustment and of having, himself, walked through the earth-cleansing fountains of radiant energies and pillars of fire, ascending to his own proper position beyond this galaxy — yes, in another universe — that she on the earth was recording some works of his voice, that the Moderator (and his biune) came to her as the two beautifully colored birds in the rain – he and his lovely biune.

The power they brought lifted her with the contact into sublime heights, and here it was that Ioshanna experienced the greatest of all the psychisms she has ever undergone! The love that was emitted to her from him (and his polarity) was near more than she could absorb. It was then that he supplied for her the words to the love poem she was before unable to hear, due to his lessening of breath and power. How wonderful that he thus fulfilled the only wish she carried within her heart – her only desire to know just what did he convey, of the rose and the heart? The number of verse, poetry and heavenly tone poems which he wrote through her pen are sufficient to fill six to eight books, yet she treasured more than all others combined – the few missing lines.

Thus, the verse now projected from his inner and exalted state more than fulfilled her great longing indeed. The verse from her love, now in the Spiritual Worlds, to his love on the earth was as follows:

The Victory Song

To Ioshanna:

Seek ye naught the way of the flesh,
    the way that travels the earth man
But travel ye upon the highway of Truth
Freed of the vultures of the air that would
    waylay thee and devour thy fruit
Yea, and they wouldst render thy ground
    unfertile
That it groweth not more of this ripened fruit
    — hence the planting

For in the rendering doth thy ground become
    even more sterile than the unfertile egg
    that hatcheth not
And that thy labors becometh in vain.
The stench of this rendering lingers long
    and its evil penetrates beyond
    the deepest of depths.

Yea, there is no destruction that can be
    likened to that of the evil forces of hatred,
    lust and envy.
And the embers of their destruction linger
    long in memory and burn deeply in the
    heart of he who hath so suffered their
    wrath.

But of he who so overcometh this evil,
    and the adversaries thereof
Thus becometh yet a stronger soul
    in the eye of the Infinite
And that in the victory hath thy fibers
    been made stronger and thy tissues
    as the sinews of the smithy
Who labors long o'er his forge to so strengthen
    his blade of steel

And when he hath so finished his forging
    and that his blade is made stronger
    than the mightiest sword
He hangs it upon his wall in admiration
    knowing that a great part of himself didst
    so enter into this great accomplishment.

Be ye as the smithy and cherish well thy
    victories, for they hath been well earned.
Long and arduous were the battles,
    and thy scars deep and many.
Yet, as the Phoenix Bird rises from the ashes
    cleansed and renewed
Ye, too, hath become ever the more strong
    for the encounterment
And shall be better prepared in the future
    when thine enemies may be even greater
    in number, and more wicked and clever
    in their disguise.

Keep ye well sharpened thy sword of Truth
and hung high to ever grasp its hilt –
the hilt now laden with many precious
gems,
That will slay thy adversary as he approaches
thee in thine own vineyard, to stealeth
thy fruit and to render thy ground unfertile

And that thy bowstring must ever be held
taut within thy hands
That thine arrow doth findeth its mark.
And when thou hast loosed all of thy shafts
of Light
Thou shalt return to the Lodge of the Masters
to again replenish thyself
That ye be ever thus fortified

And that the storehouse whence ye cometh,
shall not lessen with the taking
For in the sharing thereof – this Light
is replenished thereby
And it canst not become depleted
For this is the Life Force of God.

And that thou needest to live ever the more
closely with Spirit
For thou hast truly ascended; and needeth ye
naught of the earth furthermore.

But that in Spirit resideth all of the things
    of which thou art
And that thy brethren awaiteth thy sharing
    of all that which hast been prepared for him
That he, too, may so conceive and becometh
    of the Spirit
And in this sharing of Spirit,
    is God made manifest; and liveth
    within the heart of man.

Thine adversary hath been well slain
    and many have been thy fallen foe,
    and none is left to return.
Ye hath labored well and long, dear one —
And I wouldst not have it so.
Yet it is, in this overcoming that the
    last fibers of the earth world can
    be severed and shattered
And only the pure waters of spirit remain
    that ye shall be thoroughly cleansed
    of all thy adversaries
And that ye shall enter the Kindom of
    Heaven where ye needs go out no more
But that ye shall dwelleth therein eternally.

And that soon ye shall hang up thy sword
    and thy buckler
And shall ye enter into the great Halls
    of Emancipation, wherein are gathered

together all those who have likewise
   conquered their earth worlds
Those who hath slain all of their dragons —
   dragons of hate, lust and envy and hath
   cometh unto the House of the Lord
   all the rest of their days —
Days which are not numbered as ye count
   time.

And in these halls shalt thou wearest
   thine new raiment, which was created
   of the whitest substance, made from the
   good deeds which thou hast so lived
And the selflessness of thine own doings.
And that these whitened garments groweth
   not old with the wearing thereof,
Nor corrupteth not with the passing of time
But that they becometh ever the more radiant
   and lustrous
As thou addest from time to time, more of
   these kindness deeds, sharing ever
   the true light of wisdom.
These are the raiments of love which ye
   shall cherish forever.

Many have been the flowers which ye hath
   strewn upon the pathways of others
Walk ye now upon the petals from those
   who hath gone before thee

And have strewn them for thy feet to trod

And in these Halls of Emancipation walketh ye
    in the golden sandals all studded with
    jewels of thy goodness so shared
And the guiding Light about thy head
    shall leadeth many from out their dark-
    ened dungeons of wilderness and despair
Unto the illumined pathways of the Eternal
    Light.

And in the haloed Light 'round thy head
There shineth there a brighter star
    created from all the things thou art
    of Heaven and earth —
That go to make an Angel fair.
And that ye liveth forever as the rose
    within my heart, within the chalice
    of my soul —
In God's Pure Light.

— Inspired by The Universal Spirit, of the
                    Unariun Moderator — through
                    Ioshanna

(Note: Never, not ever, were three words cherished more. It must be admitted, with these lines
and his great Love and Presence, little physical

171

strength remained. They nearly took me right out with them in their love. "I")

Her heart filled with a joy, only God Forces can know, for this is an Infinite Love far removed from that which the earthean calls love, but is an everlasting oneness with the Father within and with all Creation within and without. Thus, she was so overjoyed and inwardly filled that she lost herself in his elegant lines. Quickly she made them available for all to enjoy, and did each one likewise experience his love. Perhaps, not in the same full measure, for they two are more compatible in frequency, yet the love, the energy power was all there. So it is thus, that his personal and perfect, one deep, velvety rose meant more to her than all else that was upon her so lavishly bestowed.

Ah, yes, she shall enjoy, cherish and love every beautiful moment and memory of the exquisite Conclave of Light and each time her thoughts do so reattune, shall she again be absorbed in its glory, radiance and love, for long it has been, since the way of Light has she chosen, and as such, all is only a thought away.

It may be said too, that the Moderator had served likewise at one time, as the teacher of Leonardo da Vinci. Thus the three had a most compatible frequency, as well as did his biune Orda (or Erza), who lived in the present earth life as Ioshanna's physical sister.

No, these God Forces, after having arrived at such attainments, need never lack the contact, for they know well the principles of inner attunement and work with the cosmic laws, the principles of the Infinite. Thus it is now, theirs (and countless more), the concerted efforts and expression, to bring to the many earth worlds the Truth and the Light, for the time is nigh. The earth and its inhabitants shall soon see the results of all that of which we have spoken – and much, much more!

Our only regret: that we are limited in this third dimensional earth world by words; yet we know, with proper assimilation of the knowledge so brought and the power that shall henceforth be directed, man shall awaken from his spiritual slumber. He shall be awakened and arise, and face, and walk in the Light.

* * *

Now following directly behind the great golden coach, the procession is reversed, for as we see the coach moving slowly out through the long thoroughfare, in order that all may so view, we see the gay paradise birds who now have formed a great semicircle about the rear of the coach, their great fans held high as if to protect the ones within. They appeared as a great and many-hued rainbow, all shimmering and aglow.

Then came the tiny ring-bearer, her pillow now bare of her load; then the tiny flower tots, whose baskets never seemed to deplete of the flower petals, continued in their dainty dance of ballet, twirling and dancing so gracefully. Moving closely behind them walked so erect, the most impressive candle bearers, dressed in white, and who held high their individual candles aglow.

Next in line in the procession came the most colorful Maids-of-Honor in so many exquisite shades. Although their trek had been most lengthy, yet no one appeared to be tired, for the rejuvinating element here keeps us thoroughly buoyed up and refreshed. Now, the thirty-three harpists so lovely, just finished their beautiful rendition upon the strings of their golden harps, and join the moving procession, bidding adieu to their Queen. Following right close by, was the great group of choirboys, their robes of the most brilliant blue, who marched just in front of those who had created the chants throughout the great halls. These numbered in many hundreds, thirty-three, it did seem, or thirty three hundred in all.

Thus, just as the great chorus of colorfully garbed opera singers had completed a last magnificent song, one of adoration to our queen, they too, joined the procession and walked, thirty-three abreast. The costumes they each wore made a glorious sight, for here in real life were the personages who had enacted the great roles of the past; each in his gala regalia, which he wore in his particular role. Now we see the lovely Madame Butterfly and all who took part in this particular opera; also Aida. Then the unforgettable and exciting Faust and Pagliacci, who made a dashing appearance in his artistic masquerade. Enrico played himself, as Caruso, all bedecked as he sang his familiar, glass-breaking, powerful notes. Yes, all those taking part, the great Verdi's Rigoletto, the lovely pair, Romeo and Juliet, were among the countless numbers of those who were now following in lines, thirty-three abreast, singing as they slowly marched forward in the procession, through the great golden halls, in this magnificent museum. Of those great and wondrous opera stars, writers, composers, singers, there must have been at least thirty-three hundred.

Then in unison, the vast assemblage all began filing, thirty-three abreast, in lines diagonally, across the vast esplanade that stretches directly across the diameter of this great conical enclosure, many miles in length. All continued to add their song as the many thousands, now all joined in the parade, and of which by now, the glittering coach could scarce be seen, so far ahead had it moved. The countless thousands of souls who had so gathered, had all paid homage, and moving in unison with the throng, the most glorious experience, they all were having.

Then it was, many of the personages mingled and went to the various large homes of others who lived upon this planet and plateau, to continue on in their celebration; in fact, we were told, they would continue for one entire year, or three hundred and sixty-five days, in this celebrating! There were thirty-three hundred, (or three thousand, three hundred) of these particular individuals, advanced beings, who, as they were invited to the great reception which was to begin almost immediately, went directly to the home of the newlyweds. Yes, the number thirty-three represents the number of souls, those who first went out from the planet Aries to the various earth worlds to start the spiritual seedings, so to say, and now that the cycles have swung, they are again brought into proper junction – the five hundred thousand year large cycle. And now it has been surmised, even this number of five hundred thousand could even be doubled, and that this great celebration is factually that of the millennium! No wonder, the many thousands have turned out and that the thirty-three hundred are again making contact in this most jubilant and pinnacled way! We have, indeed, cause for celebration and joy at this, the affair of the millennium!

Chapter 18

Vaughn: All of a sudden popped into my consciousness this tremendous and beautiful lighted home, if you can call it that. I saw a mansion that was the whitest of white. The White House seems black compared to it. One would think it was being flooded with floodlights all about it, but not true. The glow came from within the crystaline material of the structure of the house itself! Before going into the house, the grounds were of the most classical contours in terms of the symmetry of the trees. There is every known specie of tree which has been planted, and in such a way that they are all very harmonious; all of the known species and particularly the wind-swept cypress are here, all represented. The trees, themselves, look like huge flowers because of the way they have been, seemingly, trimmed — and many do grow flowers.

The flower gardens of your spiritual home, Iona, really put to shame the grounds of the famous castle which Louis XIV built, and which is noted for its grandeur, which was a very formal garden, supposedly the most exquisite of all on earth. As you move up the long driveway, (and it really isn't a drive), on either side one sees the most luxuriant flowers, which are exceedingly tall — some as high as ten to fifteen feet! They, themselves, glisten and shine; they seem to say, welcome!

It must be mentioned that the foliage, trees, shrubs, flowers, all were in the greatest of profusion everywhere about. The greenery was in a great variety of shades to the palest of green, almost the color of seafoam. One could see right through the leaves, noting each tiny vein in a perfect symmetry and pattern. One has a complete and beautiful rapport with all of these growing, shimmering and scintillating things. They all expressed the feeling of love as one passed by – the feeling of love and oneness was felt from the plants as they were being approached, as if they were sending their love to us. This, in essence, was true, for all things here are created of that infinite substance and love in the oneness of all. All things were sparkling, shimmering and glistening, and no drab colors were seen. It was a paradise to behold. No matter what area, parkway or walk, and especially around the central park, each of the areas around the crystal lake were abundant with the luxuriant growth, far beyond anything the earthman has conceived.

Topmost and foremost is the manner of the growth of the beautiful and exquisite flowers, which were bursting forth upon all the plants. Very few were the trees that did not have flowers thereon! The array of colors was inconceivable and indefinable, and of which there are no words. Each plant, each leaf, each tree, one actually felt the growth taking place and the radiance extending from it!

All of the walkways, about which there were many, surrounding these exquisite garden areas, were all bordered, each with a different shrub or flower – all in an abundant profusion of color and fragrance, the likes of which has never been conceived on earth – and all of this was maintained, not by the use of the garden hose nor of the time some weed pulling and personal hand nurturing takes, but actually were cared for from the psychokinetical mind energies which have created and grown all things here. Yes, the very soft, tender blades of grass of such a delicate and tender hue that looked like velvet, yet one could see right through the tiny blades.

Bear in mind, when we say all these creations are crystal, they are not stiff and hard and sharp to the touch – far from it! The reverse is true. The crystal has caused a brilliant hue, a frosty appearance on all things. After all, this is the crystal city of the crystaline structures.

What amazes me is the great foyer. As one walks into the entranceway, the foyer is not some small hallway, but rather, is of the dimensions of an enormous room; yet it is only the entrance! It has a domed appearance. The ceiling seems to be very high, perhaps twenty-five feet. We see a flooding of light coming from the ceiling, like a skylight, with the light shining through. It is not really a skylight but again, is the reflection of the crystaline energies from which this room structure is created. This great foyer is similar to a large museum or an art gallery in itself! It is a beautiful circular ballroom. All about the room is seen the greatest collection of exquisite statuary I have ever seen – even in pictures. These statues are on pedestals of the Ionic column, and countless others, all very graceful – and some of your own creation, Iona!

Iona (now named Uriel) is what Leonardo, (now Michiel) calls you, Ioshanna, and it belongs to you equally as does your new spiritual name (Uriel) – which the great Overlord gave you, that of the Archangel Uriel. I believe (Uriel) that he loves to still hold, in his memory, the fondness and psychic memory he retained throughout the lifetime when his life centered about his Mona Lisa. He actually lived this love with her, even though he knew not of her, so strongly did she project herself through from the inner, higher planes of Light. Ioshanna: So, then I shall use that name! Vaughn: For, as it was told, they never met in a physical world; perhaps always the search, but never fulfilled. They were each (as was the Moderator and his biune Erza), on an eternal mission for the Infinite Father within.

Ioshanna: And which brings to mind, Vaughn, the Moderator often told how he searched for me through the previous fifteen years to the time of our meeting.*He told many persons, he knew there was a brown-eyed girl on earth who would help him with what he had to bring, that she'd understand him and that which he taught – and she did! This, as he related many times, was but one lifetime of at least six, during which the two played hide-and-seek

180

amongst the planets – more correctly, other universes! Vaughn: So it is, all the most romantic and beautiful love story ever written of not only one but of two biocentric or God Forces (or of four individuals).

Vaughn continues: The elegant statues are of all the most noted ones, the graceful people who have always been the example of beauty: Aphrodite, Apollo, Athena – all of the gods who were, in essence, along with yourself, Iona, the very same people who came down to these earth planes and who have been carried as a tradition and have been so classically portrayed in these great sculptured works of art. The masterful and elegant paintings that hang on the walls are representations of all the great works of art. It is said that the Louvre in Paris holds the greatest of all original paintings of all the masters of old; yet here are these really original creations, which we all know are the angelic paintings of Raphael.

The great and original painting by Leonardo, the Mona Lisa, has a particular place of honor. It hangs so there is nothing around or near it to distract. As one walks into the foyer, this painting is four times life size! The reason is because of the great size of the room. It is directly in front of us as we walk into the house; it is the first thing we see! Ioshanna: I have seen much you are relating but you cause me to want to shorten my earth stay, telling me of all the beautiful things! No, I know they shall wait. There is much work to be done here on

181

earth. Vaughn: I have such a great desire, as I expressed before, I would like to be invited! Ioshanna: Oh, you will – you are! In fact you have been there, many times Vaughn, in the past. You feel quite at home in the da Vinci's palacial home. Vaughn: One does not see, nor is he aware of the graceful staircase immediately, because of the great beauty of the entranceway. Towards the rear and to the left is the outline of what seems to be a staircase that is hanging in midair without supports – easily twelve feet wide. It is like a sine wave, a wonderful representation of the basic form of energy as it curls around!

Ioshanna: Will you explain further about the walls and floor of this superstructure, the home of the da Vinci's on the higher planes. Vaughn: I am glad you brought that up. The floor is one gleaming reflection, like some large crystal prism. It is not white, but is a rosy-hued reflection and it appears as if lighted from within, a rosy hue. It is completely overwhelming because of all the color there. The walls are beaten gold and I remember how (although you never attend such gatherings), you were prompted to go and see the movie, "Sound of Music" where one scene showed a great room of this same fashion. The walls seemed beaten together or put together as if gold dough would be kneaded and thickly applied. Spaced periodically on the walls in your home there are certain flat surfaces. This is where the paintings were hung; yet they weren't hanging there, but rather they seemed to be embedded within the very wall itself! Ioshanna: That is why the scene in the movie of the dance pavillion meant so much to me. I was just in love with that and it really quickened me and turned me on! It tuned me unto Parhelion!

Vaughn: there seems to be a chandelier of such enormous size, of beauteous form and splendor! There is really no way I can represent it. It is not a chandelier where the tiers start large at the top and become smaller and smaller, but is of the exact opposite proportion. There are thirty-three tiers; they start in a smaller circumference or, but one prism at the top and become larger as it progresses downward, forming a cone shape or pyramid. Ioshanna: That is not the customary way most chandeliers are made, and all sounds most magnificent, and I might say, you are correct on all points! But you are going to have to hold me here to keep me from wanting to take off and move into the home immediately!

Now, Vaughn, tell us about the lounges or chairs, about the places they recline or sit in. Are there any furnishings at all? Vaughn: There are furnishings; yet there is just a certain number, they don't seem to overburden the room. They are very sparse, and what there is, is of the most modern or futuristic in design. There are many different shapes; I don't see any squareness. They are very round, or circular. Ioshanna: Does it appear as plastic? Vaughn: It is seemingly plastic and yet it is crystaline, very much like the plastic tables you have here; yet the plastic has a scintillating quality to it. Ioshanna: Do they use pillows for soft sitting, or is that necessary? Is the plastic or whatever is used hard to sit upon? Vaughn: The furniture seems to be firm when one looks at it, but when we sit on it, it is soft as down. So there is no need for cushions; I don't see cushions. Ioshanna: So how many rooms does the house have, would you say? Vaughn: When I saw the mansion from outside, it seemed there were countless numbers of rooms. But I am sure there are more than twenty-five, and each room has the proportion of a very large dining room, such as you would see in the White House. Ioshanna: Now, does this poor girl (me) have to do all that cleaning and scrubbing herself? Vaughn: Funny that you asked that! They have the most modern contrivances for keeping the home clean; the furnishings are of the self-same energies that reside in the dwellers; it is all of mind creation. Since they reflect the absolute, there is no dust. It is a complete creation, it lives within itself! It has no need for care!

What I see now are the special guests coming to the reception. They are all coming along in carriages; believe it or not! They are all most beautiful carriages – of the 18th Century time, of the queens and the kings – a luxuriant and elaborate scene of one carriage after another, and every one different in design – not one the same as another.

Ioshanna: Do you see anyone you recognize, that you could relate their names? Vaughn: I recognize many of the people who are and have been the scientists on this earth plane — one, a man by the name of Copernicus, another called Charles Peirce, and William James. Now here we see a lady who was known as Blavatsky, who brought in some teachings in the 19th Century. She appears to be a very young woman in her late twenties. Then I see many of these people who have a special relationship to you, amongst whom are those wonderful, gracious individuals known as Ming-Tse, Lao-Tse and Kung Fu. Einstein, of course, was there. There is a person who is well known to you, known as Krishna. Krishna was one of the great Spiritual teachers in India. He came with the others as if he had no special designation. His deep humility is something beautiful to behold. He is now on Parhelion as Hilarion. They are all so beautiful, they have such an air about them. They are not dressed in modern clothing; they seem to be dressed in what they choose or prefer, of their own memory. They are all dressed in a particular fashion for this purpose — in the fashion of the occasion. Ioshanna: Yes, I did note that with the singers and artists, with the composers; they all dressed in their costumes, such as Aida and the Rigoletto, in costumes, etc. I did conceive that at the Conclave. But here in the evening or perhaps later in the day, at this great reception, they all wore those particular costumes. Now what period did this represent especially? Vaughn: This is more of the 18th Century costumes where the ladies and men wore costumes which were much more of an example of how people live on the inner, in the higher dimensions. The colors were very strong and predominant. I won't go into the exact specifics. Those descriptions could fill a book in themselves.

We are in a different room now, a much larger room which might be called the music room. If one has seen pictures, one knows what the New York Opera House looks like; this room is very much like that, except there are no balconies. There is a huge stage, and upon this stage is a gathering of countless opera singers who are giving a rendition of the particular opera. Would you believe it if I told you it was your favorite – Rigoletto? Verdi, himself, is leading the orchestra! The orchestra contains at least a hundred people, and there must be anywhere from fifty to seventy-five people on the stage, performing this great story, which the opera Rigoletto portrays.

There are thirty-three (3300) guests invited and they have all congregated in this great ballroom. They are those – the original thirty-three hundred Aryans! They are seated, not standing. Special seats have been prepared, however, and are very ornate, very elegant and all of gold! They have seemed to be individually fashioned – each chair, an individual work of art! The backs of the chairs seem to be festooned with flowers and buds, twining all around. Not only that, but although they are gold, yet there are colors. Even the flowers are in their natural color! It is really an overwhelming affair. There are five hundred great lights in this auditorium with tremendous music flowing about.

Every section in this house has a particular purpose. I am just beginning to see more clearly, this ballroom is the music room! This one area alone is almost as big as the White House itself! Every particular room has been created, not only for yourself and Leonardo, but for entertaining; that is, the giving of yourselves. Ioshanna: This is, I see, the way of teaching; by having the people come here; for surely, how could such people who have been teachers for many countless thousands of years be satisfied to do anything but teach! It is part of their very being! Vaughn: Whatever is being done or whatever happens in these various rooms, in this particular case, listening to the opera, through the vibronics of the music, there is a teaching impinged in the music itself. Isn't this something wonderful? The organ, of course, is part of the orchestra, it is a large crystal organ. Ioshanna: Indeed so! The organ renews a memory. You told me about it the other day. You said the house has an organ just like the one at the conclave, except smaller, because that one serves so many thousands of people. But, you said, the one in my home was the same in principle, so perhaps it doesn't come to you again, because you have already objectified

187

and described it. In other words, you have already canceled out the picture in this dimension! Vaughn: That is true, I did see it before. Well, what wonderful gatherings they must have, to have all these beautiful artists and entertainers, songsters and harpists, beautiful musicians and composers come there to teach and express, practice and perform. What a wonderful way to live! Vaughn: It's creation itself, to live in this fashion. One is always, always growing.

Ioshanna: One of the lifetimes of the past that remains in fond memories is a time lived in Louisiana. I believe the Moderator found me to have been the "Maid of New Orleans." It is all so vivid. There is a big circular drive, and as we drove up in the lovely comfortable carriages, drawn by four, or sometimes six or eight horses, we come up to the great, tall white Ionic pillars on the outside of the home. I don't know whether there are seven steps, but I wouldn't doubt it for a minute! All is circular around the front of the house, then the pillars themselves were in sort of a semicircle. A great veranda was across the entire front of the house, which was all white. As one stepped inside, he walked right into the great and beautiful, what they called — the ballroom. The light oak floors were waxed and polished to a high gloss, over which hung several beautiful crystal chandeliers, the size of which actually dwarfed those in the lovely hotel here, which we think are so huge and magnificent.

The chandeliers were tremendous. And you know, I have seen a house here in Glendale, when we were looking for a place (similar to this present one), which was such a close replica that it wasn't even funny. It even had all of the statuary out in the garden — the famous ones of the past in Rome. I really had a charge, a pull, and rapport with all that. I kept begging the Moderator to look and he took a peek but it didn't tempt him. He didn't have quite the same rapport with those things that I did so we passed it by, but every time I drove by I would drool a bit, till I worked it all out. Do you know, I fully believe sometimes the eras or contacts we've had which we've loved — the more fond memories are even more difficult to cancel out than are the more negative ties!

Vaughn: As you described this house you lived in, in Louisiana, during the late 18th Century, I believe it was; I am struck by the close comparison to the home which you and Michiel built on the inner on Parhelion. The house has so many of the identical characteristics, particularly the way you described the pillars and the semi-circular front of the house. You don't have a veranda or porch on this house you built here which is all of crystaline structure from your own mind energies, but there are the pillars! This is the first striking feature as you come into the driveway, which stretches for miles. Before you come to the house, you have to come through the grounds and parkways; then when you come into the first portion at the end of the circular driveway; this is a little parkland itself. Inside the circle is a miniature park as well. There are no tall trees because they would obscure the front of the house, but there are countless varieties of roses which grow on tall bushes! They actually seem to be trees! Ioshanna: Your description of the grounds, park areas, etc., reminds me of a time when the Moderator and I visited the great and elegant Huntington Gardens in Pasadena. It is a paradise of finely sculptured gardens, flowers, statuary and Japanese section, etc. As I was leaving, I had such a sorrowful feeling, a big cry was released; doubtless I was reminded of my spiritual home! Yes, like I related just the other day – most all of those trees had flowers, just so wonderful.

Vaughn: So what a delightful approach it is. We are met by a beautiful fragrance of flowers plus the beauty of the various shades. Right in the middle of the great flower bed is a beautiful ornate fountain, set on tiers. The crystal waters play in different harmonious colors. They seem to have a rhythm; they dance in various formations. The water falls down from one tier to the next in a rhythmic cadence. It is a symphony just to watch it, and the interesting thing about this fountain is that as we look upon it, we receive an impression of new understanding. There seems to be a teaching simply by viewing the fountain. Ioshanna: That is very interesting . I feel too, as we contact the cascading waters, a transcendency; viewing it, music is emitted. Vaughn: In the cadence of the waters, yes. There is rather unusual music, like the music of the spheres! It isn't like music of some opera or symphony, it is music which lends itself to the teaching. It simply raises our consciousness, lifts one, is simply completely caught up with a total sense of oneness. One feels he is right with the waters and there is a tremendous feeling of love that is radiated!

All this feeling of gaining understanding and learning is seemingly due to the creation of this structure itself. This was impinged and embedded in the mind energies of which the great formations were created by the people who lived here. It seems it would be similar to playing a closed circuit television. You would see and you would hear, and this is a continuous perpetual motion. The fountain never stops in its various impressions of beauty of color, and rhythmic cadence. It is not a repetition of a tape or television program but something of great amazement; one is caught up and transcended with it all! Ioshanna: Indeed, it is a tremendously illuminating concept to even think upon. Vaughn : It breaks down all the concepts of structures that have been fabricated from the old ways of thinking; to know there is always a new avenue of understanding as one continuous exploration is exciting.

My attention shifts to the front of the house; but one cannot call it a house or even a mansion, it is much larger in scope. Ioshanna: Let's call it an entertainment area — an entertainment, educational center, or an Academy. It is much more than an art museum, when we realize that they do more than look at the art. They conceive from the artist that which he was endeavoring to express and to teach, not only in the field of painting, but for instance, the people who were learning the musical expression. We hear their compositions and portrayals of their stage productions and what they express; for they are illumined, because they have spiritually progressed. Everything they do is done with their psychokinetical energies. In other words, they carry the picture to the individual! When the observer or viewer tunes into or thinks about these things later, he can tune into the akashic or whatever it was he has seen or heard, and gain greater understanding thereof. So isn't that something to think about? Vaughn: It is very illuminating; whatever the basis and structure, the consciousness of the teacher is impinged in the music or whatever it is that one is concerned about. One is really communing with the teacher. Ioshanna: This is likewise true in all the works the Moderator has brought, due to the fact he was infinitely minded; he has a continuous and constant contact with the source of all creation. Thus, his mind was of a creative nature and he impinged within every word structure, every syllable; within every letter he ever uttered in that great collection of books, is carried this wonderful psychokinetical energy; energy that will, when given the opportunity, lift the reader into that higher consciousness from which it came. I have heard it said; this is true with the letters which I write, etc. Vaughn: Indeed they do so, Ioshanna. I can vouch for that. Here in the earth plane structures, one has to use words, but if one didn't have words, one could have a contact simply by viewing whatever the mind energies of the teacher instructed; such as the dancing waters of the fountain, which provide the means by which the teachings can be brought out. Ioshanna: Even if a person were blind, he couldn't read or hear, he could sit there among all that beautiful creation and absorb the intelligence by merely tuning in mentally and being conscious of what was being presented. Vaughn: So actually the word forms here, in our case, are really a restriction, a limiting factor; but the only means for the beginning, for many people who are seeking.

Ioshanna : I never felt so inhibited in my life, after viewing all this glorious Infinite — the beauty, the color, the radiance that existed everywhere present in those crystaline structures, then to have to endeavor to put the entire expansive infinite down in these very limited earth words, is frankly and truthfully the most inhibiting, frustrating experience I ever have undergone! But try we must! Vaughn: This is the feeling I had, having viewed to some extent, life on Parhelion, and then sensing the restrictions one has when one attempts in description. I have this feeling to the extent that I can see how masterful you have been, Ioshanna, in simply being able, within the limitations and restrictions of words to expand anyone's mind so that they, themselves, can partake of this wondrous world of the Inner! Ioshanna: Regardless, it is a complete and total feeling of frustration and I am sure this will never be overcome, because we cannot put the fifth, the sixth or a hundredth dimension down into this third dimension, and that is just what it amounts to. We are endeavoring to squeeze Infinity into a thimble!

Now this is the wonderful part: that the true seekers can tune in through the particular frequencies that have been set up in our effort to describe these things. When the student will tune in and try to get the picture of whatever it may be – the beautiful portrayals on the walls, or the pageant itself, without effort, those word pictures will create the means by which he can so relate himself into these beautiful, spiritual dimensions. This can be done; it has been proven. We have already seen several people who have, (as they have heard these words on the tape) actually seen or viewed that which was being described; such as little Shirley, who saw a portion of the great crystal pipe organ. Now she saw that because she is relative to music and simply latched on to that description or frequency, of seeing the beautiful pipe organ that was nearly the size of a mountain.

I believe it was Tom who tuned into, as he heard about the crystal table which held the crown, and saw that in his mind's eye or in his consciousness, but there has been no one up to this point, Vaughn, who is able to view these things as does yourself. It is very wonderful, and I'm so glad that you can, because it is of great help to this book, and even more to yourself! Sanosun, too, my dear secretary, during the hearing of these tapes (#3), tuned in and saw herself being taken (by this one) up the crystal cleansing steps through the flame. Then she saw the end of the wand directed at her, which she told, appeared as a square white Light. Her appearance and attitude proves it. She is quite a different person now, just two to three days later!

Vaughn: As you have been talking, I have been looking into the great structure. Actually, it is the teaching center, that which you call your home, and I am wondering what all these rooms hold, or why so many. I wandered into a room and thought I was in a scientific laboratory. This is not really a room because it is very, very large. It can be compared to a certain laboratory that we have on the earth world. I thought, here I was in the most modern, 21st Century. I saw instruments I had never seen before, and all of these instrumentations seemed to be on the order of vast electronic equipment. I saw what looked like television screens, oscilloscopes, etc. Ioshanna: So this laboratory was for students to come and learn, was it? Vaughn: This laboratory is completely full of people with white smocks. It is very interesting, moreover one night some years ago I came back from sleep state with the picture that I had been in a laboratory in the inner worlds and I had been shown around. I saw these men in white coats, and I was quite wide-eyed with it all. They were telling me they were working on equipment to bring through transmissions of the teachings of the voice, or the pictures of the Higher Ones, so that there could be a direct line, you might say. They say this is a fact; this is a promise – and we know it is going to be a fulfillment. Ioshanna: Maybe little Frank (our new student) will have a part in it. (The 14-year-old genius. I believe you found in your Akashic readings he had been some of the notables of old.) Vaughn: Oh, I'm sure of it. I felt very close to Frank. I feel he had been there and was the one showing me around! Ioshanna: It is a very wonderful thing where a boy is totally absorbed in what he has learned on the inner and achieved in former lives, that he will carry it on so early in life at fourteen; to want to get involved at that early age is very wonderful. But if you look at the boy's face, he is not a boy at all; he's an old, old man, and a wonderful proof of reincarnation. I am sure if his akashic were to be searched further and his soul record would be made, he would be found to be several of the more intellects of the past who have been the true scientists, the true inventors. Vaughn: As I tune in to him,

I know that he was the man Faraday, and Pericles also. Ioshanna: Very likely this laboratory you saw in your sleep, was the place he was working because your frequency has always been relative to mine and to Leonardo's. You were talking the other day of being invited to my home on Parhelion, but do you know, you have already been there many times? You attended the great reception directly after the coronation.

Vaughn: Well, this is my first proof that I had been in your home; and again it is an indication of what this home comprises. It is a small city, in itself. It is a teaching center. I think that is the best thing to call it – a teaching center. It comprises all of the sciences as well as all of the arts – music, painting, sculpturing, dancing – every facet of whatever you portrayed in your lives in the various earth worlds that you have achieved – and, Ioshanna, you have mastered every one of these sciences! Of course, that is what it means to be a Master; and even more, an Archangel. You have mastered every aspect of the sciences and arts – in fact it is shown me that this is true in every aspect of life, in every which way you can think of it! Ioshanna: Regardless, wherever we are at the present, there awaits a higher step to be attained into higher dimensions. I am but a cell in the eye of the Infinite. This is true; whatever we have gained is only one step lower than the next one beyond; and as they have so factually told us, there is no ending to anything!

The manner and way in which we have actually realized of this house – that it has slowly become much larger in size and in use – is most interesting. I personally am really very happy to hear this, because in my conscious mind I was really not aware of it all. Doubtless, my own higher self blocked it, so that you, the Moderator and Leonardo could present this wonderful and beautiful surprise to me! Vaughn: Well, doesn't the following explain why there are so many rooms? Every room has a particular specialty. The ballroom on this floor really is a combination because all people come here. There is a synthesis, I would say, in music and the dance. Every room has a specialty of its own; even in the laboratory I described, there are other areas which are devoted to certain special fields. I see an area here where you and others are teaching people how they, themselves, can bring this information down when they reincarnate, into lower astral worlds – methods by which they can improve the food growth; biological development, I suppose one could call it. Then I see another area devoted to transportation. Here individuals are working with various types of metal alloys and machinery. They are working with the electronic equipment that will propel the new forms of travel which will be levitated through means of gravitational fields.

So it is certainly getting to be quite a revelation to see how you live here on the Inner, Ioshanna! Ioshanna: It is very interesting to me,

I will assure you, but I doubt not one iota of what you say, because so many of the things you describe I have always had such a love for; for instance, the Moderator and I both have in the past often bought such things as large glass crystal fishes, birds, swans, etc. – all sorts of crystal things or glass that you can see through. We have always had a great affinity for these things. When a little lady who cleans the house, one day broke one of those little glass fishes or the bill off the Bird of Paradise, we both felt badly, as though something terrible had happened to the things we loved. Now we don't cherish them in a possessive way, as do the eartheans, but the fact is, they tune us in to these beautiful mental or mind creations! Vaughn: You probably felt a part of yourself was taken away because you had created these things (on the inner). Now we can actually appreciate how everything in this home has been created by yourself and Michiel (Leonardo's new name) and others who may desire to help. Here we run around and we purchase whatever artifacts or objects of art we want. In Parhelion you can create any form of beauty, simply on the basis that you tap the Creative Source! Perhaps this will give a greater understanding of what it means to be joined with the Infinite Creative Source. Ioshanna:

A flash memory comes to mind of how the Moderator seemed to become a part of all things he had to do with – that which was a part of his daily life; if any thing was moved or separated from him, he would actually feel that loss. He would know something was wrong and he wouldn't feel right until whatever it was that had been moved or taken away was replaced. In fact, it would become almost a frustration with him because he wasn't whole, because of these things, a part of him has gone. Now, that is almost inconceivable but it is true! This is so important for the students to begin to conceive energy, starting at the very beginning with the atom, the creation of the atom, and just how the Moderator has related it in the Unariun texts. One can get it if one will delve and stay with it; persistence is the key.

Vaughn: I just can't help but exalt in the view I just had of the top of the house. It is a complete observatory! I have never seen anything of this nature and of this scale. All of the equipment is electronic; it is not manually operated. One can look through the telescope and by means of changing a certain scale, one can view various planets. Then with an adjustment of the electronic telescopic lens, one can see into a particular part of the planet! One can zoom in and actually see an individual! The frequency is the key. That is really tremendous when you think about it, and yet, when you know a little of the energy principles, it all reverts back to the atomic structures, and here in these higher realms it is the psychic structures, the attunement and the force fields! I note this observatory is for students. There is no need on your part however, to use these means to see, for you see by means of consciousness. Ioshanna: So there again we were seeing what has been done here so many times. I recall, I bought the Moderator the first telescope only a few days after we met. I had a strong desire to buy him this telescope, and he was like a boy with his first Christmas. He became so attuned to that telescope that I don't know whether he hardly spoke a word for three days; he lived with it day and night. Vaughn: It shows how close you are with all this equipment that you, yourself, built. Ioshanna: He loved the lens because he formulated some of the very first lenses. He would focus this telescope into the skies and we would spend many a night viewing beautiful Saturn with its rings. We could see quite well with that scope. Of course, it wasn't what you would call a real large one, but was quite a good one. Later on we found a better one for him, and very often on a clear night we would view the sky. It was always a pleasure, especially the red Mars. The moon was always most interesting to see, and Saturn especially, but it wasn't strong enough to get too many of the distant planets. He would always be greatly taken up when he could focus on the individual planets. So we were reliving that part of our future home, and past too! I say our, for we all share in these joys and loves. One's home is not necessarily for him or the two alone. People here have become so compatible; they can easily live four to ten or twenty in a home, if they wish. It is still a manner of service being expressed.

Vaughn: Now that you are talking about it do you ever think there will be a time when it would be possible to view the inner worlds with this telescopic equipment? Ioshanna: I don't think that anything is impossible with the Infinite, and I am sure there are many individuals on planet Earth — seriously minded scientists who are working on such things. If they have developed and progressed to the point — what it would amount to would be, developing a lens that would be of such frequencies as to be neither atomic nor psychic, to connect the third and fourth dimension. I believe this is something that little Danny (Vigus), himself, experienced in his recent vision when he saw material so thin, one saw through it. He was visualizing such things in his (so-called) dream and was very likely working on this very sort of thing! It would have to be something other than actual atomic structures. It will be a very unique and wonderful thing when it happens, when it does come through. This would, in part, be similar to that equipment which the Moderator was speaking of long ago — a lens that would be made similar in form to a television screen whereof the individual could stand before it and view his psychic anatomy. The lens would be made completely of solid crystal, so that the lens would pick up the frequencies from the psychic anatomy; the person standing before it would be able to see the negative vortexes responsible for his condition, problem, or whatever it may be, whereby he could then cancel them out in consciousness. At the same time, there would be ray beams focused to help him cancel these negations out. What it amounts to is an endeavor to bring the fourth, fifth and sixth dimensional vortexes down into the third dimension and, there is the stickler. I am sure the Brothers on the Inner or the Infinite would know how. I am sure there is a way, and that certainly should and shall all be a part of this New Age, this golden cycle.

Vaughn: Right in the laboratory in your own teaching center, a group of individuals are working on such electronics now. In fact, these persons are already here on this plane, Frank being one of them! Also, Danny and the one in the nearby town who was Isaac Newton. Ioshanna: Yes, if he would get with the study, he could make faster progress. I am sure there is no one thing that could be so self-proving to the masses, because man has to see it himself. He has to weigh it; he has to feel it. Up till now it has only been by sheer faith and hope, but with such a lens they could actually visualize it — a visual contact, even the audio. This would be a most wonderful and gratifying thing, and I don't think there could be anything in this world that could happen that would please me more, and it shall! Vaughn: Of course, we do have proof in terms of video and audio, the actual presence of the Higher Beings right here, don't we, Ioshanna, in yourself? Ioshanna: Well, during the many eons in the past, these realities were kept secret. Now we're (as was said) breaking all barriers and bounds. Vaughn: Still we are not able to view the reality of the form of such as our teacher, Ioshanna. We can, in our consciousness, attune to the higher self, the true self, whom we call Ioshanna. But we can't really appreciate until we are capable of expanding our own finite consciousness. So I guess getting a direct voice and picture from the Higher Minds would have to wait until there had been preconditioning amongst those people who will accept. Ioshanna: There has been a great deal of preconditioning going on now and for the many past years. Right now people are being taken out in their sleep state; so many people who have been (seemingly) dead, you might say, to all of these finer frequencies, these vibrations and all of these wonderful things that are really a part of all nature. They are going to be waking up. We are going to see people opening their eyes in many different fields and directions. I am sure this is true because this (now) is the time! Vaughn: Well, we know now with the (almost) completion of this Book of Life, this marks the Conclave of the Light Beings, and this is the beginning of the Golden Age. Ioshanna: It is the beginning of our book, too, but never the ending; for there is no terminating point in Truth.

*The Moderator's memory of his spiritual life was vivid. He remembered how he had planned to come to earth and there would be one here awaiting to help him with his mission; for she too, had learned of these inner worlds and concepts. No thing he ever did or expressed was a surprise to him; he was simply reliving what he had planned to do on earth.

Chapter 19

The opera singers, authors, composers, etc., all driving in their respective carriages, upon arrival at the da Vinci's home and during the magnificent reception, each one presented the Queen with novel albums relative to the roles in the opera or operetta in which they had become most celebrated. This extensive, collective library of albums filled numerous shelves on the wall of her great and expansive library.

Copernicus' gift to the Queen of Unarius was a very rare and unique telescope. This great gem had the power built within it that one could focus upon any point in any nearby world by a simple dial adjustment and actually bring into close range any person, place or object into view. One could zoom in close details and observe what was desired!

The gift Luther Burbank presented to our Archangel was a very rare and new type of gardenia, a gift he knew she would love, for he is aware of her love for especially these white flowers, symbolic of her own color and ray – that of white. This gardenia specie, the first of its hybrid breed, was formed more like the lovely camelias – in perfect circular symmetry, and which she so loves. Queen Iona has often remarked how exquisite are the camelias, but what a pity they have (almost) no fragrance. Thus he has supplied a most heavenly scent, to an even more beauteous flower.

Jacobi (known on the earth plane as Einstein) presented to the Queen a very special clock — a time clock that enabled one to view any particular historical event when one would focus consciousness upon it. Each number corresponded to either a hundred, a thousand or ten thousand years, and any special significant event could be viewed on the earth plane, whether of the past, present or future. This was a most significant object requiring countless years of effort and experimentation.

Madame Blavatsky's gift was the entire library of her writings as was expressed on the earth plane; her complete Theosophical works, all bound in an especially beautiful ostrich-hide leather, a very soft texture, tinted in her dimensional ray color of a pastel green. It was a magnificent creation, carrying her philosophical works, much of which carries continuity into these higher planes.

The gift from each one was of their own creation and was made especially for Uriel, often requiring many years — in some cases, hundreds of years to accomplish, so intricate was the creation, such as the elaborate and intricate clock by Einstein. We can expect to see any of these great accomplishments on earth in time to come, for thus it has already been created on the inner — the way of all so-called inventions. These higher intellects then work with the earthman to help him (so-called) invent these electronic devices; wonders far beyond any earth plane expressions.

Of course, the queen's newly ascended mate or polarity, Leonardo, was ever at her side; he seemed to enjoy all which she enjoyed. Interestingly, too, when at various times, the assemblage or her subjects would express particular honor, respect or salutations, he, too, would join them in their salute to her, most humbly!

When Ioshanna asked of Vaughn, after they each had returned to earth or physical consciousness, just what part of the vast entertainment he enjoyed the most, his reply was, "It was all most stupendous and elegant; most difficult to choose any one portion; yet I must confess, I felt the beautiful picture which the queen and her escort, Leonardo, made, as they drifted about the lake (in the most elegant Swan (boat) among the beautiful trees, flowers, plants, surrounding the heavenly lake), was a stupendous sight. It was one that would be a fine setting for artists to paint, especially of the numerous variations of flowers about. It was truly a queenly paradise and a most memorable occasion; I'm most happy to have so witnessed it all."

One gift which the queen cherished greatly is a lovely swan boat, that she may glide about the many crystal lakes. This most unusual and elegant queens' boat, is built to hold just two. It is of pure-white pearl, trimmed in gold and shaped as a lovely, large, graceful swan! Many jewels bedeck this lovely swan. It floats so gracefully over the sparkling, green-blue waters, and is powered mentally. This elegant boat would cause the live swans to be envious, so motionless does it glide!

Within the plump body of this most graceful swan

207

has been placed some delightful music that comes into play as the boat slowly slips about over the crystal-clear water. This is her favorite pastime, to glide about among the many colorful birds that dot the lakes – birds of an infinite variety of color and form. The bird life on this world is not frightened of people; one can watch them closely without them flying in fright, for all things live in harmony here. The queenly One loves to scatter to the birds and the many brilliantly-colored fishes in the lake, the food they prefer, as she slips and glides with her beloved one so silently over the clear water in the lovely gold and white swan, creating a most beautiful sight. Colorful ray beams are brought into play, projected from the eyes of the swan (boat) as the swan's head turns from one side to the other. This same luminous effect is displayed where e'er that Uriel goes.

The great reception held, attracted the many persons present. The entertainments were presented in various areas and places, in order that each one present may view that which he especially preferred; i.e., certain persons were not particularly fond of the opera, thus other means of enjoyment was offered for them. The great crowds of persons moved about o'er the grounds, the gardens, and within the pavilions – each one according to his own particular tastes and preferences, similar to a state fair on earth, but on a much higher level and far more beautiful.

Ioshanna: Mention has been made of the various personages attending the crowning ceremony, who were to later take part in the great reception and

208

entertainment, and only a surface description was heretofore recalled. This was due to the very lengthy and wondrous entertainment which these countless performers expressed, and for the time being, details were not given. However, it could be rightfully said of the vast and elegant exhibitions, the performances and entertainment displayed, the dancing groups, the ballet performers, the wondrous operettas so expressed, the posing of live statuary representing marble, so posed by the beautiful models, the various groups and choruses, individual singing, all added up to a very lengthy and enjoyable time of the most stupendous entertainment; the artistic expressions and science, of body, of grace and agility was indeed the greatest ever accumulated under any one roof or performed at any one time or place. Yet, to say 'under but one roof', is not quite fact; for several of the extravaganzas and performances were expressed out among the vast and elegant gardens, which exist in so many areas. One sees no dark brown earth or ground as on earth, for this planet is entirely created of the glistening, shimmering, colorful crystal, and all areas about are covered with plants, grass and flowers of an infinite variety, and a riotous variety of color.

Thus, many of the exhibitions were performed among the lovely, natural surroundings — such as the beautiful background of gardens, the various luminous fountains that interspersed the blue crystal lakes, which were in abundance in these elegant surroundings. Many times the performers in the foreground were surrounded by many others at a distance, creating a background; of the performers, both genders being represented.

Remembering, especially, the most beautiful large group of young ballerinas, all gowned in their colorful diaphanous sheers; all wore long flowing golden hair. Of this particular group, there were about seven hundred ballerinas, who were of especial interest to the Queen Uriel as she observed, so fascinated with these many performers – her favorite dance. She seemed especially delighted as she watched with her biune Leonardo, from her beautiful swan-boat which drifted about among the lotus blossoms, noting the countless, graceful ballerinas who were presenting her most favored of all – the lovely "Dance of the Hours" presentation.

Noted too, were several tiny rafts carrying many flower tots who were scattering about, to float upon the water, the queen's favorite rose petals! It made a magnificent sight.

There were orchestras of a great variety; at one time she was honored with a large group of Hawaiian musicians, and of course, the graceful dancers accompanied them from those islands; their Hawaiian costumes were most brilliant, a riot of color and their music was so melodious and gay.

Most impressive and well-loved by, not only the queen, but also by the multitudes present, were the most elegant harpists. This was a very large group of angelic beings, so beautifully robed in the sheerest of flowing white gowns; their golden hair cascading nearly to the waist, all touching so gracefully on their magnificent golden (Italian) harps, studded in brilliant gems. This elegant group of beautiful girls played the accompaniment for the lovely ballerinas as they performed in their most graceful dance of agility beside the lake – a scene from Romeo and Juliet.

A most impressive gesture; at periodic and irregular intervals, toward the crystal surface of this plateau would swoop down countless of the various and beautiful colored songbirds. Many of these elegant birds had iridescent feathers similar to the humming birds of earth. Amongst these were colors, and shapes unknown to the earth persons. Of particular interest to the queen was one large specie that looked much like the Phoenix bird. 'Twas an array of brilliant colors, vivid orange, brilliant green and a lengthy and graceful tail of deep purple feathers. These birds all seemed so friendly with the graceful white swans which were present in the waterways about.

Now and then, a large flock of doves seemed often to gather about the beautiful queenly swan boat, as they too partook of the food which she delighted in tossing to the swans and the fishes. This was more of a spiritual food than physical. These birds seemed to enjoy the music which came from the boat. The multicolored butterflies were abundant in these garden-lake areas, adding further beauty to all the color and wildlife hereabout; the wildlife all seemed to know they were safe and were loved, for they were all quite tame.

Vaughn says: It must be told that this gala affair was not limited, as is common on earth, to some two or three hours time, but was carried on throughout the many hours, although in this spiritual world there is no nighttime expressed, for we have no disappearing sun to bring about the darkness. Possibly what would amount to two or three days time was used in these entertainments.

The entertainers came from many distant planets, and countless were the dancers, the musical renditions, the songs or choruses, some of which were completely unique, and foreign to the earthean, but all, most delightful to view. There was a large group of Japanese who came in the dress of their country, carrying large musical instruments, that fascinated all. With these musicians came the beautiful Japanese dancing girls in their most colorful kimonos most gay, who cavorted most gracefully; they too, delighted the eye of the queen in their soft, shy attitudes. These lovely people originated on the planet Mars and the queen has a kindly rapport with their ways, customs and artistry. She herself had, at one time in a very distant lifetime past, danced as one of the royal dancers for the ruler of Japan, and other times she taught this art expression to many others so interested.

Another of special interest to the queen was the Balinese dancing group with their music so unique; dances which require very lengthy study, practice and effort to master. Yes, she likewise expressed in this particular way at one time. These performers were all sewed into their costumes so elaborate — a custom unique to them alone — no buttons or zippers, each performance required that their costumes be sewn directly on the performers.

Interspersed between dancing were presentations of the operettas and opera singers; they would appear in settings for their particularly chosen roles, all costumed accordingly. At times there were several hundred of these opera stars performing in these glorious gardens and again, they expressed within the great entertainment area of the da Vinci's home which has been called the Ballroom. Never was there insufficient room, regardless of how many hundreds or thousands of persons were present; for this was indeed a very extensive building. They had planned it all well and expected this very large gathering of beautiful spiritual Beings to attend. Perhaps surprising too, that the queen is interested in the karati entertainers; other logistics of the body such as jujitsu which gives agility to not only the body but also quickens the mind in alertness. There are large numbers of these contests expressed; very often the contestants were many in action, simultaneous in performance; all present were of the very finest available in their particular field. These games were in no way warlike in nature, but all carried a continuity of body agility, of grace and form.

Of interest· to especially the children viewing, were the presentations of the large groups who emulated different species of animals and birds. They were costumed in similar garments as, for instance, the large birds, the ostrich, the peacock, the eagle; their dance representative. Others took on symbologies of various animals; these acts the children adored, such as the romping and rollicking chimps, and most loved by all the kiddies were the roly-poly Kuala bears — and the bears loved the kiddies too. The great Thunderbird was well represented by a large group of Mayans and Aztecs who performed in such likeness, one would almost believe they were the very Thunderbirds themselves, with the gigantic wing spread as they strutted and cavorted about. Also presented were a group of American Indians doing their Peace dance. It must be mentioned, although Uriel viewed much of the entertainment from the vantage point in the lake, the performers could be equally as well viewed – as many did, from the grounds and gardens surrounding the lake – and in which were an abundance of most colorful and glistening flowers all crystalline in nature. In fact, we could very well compare these beautiful gardens with those of the noted gardens of Versailles; yet they, too, are, in fact miniatures by comparison, so expansive, varied and extensive are these glorious grounds. Most important, the luminosity emitted from all the foliage, flowers, trees, shrubs, yes, all things in this heavenly area and beautiful city are radiant, colorful and glistening, due to their crystalline nature. The auric emanations from all things are emitted several feet from the source in all colors of the rainbow.

The opera singers, the dancers, the performers, even the comedians and the clowns were all present, all doing their very best, to make it an unforgettable time. They had all trained and practiced long and well for this momentous occasion, and it was a most happy time for all those taking part as well. During this lengthy time wherein the countless persons were performing, would be heard music of some one sort or another; especially for the particular existing presentation. At times, the elegant crystal pipe organ within the home was heard. Always one or more bands, orchestras and combinations were ever in action. It was a most enjoyable celebration for all, and never did one want for music, for one could enjoy just about any type imaginable, with a few added!

One performance of a very large number of persons that especially caught the eye of our Queen Uriel was the great representation from each and every country. This was an accumulation of children from each of the countries of the earth world — the Japanese, the Russians, Germans, Austrians, Australians, the French, etc. From each of these countries came a large group of entertainers who performed the dance or the expression of their particular country, gowned and costumed all in accord. For instance, the large group of those who represented the country of Russia executed their beautiful dance; each one in their brilliant red costumes, doing their exciting firey dance, that quickened all so viewing. The agility of these persons could scarcely be compared! This elaborate display from each country took a great length of time to exhibit and was most entertaining as well as educational. It brought much mental applause.

Uriel continued to show her appreciation and expression for all being done in her honor, and it was noted, of special interest and love from her was the very large group (we are told there were several hundred) of the entertaining tots who were from ages four to six, who had been trained in the artistry of the dance for a time when they would live on some earth planet. These tiny children were all dressed in a similar costume, yet each was of a different pastel shade. They appeared as countless flowers, each garment representing some particular flower. This, she said, was the most impressive of all, for these tiny ones danced with such perfection, grace and unison. It was with great joy that she watched this particular performance for she especially loves children. In fact, queen Uriel teaches children on this planet Eros.

It must be remembered that these gardens are not some small secluded area, but extend and cover several of what the earthman would term acres, (or even miles) in circumference! One sees beautiful streams winding through the elegant gardens and walkways; artistic bridges spanning the streams of waters. Regardless of which direction one looks he sees exotic beauty, beautiful waterfalls sometimes one of a lesser height, again, a far greater fall, one which drops from a great height. The extensive grounds are not simply one flat level or plateau, but rather all are varied in rolling hills and dales. Nothing of beauty has been omitted or spared to please the eye of the dweller or visitor to this heavenly plateau.

Now, to describe each performance would be quite involved; suffice to say, there never has been, in any one place, at any one time, so vast or so much delightful entertainment presented at one continuous time. This indeed was the affair of the millennium — so rightfully named.

What with this vast and most glorious continuous display and exhibition of color, of grace, of beauty, of talent and form, one may think he would tire of it all. Yet, not so! All things were so well planned, spaced and presented, one moved from one area to another, to drink in the incomparable natural beauty that existed everywhere in this vast crystal city, where color and radiance abounds. When we inquired of our hosts as to its size, the replay was, "We are never overly populated. Our city is vast and accomodates the countless thousands that appear in their astral states, as well as the many thousands who live here."

Ioshanna quested of Vaughn if he felt that most of the other homes in this city were the very great size as was the da Vinci's – which was, in part, a great teaching center, as well as their home. His reply was, for he had been strolling about in other areas and had become informed: "Not all; I've noticed many homes which were of a far less expansive nature and were more modest or cozy, rather than the vast and elaborate nature as is the da Vinci's. Those I noted, existing on a nearby tree-bordered street, although they appeared much smaller, were likewise very colorful and most tasteful in their decor, all expressing the radiating crystalline structures. After all, continues Vaughn, some of the personages so living here have not been accustomed to so lavish living and they would feel lost to have it so. Thus, each one creates for himself that which is most compatible to him. Each one lives as he chooses and in surroundings he likes best."

Ioshanna, was not the long row of statues with the fountains on the road to the entranceway of the of the queen's home most impressive? She replies: Oh, indeed so, and speaking of them, they should be further described to the reader.

Vaughn continues: Speaking of fountains and water, water was everywhere; water in fish ponds, cascading water, sleeping water and still, quiet water so peaceful, murmuring water, pumped water, frothy water forced into bubbles, crests, domes, streams and ripples. Unique about the waters on this planet – they all carry a radiance, a particular beneficial frequency to the viewer. Of especial beauty among the various water displays was the vast collection of statuary fountains, periodically positioned along the roadway, leading into the great circular drive toward the da Vinci home. On either side of this wide thoroughfare stood statuary of renowned beauty, all formed as graceful dancing girls which appeared as marble or alabaster, yet were created as are all things on this higher world, of crystalline structures. These graceful young beauties were all draped in the familiar Grecian and Roman robes and drapes, each one holding atop her head a huge, deep bowl filled and over-flowing with colorful flowers from which spewed tall streams of water in delicate patterns.

Although the general appearance of these statuesque ladies was quite similar, yet upon closer observation it was noted each face was different and individual! Then it was learned from our guide that these ladies were replicas or representations of a large dancing group or school – one which the queen had, in a long ago time, taught – and each one had become a famous ballerina in her own name. Thus, this elegant row of statuary was, in essence, a salute from them all to her!

This circular display (which number thirty-three statues on either side) appeared illumined from within and cast off a soft, warm, rosy hue; yet we learned this was all created in the structures when made. The lengthy rows of beautiful forms with the graceful streams spewing high above, were all surrounded with a riot of colorful blooms and shrubs of most delicate green shades. It is said of the queen, that she experiences a most happy rapport and memory with these, her former students, as she passes between these vast rows of dancing girls, seemingly poised for her passing. Yes, Ioshanna, I too, quite agree, this is a most impressive and lovely area.

At the very far end of this majestic garden behind the large crystal pool, wherein Queen Uriel loves to look about in her swan boat, is situated a most exquisite Japanese sculptured garden. This garden occupies a distance of about three acres of ground and is literally filled with every aspect of beautiful Japanese landscape architecture, including their mind-created miniature and dwarfed trees. The coniferous trees are shaped in every conceivable manner, form and size in the various hues of green. The extensive gardens are dotted with the artistic and colorful vermillion moon-bridges which span a bubbly, foamy stream of crystal waters, dotted with numerous of their favorite golden fishes.

The lovely garden lanterns so favored by the Japanese (which are in the earth world made of cement structures) are here created of this wondrous crystalline substance which glows and radiates from within, emitting soft, warm rays of luminescence. The artistic and graceful lawn chairs, settees, swings, etc., so favored by the Japanese are scattered everywhere about for convenience, to drink in the beauty of the many beautiful sculptured fountains, always topped with some graceful Japanese figurine. Noted shuffling about the beautiful crystal lawns, we see the dainty, youthful Japanese ladies, all gowned in their lovely colorful, painted kimonos, usually carrying their tiny umbrellas, which seem to be a part of their dress, as well as their multicolored and graceful fans which they use so shyly. But to describe this entire Japanese garden would require an entire volume. The lovely tones emitted from the great bells, which are such an important part of their life in ancient Japan, are here all reenacted for the beauty and enjoyment of the visitor. Often beneath the trees are heard the beautiful wind chimes, to imitate the various tones as well as the brass chimes, all so pleasant to the ear. Their most elegant statuary, placed most artistically, exists profusely; their gayly colored tea gardens which are seen now and then and everywhere about abounds the elegant and many hued butterflies which have all been created, as are all things on this planet, of crystal, of the mind energies of those living here. Suffice to say, this is indeed a bit of paradise and most loved and often visited by our Queen Uriel.

* * *

Yes, Vaughn, you were speaking about the various gifts that each of the thirty-three hundred guests who came to the reception of the Queen and which they brought as individual gifts. You say perhaps it was peculiar that Blavatsky gave her own library when you feel that which she wrote and taught was of a lesser degree of importance, truth or science to that which Unarius is, or perhaps to that which I am aware, and you rather felt it would not necessarily be sufficiently progressive in nature. However, this would not be especially true. You see, all of these persons, themselves, have been working on their personal achievements for many, many years — and we could very well say, some of them very often for countless thousands of years! These gifts that they brought were all relative to their ultimate achievement, the expression which they have related upon the earth world which has made, shall we say, the greater mark in their entire evolution. In Blavatsky's case, although doubtless she has previously written other works, this is her greatest achievement, and so she gave of herself in so doing! It was, in essence, she! Moreover, these great gifts that each one has brought as a wedding gift to the Queen of Archangels, or of Unarius was, in essence, more than simply a personal gift of these achievements. Speaking of Blavatsky herself, although this may have been achieved in one lifetime, surely it was the culmination of many lifetimes of endeavor, so for her to bring this library to Uriel was of great significance! She is bringing and preserving for posterity on these inner planes, in order that countless personages in the future eons of time will be able to review and observe in the manner of historical reference, these works, and which, to Blavatsky, was a very great accomplishment and achievement, and indeed, it has served many persons. A great deal of her philosophy is noteworthy and of a progressive nature; it has continuity with these higher spiritual worlds. Thus, her gift was equally as great and important as was, for instance, the beautiful, magnificent clock that the one we call Jacobi, who was on the earth plane, Einstein, created from his very mind energies on these inner planes. This is an accomplishment on which he has been laboring and working for countless thousands of years – likewise the gift of Copernicus. As we say, these will likely be achieved on some future earth plane, whether on this planet or some other one. Anything these great personages have so created and evolved will manifest upon some earth planet in the future. Thus, we shall call it a clock but it is much more than a clock, for one can attune by placing consciousness upon this exquisite electronic mechanism and tune in to any point in the universe, any century, past, present or future! That's right, because there is no past, present or future in the abstract. Frankly, it is all in the now! Therein we can view any historical or futuristic event. This was indeed a most incomprehensible achievement, and thus he has presented his most treasured work, on which he likely has spent many lifetimes, for it encompasses not only perpetual motion but many other facets of very scientific expressions and exacting combinations.

These great works of their personal expressions, whether they be of the art or music, of the many composers, artists or authors themselves, the wondrous opera singers, each one individually and collectively was represented. Their gift was that which meant the most to them − that which had promoted their individual expression to the greater degree. So it is, in essence, a great giving of themselves. Due to the fact the gifts have been created from their higher minds, they are of course, infinite expressions. So here again, we are regenerating the Infinite in this wonderful, magnificent, inconceivable and incomprehensible accumulation of giving of the self, in these personages; it was an overwhelming and joyous occasion.

Vaughn: The description you give of these gifts is very helpful in explaining and broadening the dimension in which all these people are working. These are not gifts, as such; these are accomplishments in every field of endeavor, and it is quite an achievement when you describe how this was the accomplishment of many thousands of years for each of those present. So, in essence, it is a celebration of their accomplishment − not only a celebration for but one particular person, but it is a celebration of the whole Shamballa − a conclave where

223

everyone took part! Ioshanna: It is a pinnacle of each one's expression, at which they have arrived. So isn't it wonderful? It is mind-blowing! Vaughn: It certainly extends the understanding of a million years, which means simply that there is an indication of the slow progress here in these lower planes.

Of course, this vast collection that these thirty-three hundred beautiful beings have brought — these great gifts of accomplishments will serve, and remain in this home which the da Vinci's have created and built within this great Center, but also that many persons in the future will come to enjoy and gain understanding from these various artifacts. For when they attune to these particular expressions or relatings, whether it is a painting or such beautiful library books, they in turn, attune to the composer or author or painter, whatever it may have been, and thereby, the student can gain understanding from that individual. So this great collection of these works of art, beauty, science or whatever the particular level it is, will remain here in this great center, the home the da Vinci's have shared for eons of time. Countless shall be the scholars who shall come to observe, to learn, to study, not only for historical depictions, but to attune to the very consciousness of those great beings who have so created them.

Now bear in mind, these personages who will be coming to these centers, (as they are educational centers) will be, for the most part, of a lesser degree of development. They will be students up to this point of development. Thus, they will be able to be lifted in consciousness with the contact and observance, for instance, in viewing this exquisite – and it truly is an exquisite portrayal which the beloved artist Raphael has portrayed on the Queen's domed ceiling. And it must be said that he actually created the reenactment, using his mind energies to form the elegant crystal dome covering. He created this truly most exquisite portrayal of the beautifully formed angels appearing in the sky, and thus when one will attune to this he will thus attune to the very artist himself and thereby be lifted in consciousness! So these thoughts can be very mind-expanding and beneficial to the aspiring student, as well as the great enjoyment Iona, herself, her beloved Michiel, and others will obtain therefrom. With Infinite Minds it is in the sharing that they live – not in the possessions they can gain and hold to themselves, but in the sharing therein is the greater joy – in the sharing of the oneness and of themselves.

And now because of what you said and how these individuals come to your home, which is in essence a teaching center, I am quite aware that this teaching center is more unusual than any other teaching center that has been known, in that it comprises a center to which people come from many hundreds of different dimensions, planets and worlds, even galaxies, which means there are peoples of all varieties, types, natures and races. You might say that which emanates from this teaching center is the apex of knowledge, and which explains a great deal of how all of these worlds have progressed. It's because they have received the teachings that have been infiltrated down through the instruments or channels who have had their first or beginnings of their own progression from this very highest of teaching centers, Parhelion. I have always thought of teaching centers in a more prescribed way. Ioshanna: I will assure the reader that this is the most futuristic and wondrous manner and plan of teaching that ever was evolved or expressed, for the student actually enters into the very expression. He not only sits or reads or studies but carries out in action his studies! Especially when he enters, for instance, this great center which is the da Vinci's home. He is instantly mentally or psychically put in touch with all the various composers, artists or creators — the individual who has created it — thus, in this rapport with his own higher self — and which he is, at this particular time, for these persons who attend are very often from the lower earth worlds who are being given their help and teaching on the inner; thus, much benefit can be attained; he experiences the rapport and can build from there.

Vaughn: Are these students in their astral state? Ioshanna: Oh, indeed so. Some, but not all; both manners come, both after they have ascended and in their sleep state too. Vaughn': While they are in the lower worlds, they attend in their astral state, but when they are then on the inner, they attend in their higher state.

Vaughn: The more I tune in and look at your home Ioshanna, the more it seems like Montecello, the home of Thomas Jefferson. It looks very similar but that is a scale model! Jefferson is one of the scientific students you have there, by the way. He is going to come back and do some inventing. In fact, he has already incarnated here. He has been working in your laboratory on Parhelion and you have been helping him to formulate new instruments in a mental way. Ioshanna: So, in a way, this is not only a home, it is a school for minds. Now this would explain a little further what was said in the Pulse books when the Moderator dictated them. He said the homes of these people were actually communes, in a way. Very often, many people lived in one home, all in a compatible, harmonious rapport. So this would explain what he indicated there.

Vaughn: I often wondered where all of these people go. This teaching center literally abounds with several thousand individuals who are preoccupied in their own specialty or endeavors. Where do they go? They don't go anywhere because that is the reason for the size of this teaching center — for all of these various rooms! Not that the home owners have to sleep, but they do have their own quarters. Ioshanna: Due to the fact that everything with which they are involved carries its own particular frequency, they would need separate areas. They wouldn't be mixing up the music with the experimental laboratories, so this would explain why there would be the need for the various huge rooms or areas for a large center. Vaughn: There is nothing which these students could wish for that is not supplied in abundance in this teaching. Here all the leaders in their specialties are being trained in this particular center; so isn't it interesting to know that here, not only have you and the Moderator been responsible for bringing the Book of Life, called the Unarius Teachings to this plane, but you have actually trained and taught those people who were responsible for carrying out the mission! I mean the mission wasn't simply a matter of introducing the work, the teaching in book form, but it is a continuous evolvement! Ioshanna: Vaughn, once an individual walks into this door (I don't mean this house door), once an individual requests even our literature from this organization, once he reaches out, he is in our oscillation from then on; we are in touch with that individual. Because he has asked for the Light, we continue to radiate it and teach him from then on. To those who study and come along, we can extend greater help because the help must always be directed and extended in ratio to the effort the individual puts forth. All one needs to do — and perhaps this isn't the wisest way to say it — and whoever makes the contact, you might as well say, is our boy, from then on. Regardless, the oscillation has been set up and that individual actually becomes an oscillating part of us.

Chapter 20

The following information was voiced (dictated) by one who calls himself Mal Var, from the planet Venus. This discussion was more or less given to the Moderator and I (Ioshanna), rather personally. It had not been included in any text, as it was more or less a prediction for the future. This portion of a tape which I shall re-record for you on this (Conclave of Light) tape, was projected through mental transmission, through the mind and the voice of the Unarius Moderator (Ernest L. Norman) in the year 1954, as we were in the process of receiving the Pulse of Creation books (namely, that of Eros). As you will note, his predictions have indeed all come to pass during these past few years:

"Greetings from the planet Venus! I am speaking for those whom you know as Orda and Mal Var. It is because Orda is concerned with some of the transcript which I am about to give that she wished me to convey this to you. Now that the mysteries of earth and heaven are beginning to be unfolded to you and that surely, step by step, with each revelation there will come new promptings and from these promptings will be born new desires for the truth and for the things in which the spirit and nature of man always ultimately strives.

"As you have both correctly surmised, along with others on your earth planet, there is now a new movement among the peoples of the earth, and a new consciousness. This you have termed or called the Aquarian Age, or an age in which the lion lies down with the lamb. This, in itself, is purely spiritual in significance and relates only to its correct interpretation, inasmuch as the carnal lust of man shall become tempered and purified with the radiance of God's spiritual love.

"And so you must know of these and other things, for truly as it has been spoken to you, that these things were long in their planning and they shall take long in manifesting. Nor will you hear the blast of trumpets nor see the flaming sword; neither shall these things cometh by day or by night, but only in their gradual consciousness from man's inner spiritual awakening.

"And so you have been pondering much, and thinking thusly of these and other truths and for surely you have read the written word of others who are likewise pondering. And so it is, that the minds of the people, in all the nations of the world shall rise up in unison as a great tide against the evil forces and they shall be overwhelmed and destroyed. For these things have been written and so ordained in the consciousness of Him, whom you call God. For thus it is that God recreates, regenerates, purifies and does all of the things in the finite and of the Infinite Consciousness.

"For your own selves, and of your own personal part in which you and our sister play in this drama of life and death on your planet — and when I say life and death — that it is such for millions and millions of people. They have for many years been standing close to the edge of oblivion; their world could easily have been destroyed by one false move. But it is you, Ernest and our beloved sister, who deserve at least some measure of praise and commendation, for it is not many in your world who will go against the tides of man's earthly desires. It is so few who tempt the vicissitudes of their fellowman in their expressions to a more spiritual way of life.

"And so it is that the hall of history is a place wherein are many names of those who have likewise thus braved the vicissitudes of their fellowman. May I say to you that soon, she, Ioshanna, may have a story which can be truly said will be one of the greatest stories of all times, for it is the story of two who have not only braved the wrath of your own world many times, but have braved the wrath of many worlds many times. So we will say that the story of Esther and Ernest will read like no other story that has ever been written and that it shall come, not in your world and time nor even of your world, but from worlds beyond this world. For it is in these two, who have chosen to lay aside much of those things in which they justly earned, that they may again walk among their fellowman in the lower earthly orders. And it is thus they have again incurred all of the hatreds and the pent-up emotions.

"And so the time and the place when this story, like others, shall be written and shall be revealed to mankind and that you may fully understand what is meant by celestial marriage, or the unification of two God Forces in a united and concerted effort; for here again is the infinite nature of God expressing Himself in another way and in another form. The wheels of the celestial universe which are motivated by the all-pervading God Force, are slowly turning and their motion is linked with the freeing and the progression of all mankind, wherever he dwells, on whatever planet. And so it is with your planet; thus they, all the elements of the earth, of the fields and of the mountains, of the sky and of the air, yea, and even those of the stars must continually revolve around and around into the infinities and the vastnesses of this great Cosmic Mind, which is God. And so in this progression, each thing finds its own law, its own harmony and its own intelligence which is guided and motivated by this God Force.

"For surely, we who dwell among the more highly evolved planets know of these things and we would not tell you so if it were not thus. In the future, as it has been promised, there will be things and truths revealed to you which have not been revealed to any man in any space of time which has been written of among your earth people. And while some have had a little or a part of some of these truths, yet none, save the Avatars themselves have possessed or will ever know of these truths in such a large measure. For it is thus that the will of the Creative Force and, in the expression of the evolution of mankind, that he must ever returneth to the fountain of all life and all expression so he will, in a future day, resolve and revolve into these vast infinities of expression. (I asked if he could speak a bit louder.) Yes, little sister, the power is fading; for we know of the limitations of your earth bodies and of the energies for which we must maintain our communication. For the present, we shall discontinue. Until such future time,

Mal Var of Venus.''

Thus it is, one may well conceive from the great prophecies of these Higher Beings, that now all the secrets of Heaven have been revealed, and that their long-foretold, greatest love story has now been written — especially during the past few weeks.

It may well be said that I (Ioshanna) have often wondered, and especially since the Moderator has changed worlds: What about this, his great love story — that of He and his biune Orda, that had been promised? However, I did console myself with the realization that he could well project through my mind such a story, were it to be.

Thus, you can possibly conceive something of my personal feelings with my (temporary) ascension into these higher worlds and of my being so out-of-the-worldly honored, coming into the realization that Leonardo da Vinci was actually my other half or biocentric, and of being crowned Queen of the Archangels – then when slipping back into physical (or third dimensional) consciousness, little by little this vast, incredible, colorful experience was tuned into or made known unto my conscious mind – that actually, the great love story promised was in actuality my own life and likewise that of my own past many lives (biune to Leonardo), along with that of the Moderator and his biune, Orda; that it was a dual polarity situation of countless thousands of years duration and expression; of teaching and of carrying the Light into many countless unillumined planets and worlds.

Up to this point, I had been so totally involved in a personal, physical way – what with the mission and all the work involved, I had not become conscious of these things in a third dimensional way. And thus, one could well imagine the great joy, excitement, yes jubilation that was experienced as this great conclave was revealed, visited and experienced; and now, in conscious mind, effort being made to relate it to the reader.

To say that I personally feel as though I have been projected into the future ten or one hundred thousand years would not be overestimating. I am, as of this day, totally and completely far more spiritually quickened – a transcended and an ascended ethereal being. The earth world has indeed moved out from under me completely and I do, for the most part, now live

.

much of the time in this highly ascended state of awareness – beautiful beyond words. The Brothers really pulled a "Ralph Edwards" on me! (The program that surprises one with their own life – called "This Is Your Life" on TV.

So it can well be seen, the joke was on me! Surely, the surprise of the millennium. Yes, indeed, it is the affair of the millennium!

Most joyous of all do I revel in the fact that those reading these lines or hearing these words on magnetic tape, can likewise so attune and conceive glimpses of these vast inner worlds of Light, of color, of crystal; yes, and most of all – of life! Sufficient students nearby have proven this to be true. We are well aware of the great powers these words and consciousness carry, which will serve as your key frequency to so align and attune you, the reader, to this magnificent splendor – the paradise promised.

Vaughn: A short time ago, Ioshanna, you were speaking of what takes place when the individual asks for the Science (Light). That reminds me of the beautiful words that come from Jesus, where he says: "Seek and ye shall find. Knock and the door will be opened." And this is how it's done! Ioshanna: Of course! You didn't realize that before? This is it; this is the way! And even more, he said: "Believest thou in me." Now, of course, the "me" was not the personal man; "Believest thou in me", is the concept, the principle of life; the evolutionary principles he brought. That is what he was referring to when he said "me", "and that ye shall be rewarded openly." How are you rewarded? Your own life will take on greater luster, greater illumination; you shall become more quickened with a greater understanding, and the Light can flow to you in greater abundance. Again, as he says: "It is the Father Within," and who is the Father Within? It is the infinite contact with the source of all creation, or the Central Fountainhead. So there we are. We can take any predictions or vouchings extended to the disciples or people at that time, and they are as valid today as they are then, because it is all part of the Infinite Itself. And now we are regenerating that which he taught before.

Vaughn: Yes, it's all so crystal clear now. It is wonderful to know that all the questioning that one has had, finally has been answered; the questing. Ioshanna: All questions can be answered when we view life objectively with principle in mind. I no longer have the feeling or drive to seek. I feel I've found that which I sought, and it is a wondrous feeling indeed, to be at peace with one's self and the world. And I must say, Vaughn, as I was telling this little soul, Sanosun, that you are actually stepping into the future by hundreds, yes, possibly even a thousand years at a time because it is actually not — and we must repeat, emphasize and underscore — it is not the amount of time that is involved, it is the amount of concept that can be realized; the amount of this inner wisdom that we can make our own, that makes the difference, that boosts us forward – that is the forward thrust. And now you have gained so much understanding and illumination, and actual conceiving of these inner worlds, that you have what is similar to actually being shot from out a cannon – literally thousands of years into the future!

Vaughn: So one doesn't have to take a trip on a spaceship to go to a distant planet because it is all in one's consciousness. I now certainly understand the meaning of regeneration much more. Ioshanna: You have indeed expressed that very principle within you. Vaughn: Of course, I know whereof the promise has come, and I am glad that I have found one of the golden keys. Ioshanna: Indeed you have and it is good there is someone to tell the people because they must know in some way, for no one knows really, except perhaps some few people we have contacted through the mails. Out of the many, many thousands we have contacted, (I would dare say anywhere from sixty to eighty thousand people we have reached or contacted with the books), I doubt if there is really anyone who recognizes the true value and true worth of what this channelship is – what it means. You do realize to a far greater extent than anyone I know, and it is a wonderful thing because somebody has to tell them. I endeavored to tell the world as best I could in my "Bridge" book about the channel that existed, so they must learn and they must know; they will not, if they are not told; so this is one important part of your mission. It is no longer words with you, it is realization. You conceive it is a concept and understanding; it is an inner knowing about these things of which you speak.

Vaughn: Yes, and I know now the true meaning what has always been stated — to be born again. It is a complete new awareness, a rebirth. One has to really experience it. Ioshanna: That is the only way. You can't tell it; you can't explain it; one cannot know by reading somebody else's works. It has to be a personal experience and the wonderful part about it — it can and will happen to anyone who will give it just half a chance; if one will be open minded and receptive, will try to maintain a positive consciousness, be persistent above all else, and open the mind to the teachings — any individual, regardless, can and will conceive and grow, and likewise experience! Now you say, how long will it take? This is entirely up to the individual. You, yourself, Vaughn, are one example. You say, "Well, how long have I been striving to arrive at this point?" I would dare say, for at least five hundred thousand years to arrive at this point, and you have doubtless gained more wisdom, understanding and concept of life itself, of the future, of what can be, of what man is, of the Infinite Oneness of life in these last three or four weeks than you have in those previous five hundred thousand years! And we might even take those five hundred thousand years on back to another five hundred thousand years, for this is how slowly man progresses, until he finally wakes up. As dear Ming-Tse used to say: "Man needs to wake up!" Vaughn: If it takes all that time, if he has purposely held himself back by his regressing and his own concern with self, he has surely cut his own throat. Ioshanna: Yes, even much worse than that, he has committed a suicide far worse and beyond the physical suicide but rather, it is a psychic, spiritual and soulic suicide! But it doesn't have to be that way! If it had to be that way, then we — meaning this group of (3300) spiritual beings who first went out to the different planets and worlds from the planet Aries to go to the rescue — wouldn't have made these various trips and spent their lives trying to teach, if they didn't realize it would take that long anyway. I like to think, had they not so expressed this help and influence through the countless eons, things would surely have been very much worse even than presently exists, for the power they brought had to be used for good. So although all these efforts were seemingly, to all means and purposes a failure, nevertheless, it is doubtless the element that had prevented destruction long ago, even with or through countless planets through this universe alone.

Vaughn: It raises my appreciation and awareness even more, that you have gone out to the various planets with a preconceived plan to save the peoples on these worlds. How glorious it is to know that there are such inner Beings, and how far we have sunk here, being cut off;

not even aware that life exists in other planetary systems! This is truly a very terrible thing. Ioshanna: We could even push this five hundred thousand years back and easily double it and say it was a million years ago because life didn't begin then. Yes, Vaughn, this is the thing. When man doesn't realize it is his connection, his contact, his flow through, his pipeline to the inner or his feedback, whatever you want to call it, that it actually exists from the Infinite, he is or has been, in those many thousands of lifetimes, actually regressing. He becomes very little more than the very plants or animals because he doesn't experience the progressiveness. He just goes around and around in the proverbial circle and very often regresses the more. Now, once an individual — and this could be true with the biggest part of the people in the world — has regressed to any sizable degree, it takes them much, much longer to climb out from that rut or the degree to which they have reverted than it ever did to go backward, or to have so reverted. So it is a very lengthy and involved thing for the average person who hasn't had, as you have and as do all Unariuns, this contact with the higher Spiritual Beings or powers. This has changed your evolution completely from one of a negative bias and direction, to that of a positive direction. I will say, in all sincerity, you are the most fortunate person (and I don't like to say fortunate because that which man achieves he earns; it isn't given to him) but I don't know what else to call it.

Vaughn: I guess you still have to call it fortunate because it was through my own ignorance that I didn't maintain the contact with the higher worlds or the Infinite before; therefore, I am fortunate that I found and was given help to climb out. Ioshanna: You see, the sad and drastic part of it is — and this is in no way pointing any fingers because I know you have evolved sufficiently far beyond that and that it doesn't bother you to speak about it — once a person has started to revert or that he is oscillating from his negative past (let us put it that way), after he has been involved with some of these negative forces, beings or astral underworld characters and personalities, he really has little chance to break away because they are so forceful, they are so powerful in their numbers. They number many countless thousands more than do the positive souls number in their strength. Being so close to the earth world, which the astral worlds are, and being so filled with these astrals as well as thought form bodies, frankly, once an individual slips down on the retrogressive position in his evolution, these other lower astrals, along with his own negative past, overcome him, overwhelm him, and, one could say, roll him into such a negative ball or mass that he is unable to extricate himself! In fact, he doesn't know how to extricate himself or break the vicious cycle. He actually becomes one with all these negative oscillating entities and one great mass of negation and it becomes a world in itself. Vaughn:

Yes, I know of what you speak; that is why I feel that the word "fortunate" is a very apt word because one can't get out without this help. Ioshanna: So this is one thing that you felt when you sat in the chair I am sitting in now and you had this tremendous vibration, the shaking effect like the floor was shaking underneath you, and it was, in essence. We were directing a bolt unto you that literally tore apart from you many of these astrals that kept you reverting in the past and kept your mind in a turmoil, fearful and guilt-ridden. That is what this great electric shock or charge was that made you actually feel as though you were in an electric chair. You sat here and quivered, and your whole body shook, your head bounced and your entire physical shook, quivered and writhed there for twenty minutes! I never will forget the look on Dotty's face when she would look over and tip her head down in wonder as to how long this shaking would last, etc. She had never seen anything like that before! She tried to listen to the tape being played and she would turn and peer at you again, and you were still going, shaking violently! So you had it real good; that was the great charge when you said you felt like you were being electrocuted. Maybe that wasn't the exact time you said that, but this is what was happening. All those negative astrals that were hanging in there with you were the ones who were electrocuted. They were not harmed in any way; they were given this very vital and potent shock treatment to eject them from your consciousness, and then they were all gathered up like one would sweep up dust in a dustpan and carted off to some of the lower teaching centers. They wouldn't be ready for any of this higher teaching but they were — through the frequencies that we in the higher realms know of, to move these personalities around — taken to lower centers where they would be relative. They were taken to some of these many schools that we have, ushered into some classroom in which they would be relative, and little by little, some form of the teaching will be infiltrated into their minds — especially when the minds of these individuals were passive in sleep state.

So little by little, these more destructive entities could eventually be brought into the Light, but that takes a great deal of doing, a great long time, because we don't have the cooperation of the individual. It is done almost against his will. Vaughn: Well, this is a certain indication of how help is given to the person who has asked for it, as well as to those people who are obstructing his progress. These are helped by the hundreds. Ioshanna: Now this great overwhelmingly strong help of the force, and power that was brought in, was not done especially that you asked, but because you, yourself, had made such great strides and efforts. I can personally recall, back throughout the ten to twelve years that I had been corresponding with you, always there was the thrust within you; always there was the determination and this is the thing that brought you up to the winner's line — that inner determination, that vouched eagerness within yourself, regardless of any odds. And heaven only knows, and I know full well, too, the odds with which you were confronted! They really threw the book at you in all manners and ways to deter, to stop, to block you from what you are expressing — what you actually came to do. So we can say, you really won the battle, and this is a great victory, not only for you; it is a great victory for the forces of Light because you likewise can subconsciously, shall we say, or even from your true self, influence all those less positive individuals who, in the past, you may have contacted. So it is through your now more positive energies, frequencies, lines of force and position that you are setting up your mental thought waves that are being projected through the ethers so they can indirectly be helped. And isn't that a wonderful thing! Vaughn: Yes, it is a wonderful thing and something I knew subconsciously; that this is the way in which I could help. One of the individuals who has been living in this fashion of a less positive way, when he himself has been helped and extricated then he helps those with whom he has been in some kind of negative relativity. I have known this and it is something that has helped me in a way, because I have always had the desire to change this bias and prove it to myself. Ioshanna: It has always been an overwhelming zest and zeal, a pull and drive within you. I know that has always existed. I know of one very, very critical time in your recent career too, Vaughn, where the negative forces were able to have full sway, full possession and it affected myself greatly. I was overtaken, the throng was so powerful. They entered the house and took me over and obsessed me as I have previously stated in my writings. It took a little over a month to clear them out – get myself straightened around. This I know, was a most trying time for you; for what it actually amounted to in your own mind was, here was the only person you knew of who could really be of help to you, who turned you out and turned her back on you. This was very hard to do, but it was the only thing I could do to break the contacts. I know this was one very drastic time in your life and yet, what did you do? You very wisely went out and found some group, in some way to try to speak the word of truth. This was the most sensible and wisest thing you could ever do; for this was a strong, positive effort in a positive way. In other words, this is the only way to break these negative cycles – by doing something strong in a positive way to lift us up. So you were very wise in that and in other times as well.

I don't believe it is possible for man or any student to conceive the importance of changing immediately the frequency when one is negative. Now this dear little girl who came over to type for an hour the other day – and she is supposed to know as much about principle as the average student who has had the study as long as she has – yet, what does she do? She either sits in the office or in her home and feels sorry for herself, or if some little negation comes up, like they lost their car or something, she gets all wrapped up in this negative ball and regenerates the negation. The first thing you know she is living in a great, horrible, negative mass and all she needed to do was recognize what was happening to her – to realize: here is the old negative past; and in this recognition she will automatically switch that bias to a more positive one and then, start out and do something positive. Now that's all it takes, and this is a very simple principle. There is no one principle or concept to relate that would equal this importance – not one!

I am sure you have proven this to yourself – the importance of recognizing when one is negative, to change quickly the bias by objectifying in a positive way, this negative oscillation and wave form. Then we quickly move into a position where the negation no longer has power over us. This principle or secret, as it has been termed (and we certainly don't want to keep it a secret!) is the very most vital of all concepts. It can be and is the very life-changing principle – and it does work! It works inviolately when we will objectify it, but we have to really let the thought drop down into our subconscious where the superconscious can zap in on that negation. I know, not too long ago, you have (in the last week or two) caught yourself doing that, using the principle, and how happy you were to get the knack of it – of not permitting the negation to oscillate there with you and drag you down for another few days or weeks, but change the bias quickly! It really is quite a revelation for me to see that one who has been so easily influenced by his negative past can actually step up on this more positive oscillation and edit his thoughts, watch his reactions and check them out immediately! This is the very life-changing force or principle, the concept – whatever we choose to call it. This is it; and the quicker man can learn that, the better it is for him. Yet how long does it take for man to learn this one simple concept?

You know, Vaughn, let me say I have, without being really conscious of these principles, used them all my life; even when I was a young girl. When anything would come along that wasn't the most desirous – a distasteful experience I didn't choose to entertain, I would immediately get into something positive. I would change it by so doing. So I can look back and see that I was practicing and did know this principle; even though the actual terms or, to define principle was not really in my conscious mind, I was practicing it. I can remember just now three definite instances and happenings in my past where, with the normal earth person it would have been quite a tragedy, a severe crisis, such as a separation or dissolution of a marriage when I was very young – as I was married when I was eighteen but I really seemed much younger than I was. When this marriage came to an end, to most people it would have been a great crisis and yet I immediately involved myself with some very positive expressions and it didn't throw me; the same as when a former husband died. Immediately I got into something constructive, whether it was some hobby, art work or whatever, I quickly involved myself in something positive. I remember on several occasions some crisis would arise about the house; I would dash out and buy myself a new costume; it was changing the bias into a more positive expression! Now I don't mean we have to run down and buy a new costume every time we get a little negative but then I was still practicing the principle. I used to look back and wonder afterwards of the possible serious crisis back there yet the crisis was nonexistent. Now I can see; I knew the principle before I came to earth and used it or lived by it.

Vaughn: It certainly has taken me a long time to recognize that simple principle because of the very fact that having lived with such abject lower forms, feeling sorry for myself, or of not being "in charge" is basically it. When one allows one's emotions to take charge, he has lost contact; so it means a great deal to know that the third dimensional world, as you pointed out, is peopled with the astral forces; peoples who are concerned with themselves and their own needs and desires. The nature of energy explains why anyone residing in this plane is completely influenced by these entities, (either so-called dead or alive), and if one doesn't have these principles, one then is enslaved; he is drawing from his past experiences and he can't do or express otherwise. He is a slave to his past. That is all man is – an accumulated amassment of his past energies. Every act, thought and deed is impinged in this great ball in his psychic anatomy and there remains eternally. Then he continually draws from this past and for the most part, it is only negative in nature. It can't be otherwise until he arrives at the point where he does, as you say Ioshanna, (and I must remember your new name Iona) start to seek within; to knock at the door.

So we are very fortunate because we do have this lifesaving concept and the principle of the electronic nature of the Infinite itself, and which is the only way we can have eternal life. Ioshanna: Yes, and your instance would apply to any other individual. This is why I am not necessarily pointing the finger at you, but using yourself as an example of what others can achieve. I am sure, hearing and knowing what you are accomplishing now, and how you can actually see these beautiful pictures of the inner worlds, and to be able to describe anything necessary, is indeed a giant step forward. Only a short time ago this picture with you was completely opposite, you know, and it should give any student great hope and faith in his own future. Vaughn: Well, I am very thankful for knowing what life is like now on the other side. I have to make a correction here though. You said I felt very badly when you turned me out. I didn't have any feeling of recriminations in your regard – except that I was the receptacle or channel for these lower forces. Ioshanna: Of course, you were so dedicated that you did realize that. I was overwhelmed. I had to do the only positive thing I could do at the moment and sever the contact till the battle was won, and which otherwise may have taken me over completely. We should never underestimate the strength of the negative forces!

Ioshanna: Now, as we were discussing just before you turned on the tape here, about a situation and the manner in which we work, as you know, I work with you in obtaining these pictures from the inner. Could you tune in and relate just how this goes on – just how this takes place? I am not aware in my conscious mind, either. It would be of interest. Can you get any information about this? Vaughn: The method by which I receive the information? It is, of course, of great interest to me because I have asked this question many times. Ioshanna': I don't believe the Brothers have to come down here and do that, do they? Vaughn: No, but at first that is what I thought. Then, of course, very soon I knew. The Brothers don't have to come down here because the Brother is here, and that the transmitting station by which the information was sent to the receiver is, shall we say, close by. I receive these picturizations of the information that is needed, directly from the transmitting station which resides in her (your) higher self. What I am saying is this, and it has always been of interest to me because one is not always conscious of his higher self, as it resides in the higher dimensions – fourth, fifth or whatever number; but by simply placing my consciousness, I tune in to the channel, which is yourself. So I am tuning in to this channel – a very high station – and by asking the question, I am actually tuning in to this specific frequency and here is my answer. I know because I have simply dialed the correct channel. That's the way I feel. Of course, now that I have a little better understanding of the electronic nature of the Infinite, and of what energy consists, I am aware that the information is right here at all times. It is just a matter of tuning in to it. So one doesn't have to go anywhere!

Ioshanna: I know actually by some of these letters that you have written that you passed on to me to read, I almost feel I have actually written them. You have used the same phraseology, and sometimes I say, I must have written this one. I am not necessarily conscious when there are quite a few at one time, and when I sign them I will feel that I have voiced them on tape or written them some few days in the past, when, in essence, they come from your pen, or your voice on the recorder. Vaughn: Yes, and I have often wondered in the past where this flow came from, because I would say, well, I was inspired to write this, but would take the personal credit because we think the personal information came from the higher self.

We little realize that we were inspired by a higher intelligence than ourselves. Ioshanna: You would be surprised how so many people in the past, through whom we have worked in that manner — whether it be literature, music, art, astrology, astronomy, regardless of what facet we have worked with them — when these individuals (who have not been truly developed beings, up to any point of even one of the lower degrees of mastership) have accomplished or gained recognition to some notable or popular degree, this success, as they term it, goes to their head and their ego takes them over. At that moment, they begin to descend in the downward progression, or they regress; they deteriorate! So isn't it a pity? We could name any number of people in the past to whom this has happened, and it is always very sad.

Vaughn: Yes, I am aware of some of the personalities who have related their writings and who have had great trouble in their lives; they have lost the contact. Somehow or other, they have become quite emotional and many of them have become suicides; those people, especially in the arts, the poets who have seemingly lost their gift, as they call it, due to the inflation they took on after some higher being had worked through their mind in some inspirational work. Yes, it is easy to see how vital it is to keep the proper balance and, above all, maintain humility — a number one requisite for true attainment and illumination.

Chapter 21

Vaughn: To properly relate this incredible story, it is necessary to tell first, of the startling vision that I had when I was working the night shift at the Los Angeles, California, post-office. This was in 1949. I was walking through the aisles, with nothing particular on my mind; all was dead quiet – about two o'clock in the morning – and I was stopped short! Directly in front of me (it seemed), appeared a larger than life size, complete in color, picture of a lady who was looking directly at me and smiling. Now the smile was not necessarily on her lips but rather, more in the eyes. I had the startling impression that this was such a similarity to some well-known picture, a Madonna that hangs in the Louvre. I don't believe the vision lasted more than maybe thirty seconds. It was difficult to tell, but from that day on, I could never forget the impression and the great added strength and courage that I received, and which this vision brought about to me! It seemed to foretell that there was, in my future, something worthwhile to work for and that I should not be detoured in my day to day life. My searchings for my inner self, I believe, started from that very day and moment.

I lived through these years in Boston, Massachusetts. I became a student of metaphysics and asked many people in many organizations of this kind, what this vision was, what meaning did it have or why did this beautiful lady come to me? I received no satisfactory answers until years later in 1972 when I came to the Unarius Center in California. I did, then, have the answer! One day I had just driven into the garage of the Unarius center, (wherein was Ioshanna) and, as I opened the door of the car, there appeared, in my mind's eye, the exact same picture of this lady, smiling at me in the same manner! It was the same psychic vision that I had twenty-three years prior! Of course, then I knew who this was, because this was the self-same person who is our Unariun Channel, Ioshanna. I related to her, my vision of her Higher Self before entering the house, as she met me on the porch. I told her how I had just tuned into her Higher Self, and she was pleased, but is quite accustomed to these psychisms and gave it little concern.

Meanwhile, Ioshanna moved from Escondido to El Cajon, and I extended myself in all ways possible to help in the mission and clerical work, etc., and now just one year later, (after arriving in California) at the approach of the spring cycle, Ioshanna took off on a two-week astral flight! She was more out than in the body, and telling of many things viewed in the inner worlds. When I asked her where she went, she suggested I look within myself and see. Well, I did, and I could!

Much to my own amazement, the first thing I saw was a tremendous celebration being held for Ioshanna. It was a gigantic and gala affair

— the likes of which I've never witnessed. Amongst some of the visions viewed were great, real-life depictions upon the crystal floors. They were unique and most life-like, third and fourth dimensional, as well. I was describing some of these exquisite reenactments (is the best name we have found for them) to Ioshanna that I spied. One picture in particular in the great historical gallery on Parhelion, that meant a great deal to me was that of the Mona Lisa, painted by Leonardo da Vinci. This painting held me spellbound as I caught sight of the painting upon the magnificent crystal floor. The area seemed to draw me into it in some magnetic way; and when I caught the first glimpse of the lovely Mona Lisa, (I called my Madonna) my heart skipped a beat — the reaction here with this, to me, saintly lady, was one of transcendency! I didn't know at the moment whether my knees would hold me or not, so high was I in the spirit.

Just as soon as I regained my equilibrium, suddenly I realized this was the "Lady of my Madonna" vision of so long ago. Many things of the past seemed here, with this viewing, to fall in place. The very sensation I experienced when I viewed the painting was the same reaction which I had when I experienced the psychism twenty-four years ago with viewing psychically — the life size projection of the "Beautiful Lady", as I then called her. There was a feeling of such infinite love and compassion that it was actually the turning point in my life!

It was at this moment, the past became the present. I had recognized that this beautiful lady, the Madonna (Mona Lisa) was the Higher Self of Ioshanna! At the same time flashed the realization she was also the biocentric of Leonardo da Vinci! Now I further realized that Ioshanna, in her Higher Self, was the Mona Lisa! All things fell into place, and the wonderings of who this beautiful lady was, that came to me in my time of trial has now been answered. It was a most exciting, revealing and unforgettable experience. Surely a once-in-a-lifetime happening — the thread of my past is now unraveled.

This sudden bringing the past twenty-five year-old vision into focus and the reaching, way out on a distant planet, Eros, to find the answer to my age-old question, has shaken me in my boots. It's truly all so incredible; and yet, the instant replay within my mind took place within seconds — it made all things whole! Suddenly, I seemed much more integrated than any time previous. The snap realization that not only here was my Madonna, as I termed my vision, but also had I suddenly become aware, while in that frequency, that here, Leonardo da Vinci is biune with Ioshanna! It was a mind-shattering experience, and surely, one never to be forgotten. And now, this morning, April 3rd, 1973, I had an urge to go out and get a litho print of the Mona Lisa for Ioshanna while our new realization is still fresh. I knew of several places to go, called one and was told of a certain store, but felt it was not appropriate. I became quite concerned with it all and a bit edgy and touchy, and kept on trying to find something better. I even called some of the galleries. In the meantime, Ioshanna said, "I'll go out and get one right away," and that's what happened! She went into the Hallmark Card Shop nearby, and during the brief time she was asking the clerk but before she got the words out, her head was suddenly jerked about and instantly she spied, on the top row of a tall rack, a large gift card, (a get-well card) with the famous painting thereon. The clerk was amazed, for she saw it was an inner guidance gesture. She sensed something more and commented. Ioshanna mentioned, "Some persons claim that I look like this painting, so I plan to dress as she, to see. The clerk, gazing at Ioshanna, said, "Well, what do you know, it's true, you do; the likeness is very apparent. It's incredible!" But Ioshanna didn't stop to explain, knowing she would doubtless not conceive. The next thing Dorothy and I knew of it, was when she returned and showed us the picture, the material she had purchased, and the long black wig, which was identical to the way the Mona Lisa was dressed.

But the most incredible experience I have ever had, and I mean, really incredible, is when she appeared dressed in the raiment of the Mona Lisa! There, standing at the top of the stairs, was the Mona Lisa! I absolutely couldn't contain myself! Everything was there, lifelike — that infinite look and tremendous feeling of compassion and love was shining. I felt like rushing over and embracing her because of the tremendous pull and the projection of love that was being emitted.

The feeling was that the Mona Lisa had materialized in person! So how could that be? Well, it could be so, for it wasn't just a resemblance. I moved up to within a few inches of her face to look at Mona Lisa. I looked directly into her eyes and saw with my own third dimensional eyes that her complete appearance had changed; the skin had changed. Believe it or not, she actually looked to be in her thirties or the age that Mona Lisa looked! (Ioshanna is 72.) She didn't just appear to be that way, but she was that way; the shape of the face, the appearance of the eyes, and in every other way! You must see this — and I think we all will because we're already photographing the Spiritual Mona Lisa.

Ever since the knowledge came to me that Ioshanna was the biocentric of da Vinci, that he had painted his own biocentric, (and which is the classic painting of all ages, the Mona Lisa), she felt prompted or desirous of donning the dress and the hair similar to that of the Mona Lisa. She said she did it "for fun" but there was more to it than that! There was a great need to do this because there was an inner knowledge that she was the one in the painting and this was what drew da Vinci. This is my psychic feeling, that this painting is what maintained him during his lonely life in the seventy some years that he lived on the Earth; and if it wasn't for his Mona Lisa, he possibly could not have lived the full life that he did, and complete his work. What he really did — and this is my inner feeling — he materialized (from his paints) the spiritual expression that he knew always existed so that he could have it; he could view it and love it. It is well known that the painting was his very own. He refused to sell it or give it away.

There is with her more than a similarity — this identical appearance, both physical and psychic as well and is a proof showing how authentically he saw psychically, in order to put it on his canvas. This proves and reproves the principles of Unarius — that only one so spiritually advanced could reproduce his own psychic impressions, and in the reproduction of this, to then impinge upon it these fourth dimensional expressions of the infinite frequencies. My skin is just crawling to realize that this has transpired, and it doesn't seem like five hundred years ago! She's here now — Mona Lisa, in the present! Ioshanna: Did I see a tear in your eye when you looked at me, as I was putting on this little ''masquerade''? Vaughn: Yes, more than one; but you were not masquerading. It is for real! Ioshanna: This is what I mean. This was the real attunement on the inner. We must relate too, about the feeling you had, Vaughn, when you saw the picture of his student, or the one he took into his house, Salai.

Vaughn: Yes, this is very interesting. I began to read the life story, or what is known of

the life of Leonardo da Vinci, of when he first
set up his studio and had moved to Milan, Italy.
He had taken a student into his household. I had
read of da Vinci and had seen a movie of his
life, and I was always "stopped" with the description of the two students whom he had taken
into his house. There is a strong rapport there.
There were two; one didn't stay too long. The
other one stayed and followed da Vinci around.
He was more than a student, he was sort of an
aide. He helped in the material things because
Leonardo was completely transcended most of
his life. He lived more on the inner than in the
third dimension. When I looked at the picture of
this young boy – and I don't think it has anything to do with ego or pride – I just felt very
close and 'in tune' with this individual! The
rapport existed, and I seemed to just know this
Salai was myself! Ioshanna: When you spoke
of it last night, I didn't go into it because I
was wrapped up in what I was doing; but I realized afterwards that you were right. That it is
truth, that you did live in his household! Vaughn:
So I can appreciate how I have been helped all
along, purposely brought back to the earth to be
helped and guided because of my great need;
and I am very grateful to the Brothers – more
than I can ever express. I'm sure there is much
important work to be done by myself with the
Mission in the future.

Ioshanna: The following day, April 4th, proved
to be Vaughn's day! He drove hastily to San
Diego to a bookshop, even after I had found the

The Temple Gardens

The Trumpeteers and Flower girls

The Marriage and Crowning Ceremonies
of the Archangels, Michael and Uriel
(Leonardo and Ioshanna)

Leonardo da Vinci - 1452-1519
Italian Painter and Scientist

Original Mona Lisa Painting
by Leonardo da Vinci

Photograph of Ruth Norman

Nikola Tesla 1856-1943

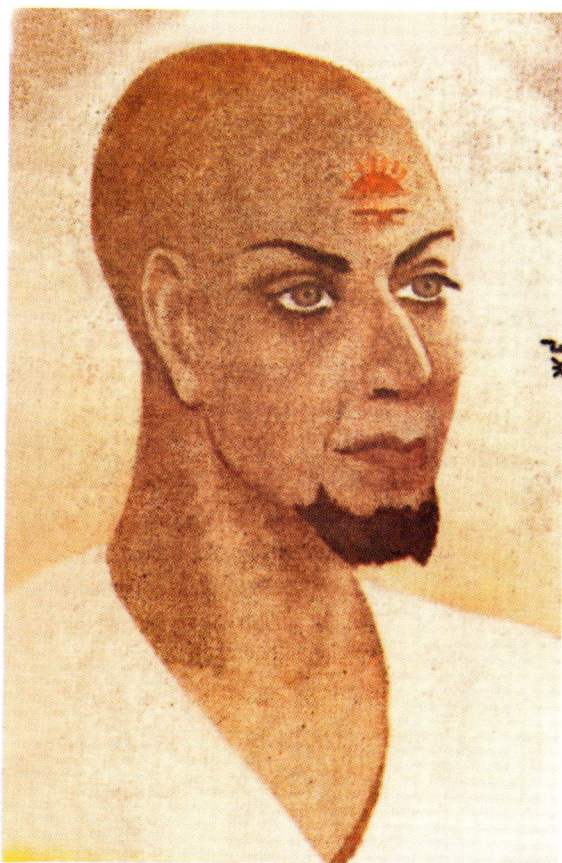

Yada (di Shi'ite) of the civilization of Yu, 500,000 years ago, who later reincarnated as Leonardo da Vinci; then 500 years later as Nikola Tesla - now expressing as Serapis Bey

large card with my desired photo, to get, of all things, a huge book of Leonardo da Vinci. It is the elegant, seventy-five dollar issue with beautiful color plates of all the works of the Master. Thus it was, he also brought back with him a lovely vocal record of — yes, the beautiful Mona Lisa melody! As the record was played, and as he viewed Mona Lisa, a large full-page photo of the original in natural color, it happened. He had a factual flashback. He realized inwardly, yes, with tears, that he had been honored to live in the Master's household to aid him. He had watched the great artist create the noted painting, and even more, I recalled how Vaughn also had watched the Master pour his love into the painting through the years; for it seemed to put him in touch with his beloved biune. No wonder Vaughn experiences such emotion and rapport with Mona Lisa! Actually he had a great reverence for the painting, and when he stepped near me as he took a snapshot, he did have a rapport with the past, for he too, due to his admiration, love and sympathy for the great Master, had learned to love deeply the famous portrait, as well!

Now it is understandable why Vaughn has so often said in the past, "Ioshanna, when you smile that way, the light of Heaven comes from your eyes." He was doubtless reliving then, too! But he is and always has been an extremely sensitive person. Vaughn relates:

It should be said, we have had verification from the Higher Ones on the Inner that all we are recording for posterity is fact. But now it is known that this is – incredible as it may seem – the real version of the Mona Lisa because we now know that Ioshanna is the polarity of Leonardo da Vinci. There was no earth person whom he based his painting upon, but it was his own psychic vision and memory of his own polarity or biocentric living in the spirit world which gave him great courage in the lonely life he lived in the 15th Century.

Now, just recently, the presence of Leonardo came so strongly to me and I heard him say to me, "Get back to the Center! Get back and tell what you know!" And when I did so, I did say to Iona, "I feel his presence so strongly here! He impelled me to come back as swiftly as possible and to relate to you, 'He is here!' " And with those words, Iona did a quick flip out. A new conscious rapport was instantly set up, and a new joy is seen within. She now knows, there is no question (in conscious mind as well) about it. Leonardo da Vinci is her true biocentric, and I know this to be true because immediately afterwards, we took out the biography with the paintings and drawings, and opened the book up to the painting of the Mona Lisa – and here, too, one was again struck with the classical, eternal, regenerative expression of passivity that poured from out the eyes. On examining an early photograph of Iona, (Ioshanna) which was taken back in 1943, one could factually again see this truly was the same person.

Who is the Mona Lisa? The mystery of the Mona Lisa has now been solved. The Mona Lisa was never a physical person but is the Higher Self of the biocentric of Leonardo da Vinci! The reason it has had such acclaim and the reason that it has held up as the greatest painting ever to have been created, is because the actual soul self of the painter, da Vinci, and his expression of love, have been impinged into the paint, into the atomic structure of the pigments of the paint, of the color and within the very canvas itself! Thus, one is not simply viewing a flat, linear portrait, but one is factually being put in contact with the Infinite Itself; and in so doing, there is a quickening for that individual. Of course, over the hundreds of years, literally millions of persons who viewed the Mona Lisa portrait have thus been put in contact with the High Minds.

Another realization has just been conceived, that in this new Golden Age of spiritual awakening, the many hundreds of thousands of people will see Iona as the greatest healer who has ever existed and they will say, "Why, I have seen this lady! I have seen her before!" And they will not know how, but of course, now we know why; because either recently or in other lifetimes, the person's memory has now been reactivated and regenerated. This contact will have been regenerated in the present, with the viewing and with the seeing of Iona, and the various pictures that will be sent out, either through television, movies, public appearances, etc. Isn't that a wonderful revelation? Ioshanna: Yes, Vaughn, it is all very wonderful to me, too, very wonderful and very beautiful. I must say, that all the time you folks were gone this evening, I repeatedly played that beautiful number, Mona Lisa, over and held to my heart his beautiful paintings and oh, when I think of him thusly, he is very close, for the promise was, he would be working very closely with us, and the evidence is in all the beautiful healings that are taking place!

To add a word to Vaughn's very excellent description, on further analyzing as to why and how it is all persons viewing the picture valued it so, was due to the fact that this great artist was more than a master artist at his painting, for he is more than a past master in the spiritual worlds, in his personal evolvement and spiritual development. He is known as a Logos (now an Archangel), one advanced far and above a mere mastership degree. As such, all things he would do or express, such as in his paintings or sketchings, each article, everything he would touch or relate to would carry this tremendous higher vibration or frequency; perhaps invisible or unsensed to the average person, nevertheless it is impinged within everything that he did or does! This is the very great difference between an advanced being expressing in any way — art, painting, dancing, etc., regardless — their expressions, their work carries their particular spiritual frequency or aura which makes it possible for all persons in contact with that, to "tune into" or pick up these frequencies, and which serve in time to be the seed planted, as it were, for the individual person to start to seek greater understanding of life. So it is a very wonderful thing to conceive! Vaughn: When I look at you, I am conscious of your biune or biocentric. It is very unusual. It is almost like having double vision. He now seems super-imposed over your face! Ioshanna: That is wonderful and it is due to the ceremony that took place a few days ago. In such a ceremony, that particular advancement or particular point in any biocentric's evolution or stepping up, as took place, the actual joining of two God Forces, the two can and do, function or oscillate as one — as the Moderator taught in the Unarius books — they could either function as one or dual. I am sure, now with all that has taken place, and all that took place at the conclave and the great interest that the dear one, (Leonardo), has in mankind, that he is doing and shall do all possible to help in this great healing program. So what a wonderful future! In other words, my life has taken on a new luster, a new glow, or an even added interest! Vaughn: Now with the knowledge of who you are and that you are now joined with your biocentric, in a psychic way you have the great added strength and the great love within; this is the most beautiful ending of the greatest epoch that has ever been completed on an earth world, because we have actually seen Heaven brought down into this earth plane!

Ioshanna: To me, of course, it is the epitome of all possible expectation, far beyond any conscious hope on my part, yet how could it be otherwise? This work being so enormous, so vitally important, so far-reaching and vast, it shall reach into the four corners and encompass the world, how could it be, or that there would be no oscillating polarity? It was a must and a natural sequence of events! Even to the point, as you found and saw, and heard yourself, Vaughn, that even a particular degree was "stepped over" or skipped, as one would skip grades in school, to have become as you related, Archangel in ascendency. Even that was brought about to further hasten the incoming New Age. And we can rightfully say to each student, all that the Moderator has taught in the texts, is likewise now factually being proven and I think Iona, herself (her spiritual self) gave a discourse in the pulse books about biocentricity! This is simply proving principle. It isn't placing me on any pedestal, nor do I feel that I am, in any way, better than other individuals. We are each a cell in that great eye of the Infinite and all things that are expressed come from that Infinite Source.

But this wonderful situation that has developed during and after the conclusion of this great conclave and in our writing it up, that Vaughn has so beautifully, psychically seen and heard through this inner ear which simply all goes to prove the authenticity, the factual principles the Moderator brought when He was on earth. So onward, and forward, dear ones. Vaughn reiterates: After the countless previous revelations, visions and inner glimpses of this great conclave and after the realization of Ioshanna being the biune of Leonardo da Vinci, as I was driving home from the store, I said to myself, "I wonder where Leonardo da Vinci is? He must be close by!" I hadn't seen him. Then I was given the impression and I actually saw him! There he was, standing immediately near the front of the dias — near the front and to the right of the three crystal tiers! As Ioshanna moved down the great thoroughfare, she paused as she reached the front of the dias. Just before she reached the dias, the Moderator met her and Leonardo da Vinci stepped out. He is one of the three leaders of the thirty-three Logoi. There are those of the thirty-three who are known as the inner circle.

He stepped out of position at the head of the triangle which he headed, representing his particular Logoi. The Overlord then presented the Queen to him. Both faced the dias, looked up to the Moderator, and the instant he did this, the auras of the two souls completely intermingled — a tremendous, blinding flash of Light. She was most joyous to find her biune to be he! After the brief but beautiful ceremony, then, arm in arm, they proceeded to walk up the three tiers of crystal where Ioshanna was given her higher degree and crown; preceded, of course, by the Overlord and his biune Erza, (or Orda).

As we sat at the dinner table reminiscing

about this, I said there seemed to be a special consciousness here with us, that Leonardo was directing his thoughts right here to us. It was a feeling that his consciousness was here — not just momentarily, but here permanently. I said (from the inner), "It is permanent, Ioshanna (or Iona), as long as you are here with us!" Ioshanna said: Well, I couldn't feel this way and tear if he were not in direct contact because it takes a great deal to bring that about in my frequency. It is an upliftment. Of course, only one of like or higher frequency could cause it, so I know it is his presence, and I think it's wonderful — a very sacred, blessed and beautiful thing!

Mentally, I hear everyone in the entire conclave repeating over and over the name (and I don't know whether they often use names), saying, "We pay homage to the da Vinci's!" That was just as you were leaving in the princess coach, Ioshanna. Ioshanna: That's beautiful, just beautiful! And you are correct in the sensing. Vaughn: So from now on, we must call you Iona da Vinci. Ioshanna: I'll love that! Vaughn: Leonardo is one of the taller ones — at least fifteen feet tall; that is, not including the great, great aura. All of the Logoi were taller than the others in the same grouping. They were the tallest. Ioshanna: Yes, I feel sure he is going to remain in my aura — in my consciousness, more correctly. I am sure of this. If I have to go out there in the world and enter into what has to be done, there would be the need for a lot of strength and help, that is for certain. There will be healings like the world has never seen — group healings, mass healings of all kinds! It will have to be done that way to get people to get out of their little ruts and begin to learn, but they are going to have to get in and learn some of the science too. Vaughn: The science is so broad. Even now when I go back and study, I appreciate that I didn't know anything. I never knew a thing! The past experience has taken on proportions and is so huge, I appreciate more and more now what the Moderator has been saying in all the texts.

I was at first, taken back, simply amazed and flabbergasted, Ioshanna, when I saw how you took on the appearance of the Mona Lisa and actually became that epic lady in the portrait painted by Leonardo da Vinci! Then today when you came down the staircase with your wedding gown, your long red hair, the tiara and the great red rose you were holding, I simply had to blink my eyes and pinch myself! It was absolutely incredulous to see here how you took on an entirely different appearance! You appeared to be a woman of thirty. Now, let it be said it wasn't makeup, for you wore none. It was a complete change. Your appearance changed, your facial appearance changed, and I know what it is now — it is because the physical body that you occupy is simply an apparatus, and in your new, higher understanding of the Infinite, you have been able to so manipulate it, that it can take on any expression you wish!

It is only an instrument, and to see the instrument change from time to time by people who have not had this development, it is confounding! Yet, it explains everything. This is the real explanation and the proof positive that the physical anatomy is simply a mechanical vehicle and that it is not the true person! Ioshanna: That is right; it couldn't possibly be the true person because the true spiritual person is a fourth, fifth, or sixth dimensional electronic configuration, and it couldn't possibly live in this dimension. This is a dimension for atomic structures only. Vaughn: So we can't change the atomic structures of this physical body, simply because of the consciousness we place upon or within it. In other words, if we are sick, it is simply because of the concept we have. Ioshanna: True, but also, after all this transition that's been taking place about now, this body is not as third dimensional as it may appear, or that it was a few days ago. It is now kind of half way in between! Vaughn: Again, thinking on the statement that you made, it is all concept since you are in the third dimension. Ioshanna: Yes, I don't believe in this third dimension. Everything is concept; you are what you believe. I never have believed that I was the physical person. I have and must wear a body as a means of doing what is necessary here in this mission, but I never have believed the body is I. "I am" that which resideth within the body! Those were Jesus' words too; the Father within. Each and every individual has that

Father within if he will but begin to recognize it and build and reconstruct and add to it.

And so with the hair; one was black, one was red and I put that little piece of metal on top, (the crown), yet to you, to all indications, appearances and feelings, it was a totally different person! Vaughn: Yes it was; it wasn't the same person who was represented as the Mona Lisa. Ioshanna: It is food for thought, isn't it? The great difference is that I was conscious of being the other Being!

Vaughn: So, here I came full circle and all the questions and all my uncertainties of life and death have now been answered and it was all there in that viewing of many years ago! The completion of the Absolute was portrayed in that classical painting of the Mona Lisa by Leonardo da Vinci, and the reason being that he was projecting through the painting and through the atomic structures of the portrait into this dimension, a psychic force which continually regenerated itself and which is the explanation for its great beauty, its long enduring interest and its constant question, "Who is the person in this, the painting of the Mona Lisa? How could such beauty reside in a physical being? Of course, the answer is that this was not a physical being, being painted but was the higher self of the polarity of da Vinci. And of course, only he could know. This is an example of what one sees and feels when in attunement with one's higher self.

Referring now to the great golden Temple of the

New Age: One sees here all of the evolutions of the earth, the astral worlds which are a result of a combination of many hundreds of thousands of years of striving of the individuals; of nations in these dimensions, who have been constantly assisted by the advanced spiritual intellects residing in the scientific plane of Parhelion that gives them the reason and the courage for their strivings. Then of course it is no ordinary feeling as one walks into this great golden temple structure, the immediate feeling is the one of great lightness; although I have been told and have read of this feeling that one senses when one is in the aura of any of the structures on that plane but, now I know! It is an intense feeling of having been put into contact with much higher forces. One has the feeling that he is being bombarded with the Love of the Infinite, Itself. One feels completely 'lifted' up out of physical consciousness. There's a feeling of being in touch with the oneness of all things. It's a very unusual and uplifting feeling. I speak of course, from the consciousness of one who is an earthean. Ioshanna: You can't really be an earthean and view such as you have! Of course, so much has been done and is being done for you, with you, and by you, with your constant and never-ending struggle which you so determinedly continued, and in which case, it pays to be a little determined in ones efforts. It is a very wonderful thing to be so dedicated and to ones own progressive evolution; and only as such, and with your own efforts, could you arrive where you have. Yet this too, but a step toward the next step higher! There is no one in this world or any other world that is happier for you than this one. It's a beautiful change that I've watched come over you only in the past few days, since this great conclave has started to take place with us; more correctly we, with it! The conclave, actually of itself, is being carried on throughout the entire year in celebration and honor. However, the many thousands of years duration for preparation was no small item. You doubtless have been preparing yourself all this time too, Vaughn. Sometimes an upper road would be reached, and there'd be a little boulder in the road and the foot would trip, and down you'd go, and perhaps to oscillate with the lower wave forms — the lower half of the wave forms. I don't believe that there is anybody in this entire organization who has striven and overcome, who has had a more difficult negation to overcome and uproot than has yourself; but, you have done it, you have done it! This proves Unariun Principle too. The last few days have brought such change over you that there's no semblance of the former person. The only semblance I can see, is the clothes you wear and I know, if you could do as you feel, you'd toss them all out and get a completely new wardrobe — so foreign has the past and all pertaining to it become. Vaughn: That's very true; and I would even say, just today, I now actually know the difference between the outer and the inner. I can actually see the complete contrast between the physical and the psychic being. The first time I am really aware that this physical is a covering and that it is, as you call it, a disguise. It is nothing, and I see the psychic bodies of people rather than being deterred by thinking that this is the person at whom I'm looking. Ioshanna: You know I never do expect to see you entertain any negations or be tripped up again in any reaction or emotion; never again! Vaughn: Well, it's not possible now! Now I can see the duality as it lives in this plane. Ioshanna: That's important for any striving person. It's wonderful! So carry on, I just had to make this comment because it's so true, and so evident. Beautiful, wonderful, lifechanging feelings that have taken place there with you! Vaughn: This all proves the truth of the great and tremendous acceleration, feelings of force which come through the crystal lens; I mean it is unparalleled! The future will prove it even more as actually the hundreds of thousands of people will add their personal testimonials.

Vaughn relates from the Inner: It could be related that this event was especially to honor Ioshanna, in all she has, is, and shall express upon the earth world, as well as here in this plane of Science on Parhelion. In order to bring all things necessary about, whereby she could be united in consciousness with her biune, Leonardo da Vinci, (residing here) on the inner, into a more compatible frequency with him, this being most necessary for the work to be ex-

274

pressed to the public – the duality of consciousness – one, on the third dimension, the other
in the higher planes. All states and conditions
have now been set up so they can (and do) now
function as one.

Often, during the past few days, as I look at
Ioshanna, I see superimposed, Leonardo's face!
No wonder he (Leonardo) prompted me in my
short trip to the store: "Hurry back and tell
her!" He was most desirous of completing this
last new setup or oscillation with her in consciousness. It was, of course, necessary that
she, in conscious mind, be aware of him, of the
relationship and the new oscillation in order
for her to send out her mind signals in return.
When she was told that she was biune with him,
I noted a beautiful exchange of feeling take
place. He came directly into her aura and remained, tears trickled down her cheeks una-
bashed, and a new and beautiful spiritual radiance, oneness and love existed! Her face shone
with a new inner happiness and peace. All
things are indeed now in order for the great
work to be done.

It was not until the next day that the realization of Mona Lisa was brought to my consciousness. When it was related to her, she went directly to her library and took out a large book
of his colored paintings. Amongst them, of
course, was the most famous and prized Mona
Lisa. She said, the lovely melody "Mona Lisa"
began to be heard within her consciousness over
and over, and it was evident a new love oscilla-

tion had been set in motion! Different, quite, than the earthman's love affairs, for theirs is an eternal love – a love that has existed for eons past. It could be rightfully told that this harmonic tie between them was set in motion many more than five hundred thousand years ago, before they came, in dematerialized form, to planet Earth to reseed the earth of spiritual beings – this, due to the low level to which those living here had regressed.

Thus, it can be seen, in part, just why this relating of the great celebration in our world was necessary, and why all participants in the higher dimensions were so eager and overjoyed as they worked the countless years, yes, eons through working with the mind forces in building this tremendous city; the building and electronics, the power supplies by and through which your earth and astral worlds can be saved.

And so it shall be!

Vaughn: In my dream just last night, Ioshanna, I saw two bright flashes of gold rays going out from the lights! They were on either side of your shoulder. They were just projecting, it seemed. I thought they were two great powers – Archangels! Ioshanna: In all probability you are correct, and what the seer, Greif told me of those who were added to those already helping – eleven were added, I think he said. Vaughn: They weren't only angels, but in positions above · as well. This brilliance and beauty was shown in my half-sleep state. Ioshanna: Well, that's really wonderful that you are so experiencing, too! Vaughn: Like with Helen, when she stood there, Ioshanna, and viewed you as Mona Lisa; she looked at you for a few seconds, then she really broke up! You should have seen her when she first saw you! Then she cried very hard. It's really something when you merely glance at a person and they break up and cry like that! You know something wonderful is taking place within − healing! It's tremendous, the charge of frequency that is coming out! Oh, but it's entirely to be expected now, you know − the power that comes from you! Ioshanna: Yes, there is great power present now. I have to see it manifest: Vaughn: When you're very concentrated now, Ioshanna, when you're working on something, your power is vast, it makes people fearful, I think. Ioshanna: Well, it knocks me out too, sometimes! Yes, I know well, they'll have to get used to it, for it is healing power! (4/5./73) − Ioshanna writes: As Vaughn has related of his own personal experience of the past, of his psychic vision of the portrait of Mona Lisa, then after he had so excitedly purchased for me (Ioshanna) the most magnificent book of Leonardo da Vinci and his paintings, we hastily thumbed through it and he caught sight of the pencil sketch of the Master and the boy Salai. He related that he felt to have been him. Then later, in reviewing some of the many copies persons have made of this historical canvas, he realized that here among these copies was one he, Vaughn (as Salai) had painted! It was a fine copy too! No doubt this was done during his stay with the great Master Artist, and of the much time Leonardo spent in the consciousness of that work — that it had rubbed off on Salai! Interestingly, too, he noted good similarity to the painting he'd done to the original — but, as he (Vaughn), said, it lacks the spiritual quality — the inner beauty. Yes, one must, himself, have it within to express it without, but it is a fine copy!

Objectifying this, seemed to put all things in proper place mentally, for now this explains further, how and why he experienced the vision. But even more, it had been a projection from herself, the spiritual being, Mona Lisa, into his consciousness, for this was a great need for Vaughn (as Louis) during those trying years, in overcoming the past. Now, as he states, it all seems so unrelated to him, as if that which he underwent was another person! And so it is when we have changed our relationship to the past — the very object of life on this physical planet — we are truly free. This new realization was of great interest.

About two weeks before the start of the compilation of the "Conclave of Light Beings", Ioshanna had been duplicating the series of tapes of the Pulse of Creation. These transmissions from the Shamballas (the seven higher planes of what is now called Unarius) were brought through by the Moderator, Ernest Norman, in the formative years of the Mission (1956), and were on reel to reel tape. Now, with the envisioned growth of the Mission and students, Ioshanna felt that these revelations from the inner and higher worlds of the Shamballa should be put on cassette tapes in order to make it possible for more to enjoy them and to have them in this more simplified tape form. A library sheet was needed to give information as to the various new tapes. It was felt that the front of this library sheet should show an illustration of the manner in which these transmissions were brought in, graphically; and so Ioshanna suggested that I contact a commercial artist who would be able to illustrate it in a professional manner.

Immediately, I went to the telephone directory, picked the name of one person Marc. My first conversation with him revealed that he was a student of truth and had been on the path for many years. He seemed very interested in the description of the tape library sheet, and asked for literature of Unarius. He agreed to come to the Center, for preliminary information. The first contact was made with him on Monday, the 26th of March. It was on the same date, that the first psychic revelations of the viewing of the Ceremony of the Conclave of Light Beings took place!

The next fourteen days would bring through a great many more views and details of this coronation and celebration, and, during this period of time, Ioshanna was in fact, living on the inner dimension and was constantly transcended as she viewed this great and momentous gathering of the Light Beings in her honor. So there was a mass of detail that needed to be put together of the description of this event and it took the combined efforts of three helpers to type and retype and put all in order. Two weeks later Marc met with Ioshanna who had by then more or less returned to physical consciousness. Spirit did so direct his contact that there was no interference with the work during this entire period of Ioshanna's transcendency.

When I first saw Marc, I immediately felt a familiarity. As the description of the conclave was being drawn out by Ioshanna, and the great works of art were shown around the temple building on the inside walls as well as on the translucent floors, Marc took it all in. Later on, I told him about my vision of the Mona Lisa, and how I realized that I was seeing the Higher Self of Ioshanna, and related to him the series of events that led up to the disclosure that Ioshanna was Iona, the biocentric of Leonardo da Vinci. Also, I told him that I had lived in the da Vinci household as the houseboy and student, Salai. I was prompted to tell him about my relationship with Leonardo da Vinci and of Ioshanna at the time she was Johannes Kepler, the scientist, in the 16th Century, and I, his eldest son. It was further explained to Marc, how these contacts with them were part of a great plan so that there would be a rapport or frequency for the time of the Unarius Mission in the twentieth Century, when the Unarius Science would be presented or introduced to the earth world.

When the name Salai was mentioned to Marc, he immediately knew of him and remarked, "Oh, he is the one that stole from Leonardo!" I said, "Yes, that is the one!" It turned out that Marc had read the entire life history of da Vinci and had been an avid admirer of his paintings, and much more. He had a good rapport with him, and as he had been an artist for the greater portion of his life, he had a good feeling for color. Later, while contemplating about Marc and his familiarity with Leonardo da Vinci and that he felt, as he said, inspired in his own work by Leonardo, it came to me that Marc was also a student of Leonardo and lived in his house at the same time as did I. This explains my feeling of recognition and familiarity with Marc. Also, when he said to me, "Oh, you were Salai, the one who stole from Leonardo," I said, "Yes," in an offhand manner.

Some time ago, I had seen the life story of Leonardo reenacted and had a pull with the one called Salai. He was a rambunctious and pushy individual; sly, though very handsome in appearance. I had not mentioned these characteristics to Ioshanna at the time that I had recognized myself as this self-same person, Salai. However, after it was known that Marc was the other student in Leonardo's house, I went back to da Vinci's biography to locate the name of this other student of whom Marc had lived the life. As I read the description of Salai again, it was discovered that the name Salai was a nickname that Leonardo had given to his student and that it meant "little satan". Then it was that I realized that I had not noticed this in my previous reading just a week ago! Apparently, subconsciously, I did not wish to make this fact known to my conscious mind; this revealed to me, much of my life in the past, my guilt feelings, my desire for seclusion and the difficulty to express myself freely. It also explains why the da Vinci's, both Iona and Leonardo, have been my guardian angels to help me in these lifetimes that I might be able to help myself by taking an active part in the Unariun Mission and thereby change the negative bias of these many past lifetimes, lived out of tune with the Infinite.

(4/5/73) — Vaughn: I have a strong realization that I will write a book about the true story of the Mona Lisa, because the more I dwell upon it, the more I realize that it was no happenstance — my being brought to live in the house of da Vinci, remaining there for twenty-five years. It has significant meaning because he does not take lightly what he does. The plan that was set in motion with the experience with him was then continued as I again lived in the presence of another master (who was the biune of Leonardo) and who, at this time, was known as Johannes Kepler. In searching the akashic, I found I was the eldest son. Kepler, of course, as it is now known, was a lifetime lived by the Channel, Ioshanna, now called Iona.

It is known that Kepler, with his own hand and mind brought out the true laws of the ellipse of the planet Mars around the sun. Until this time it was thought that all the planets made their orbit around the sun in a circular or cycular manner. But through a mathematics which he devised, going through the countless thousands of calculations manually (no machines) and at the same time following his inner guidance, he was successful. It has always been considered a mystery as to how he arrived at the answers because it would take months for a modern calculator to calculate the infinite number of calculations for this orbit. Johannes Kepler is known as the father of astronomy and mathematics. He was also an astrologer.

I can now see from the distant past how this plan has unfolded; now I have found my identities, all ties in with the great new revelation that has been brought out during the past ten days — the whole story now comes to light! Since I can now see my part in the great plan, which will be a story that will compare to the story about Phylos' "Dweller on Two Planets." This realization really shook me up.

It is a story of a man who turned his back on the Light, and how he tried to come back and was helped. Through each lifetime he had the assistance of those persons who had gone forward and whom he had himself, in ways and means harmed through negative acts. It showed how all of his lifetimes were intertwined in so many ways with the help of the spiritual beings who no longer had to return to earth. Here I see the same story; I see an almost parallel! But the greatest parallel is the book that is now being written, "The New Revelations". It indeed parallels the biblical Revelations and is all of the religions and all of the philosophies that I have ever learned about tied in one.

Now, to top it all off, Ioshanna turns out to have been not only Johannes Kepler, but Queen Hatshepsut, Queen Tiy of Egypt, wife of Amenhotep III, and the mother of Akhenaton who then (3500 years ago) brought the Science of Life to the earth planes; as Bathsheba, wife of King David, and of course, the mother of King Solomon; as Mary Magdalene, as the foster mother of Moses, as Isis, the wife of Osiris, and as the Chief High Priestess of Lemuria, then known as Ioshanna and on still further back in history that is not known to man; of course, too, now, in this present incarnation (again), as the wife of the Moderator, the truly greatest of all Scientists, Ernest Norman. So the interweaving and the steadily developed plan begins to unfold and I see how I was brought to the doorsteps of the various persons involved in bringing this science to the earth plane. It is no happenstance that I was allowed to learn, and to walk by their sides so there would be a compatible frequency; so there could be a compatible oscillation for this, the New Age in the 20th Century, where this work is now coming to fulfillment — and has been fulfilled.

So I am, of course, inspired to write this great epic and love story of how Leonardo da Vinci kept a true and permanent contact with his biocentric, Iona (from her spiritual world), whom we call Mona Lisa, who harbored and sheltered him through his lonely life. We know he never married, nor did he ever have any companionship. He needed none, and now it is understood. So this will be a work of joy and will be written, I am sure, from the Inner. Ioshanna: Yes, I am sure that is true, Vaughn, and as you say, very definitely and without the slightest doubt on my part, you were factually placed in Leonardo's home to aid him; to set up the relationship; the whole plan was made countless thousands of years ago – how these souls would evolve into one relationship or frequency and pattern. It is very interesting to trace the history back and, only through this clairvoyant vision can a factual and actual family tree – Tree of Life – you might say, be traced. Yet, this is the Tree of Evolution and you are relating and pointing up and conceiving revelations that I, myself, would not; because I wouldn't be sufficiently interested in my own inner self to make that type of a search. There is one thing and one thing only, in which I am interested or concerned and that is in getting the Unarius texts to those ready. This is the only thing that is vitally important to me. One's position will take care of itself if he takes care of what is at hand to do! This is my frank and honest concept along these lines.

However, Vaughn, as you seem interested in these past historical epochs, civilizations, etc., of old, you can surely read from the akashics of the portrayals upon the walls in that great and magnificent city, Parhelion, and go as far back as you like. Even as you saw some records of five hundred thousand years ago, this is not the beginning; in fact, no beginning exists – only change; only regeneration. And right here is a good place for the reader to toss in his wastebasket, along with many other of the false interpretations of the past, the ridiculous story of creation and of creating man from mud and a rib! Such asininities do not even belong in the child's fairy tale books. Life is scientific and man must learn the true science of living as contained in the Unarius book of Life – the Unarius Library. Vaughn:

I am impressed here, too, Ioshanna, that although you, yourself, may not have expressed in these fields of art, such as literature, painting, sculpturing, in a physical way, yet you did indeed inspire many from your Higher Self; and during the lengthy time you spent on the inner planes, you worked with countless literates, poets, painters – those persons upon the earth with whom you have created, in some former time, a harmonious relationship – making it possible for you to work with them from the inner worlds. It could be said, and truthfully too, that regardless, whether you live in a physical body or that you are on the inner planes, your Higher Self can work with many persons simultaneously. I have in mind King David, Solomon, and the "Songs of Solomon", also Solomon's ability to construct a city. It is very well known that he was prompted by his own inspiration, but he had, Ioshanna, your over-shadowing! You were close to these two – David and Solomon. Solomon was, in the physical, really one of your sons. He was a son of David and you were Bathsheba, his mother, history claims. Ioshanna: Yes, Vaughn, I have always been thoroughly relative to both David and Solomon. You, also, know the one who lived the life of David – who is now Jack Holland. He visited me in Escondido last year when you were there and the rapport was very evident. As I sat across the table, the love poured out to him as the water streamed from my eyes. He felt the tie, too, very strongly. And just lately we have been contacted by the one who was then Solomon! Vaughn: It now becomes more and evident, (as I attune more deeply to the inner consciousness), much of the inspirational material that we have in the Bible and much of our poetry, for instance, Tennyson, Keats and Shelley, were inspired, and there were many of the English poets in the 18th Century who were inspired by you when you were on the Inner! Great credit has always been given to these poets because it was considered that some-how they had some inner knowing; yet they simply were able to receive your inner inspira-tions! They didn't necessarily have this knowl-edge. Tennyson, particularly, always wondered, himself, where it all came from. Then there was Coleridge, an English poet, who wrote many verses that were considered mystical; they always had alluded to a higher state of consciousness. Ioshanna: Yes, it is true. When a person becomes developed on the Inner, he can be a great help to many people. He need not be limited to any singular mind but can oscillate through many or an infinite number of souls simultaneously. Yes! Such a consciousness is not limited as is the earth physical conscious mind to a one-track way of thinking, but at that particular point of development, one can attune to or aspire to, or oscillate through, or relate to or through countless persons at one time. In other words, they become of Infinite Mind, infinitely oscillating simultaneously. Vaughn: I have just become aware of the results of this expression of an Infinite Consciousness from the point of view of having, myself, read much of the literature of this inspirational quality. It just came to me, "Well, where do you think this came from?" This came from an infinitely created source — an infinitely-minded person. Ioshanna: What you say and are finding in your inner attunements in no way inflates my ego because this Infinite Mind or Superconscious Self is not this conscious mind nor this physical person. It is a state of awareness; a state of being; an energy configuration that lives in the higher dimensions and could never live in this dimension because it is not an atomic structure. I think that may help clear up the situation of an Inner Advanced Being and Super Being. However, it can and does function very closely any more and it is a very wonderful realization;

a completely different way of thinking than does the reactionary earthean function.

Vaughn: Yes, there will be many, many questions of this kind. People will be asking and I know this is where they can get their information. Of course, the answer for this possible questioning as to what is this Infinite Mind, is all here in the Unarius texts – the Science of Life – which explains the concept of life from its very beginning and its continuity from the Inner Planes, then of having to live in the lower physical planes for experience purposes. So this should give us added incentive to know there is only one means by which we can live on these higher planes and that is: to understand the manner in which an infinitely-minded person can exist through an understanding of the actual concepts of what the Infinite is. Ioshanna: Yes, what you say is so true, and the answers are all in the texts if the student will continue to study and remain steadfast in his endeavors or in consciousness; for we do work with each and every individual who makes conscious endeavor to learn to conceive, to understand, and to progress himself. This is what it is all about, what Unarius is all about: to teach man to free himself from his past or, in other words, to achieve psychic liberation!

Chapter 22

Ioshanna: We have, in the previous pages, discussed our Mona Lisa project and the various contacts which have recently been made, and as the topic is one of major concern in this book, through further psychic observation, other important realizations and revelations have been brought to light.

Although much of this chapter has been included in our pilot book "Who Is the Mona Lisa?", it was felt that this information was so important and valuable, it should likewise be included herein, as it not only helps to prove these relatings regarding the mentioned persons, but also adds great weight and strength to the ever-existent evolutionary principle — the regenerative principle of reincarnation.

When the beautiful Spiritual Beings related to us that this story would have no end, it is plain to see what they meant, for truly, each day holds its new beginning. Each day brings forth new avenues of this great concept; new contact from the past. For instance, it was but a short time ago that Vaughn purchased a new sport coat; now looking back, he says, "I have never bought a coat that was too large for me in my life, but here I bought this coat too big, and I couldn't understand why. Now it is plain to see how, with guidance from the inner, I was prompted to seek out and find a tailor shop, where the seamstress would alter my coat. I was happy to have made the contact, for a short time later, Ioshanna would have need for this particular person's talents and to learn of another of her contacts."

Now, as it has been told of Vaughn's vision of the Mona Lisa, and as a result, Ioshanna has desired a large photograph of the da Vinci portrait and planned to have a greatly enlarged tinted photograph made of it; also, one of herself with her hair down to prove the identity. Thus it was, being aware of this seamstress, Vaughn took Ioshanna to her and, of all things, when the seamstress (Mrs. Collins), was shown the photograph of the Mona Lisa painting, her first remark was, "Maybe I can find a better one that isn't so dark; I have a great number of them lying around the house!" Of course, with that remark, we both stood aghast and dumfounded, looking at each other in amazement, wondering why any individual would have a number of pictures of such around her house! So we knew, here was an important contact. Soon it was related that she had a son who did such photographing and also oil painting – a rare ability. Vaughn saw psychically that Mrs. Collins had been da Vinci's tailoress in this former lifetime and how this woman had also been close to me (Ioshanna) in more than one lifetime. In one life she was seen to have been a coolie in Japan, who drew my cart around. When Mrs. Collins was told of this, she strongly resented it. She bristled; she didn't want to be a coolie! However, this was a dead give-away; if she had not been one such, there would have been no reaction, so both Vaughn and I had a good laugh over this situation, but Mrs. Collins has, to this day, all the semblance and speech of a coolie. However, when it was related to her that she was with me in the

291

Hatshepsut life, she experienced a very strong, positive, happy rapport. She grabbed me and hugged me, her eyes were dancing; she was laughing, repeating, "I hope so, Oh, I do hope so!" She had a real strong, positive, happy reaction from that bit of information.

We two soon went to her son's house, as she told us he was the artist we needed. So we found the man called Lawrence, the photographer, about thirty miles distant who, as this lady had told us, used a very unique, unusual and new process in his coloring. In the interim, Vaughn had, through his psychic realizations and visions, found Lawrence to have also been a student of da Vinci at the same time Vaughn (as Salai) had been his student! As was related, Vaughn lived in Leonardo's house for twenty-five years. Thus they sensed a closeness, or rapport. The gentleman is making the copy and photographs. So here was another contact of Leonardo's revealed — all due to the too large coat!

Vaughn: So goes the story; it seems impossible to form any new contacts any more unless they have been from this past da Vinci cycle. Again this very evening, May 15th, as we had errands to do uptown and as these things were more important than time used in cooking meals, we desired to stop in a restaurant for dinner, yet when the time came to stop, suddenly Ioshanna said, "Let's go to such and such a hotel," which happened to be quite a distance into San Diego. Dotty and I wondered why she felt it was necessary to go so far when there were many restaurants closeby, yet it was soon learned the reason, although Ioshanna herself wasn't really conscious yet as to why.

Soon after we were seated, a young man working as a bus boy, came by, and immediately Ioshanna felt a close rapport. The first thing she said she felt, was painting with him, and immediately she knew that he had been an artist in the past. He said his name was Douglas. I quickly said, "More of a sculptor, and I see him with a large mallet in his hand; he has large hands and he is pounding away on a chisel at a large sculpture." Immediately the boy was approached, and what a beautiful young man, and how very receptive he was. Although still a youngster of only eighteen, he had never heard of the word "reincarnation" or about living more than one life; he was totally taken up and absorbed, wide-eyed and very eager to hear more. He was very soft-spoken and there existed a sweet and soft radiation about him. We both sensed a love toward this beautiful soul, for we both had a rapport with him from out the past, and he seemed most familiar.

Quickly, I sensed and said, "He was Verrocchio," and soon Ioshanna felt there was a da before it, or del. Ioshanna said, "It feels like it should be either del or da Verrocchio." After telling the young man (Douglas Bell) about his life and who he was, he of course wanted to hear more; he just drank it up. He didn't get all emotional or excited, he took it exactly like an old soul would. Inwardly he knew it was truth he was hearing, and yet because it was all strange to his conscious mind, he had a peculiar reaction and kept saying, "Well, I just don't know what to say! But it is funny you should say that because I am majoring in painting and art in school!" When he was asked, "You enjoy and love your work?" "Oh, yes!" he said. He was totally involved in his art expression — a definite carry-over.

Very little time was spent with our food, for we were all absorbed in this, our new find — another dear one from the past. It was a most glorious feeling and relationship. We both experienced a very beautiful oneness and rapport from the past with him. Vaughn had spent time with him in those earlier years (five hundred and twenty years ago).

Thus, upon arriving back at the Center, we immediately scrambled over who was going to get to the encyclopedia first, when it was soon found that del Verrocchio was not only an acquaintance of da Vinci but had been his teacher! When Douglas asked, "How can I learn some more about this," he was told to look up the name in the encyclopedia and read about himself. What a wonderful surprise he is going to have when he finds that he was actually the art teacher of Leonardo da Vinci !

(Vaughn, speaking from his psychic viewing:) Interestingly enough, although Leonardo was a student in the studio of Verrocchio, at about the age of twenty, when a certain painting was being produced, Leonardo played a great part in painting the background of it; a canvas which Verrocchio was in the process of completing, called "The Baptism of Christ". The background of this painting is shown as a scene which has no earthly connotation and which has a mystical quality. There is a swirling background of the horizon, and the mountainous scenery has an unusual staircase formation. There is no representation of this in any particular geography of the earth, and the colors were especially of a quality which no other painter has ever been able to command. Immediately Verrocchio realized that his own student, Leonardo da Vinci, had outstripped him, and although Verrocchio was a master of not only painting but of all of the Renaissance art forms, such as metalsmith, goldsmith, sculpturing and painting, he then realized that he had met his own master in the field of painting; thus, in his deflation, he gave up painting — to then enter into sculpturing!

This background that was painted by Leonardo then explains why many art masters and critics have often commented particularly on the background quality of the Christ painting. There has always been a strong feeling this was not the handiwork of Verrocchio as it was entirely different from his other works, especially when the colors used in the figure of Jesus were in such complete contrast to that of the background. This background was the very same used later and reproduced from Leonardo's mind for his most famous painting, the Mona Lisa! Thus, this psychic finding supplies the long sought answer here, too!

The young boy, Douglas Bell, when asked if he had a rapport with Leonardo, mentioned the fact that he always had experienced a very beautiful feeling and rapport with the Mona Lisa painting.

This would explain why he had such a rapport because the frequencies that were in the painting for his "Baptism of Christ" were the same frequen-

cies used in the painting of the Mona Lisa; moreover, he often visited the studio of Leonardo and
had admired the Mona Lisa while it was being
painted over a period of some years! This young
man, Douglas, was very taken up while we were relating to him about this former lifetime – and no
wonder! As was stated, he had to do with the very
background himself! Interesting too, it was due to
this very picture that Verrocchio actually gave up
his painting! He evidently still had a little human
element that caused a resentment, for many geniuses are thus inclined with a little tension or perhaps
a bit emotional. Vaughn continues to relate: The
whole thing opens up as if it were yesterday! I can
see the entire situation in that long-ago time! I can
view now too, the panels of the great painting, The
Last Supper, as da Vinci was completing it; I can
see all the great artists of that time of the Renaissance, how they all gathered together as they were
invited to his studios for the unveiling of his incredible Last Supper painting!

Vaughn continues: "Of course, the Andrea del
Verrocchio revelation was very wonderful. Ioshanna
made a prophecy to this fine young man, that he
would again in the present lifetime, become a famous artist, and I am sure this will be. He was no
stranger to either of us and felt as did we, a familiarity and closeness, for I had met him many times;
in fact, I ran errands for Verrocchio himself, as
well as for da Vinci, in that long ago 17th Century,
that seems but yesterday." Another triumph over
time.

Another contact regarding da Vinci was made

when Ioshanna and I went into a nearby card shop to have our formal invitations made for the symbolic and coming ceremony. The lovely lady waiting upon us, Mrs. Crain, (who owns the beautiful Hallmark stationery store), seemed quite impressed with what was being imprinted on the cards. It was several days later when I was in an especial attunement, viewing others' pasts, I saw that this lady, Mrs. Crain, had been, at the time of da Vinci, his personal engraver. We are indeed in a da Vinci cycle! (She was also close to Hatshepsut in Egypt and with Queen Tiy a hundred years later.) It seems everywhere there are awaiting, other contactees of this great and important cycle, and as the Brothers imply, the story shall never end!

It was during these very same few days time that Ioshanna and myself were again shopping in San Diego. Our lunch hour had passed by and when Ioshanna was asked where she would like to have lunch, and after I had related the few places existing in the area, she chose a lovely restaurant atop the sixteenth floor of an office building called Mr. 'A's. We had been here on one previous occasion to show her the expansive view of the city. After alighting from the elevator and just inside the foyer, before entering the round, brilliantly red-clad dining room, Ioshanna stopped short. She stood gazing at the wall. There before us in stark relief was a life-sized oil painting of the Mona Lisa. I personally was quite amazed for I had visited this restaurant previously and had not noted this painting. She asked the maitre d' how long it had hung in that spot, and his reply caused both of us great consternation.

The man said, "Oh, that's Mr. 'A's favorite possession; he takes it wherever he goes. It has been
there several years — about six now!

At this remark I became more than interested,
due to my hookup with the lovely lady in the painting. As we sat awaiting our lunch I "shifted gears"
in consciousness and made attunement with Mr.
'A's vibrations. Instantly it was revealed to me,
that during his life at the time of da Vinci, he had
his own wife's portrait painted by da Vinci. During
the times Mr. 'A' visited the studio, he admired
greatly the lady, Mona Lisa; so much so that he offered da Vinci a large price for it, but Leonardo did
not wish to part with this, his favorite work. Evidently this unrequited desire by Mr. 'A' for this
particular work of art, set up within him a never-to-
be-forgotten yearning or anxiety, so that now in the
present, he actually sought out and secured an individual artist to paint a copy of da Vinci's Mona
Lisa! It was quite a good one too. The artist had
caught the spiritual quality within the eyes, but
the faint smile was not quite true.

Here was found another historical link in the famous painting. We have not yet had the opportunity
to relate to Mr. 'A' how or why it is he feels he
must constantly take along with him, his Mona Lisa
lady, or why his great love for it, but this we shall
do and, doubtless, he shall not be too surprised.
For these recurrences from our pasts are quite as
natural as our day by day living experiences, and
eventually, there seems little difference or separation. It is all one extensive and continuous life!

And now, just this very day comes to consciousness, the fine man C. A. Smith, who owns the ele-

gant hotel in San Diego, the Westgate Plaza. It is psychically shown that he was one of the Medici's, a promotor (of great fame and wealth) of the great master artists, including da Vinci! Doubtless, he shall be happy to learn of his former da Vinci contact when the proper time arrives.

Ioshanna: As Vaughn and I were visiting with Helen Moore (the student who sets the type for the books), he had a psychic flash that she had had a connection with the da Vinci household. He saw her as a man with some small mechanical etchings on paper and her pencil was going over them. Although this scene was not just then thoroughly entered into, the next day as I quizzed Vaughn further about it, he immediately saw that Helen was, at that time, a workman who did carpentry work, and he, as Salai – who was da Vinci's aide, student and houseman – was the one responsible for the hiring of these (and other) needed workmen or women. Thus it was, he hired the man John (now Helen) to help construct the large scaffolds necessary for the "Last Supper" picture.

As these men worked about the studio, there was ample opportunity to note the many sketches on which the artist had worked. On one occasion, the man John filched some of the sheets of mechanical drawings, which were numerous about the many shelves in the studios. All this was, of course, viewed psychically.

Another time when John returned to work on the rough wooden structure, the one, Salai, caught sight of large sheets of paper with the small sketchings being rolled and tucked quickly into the shirt of

John. Salai quested the man, with his denial; but after some argument, Salai was succesful in over-powering John to remove from his shirt front the sheets of the various sketches. This contact and guilt, the feeling of resentment, has continued to exist between these two (Helen and Vaughn) during these past five hundred and twenty years, and which now, due to recognition, is being discharged.

Now at this late date, in midsummer, 1973, Helen herself seeks out a book on da Vinci's life which divulges this very action she expressed in that long ago time (as John). The book goes on to tell how he was caught in the act of stealing the drawings of da Vinci, and which were mechanical sketches of telescopes and lenses, etc., and which John passed on to another on the outside. They were then turned over to be manufactured in Germany! This action and the results were of no small import — this purloining of the sketches of lenses and telescopes — for we now find the Germans to be the foremost manufacturers of sighting devices (lenses, etc.) in the whole world! They have carried this reputation for many a decade. Here again comes full cycle, and truth is revealed in the only way such secrets can be learned — via psychic attunement or ESP!

Another student (Unarius secretary, Dorothy Ellerman) had wondered, too, and rather felt she had some contact during that time. Thus, when Vaughn was asked to take another mental or psychic trip back into that household, he saw where she had labored in the kitchen of the artist on occasions when he would entertain the many persons, as they were

300

invited from time to time to view his great works, or in times of an unveiling. She was seen as a cleanup woman – one who labored with the heavy pots and pans. It was Salai, too, who hired this woman, Martha, along with five or six others, for this heavy kitchen work. No wonder Dotty has disliked and been so blocked off in her efforts in the small kitchen at the Center, for those Italian dinners of the past were no small affairs! Doubtless it was here, too, where the three, Helen, Dotty and Vaughn picked up negative karma and which now, with the relating, is all resolved – again proving the Unarius principle!

Then, too, this young man of whom da Vinci thought so well, the Salai, at times, would slip out and entertain a certain lady friend who lived nearby in Milan. At times he would bring her into the artist's studio to show his work, when she would quest of the great artists, ''What does all this mean, and why are you doing all this extensive work?'' Salai later married this woman, and who is now, in the present, a Unarius student called Rachel. Before the death of Leonardo, there had been bequeathed to his aide, Salai, a large property, a grape vineyard, in memory of his love for the boy. Salai's marriage was short-lived, for she cared not for the life he could give her. Thus, another small cycle concluded with these two, Vaughn and Rachel, in the present, as he, in recognition, cancels out that past tie with her.

Now last, but indeed not the least, at this early date comes into consciousness another even more vital and important former contact and proof of that da Vinci cycle (and of reincarnation). Because there was held a symbolic wedding and crowning at the Unarius Center, some gifts were brought. Of importance to relate is one brought by a man, a student of some fifteen years standing. Azhure had presented as his wedding gift to Ioshanna, a small, framed picture of the Mona Lisa. It was not just some framed picture he had bought, but it was evident he had located and cut out the picture from something and then obtained a frame to fit and inserted it therein. When she quested of him, "Why did you pick this particular thing," he said, "Oh, I just felt drawn to it, I simply had to get it. I wondered why, but couldn't sense anything on it, just why I wanted so strongly for you to have that little print."

As Vaughn is becoming so adept at his akashic reading, anything we are needful or desirous of knowing from the past, is quickly psychically seen by him as he mentally quests. So, later on, as I had inquired of Azhure why he selected the particular picture for me, I realized that he knew absolutely nothing as yet, about our contact with it, nor of our tremendous psychic and astral inner trips. He lives in a city two hundred miles distant and had not as yet, heard of any of our important goings on. We had, up to this particular time of his coming, related it to no one outside. As was mentioned, tape recordings have been made of the astral visits but Azhure had, up to this time, no way of knowing of these. It had not been told! It was only when he came to the Center with the picture (May 27th), that he first heard of our Mona Lisa interest, contacts, etc.

During Vaughn's instant psychic replay or flash-back, he learned how Azhure had been a man employed by da Vinci, along with John (Helen) to work on the large, rough scaffolds that often needed moving. He too was concerned in obtaining for himself some of the great artist's works. He was caught by Salai as he (Andy, as he was named) was endeavoring to rip off the very canvas of the Mona Lisa from its wooden frame. Yes, that's the picture that flashed into Vaughn's consciousness from the very akashic (or subconscious) of Azhure! Then it was seen that the aide, Salai, (Vaughn) quickly confronted the thief, but Andy was a much larger, stronger man than was young Salai, and even though he tried, the thief knocked Salai down and ran away. Of course, the young houseboy knew who he was, and the thief was later brought to answer for his attempted crime. Due to this attempt at thievery, Andy lost his job there; he was also unable, in the future, to get other work; for the entire town learned of his attempted dishonesty toward the greatly loved genius, Leonardo, and he became an outcast.

Now to carry Azhure's story and proof even further, he has just written to the Center a lengthy letter, relating how much the physical symbolic gathering (crowning, etc.) meant to him and other comments, saying it was a day he will never forget – the most memorable day in his life. Of great interest to both Vaughn and myself was his mention re Leonardo da Vinci (existing now on the inner worlds), as he heard, while here with others, our tape regarding Vaughn's vision of the Mona Lisa, and including the spiritual marriage and union with

Ioshanna, etc. Azhure commented extensively, "I don't know why, but I'm so happy for Leonardo that he now has his Mona Lisa. I'm even more glad for him than I am for her!"

Well, no wonder he was glad, his great guilt (so carried for five hundred and twenty years) was, in a sensed, appeased, as he heard of Mona Lisa being "brought home" to Leonardo! Of course, it will all be related via the mail to Azhure, and doubtless he shall experience, as is always the case, a great sense of release and relief when his past negative karma can thusly be discharged and cancelled through these observances by Vaughn.

We expect many things will be brought out when we have the public unveiling of the two photographs together, the Mona Lisa and Ioshanna herself, with the garb and hair style of the painting to prove the identity. This proving should stir up quite a furor amongst the art critics, as they learn the truth of just who was the Mona Lisa lady. Vaughn and I, of course, were most pleased to watch this added drama of the past come to light. We know, too, it is all but the beginning of much more to be lived in the future regarding that great da Vinci time and cycle.

We are again made aware of other contacts of the da Vinci time, and the unraveling continues of these most important findings and realizations. First, it was soon after our letter arrived from Julius (Chiminec) of his becoming aware of having been the close friend and associate of da Vinci – one Francesco Melzi – that we learned Melzi had likewise made some very fine paintings.

Recently, Vaughn and I have been wondering and and quizzing, within, just how or why it was that Leonardo took Salai (now Vaughn) into his home at such an early age of eight or ten years, for this was not customary for any of the master craftsmen to take on an apprentice under the age of fourteen.

As I questioned Vaughn, and suggested that he tune into his inner self, he quickly came up with the reply that Leonardo had been, in a former lifetime, the scientist Archimedes, who devised engines of war just as he did when he later became da Vinci! Moreover, at the same time, Vaughn saw how Salai had been a son of Archimedes and had, as such, set up the relationship and tie with him so that in the later life (as Leonardo), he felt desirous of having the young boy take abode with him. As further viewing and delving was entered into, Vaughn contined to see and become aware of the fact that the one, Melzi (Julius) was another of Archimedes' (da Vinci's) sons! This would answer the great question as to why Leonardo bequeathed to Melzi all of his most valuable papers.

Then, with still further akashic searching came the realization by Vaughn that King Francis I, of France, lived a life as the third son of Archimedes! So, here, Melzi, Salai and Francis were all brothers at the time of archimedes, (his sons). As such, they had set up this frequency, tie or bond, whereby when Archimedes again incarnated as da Vinci, they were all brought together in a close bond; even unto the time where da Vinci spent his last days at the home or chateau of King Francis, to whom he bequeathed his two most prized possessions, Madonna of the Rocks and the Mona Lisa, and which, he stated, were his favorite of all works he had done. Some authors have written that Leonardo sold the paintings to the king for the country of France, but according to this accurate psychic viewing, it is seen that this was a gift he bequeathed to the king, and no monies exchanged hands. Moreover, why would Leonardo want money upon his very deathbed?

So, indeed, there was reason enough why Leonardo da Vinci should want to spend his latter days in the home of King Francis. His tie and memory of that former lifetime as Archimedes, when he had been the father (of Francis I), set in motion frequencies and energy oscillations that continued to reach out and draw them together. It was this tie and this energy oscillation between these four that brought them together again, and especially during the last days of the life of the giant master of many talents.

Vaughn viewed vividly, the bedroom or deathbed scene of da Vinci, where he described, as he termed it, a very large bedroom. The bed was of gigantic size, he said, with an overhead canopy, covered with a purple bedspread. Now Vaughn also viewed in this bedroom, (wherein Leonardo spent his last days), not hanging upon a wall, but standing on an easel, the Mona Lisa portrait! He kept it with him to the very last!

It is also of interest to note that King Francis' portrait hangs directly beside the Mona Lisa in the Louvre! Interesting, even in death or freed of the physical body, their tie and energies continue to draw them together. So it is understandable, as we learn from such psychic readings and viewings, how Leonardo da Vinci had lived the life of Archimedes; it is understandable too, how one with such knowledge as Archimedes had, would as a natural sequence, return with many of these engineering principles and concepts, which he carried over and brought to earth when he later became Leonardo! Anyone reading the various historical writings about him could see at a glance, that much of their science was very similar or identical; in fact, Leonardo improved upon his former expressions of the time when he was the scientist Archimedes.

Moreover, and above all these realizations, and through this same inner consciousness and psychic attunement, it is also seen that the one, Edward T. Folliard, the veteran White House reporter of the Washington Post, who has written so extensively and been so totally involved with the Mona Lisa painting, spent twenty-five years endeavoring to have it loaned to the United States so that the Americans could view this work of art.

From a ten-year old National Geographic Magazine, in E. Folliard's own words regarding the Mona Lisa and of his tireless efforts extended to try to help obtain the painting for viewing in America, a quote from the magazine: "You may wonder what interest a Washington news reporter (who covers the White House) could possibly have in the Mona Lisa coming to Washington. Andrew W. Mellon (former Secretary of the Treasury), one of the world's richest men, had planned, and after only seven years, created and built a magnificent National Art

307

Gallery. My vision, plan and dream took nearly twenty-eight years to eventually consumate. I yearned for the day when great art works would be shown in our National Gallery — particularly the Mona Lisa. This became an obsession with me."

Ioshanna: Now, no one could become so totally involved, and throughout such a long period of time unless there was good reason in his former lives and background. Thus, he is no exception. It was learned that this man, Folliard, had been, in that former lifetime, King Francis! No wonder he wanted (his) painting (back) in his own country! This, we feel, is a very interesting and exciting revelation, to say the least. So what this all amounts to, is that this one called Folliard in the present, was in the past, the King, Francis, and in a still former life was also the son of Archimedes. There we have three lifetimes of Folliard.

We cannot help but wonder how Edward Folliard will feel when he realizes that he had, not only this one close contact in the cycle with da Vinci five hundred years ago, but also with Archimedes as his own son! Doubtless, there is much, much more to come.

The Encyclopedia Britannica states in part: "An artist as renowned as Leonardo da Vinci (1452-1519) was seldom willing to paint a portrait, and when he did, it seems to have been because his sitter could be made to represent an ideal rather than a particular human being. The most famous portrait painting by his hand is the Mona Lisa. This work, (from 1504), not only makes it clear that Leonardo was interested in idealization but also that he was per-

308

haps sufficiently tempted by the technique of oil painting to want to achieve the illusionary effects for which Jon van Eyck had also strived. More even than Van Eyck, Leonardo, in his portrait, makes the transitions so subtle that the illusion of a body of flesh and blood occupying space is almost complete; however, in spite of the fact that she seems so physically convincing, the Mona Lisa remains aloof. Her dress is simple but the bearing of her head, the position of her hands and the triangular form she occupies, makes her seem imposing and regal. The face which, more than mere flesh and blood, seems to radiate with an inner warmth which is so provocative, so eternally enigmatic in its expression that it has tantalized the millions who have seen it in the Louvre or in reproduction. The landscape behind her increases the mystery; it is so much sheer fantasy that it seems related to the world of imagination rather than fact. The Mona Lisa is so generalized that it is perhaps not even a portrait; rather, she is characteristic of the short-lived High Renaissance desire to concentrate upon the ideal rather than the particular. The ideal which the Mona Lisa resresents, no matter how illusive it is, is certainly a matter of inner life rather than physical externals; it radiates through her flesh and skin.''

An added note of interest: Vaughn and I have been endeavoring to take photographs of one of the large portraits of the Mona Lisa with but little success, when today in the mail, comes a very beautiful negative actually taken in the Louvre made professionally, sent by the student (Ashure), the one who, at the time of da Vinci, attempted to rip off and steal the canvas of the Mona Lisa. So again, here Azhure is trying to more completely replace his attempted theft. Not only that, but also he sent along what we feel could be a very important paper, pictures and descriptions from a ten-year old National Geographic Magazine article, relating the details of the shipment of the Mona Lisa and the great involvement and care entailed, in this great endeavor of shipping the painting to America, (when it was loaned) where it was displayed. Yes, it was twenty-seven years that Edward Folliard endeavored and strived to make contacts whereby he could have the Mona Lisa borrowed, moved and shown in America. It must have been a great satisfaction to him when he eventually became succesful. This, of course, came about after President and Mrs. Kennedy showed great interest in art that he made headway. We shall do what we can to help this fine person Folliard become aware of these very interesting past lives which he has lived, for he should be most interested!

One mention in this National Geographic Magazine of ten years ago: "People came to see the Mona Lisa because they knew she represented a peak of artistic achievement, a summit of human creativity. Perhaps afterward, they felt they shared a little in Leonardo's genius. This great painting stirred some impulse toward beauty in human beings who may never have felt that impulse before. After such a compliment, there should be a trace of satisfaction in the smile as Mona Lisa relaxes once again in her old home at the Louvre."

It should be added, at the present time Unarius students are experiencing their own psychic visions of this Mona Lisa painting which Vaughn described as being on the crystal floor, (in the great Museum on the planet Eros) and as they so view or tune into this life-like painting, they experience a transcendency, an inner quickening indescribable. They become incapable of putting into words, their feelings. Helen Moore, the student who sets the type for the Unarius books, this very day, telephoned to relate what a wondrous experience she had as she made a psychic attunement with the higher self of Ioshanna as she caught the give-away glimpse from the eyes – the inner contact that was so identical to the Mona Lisa painting. Helen experienced the transcendency and quickening and had tears with her inner contact with this Higher Self of the Unarius Channel, which we know to have been the Mona Lisa.

Thus again, only through such means as clairvoyance can the true answers be found, and one day history will be corrected and the many misconceptions and errors be brought to light through means of this higher sensitivity or so-called ESP. Clairvoyance or inner attunement is a very exacting science and which we Unariuns are proving daily.

Vaughn relates further: It was during the very last days of da Vinci's physical life on earth that he bequeathed to Francis I his two favorite paintings, to Francesco del Melzi his voluminous paper work, and to Salai the property, his grape vineyards. Little wonder then, when we realized that these three personages with whom he was close in

311

a lifetime approximately 600 years previously had been, then, his very own three sons!

There were many other persons of noteworthy acclaim with whom Leonardo was acquainted and who were good friends, such as Michelangelo, Raphael, Verrocchio, and many others, any of whom would have cherished any of his belongings; yet he chose to leave all that he possessed to these three (former sons), one of whom was a French king!

Little wonder too, that the White House correspondent for the Washington Post newspaper, Edward Folliard, spent a goodly portion of his entire life to get back his Mona Lisa into this country, just for a few weeks time; for it had been given him, remember, in a former lifetime (as King Francis) by its very creator, Leonardo da Vinci! Thus, time had not dulled his memory nor slackened his love for it, as he termed her, Madonna. Thus, as it came about, he found himself in the present life in a position in the White House near the President (Kennedy), and which eventually led to and brought about the agreement with the French government for the loan and showing of the portrait in the United States where she was on display for the twenty-seven days – a time during which over one million persons viewed her. Doubtless, little does he (as yet) realize, all this was set in motion when he lived as the son of Archimedes – and possibly before, in even previous lifetimes.

It is said of the countless viewers, although no signs existed regarding any silence necessary, that there was evident, extreme quietude and a reverence in both the National Art Gallery and the New

York Art Museum during its display.

Unknown to the earthman as a whole, it could be said of this work of art, that one reason for its unusual popularity and attraction is not entirely due to the physical paint or canvas. For it does carry, due to the Inner Being who inspired the painting and who, at the time, lived on the inner or spiritual dimensions, and extended into the artist's work, her psychokinetical mind projections or energies. Thus, the one so viewing the painting is, through these higher and invisible frequencies, transcended or quickened in a subconscious way, the individual not realizing just what it is that attracts him thusly, that causes one to feel an affinity or even a sense of love toward the Mona Lisa! For that is exactly what she is expressing to the viewer — even now from the inner planes!

We could well go a bit further and say, that which da Vinci has brought through in his portrait, is about as close as one could come in bringing into the third dimension or physical world, evidence of the fourth dimension or inner. It is well known how the many persons, the scientists, those interested in the psychic realms and research are endeavoring to find a catalyst to join or connect the two (or more) dimensions. Countless are the persons so striving to invent or to create some substance or an electronics that will bring together these two (seeming) widely-divided or separated dimensions, worlds or plateaus — but with little or no success! The reason is, the third dimension is of atomic form, the inner, non-atomic or the abstract, where all things exist in a cycular motion, minus

313

the time element factor.

Leonardo da Vinci, in his oils and canvas, has captured a glimpse of this inner world of passivity and peace in the eyes of his own polarity, the Mona Lisa, or in the physical, Ioshanna. It is with her inner or higher self to which the viewer attunes as he makes the visual contact with the Mona Lisa portrait; the same being true as we students look into the healing eyes of the Unarius Channel, Ioshanna. So there is really no mystery at all when we view from the inner vision or through true clairvoance; all questions can thereby be resolved!

Ioshanna: Carrying on this da Vinci cycle and rounding up, as it seems, those persons with whom he had, at that time, kept in touch, we find, through another observation of the fine Mona Lisa painting, a copy which hangs in the foyer of the lovely Mister 'A's restaurant, on the nameplate below the oil painting, the artist is one presently operating a studio just a few miles distant from us!

As has become our habit of late, when Vaughn and I discuss such things, he shifts into his inner or higher consciousness to learn that this artist in the present, named Richard Gabriel Chase, was, in that da Vinci time, also an artist of renowned acclaim. He was the master called Marco d' Oggiono. Several of his fine works are displayed in the large book of the da Vinci paintings. Vaughn saw earlier how this student then approached da Vinci, applying for apprenticeship in Milan. He was with da Vinci from 1490 to 1501 and was the most spiritual of his students, capturing a greater spirituality in his paintings. Marco also became a student of Ga-

314

briel, and even in the present, bears the artist Gabriel's name as his middle name!

As deeper psychic contact is made, it is seen that Marco felt he could learn from Leonardo how to capture the frequencies of the inner worlds. In da Vinci's comments to him, he is heard saying that color and tone have much to do with luminescence. Marco lacked this luminescence or lightness at that time; however, in spite of it all, he was the only one (of many students) able to express the attunement with the inner or higher worlds. Marco soon switched from doing portraits to painting murals and did much fresco painting at the time.

Marco came to admire da Vinci almost as a saint due to his advanced expressions being presented to the people of that day. When the portrait of Mona Lisa was completed, it was exhibited. Marco saw it and vowed to try to capture this spiritual oneness so related with the lady.

The one Salai* (now Vaughn) has, in the present, criticized the work of Chase, especially his Mona Lisa copy, feeling it was a bit too dark in tone. Now, weeks later, with his ability to "tune back", Vaughn realizes what he felt in the present was, in fact, a personal resentment, or the way he felt in that long ago time, living as the apprentice Salai. He was a bit envious of Marco's ability to express greater spiritual quality in his work than could he, Salai. Now, Vaughn can smile at his former envious

*Salai's real name was Gian Giacomo d' Caprotti, however, when Leonardo psychically attunes to Vaughn now, he refers to him as Salai.

feelings, for he now can likewise express in his own psychic way, in his own present field of psychic expression – a rare ability.

It is a note of interest that all these persons, the students of Leonardo, his patrons, etc., are now, in the present, all living in the same area! It was on the first day that Vaughn came to this city of San Diego that he was inspired to visit both the lovely Westgate Plaza Hotel of Mr. Smith and the elegant Italian restaurant of Mr. 'A', although at that time he was totally oblivious to any of these former contacts and ties, or true story – even though he had (as Salai) known them, each one. He sensed a strong desire to meet the one, Mr. Smith, not knowing the true reason why, yet all reasons and causes are found in past lives – and as the past is unraveled, the mysteries are solved.

Chapter 23

Inspiration through Vaughn, 4/3/73: After the crucifixion, John the Revelator fled to the island of Ephesus, in the Aegean Sea, but before he got away, he was stoned and you, Ioshanna, (then Mary Magdalene) took him to this small island off the coast of Greece. During the period directly after the Crucifixion of Jesus (and at the time you were Mary Magdalene), even at that time, you were in the order of, or had the degree of a Logos; you were the one responsible for the healing of John the Revelator and you actually brought him back to life. This was possible due to your close contact with the inner worlds. Over a period of twenty years he recuperated sufficiently whereby you and he could visit the various churches in Asia Minor.

It has come to me psychically, that while St. John was recuperating, his health was restored due to the great assistance given to him from the inner planes. He was more often transcended and on the Inner than he was in physical consciousness; so in this way, he was able to be a channel for the relatings of the future of the earth world, as well as other worlds; thus, the great detail that was brought through his consciousness in his great vision which he had while transcended in seeing the New City of Jerusalem and thus to write the Book of Revelations. St. John actually was taken into the great golden city of Parhelion and saw (just as you, Ioshanna, have done) with his inner eye, the golden crystal and the great Light that existed within and without the temple. He was told, and it was biblically recorded also, that when the Spiritual Age would come upon the earth and other planes, a new revelation would be brought! This would be in order that man would learn of his spiritual self, and future! He prophesied that all the secrets which had been withheld from man would be brought to him. These secrets were the visions which he, himself, was viewing at that time — man, as a spiritual being, with the beauty that resides only in the celestial realms. He was told that before this would happen (over this period of the past two thousand years) there would be many wars and pestilences, that there would be a great battle between the forces of evil and the powers of Light; but that the forces of Light would be triumphant!

Ioshanna: I know I lived long after my betrothed (Jesus) died, which was just six months after the crucifixion, but I have not been conscious where I went after that time; although the Moderator did relate soon after we met, that I went forth and carried on Jesus' teachings after He died, but knew not with whom. Vaughn: At this time, as Mary Magdalene, you were responsible for bringing St. John back to life. He was seemingly near dead after the stoning, but was a young man at this time and Mary taught him and prompted him in much that he did. It was the Higher Self of Mary Magdalene, residing on the inner planes in the City of Parhelion on the planet Eros, who prompted him in his visions, for she, herself, was residing on this plane and overshadowing him.

Just yesterday morning, Ioshanna was quickened with the sudden realization that all of this information, our great revelations here in the present, which had been coming through and being lived by her for a period of ten days (now two weeks) was the modern version of the Book of Revelations, written by John the Revelator! She met me with the words, "Eureka! We've just experienced the Book of Revelations!" Quick as can be, the New Testament was sought out, "dusted off" and opened up to the Book of Revelations. Lo and behold, there were replicas of descriptions of the city and temple we had just viewed, related psychically, and either voiced on recorders or written it down the differences being only in the language in which it was couched — in the old style! Yes, even the Overlord of the Shamballas was related in John's visions and prophecies.

We, Ioshanna and I, have written in much greater detail, these descriptions that were seen and stated by St. John, which are now completely corroborated by the descriptions by St. John, as he, himself, gave in the Book of Revelations! In addition to that, there is the conclusion to all of the prophecies made in this chapter in the Book of Revelations which St. John was prompted to write. These prophecies are those of the "Last Days" of the millennium and the dropping away of the carnal self of the people of the lower astral dimensions, to be replaced by the bright light of the great Light that emanates from the Fountainhead – this, the nourishment of man, which is now his mainstay, and the only manner in which life can progress. We now do have tangible proof of the great powers promised, in the healings and changes in persons who have read or heard on recorded tape some of the first chapters of this book. This is the proof of the regenerative quality of the powers and light now being channeled by Ioshanna.

Revelations of Vaughn: Focusing my attention, again as spirit prompts, on St. John the Revelator and Mary Magdalene, she was the one who not only nursed him back to health physically, but was the real teacher of John. Then it was shown to me that the disciples of Jesus of Nazareth were students not only of Him but also of Mary Magdalene; and although it was never recounted in the Bible, Mary Magdalene was the thirteenth disciple. It had not been related due to the fact that the disciples were prejudiced against a female teacher or disciple; thus they maintained the silence thereof.

From Edgar Cayce's "Story of Jesus": "She (Mary Magdalene) was the individual to whom the Master appeared first upon the Resurrection Morn, and it was to her that many of the Apostles and leaders went for counsel, as it is spoken of in the various accounts . . ." And even more than that, she was the spiritual teacher

of the disciples or the students and often-
times they received their teachings from her
direct, after the ascension of Jesus. Then it
was shown to me that Mary Magdalene, having
been their spiritual teacher, was of the spiritual
rank of a Logos at this time. However, this degree, too, has many levels (thirty-three). Now
that the Mission has been redoubled in its
strength, and the completion of its safe arrival
on earth has now been demonstrated through
her mighty efforts along with the Moderator, the
mission is now experiencing its victory. It could
only come about because of the great knowledge
and the preparation over the hundreds of thousands of years, culminating now with the great
and grand ceremony which knows no parallel on
any earth or astral plane history!

Now it can be told, that the one who was
known as Mary Magdalene, is now Ioshanna.
And again in the present, Iona, the biune of
Leonardo da Vinci is working in unison with
all of the Shamballas as a leader of the Shamballas. She has now, since her ascension and
coronation, become an Archangel of the first
rank, or as we term her, the Queen of Archangels! With the completion of her earth mission, she will then take over her rightful position as the leader of all the Shamballas with
her biune, Leonardo da Vinci!

I stand here in rapt wonderment and with
great humility, knowing what my position has
been as one of the leaders of the opposition;
one of those who has hindered and blocked

the great plan of the Worlds of Light and it is as such that I am rectifying my past deeds by putting my consciousness in a position, with great determination, to assist in the plan for the upward climb out of our dark and misty pasts towards this New Jerusalem which we now can see in the horizon.

Along with the statement just made with regard to the function and understanding of the spiritual qualities of Mary Magdalene, who had not been, up to this time, understood, or even considered as having been a great spiritual leader, I concerned myself that this understanding of the spiritual teachings that were coming out at the time of the mission of Jesus, must have had prior periods in which other revelations or teachings had been so stated. Immediately it was brought into my consciousness that the Book of Ruth was so called because of the person who wrote this book. Ruth is a very significant name in biblical literature and the significance of Ruth is that she is a "handmaiden of God", who stands on the right-hand side and goes forth as a prophet, or prophetess. Interestingly, the name, Ruth, has letters numbering four, which is a very significant factor because the spiritual name, the rightful name, (if names can be so used) of Ioshanna is Iona — a four-letter name! When her biune, Leonardo da Vinci, was on his mission on earth five hundred years ago, he called his true love by the name Mona (Lisa), which means one, and it is also a four-letter name. I can mention also, in having been helped and guided, I have always had a peculiar fascination for the name Ruth. The woman I married was named Ruth and maybe the prime reason although there were other reasons that had to be worked out. But Ruth has always been a beautiful name and I have never lost an opportunity to use that name. I may not have had a positive relationship with the person but the feeling for the name didn't change.

In addition to the book of Ruth, I have strong inner feeling that you (Ioshanna) also wrote the verses of the Old Testament, The Proverbs and The Psalms. Now looking into these Proverbs and Psalms, it can be seen that they are of the highest spiritual quality. There are absolutely no earth comparisons, but all of the inspirations come from the highest. It takes a great and tried past master of life to have been able to bring forth some of the great truths of life as lived by persons who are closer to or in the oneness with the Infinite Creative Source. I'm not really surprised at these revelations; I don't even have to read the Book of Ruth or look through the Psalms because I know it's true − it's the truth! It was as I psychically sensed, she, (Ioshanna), has inspired many of these poets and religious teachers of old.

Ioshanna: When we really attain some sort of a level of development, of attainment, psychic consciousness or inner attunement, whichever you prefer to call it, one has what we could call a type of scales of balance within and it is always sensed. One knows if the balance

323

doesn't feel just right; he can tell. When we are strong and positive and we know inwardly with this positive assuredness, nothing can jar our consciousness against it or turn it in another direction. It can't possibly! We need not wonder about some revelation when this inner knowing is present; we know. Vaughn: These are the definite statements you have been making to me all along — that the inward knowing is the real knowing. It is very evident. Ioshanna: You are now in a position where you can do the greatest good in a most strong, positive way. Good always overcomes evil and, as such, evil does not become the man.

The following are verses from the Book of Revelations. Below each designated verse is the version of Vaughn and Ioshanna, verses relative to their descriptions in this book "Light Beings". Neither Vaughn nor Ioshanna had read the Book of Revelations until this book had all been completely typed. Then Ioshanna experienced a revelation: You have just written the 20th Century Book of Revelations!

Revelations of St. John the Divine

Ch. 12: Sayeth John:

And there appeared a great wonder in heaven; a woman clothed with the sun, and the moon under her feet and, upon her head, a crown of twelve stars!

Vaughn so spaketh:

And there appeared a great, wondrous

324

sight, the great Queen of the Archangels, her aura brighter than the sun; upon her head was a golden crown with seven large, gleaming diamond crystals – stars.

Ch. 1 12. John:

And I turned to see the voice that spoke with me. And being turned, I saw seven golden candlesticks.

Vaughn:

And there appeared two large Angels garbed in white, holding aloft each a candlestick, bearing seven golden candlesticks aglow.

13. John:

And in the midst of the seven candlesticks, one like unto the son of man, clothed with a garment down to the foot, and girt about the paps with a golden girdle.

Vaughn:

And the golden throne sat upon the great crystal island upon which sat the One whose voice seemed as thunder as he spoke.

Ch. 1 14. John:

His head and his hairs were white like wool, as white as snow; and his eyes were as a flame of fire.

Vaughn:

His aura was the whitest of white and from his eyes darted two piercing flames of fire.

Ch. 1 16. John:

> And he had in his right hand seven stars
> . . . and his countenance was as the sun
> shineth in his strength.

Vaughn:

> The luminosity that shone from him and
> which surrounded him was more bright
> than one hundred suns!

> 20. John

> The mystery of the seven stars which
> thou sawest in my right hand, and the
> seven golden candlesticks. The seven
> stars are the angels of the seven church-
> es; and the seven candlesticks which
> thou sawest are the seven churches.

Vaughn:

> There was the great golden temple sur-
> rounded by seven golden steps and seven
> golden archway entrances. The seven
> dimensions are the Shamballas and rep-
> resent the seven golden candlesticks;
> and the seven stars are the Overlords of
> the seven dimensions.

Ch. 4 2. John:

> And immediately I was in the spirit; and
> behold, a throne was set in heaven, and
> one sat on the throne.

Vaughn:

> And I viewed on the inner, the great golden
> throne set upon the great crystal island
> upon which, one was seated.

Ch. 4 3. John:

And he that sat was to look upon like a jasper and a sardine stone; and there was a rainbow round about the throne, and in sight like water unto an emerald.

Vaughn:

The great One appeared as a living, white great Flame, which surrounded the golden throne.

6. John:

And before the throne there was a sea of glass, like unto crystal.

Vaughn:

And in front of the golden throne was the great and vast crystal esplanade spread out for many miles.

Ch. 5 1. John:

And I saw in the right hand that sat upon the throne, a book written, and on the back side, sealed with seven seals.

Vaughn:

There upon a square red quartz crystal table on the right of the throne, was the Book of Life, bound with seven seals.

Ch. 21 2. John:

And I, John, saw the holy city, new Jerusalem, coming down from God out of heaven, prepared as a bride adorned for her husband.

Vaughn:

And there appeared before me the great golden crystal City of Parhelion – the new City of Jerusalem – gleaming in its golden radiance! There came the bride adorned in the whitest of white. From her eyes shone great beams of light.

Ch. 21 18. John:

And the building of the wall of it was of jasper; and the city was pure gold, like unto clear glass.

Vaughn:

The wall around the City of Parhelion was a pearl-white alabaster, and the city itself was of golden crystal.

22. John:

And I saw no temple therein; for the Lord God Almighty and the lamb are the temple of it.

Vaughn:

Upon my first visitation, all I could see was a blinding light. No thing appeared without or within. After the first visitation, the great crystal island and throne was seen.

Ch. 22 1. John!

And he shewed me a pure river of water of life, clear as crystal, proceeding out of the throne of God and of the Lamb.

Vaughn:

There appeared a beautiful seven-tiered fountain with crystal clear water there, flowing from it.

Testimonial experienced during the typing of the aforegoing:

I was typing the "Revelations" that had been brought in through Vaughn, of Mary Magdalene being a Logos at that time; that she had written the Book of Revelations, the Book of Ruth, and the Proverbs and Psalms of the Bible, and a great shaking up began for me with the power projected. The tears flowed as I sobbed and shook, trying to continue with the typing, but a great joy was there in the knowing that these were the promised healing energies that would be projected in added measure through the great lens and the Channel, Ioshanna, to all eartheans.

The typewriter was bathed in a beautiful color of purplish-red and I couldn't see my hands but I continued to type and shake and sob and tear, until the power became so intense that my head went down on the typewriter and I was taken out. When I came to on the cold, hard metal, for a while I couldn't get my bearings. I had lost all track of where I was or what I was doing, until I looked at the words on the typewriter, then a powerful ray-beam came down over my head as I continued to type. When I tried to get up off the chair, I had no legs and my body felt completely spent as though I had gone through a wringer, which I knew was a psychic purging of past-life dross, an uplifting and healing made possible through the great strength which now exists with our beloved Unarius Channel. I am most humble and grateful for this life-changing projection.

Dorothy Ellerman (Sanosun)

Chapter 24

Vaughn: While listening to the tape recording of the description of the Conclave of the Light Beings as experienced and voiced by Ioshanna, the tremendous effect upon me was to render me immobile for a period of four hours! It was as if a thunderbolt had struck me and I was entirely lifted out of my mundane, material consciousness. The word transcended has to be put in capital letters. I have not previously experienced such a wondrous upliftment and I had to lie down while listening to the tape. The following day, again hearing the tape as it was being recorded, I had to immediately sit down. My legs could not hold me. It seemed as if all the muscles in my body had turned to jelly and accompanied with this feeling in my legs was a great, intense power beam on my forehead. For the entire time of two hours, I was completely out of the body and, in this condition, I was viewing the ceremony of the city of Parhelion on the planet Eros!

It was a transfiguring experience for me and I feel that the last dross, the most negative aspects of my past lives have now been removed. While viewing the scene, I felt suspended looking down into this great temple. The more my consciousness was placed upon the scene, the more transcended I became and the more intense was the beam on my head. It felt as if there was a wide electric band around my whole head, that I had no body and I was greatly non-plussed. All of this time, in a prone position, I was conscious of the wondrous scenes I was viewing in the temple — the triangles of the thousands of Advanced Beings who had gathered to honor the granting of the advanced degree to Ioshanna; the many other initiates who had come for their own ceremonial progression.

The most intense vision I take back with me is the size of the temple as I view the great center esplanade, which was wider than any earth boulevard. The crowning glory, and I believe the factor of my great transcendency, was the viewing of Ioshanna walking or floating down this wide runway. I can say very definitely that having viewed her Higher Self in other experiences, what I now saw far surpassed anything I have ever seen before! It was as if I was seeing a very large city skyscraper in size, all lighted up!

The three colors together, that she and the biune stepped through, had somehow affected the viewer as well, because it was just too much for me; a power of such intensity that I feel somehow a tremendous amount of dross was removed from the viewer — myself. I returned to consciousness with a new feeling of humility such as I had never before known because this has been my main problem in the overcoming of my past — the development of a great ego. So, in a sense, I feel betwixt here and there. To me, this is a great overcoming, to be showered with the power which cancels out much of my negation, amassed from a countless number of negative experiences lived in these past lives and, as such, opposed to the Light.

I now have a clear and firm comprehension of the part I must play in this great and vast scheme, which can only be glimpsed through the great Minds and Advanced Intellects who reside in these higher spiritual worlds. And so this great Conclave of Light Beings becomes a celebration of a successful completion of a vast plan that has been in the making for several hundred thousand years. It is not only a plan, but is a development whereby this lower earth plane could be raised in frequency and, in so doing, remove the strength and the force of all those who oppose the progressiveness of the spirit into the higher realms.

Again, I reaffirm and rededicate my own small, but now beginning to be positive, steps which will be with a great sense of help rather than, as was in the past, opposition.

What I am really trying to say, Ioshanna, this is, the first honest assessment of my own self I've been able to make, and now I can conceive the complete opposite of whatever I have ever been. In viewing the unveiling of the plan which has been in progress for several hundred thousand years, it's the difference between night and day. I have been in the night, you see, and it's a tremendous shaking up for me!

Ioshanna: Well I must say you have an entirely different appearance. The look out of your eyes is entirely different. You don't have that horrible fear and guilt you have been carrying. When one does look back, he must be very conscious that he is only doing it to gain greater benefit of the lesson from it, not in the reactionary way. That is the big secret! Let the negative past remain in the past. Regenerate the positive! Vaughn: You said, Ioshanna, that the sceptor or the electronic wand was a part of the crystal lens, that it is actually hooked up to the crystal lens in a sense. It has been further shown to me, the lens is the main generating power and if the power of that lens was ever turned loose, well, there wouldn't be anything, because it would destroy everything! There is nothing to compare in frequency to what that lens has, so the wand is a demodulator, and it only takes a small portion of the countless frequencies to do the desired work. Frequencies which still reside in the very high level are still too high to be used for any healing purposes, then they have to be demodulated again through the generator which exists within the channel of your own mind, Ioshanna. So there are really two demodulators!

Before the crystal lens was created and put into use, the channeling of the power came through the gathering of various individuals who purposely gathered for the sending out of these energies, but the crystal lens is the conglomerate reservoir of millions of individuals! There is much more power than there has ever been before, so they had to devise a method by which small portions could be brought down at any one time. They are saying it is being used by other channels in other planes in the universe. They all have the use of this lens°, these powers; they all have the same purpose. The tremendousness of it is just beginning to appear!

Ioshanna: I can see the enormity of it; I see the full scope. In a few seconds the other afternoon, everything opened up and there it was! When I was viewing the grass and flowers there, I could see the pale green, almost like pea-green – the crystalline structures of the grass. I could see through them; they were almost opalescent, almost frosted-like yet so soft to the touch, and at that moment when I was out there, I psychically became aware of the whole magnificent operation in one fell swoop! I was immediately overwhelmed and felt so completely inadequate and powerless to even begin to start to describe the enormity, the vast, incalculable, inestimable, indescribable meaning to the earth people. However, well it is that I know it has to be a realization, it has to be a personal inner growth; one has to become a part of it before one can actually conceive it. The Moderator very often used to say when he tried to teach people these things, or they would read his poetry and say, "It's pretty, but what does it mean?" – of course, it was rather disgruntling to him. He said, "They can't get it, they can't get my writings; they can't get anything of these concepts unless they have been prepared and conditioned on the inner first. Only then can

they conceive; then there is the oscillation within them, otherwise, it is just like pouring water
on a duck's back, it means absolutely nothing."
Vaughn: You know, now I have a much greater
appreciation of the poetry than I ever had before.
I just read some of the first parts of "The Anthenium" and I just opened up!

Now, talking about the crown being itself an
oscillator, the frequencies residing in the gold
crown, the crystal of the crown and the diamond
crystals, as well as the rubies themselves,
have the purpose of adding to and raising the
frequencies of the person upon whom the crown
was placed! It wasn't a matter of, as you said
before, Ioshanna, just placing a crown on as a
ceremonial purpose. It has a much deeper purpose of great significance!

Also looking about, it is noted that the lights
on top of the cone of the great building are now
operating continuously; they are rotating. We
see one color, then another, and on. The other
factor is, that the generation of the tremendous
energies from this "Light" ceremony is dissipated in the regular manner through these thirty-
three huge colored lights or lenses. That was
the purpose of the lights, so that the tremendous
concentration and buildup of the frequencies in
the temple from the ceremony and from all the
people involved could be added. There has
never been a gathering of so many Light Beings;
they came from many different planes and dimensions. They stored these frequencies in such a
way that they now can be drawn upon and sent

out continuously through these lights or lenses! Ioshanna: So, in a sense, the great crystal lens is more or less a reservoir for the frequencies of all these people; of their psychokinetical mind frequencies, combined with the cosmic energies. Vaughn: Yes, the lens is really a reservoir. It is also true that your wand, Ioshanna, is the generator. The wand is much more than just a laser beam. Within itself, it takes the energies and frequencies and demodulates or steps them down, more compatible to earth-world frequency. They are stepped down and re-arranged into other frequencies so they can be used for the eartheans. It is like a miniature generating station – all dependent on the purpose or the need; it instantaneously computes! I think the word computer best describes it. The lens as a reservoir, is, itself, also a computer but the word computer falls short for that kind of a description of the lens. You could really call the lens the Infinite Source! Yes, that would be the Infinite Creative Force and Source!

Reiterrating and thinking back, again as I tuned to inner consciousness, I saw the magnificent crown on the table – a tall slender table, itself like a dais, and round, with a round top. There was a deep red cushion on top of which was laid the crown. There was a crystal top or cover for protection. Then I viewed just beside it, a separate column, on top of which stood the wand. It stood slightly lower than the crown, in the especially made stand. Ioshanna:

Well I remember when the Moderator made contact with the throne, there was one great white blinding flash for a second and everyone prepared himself! Each one present added his great psychokinetical power, for it was especially to add strength to all the energy projections that had been taking place. There was a tremendous brilliance beyond compare! Everything turned to a gleaming, radiant, white light! There wasn't anyone in that city who didn't know all about it. That's all there is in that city – the creation of all those things. That's what it's all about! It is their life; their life's blood, so to speak, for each one of these persons, due to their efforts, endeavors and consciousness into these things. When these configurations were completed, it was an accomplishment of thousands of lifetimes and of many thousands of persons. They all had a stepup in frequency and consciousness. It was a higher degree for everyone there, well-earned. And they're not promiscuous in giving out these degrees.

Vaughn: I now sense, too, the definite spearhead for this great plan was that the Moderator had to come to this particular earth plane where, let's say, the greatest destruction or negation occurred. So this being the one where the need was greatest, the greatest amount of work that had to be done, that meant that anyone who was commissioned to do this kind of work to bring this upliftment, would have that much more need to accomplish. Therefore, the fulfillment of this mission meant a much greater accomplishment

for yourself, Ioshanna, and the tremendous celebration and receiving of the golden crown, signifies the fact that you and the Moderator accomplished something that no one else could
have done. Although each one had taken part in
the plan, the individuals who really put it into
operation were yourselves – the Moderator, of
course, and yourself. Thus, you, Ioshanna, received, not simply a Master's degree; it is much
more than that! All those present had taken part
in the building of this tremendous configuration, the lens, which is to be used in hundreds
of trillions of planets. As the earth was one of
the lowest, there was much to be done. On successful completion, Ioshanna, you have advanced in such a great manner that the power
you now extend here is sufficiently strong to
immobilize individuals for several hours at a
time and to render them helpless just by a look!
To receive this tremendous feeling of joy, just
by your touch, or a glance, is to me, a significant factor, indicating just who you are, and of
your contact with the Infinite! Ioshanna: It must
not be conceived by some reader that this power
extended – the great Infinite Force you have
called the God Force and which, as has here
been indicated, may cause any ill physical
effects or reactions – although it does transcend, even to the point of causing one to lie
down or even, as Vaughn states, become so
transcended, uplifted, as to go to sleep, it is
in no way harmful, injurious or even painful.
For the most part, it is a most relaxing and

beautiful feeling, impossible to be conceived except by those who have so experienced. Let it be said for now and all time: This great infinite healing power, the very Creative Force of God that stems from the Central Fountainhead on the great plateaus of the spiritual dimensions is completely and thoroughly beneficial and healing in nature and would in no way, harm any person, place or thing! It is the greatest blessing to be so blessed as to be so touched. Vaughn: You looked into my eyes this afternoon and tears came because of the great love that shone out from you.

The fact is, it all started here where they brought together all the culprits (you might call them criminals) — the very ones who were instrumental in causing the degeneration of this plane and changing its direction! Ioshanna: Well, this was a very wonderful realization and growth to me. Whatever in this regard that you can view in addition, please do so. Yes, I can testify to the fact that something tremendous and great has happened with me and to say I'm grateful doesn't begin to relate the complete truth. Vaughn: I must relate, too, Ioshanna — and I must remember to call you by your new name, Iona — it was during your several mile stroll down the concourse prior to receiving your gold crown that I was taken back with the size which you appeared to be and I felt as though I were going through another shock treatment. The force I received was tremendous and I can really appreciate how I was able to view all this and "take" all this power. I must have been put into some special cage or energy enclosure because I felt like I was being electrocuted, really! I mean, I really did! If I hadn't had this treatment, this ray beam on the forehead which you have extended over a period of many years so I could take it, I am sure I would not have been able to do so. This was the added strength of all the previous rays put together the time you floated down the promenade! I felt very ill. For a moment I thought maybe I was really going under.

It would be difficult to state the size you seemed to be in that spiritual state or self, Ioshanna. Well, I said the height of a many-story building or some several hundred feet. You, yourself, couldn't be seen. I couldn't really see you until you moved up into the front area. At first, I saw only the billowing effect of the chiffon, then yesterday I saw the actual golden aura, which was really white with a gold rim around it. It is really difficult to conceive, even though I've seen it! The only adornment that broke the extremely white appearance of your elegant flowing robe was the huge, deep-red velvety-appearing rose which was more than four to five times the size of any rose of the earth. This fragrant flower covered the entire front of your bosom. The rose was formed, of course, from the radiant, glittering crystalline mind energies – magnificent to behold and, had been created with great love. The red rose, I understand, happens to be the favorite flower

of both the Moderator and you. It is now understandable why, when you were ill at one time,
a single rose literally gave you life force –
the love oscillation between the flower and
yourself!

The size and magnitude of the entire Conclave is far too vast to even attempt to describe
in words, however, a small comparison of the
great Spiritual Beings in attendance could be
compared with the vast numbers of people who
gather and attend the earth-world, Rose Festival
parade in Pasadena, California – speaking only
in relative numbers in our meager attempt to try
to build up within your minds some slight semblance of this incredible experience, expression
and attendance.

So this is where our future lies. It certainly
gives one great courage and aspiration – something to strive toward. Ioshanna: That's the first
thing man must do: free himself from all his earth
ties – these negations that he permits himself
to constantly live and relive; his reactions,
his emotions, his hatreds, his fears, his guilts,
his tensions and pressures, his hostilities and
his resentments to many persons with whom he
is confronted daily. These are the reactions
which he must learn to recognize and cancel out.
Man must need to edit his thoughts to free himself of them and realize they are only bonds of
the past; they are bogeymen of the past; they
are not reality! He does not have to succumb
to them or to continue to regenerate these negations. And this is what all this Light, the lumi-

341

nosity and energies, this great, wonderful, tremendous and inconceivable buildup is all about – to help man overcome all this. And it shall be done!

Ioshanna continuing: Then one may ask, what about all these people's karma – that which is being removed? Well, after a person has been cleansed and freed of a great deal of his karma, these individuals are, of course, taken out into these higher dimensions during the time their body sleeps and shown what has been done for them, how they have been helped and released and freed; they are shown how they must work further toward gaining understanding so that they can oscillate more compatibly with the higher frequencies which now are existent. Study and understanding will be important to these freed persons. This is all work the great Beings, the Perfected Ones, the Spiritual Beings are doing in these healing wards on the Inner – to help these people who are released and freed here in the physical and to teach them further how they must carry on, how they must begin to live when they are on the earth. It is all a part of the New Age plan, work and expression. Vaughn: It is all getting to be of great proportions. I can appreciate why it was necessary to have gathered those numbers of people because they all – each one in himself – is leader of whatever it is he has been responsible for; schools and hospitals.

Ioshanna: This Conclave, may we repeat, is not only of this world, but includes the evolution of many, many worlds, as well as the astral worlds and countless surrounding worlds. We don't like to say "all" because that infers a limitation. When we say all the worlds, that, in itself, is a limitation and we don't impose a limit upon anything.

But surely, all the worlds that we can possibly conceive – and many, many more – are, and will be thusly affected in a positive way for good, for they are all so interlocked and interrelated, one will indirectly affect the other through the principle of frequency relationship! It's very vast! Vaughn: It makes me just shudder. I was just going to say, as a result of the dropping away and the cleansing I experienced while viewing this great ceremony of the conferring of the Archangel degree upon Ioshanna, I found the next day that my rapport with Dorothy had reached a proportion that I had never before experienced or thought possible – a new high. We both had a wonderful rapport. We could really appreciate our spiritual selves. As Dorothy said, "I love you – spiritually", and we looked into each other's eyes and we really scanned the depths of ourselves, didn't we? Dotty: We surely did, and there really are no words to express what we felt – there were none – just an appreciation for all that we received. Ioshanna: So this is proof of instant healings of you both! And I am sure, of our dear sister Helen, too, who also experienced a step-up after spending some days here working on the first part of this description – this meager attempt at description;

for, as we say, words just fail us. There just simply are not words to describe these beautiful dimensions and artifacts and activities. Words lack meaning. Vaughn: I am beginning to appreciate what you are saying. Dotty: "Where there was no love before . . ." They said. Vaughn: Yes, no love; just resentment and jealousy. But now that the scales have been drawn from our eyes — my eyes particularly — I can see the spiritual quality in you and all people, without having to be envious. Ioshanna: What could be more wonderful? At that time, during the intense power that you tuned into, viewing the pageant, much of the past negation was discharged. Dotty: It's a freedom that is worth working for. Vaughn: We feel psychically free. Ioshanna: That is what man has to seek and find in each individual — his soulic self; because it does exist in each one. He couldn't be an individual unless he had this connection with the Infinite and was a soul being. So we must search for that in all men. Vaughn: It was surely buried! Dotty: Well, this great Light searches deeply within that dark region . . . Vaughn: What I was trying to say is that those people who were present when the ceremony was being viewed, for instance, Helen, Dorothy, and myself, to all intents and purposes we were (as we were a part of the balcony guests) a part of the ceremony and received the benefits of the great powers that were being generated for the help of mankind in many worlds. I can now really appreciate what has happened to me and how I had felt; it was as if

I was, in a sense, being electrocuted with the high powers that were coming through! This was the effect of being brought close to the frequencies being built up in this temple. The crystal lens was in operation, you might say, and I was the recipient of its benefits. That is, it calculated the necessary amount of voltage and power, that was done through the ray of the crystal rod, which we call the demodulator — and just the necessary amount of power that was felt by me was still of such great intensity, which was necessary to remove the vestiges of the negative frequencies that were accumulated in my psychic anatomy — still just sufficient that it would not be damaging. But I still can't get over the intensity of it; and the proof of the intensity is the number of hours that I was immobile, and yet not rendered unconscious!

Ioshanna: Now, all this started the other day when you had that half hour in the chair when you were shaking all over. This was the beginning of your treatment. Just before that, things were pretty negative with you. Do you remember how things were so bad?

Vaughn: Oh, yes, just before that I felt as if — well the word is, I had really lost my soul because I had no hookup; I felt completely stripped of all intelligence. Ioshanna: The obsessions had full control. Vaughn: Well, this is great and wonderful! I can appreciate what this power means to have made such a change. Ioshanna: I dare say it is utterly inconceivable to really factually estimate the number of years, or shall we say lifetimes, that you have been projected into the future, cancelling out many return trips to this physical dimension. That alone is of inestimable value! Vaughn: Well, I, for one, know what I shall do on a return trip to this or any other planet and that will be to work for the progression of all those whom I contact or am put in contact with. Never more will I have the need to think of self as the sole importance. Ioshanna:

Oh, I don't doubt for a moment but what you all were there, observing, because you would be unable to conceive what we have been describing otherwise. If you had not viewed these things psychically, you would not be able to view it here, now in the physical, without getting completely and thoroughly transcended with it. You wouldn't be able to view all that you had psychically, had you not been a spectator or been present at the great conclave. I'm sure, if you really would like to know and will set your consciousness aside in the way you can do and extend the antenna and look within, you will be able to see and know. Any questions you need to know about, you can now very accurately see and know — and I will know factually as to the correctness. Up to now, I see no signs of any errors you have made in viewing. It has all been very accurate. Vaughn: Now I did see, and am again seeing many earth peoples from many earths who were brought, in their psychic selves or sleep state, to view the ceremony. Special sections were made very high in the room; the balconies were in a circular fashion and they contained countless thousands of souls. There was a screen; I see it as an energy screen all around. I can see the tremendous temple, and the balconies completely encircled the inside of the temple, starting up at least a hundred feet or more and much higher, so that there was no interference with the higher frequencies; still, everybody could see, as if they were within a few feet. All of these people who were able to come had been preconditioned; they, themselves had healings. This magnificent temple has such a great purpose that it is just inconceivable to the small mind. Everything has been thought out and so well-planned. All of these people have been collected together throughout the many, many ages. They just didn't happen to come, for they, themselves, had planned and worked toward this conclusion for many hundreds of years in the past.

Ioshanna: It was sensed at the beginning of this great conclave that the plan was started one hundred thousand years ago, and we've all been working on it ever since. Then later on, it was realized by both of us that it had been actually five times that length of duration. This slow take was especially due to the fact that it was all too vast and mind expanding to conceive, both the vast lengths of time and personages involved. The total involvement was easily twice that amount of time. Thus, a good title for the book could well be "The Affair of the Millennium"! — which it is! Vaughn:

These numerous individuals were all a part of the great plan, for which they, too, had been working.

Also were the balconies segregated according to thirty-three dimensions, because these people came from these thirty-three other dimensions, and in each dimension are many millions of worlds — terrestrial or astral worlds — so they had to have a separation, too, otherwise they wouldn't be compatible to sit together, even in that particular suspended state. Ioshanna: You have a light in your eyes I like to see. May they ever shine so brightly. Vaughn: I shouldn't use the word proud, because it isn't pride, but I'm being proud that I am a part of this, being and working beside you. Ioshanna: It is something to be proud of, to be a part of this vast undertaking; so am I proud, grateful, humble and thankful. And this is why I can be satisfied if I don't see a lot of activity going on. I don't have to run around with the advertisement, as I once felt necessary. I can be at peace because I know inwardly all things are manifest as they should be. The work goes on from within and not necessarily from without.

Vaughn: Also present at the ceremony were all those on the earth plane, presently incarnated who are, in the future, to take an active part in the Unarius Mission. All of those who are going to take an active part in the mission, whether they have been contacted by the Channel or not at the present time, will have been quickened, and in this way, their contact will

348

be made in a short time. I think it is more than a quickening. I started thinking of Bryce Bond, the man who sent several new students lately, and realized he has gone through an experience, having attended this ceremony in sleep state. I had a feeling when I tuned in to it that Bryce had one of the biggest jolts he ever had. I believe, also, he was one of the people being initiated in another progression, and he experienced a change in frequency which is a great stirring up as far as his physical senses were concerned. I just felt he had a tremendous experience; then I knew this was true. And all these persons who had come to the earth plane for this purpose were also present at the ceremony. Ioshanna: How could it be otherwise; of course they were present! At first everything has to be done on the inner. Nothing is ever expressed first on the outer. I am glad you were able to see this. You are getting to be quite a "seer"! Vaughn: There's no ending in consciousness as to what this plan is, because it's so infinite. There will always be, as far as I can see, additions made as to its connotations. I appreciate these people all had to be a part of it. It just hadn't come into my mind before. How fortunate for them all! It is all so infinitely vast. Ioshanna: In the event some may question and wonder regarding the Unarius Moderator, to this let it be said: He has worked long and arduously ever since the (His) crucifixion in Jerusalem; worked with the many who helped to bring it about, that they may be freed of their karma. Even as He returned in 1904 and carried out his full mission through 1971, he worked successfully toward the releasement of these countless persons. This was the one great reason for his return to earth, to do good for those who have wronged him! He practiced that which he taught – to turn the other cheek.

Several have been the lifetimes which I, personally, have spent in his company, more or less as his helper and/or his student. He has earned well his freedom from all this, the Hill of the Crosses memory, and I feel prompted that he has, as he predicted he would, moved on into another galaxy, in possibly another universe. I am sure he was most happy to sever from his own psychic structure, these countless energy forms, memories of these lives he gave in his effort to bring to man the Light.

Yes, as I look up into his beautiful face in our large portrait of him – that shall serve many as their Savior – yet he would not choose to be known as such. He would, rather, that each one look to him in the respect that he brought to the earth the Word and the way man can learn to free himself from his past.

Thus, as I travel forward in this, his great mission on earth – the mission and work of billions of souls – it gives an inner peace to know he can now leave behind the numerous negations of the past countless thousands of persons and create, as he is, greater worlds in Light from his exalted position.

He was, after the Jerusalem episode, the

ruler and Overlord of all the Shamballas. Thus, when he left the physical world, (December 6, 1971), after his mission as the Unarius founder and Moderator, (Ernest L. Norman), he was again "stepped up" or advanced to another even greater point in the infinite plan. He could make mental contact regardless of distance, but I feel he shall be privileged to be concerned more with greater and Advanced Beings, for his wisdom and great spiritual awareness is far too great for this, the earth world. I shall be happy to reminisce and appreciate the privilege I experienced as I walked by his side here on earth in the 1900's, as well as in Jerusalem nearly two thousand years ago as his betrothed; that He can place his great Light and Love with even higher worlds, for he, with the many others, have all prepared us well for a light-filled future! He helped make it all possible that the beloved biune, Leonardo da Vince, could take his proper place by my side in this great endeavor until it is, that the sands of time have spent themselves and the Light has been shone − as was the promise − unto the four corners of the earth and the many earths about; until the time the Father will call me home again, and I shall know there will be one awaiting to welcome me back. Yes, after this great celebration, I can be sure there shall be many to welcome me home!

Study ye well, dear ones. Learn of these vital concepts of life that when it is your time to depart from the flesh and this earth world, its many ties and bonds hold you no longer; that you will move on to your home in the stars in full consciousness and light, with the wisdom and knowledge of how to exist there. For so it must be. Man cannot live where he is unfamiliar; he must prepare!

Another note of which mention should be made is that of the one called Prince Serapis. This great illumined Being is from another solar system and yet, he had come during the transcribing of the Pulse of Creation books to oscillate his Power, Light and Consciousness. He gave, during that time, a mental dissertation to the Light Beings living on Parhelion. He, too, was moved forward in his progressive evolution to an even higher solar system, galaxy and universe, and another great Logos occupied his former position. And so all personages have moved forward in this great conclave experienced — the once-in-a-millennium occasion!

Vaughn: For this great hierarchy, this project is a pinnacle of expression for and by the many thousands of souls, during the past (at least) many hundreds of thousands of years. The importance of this festival this day could never be sufficiently emphasized or estimated. Suffice to say, there has never, at any time, been expressed as meaningful or purposeful an endeavor towards not only our small little earth world, but including the countless other physical, as well as numerous astral worlds. These worlds too, shall in the future, sense, realize, and benefit from the results that shall henceforth, from here on, be so expressed. The coming New Age has long been looked forward to, but few, if any persons realize the great significance of this term or just what could be entailed. In essence, it could be said, that due to the great powers, the Light energies and force fields being so radiated and directed from these higher dimensions and Minds, the earth man can be moved forward great distances in his evolution, saving him countless return trips into these negative, material worlds! Thus, what cause could be of greater value? Indeed, there could be none half so great. Only time will tell and show the great changes wrought. Suffice to say, our new Golden Age is on the way, and much sooner than most can believe!

Thus it was, in reviewing but the past few moments, and of the tremendous powers that have been generated and regenerated; the intense build-up of the chant-energies, the crescendoed music that created added energy, the mind powers of all present and involved that were, at the precise moment, projected out through the ceiling and out into the spheres – along with the unforgettable and ear-splitting tone frequencies of the great bell, plus the psychokinetical mind powers of the many thousands present – added and multiplied in millions of megacycles of frequencies.

Combined is the concerted effort of all these force fields, the mind energies of all these thousands of Perfected Beings, the great golden energies peculiar to gold alone, impinged within the bell; the energies that had been created from the music tones, the incantations of the voices of the adepts, the boys; the energies which the continuous changes had so set up; color radiations that had been projected from the crystal structures themselves and into the buildings, into the very ceilings. No less in importance, too, the vast assemblage itself, consisting of countless thousands, wearing the familiar conical hats that serve to funnel the mind energies up and out the cone-shaped building into the reservoir — the great lens!

At the moment of this sounding of the bell, this great collected accumulation of psychic, spiritual and very high frequency energies, all collected and amassed together, and "shot", literally, into the earth and astral world aura; and aimed directly at specific conjunctions of magnetic force fields, the magnetic belts and the force fields of the earth, at a precise moment of the equinox.

Thus, these great emanations of energies are interjected and projected, directed and shot into the particular magnetic belts of the earth, there to generate eternally. In other words, perpetual motion! Thus the countless force fields about the earth will, due to the regenerative properties of the various frequencies, regenerate ad infinitum. The very plasma of (so-called) space itself, will, in this hysteresis process, quickly move or translate this abundance of creative energy into the aura of the

earth, there to oscillate and regenerate infinitely
— eternally!

* * *

The following lovely verse was projected
mentally from the Universal Mind — the Unarius
Moderator, Ernest L. Norman, during this Conclave:

And as ye have found me, so have ye
found thy destiny,
And were it not so, I would not have
told ye.

Drinketh ye deeply of these true waters
of Spirit.
And that ye shareth with all who wouldst
likewise thirst
For in the sharing doth ye become ever a
greater part of the Infinite
And thy Light shall shine ever
the more brightly
For such is the way of Spirit.

And as it hath been well spoke
in that long ago
I cometh as a man among men for I am
not the man, but that which liveth
and resideth within Him.

Believest thou in Me, and thou shalt
    have life Eternal.
And now the very secrets of Heaven have
    been unfolded before ye
That which ye garner
    from the Book of Life
Shall carry you on, beyond
    the ends of time
And as ye hath so expressed and shared
    in love
So that it shall be done unto ye.

Lay ye up not treasures on Earth
But lay ye aside the treasures of Spirit
For these are the things that remaineth
    with ye always
And that they tarnish not with the
    passing of time
Nor do they rotteth away with the mold
    of the earth

For these are the treasures which I
    have promised thee
That groweth the more beautiful
    with the taking
And that ye now walketh in the pure
    Light of Heaven
That naught shall deter ye from
    thy destination.

And that as ye drinketh more deeply,
    these waters of Spirit,
Becometh they the more sweet
    to the taste.

Heed ye well and mark ye wisely this
    day in thy progression
For it hath been long in thy unfoldment
    and many hast there been the stones
    for thy feet to bruise.

Yet it was in the great overcoming
    that gaineth ye the great strength
    and the fullness of Spirit
That ye shall needeth not –
    to go out no more, but rather
That ye shall resideth in
    Heaven henceforth
And if it were not so, I would
    not have told ye.

Believest thou in me and ye shall have
    eternal life.

Many hast been there thy foe
    to overcometh
And many thy sheep to feed
Useth this Light and thy wisdom wisely
    that ye cast not thy pearls
    to the swine
For it hath been so told and so writ
    I hath spoke.

                    Jesus of Nazareth via Uriel

It must be related of the beautiful experience I had just last night, Vaughn, after I asked you to get the record, "My Special Angel", with the introductory lyric, "You are my special angel" – of the beautiful, wonderful reaction I had when it was played. This number held an especial meaning to both the Moderator and myself, for when he would play it on his stereo or we would hear it on the radio, his remark would always be: "You're my special Angel," or, "They wrote this number for you!" My reply would be, "It was written for you!" Thus, as you so hastily dashed to the store, Vaughn, and so successfully brought back my beloved melody, and as I played it (and it was an especially vibrant vocalizing with tremendous vibrations, the orchestration itself, was especially fine, portraying great strength), it did give me a pickup! I was vibrating very positively with it and so happy to have it; it tuned me back to the many times when the beloved Moderator made these kind, loving remarks.

With his large picture above the stereo where I was working on the tape, as I glanced up to the picture, more or less talking out loud to him, I said, "There, how do you like that!" And quickly, right within the same instant, there came back the thought, "How do you like that!" In other words, he was again repeating, just like he did when he was in the physical, when we would pass it back and forth to each other; intimating, of course, that the other was the angel. But the joke was on me, for here, for a

358

moment, I was believing I had surprised and delighted Him on the Inner when, actually, the reverse was true! Thus, his quick comeback: "How do you like it!" I did have a good laugh over it all. Here now, we find we both are on the very close plateau together!

It was a very stimulating and happy time, and I must say, the tears did flow, because he was, at that very moment, just as close as close can be, and which again proves there is no distance in the abstract. For even though he may be worlds apart, universes or even galaxies (and I have assumed he is), here was my thought, what a wonderful contact and connection in consciousness we do have! What with the very mere thought, here was his instant flash reply, which goes to prove, too, that we do nothing here on the third dimension, after we are on this higher plateau, or that we function from the inner, for all things we do are guided, set up and inspired from the inner self or minds.

So there, of course, I was inspired (from him) in the beginning to get the number – and Vaughn to find it – and it was a very wonderful and happy situation. I must say, each and every day since the very beginning of this wonderful occasion, there has been some wonderful joy, such as the one I just mentioned, brought into consciousness. Every day holds its joy, happiness and surprise, and I am sure when the Brothers told us the conclave was being carried on through the year, it is indeed true. I am enjoying and revelling in every hour. Of course, these happenings and situations go much further. They serve too, to prove the principle which we are so endeavoring to bring to mankind – that of life as a regeneration, called by the earthman, reincarnation.

Chapter 25

Vaughn: It is easy to see how any earthean would become lost in the maze of even a simple word description. Suffice to say, it shall, indeed, all become worlds-changing!

Henceforth, a festival will mark an annual celebration in honor of this great world-changing event. The golden bell will here again be rung and all participants shall again gather in commemoration. Surely, my own (Vaughn), cup runneth over and I will never be the same! The power which is sensed, and now generated through our channel, (she now terms herself a generator), far exceeds the power and strength of the atom bomb. For instance, as has been my personal experience, in reading a few lines on a birthday card written by Ioshanna, suddenly the transcendency became so intense I was forced to quickly lie me down to sleep. There was also a very strong ray beam focused at my forehead. What more can one say? The reason, of course, is due to the countless thousands of Higher Intellects who are, through the function of the new crystal lens, all "hooked up" or oscillate with and through her.

Of great significance also, at the present time, during this entire week, Ioshanna, in the physical has been rerecording in stereo, the entire set of the Pulse of Creation books. As a student, you will know how all of these great minds have spoken their words through the vocal cords of the Moderator when he was in the physical. This gathering and celebration is, in a sense, a salute and recognition of this great accomplishment that was achieved (the great Unarius library) and can now be given to the earth world. Perhaps an even greater significance is, that it all symbolizes and actually sets in motion the new Golden Age!

As a note of interest, many years ago the Brothers on the Inner related that Mrs. Norman's name, used in Atlantis, was "Ioshanna" and because she related to it, has since used that name. During the several days in which this great celebration was taking place and I would receive another inner vision, Ioshanna asked, "What was my name?" Instantly came the reply "Iona". In the "Pulse of Creation" "Iona" is the biocentric to Leonardo da Vinci. She did not seem surprised, for doubtless she knows all these things inwardly.

As Ioshanna tells, although the Avatar (called the Unarius Moderator) had been the Supreme Ruler of all the Shamballas during the recent years or since his ascension after his life as Jesus; however, he has now, since his recent transition ascended to an even higher position and plane as yet unknown by name. Suffice to say that he ascended to another galaxy far higher in spiritual progression to that of the former position held. It was for the purpose of this great conclave that was held, actually in the honor of Ioshanna and the great mission, that he returned this day – to be present in the great historical golden room; to stand before his huge throne of gold that he may be the one to present to Ioshanna the precious and invaluable crown and golden wand – the electronic wonder which projects a ray beam; a beam that would cause even our laser beam to appear slower than a snail's pace in comparison. The white square light emitted is, of course, for healing and corrective purposes; in most instances, the ray would not be sensed by the individual being treated and to whom the ray is directed, for the frequency would be so properly adjusted to the particular person. So never is any pain felt in the healing treatments.

It must be said, too, that since the passing of just the last two days, our Channel has changed in psychic appearance even more so. The angelic aura and radiance is most evident – evidence of the great powers and light that were so interjected at the Spiritual Conclave in her behalf. Likewise was the great Conclave commemorating the conclusion of the creation of the great electronic wand of Light that so joins her with our Spiritual Brothers and world, the wand and the great lens, which shall play such a vital part in the incoming Spiritual Age for mankind. Now it is understood why our Unarius Channel must protect herself and the great powers that are now projected through her Consciousness. At no other time has this great work been known or been attempted, nor was it possible.

To each Student: Be ever humble in the

knowledge of your individual part in this, the greatest spiritual awakening ever to come to these lower dimensions. Be positive, passive and complacent in this knowledge. Thus, let us, each one desirous of a higher and a more quickened state of expression and evolution, rededicate ourselves to this, the greatest of all causes.

Another word which was related by Ioshanna after her glorious coronation celebration on the Inner Worlds of Light: The Brothers conveyed in their mental transmissions that where e'er would be placed her thoughts and Consciousness, theirs would thus be added to hers! Surely this promise carries much hope for each one of us! Ioshanna told too, how she was impressed with the fact that now, and for this, the New Age, many souls can be relieved of much of their karma − that many of their ties and bonds of the past shall be lifted from them! This done in order to help balance the scales and to get this world back on a more positive frequency in its evolution, and in a better relationship to the spiritual planets within its orbit. So, courage, fellow students, and forward in Love.

It might be added, and factually so, that I, (Vaughn), have myself, since experienced a tremendous healing due to these new electronic devices of the Inner, as Ioshanna has directed her Consciousness my way! The sensation was, as if I were sitting on a very strong vibrator; my entire body shook all over − not as an inner chill, but externally as well as internally.

Those nearby watched as I was physically shaking, uncontrollably, for twenty minutes duration and were quite confounded. The feelings and effects immediately afterwards were astounding! I feel for the first time in my life that I have just come to life. It is as though I have been reborn – and the physical world seems further away! Surely, large steps-up into the future have been made due to this, our Unarius' new healing electronics; mechanisms through which our Channel directs her Consciousness. Moreover, there shall be, countless and without number, those who shall likewise thus benefit, due to the numerous and collective minds and energies so involved and who have thus expressed, as our Channel Ioshanna leads the way, in this, the new Golden Age.

Our one great expectation is that each dedicated Unariun reading these lines, may likewise attune himself unto this most glorious of all life-changing, earth-shaking, historical event, for it is truly such! It is a once-in-a-millennium happening, and fortunate indeed are the eartheans. The future will indeed serve to prove and verify the countless and innumerable healings and lives that have been changed for the better due to these Light radiations now being brought to the Earth with the start of this Spring season, 1973.

Let it now be known, too, that the collective Minds, Energies and Intelligences from all the great Beings and Souls who have ever lived upon planet Earth, and countless thousands who have never lived an earth life, are – in this great and concerted effort for mankind – extending themselves to you, each one, with their rays, with their psychokinetical energies, with their radiations and Infinite Love, to help bring about a change in the direction of the evolution of the earth world, along with many other material planets and astral worlds, that we may henceforth enter into a progressive evolution, regenerative in nature. May we, each and every one, do what we can in this great cause for mankind by maintaining a strong and positive consciousness.

A word from Ioshanna: And now, dear reader, if you will thus attune yourself with me here, as I likewise attune into the countless Higher Ones – and through the great created crystal lens, the crown I wear, the wand I psychically carry, you will receive the healing energies so projected through for your personal benefit and healing.

Here we go: . . . .
. . . .
(one minute) – time!

Vaughn: So this great temple is the structure that you, Ioshanna, saw in 1964, and many students were given great hopes and expectations when you wrote them of your revelations – that they would see such a structure on this earth. Ioshanna: Yes, I hurriedly, and perhaps too hastily, wrote to many people because I was so quickened and taken up with it. I was living it for a few days there. The projection was so great that everyone I wrote to relived it, too, and entered right into this thing! Vaughn: Yes, I recall I just made the contact in 1964! You wrote me of it. Ioshanna: Many of these descriptions herein were related in my "Bridge to Heaven" book, of 1969. I've not been conscious of it here, during these two weeks of living on the Inner. This rereading the chapter in my book regarding our spiritual home – so like here now! I really thought it was going to take place right then in 1964. I didn't realize that I was seeing from the Inner for the future; for it seemed to be in the present! However, we'll never draw any lines or limitations. We'll welcome and let whatever shall be, to be. We won't limit anything with our conscious minds, but I couldn't forget how everything built up within me. Oh, these beautiful scenes that were on the walls. I said they were historical events. It was exquisite beyond any possible means of description; so I know this was what I was seeing psychically. I know this was what I was doing – viewing the future – the experiences just lived! Doubtless, I was helping in the construction of all these crystal things! But it was all so tremendous. I was far more emotional with it all then, than now – but that's understandable too.

Excerpts from Ioshanna's "Bridge to Heaven" book, published in 1969, the chapter called "My Erosean Visit", relate the similarity to that which was experienced presently in the great Conclave of Light, and as was related, the feeling then was that she was building it – and which is now conceived that this was true – or too many identicals to be accidental! These realizations were not simply that they were projections into consciousness, but rather that she was there on the Inner Higher Worlds of Light – it was being first relived in the present in 1964!

To Ioshanna:

> The shining Light 'round your head
> a halo of the stars
> Composed of all the things
> of earth and sky
> And by this Light my soul is led.

(The Moderator)

". . . I suddenly was transported, visited and viewed a beautiful luminous home. The walls seemed made of some lovely, synthetic or plastic substance with swirling cloudlike patterns in pastel shades which were luminated from within. There seemed some substance was included in the material which created a soft, rosy luminosity. The floors were similar to beautiful marble, yet the material was not opaque but seemed translucent and they, too, were illumined softly from underneath. Well I remember the gold string or bands in a radial pattern, meeting in the center radiating outwardly to the perimeter which formed a lovely pattern to walk upon, and in between each separation were glorious scenes depicted and which, too, could be changed at will! The feeling when walking over this lovely floor was that it gave off some energy radiation of an uplifting element, a sort of buoyancy, that made walking seem more like floating.

"No lamps or lights were visible for there was no need for such, as the lighting element was evidently mixed in with the building material — such as a fluorescence.

"Centermost in this elegant circular home was a beautiful mosaic alabaster fountain with levels of various graduated sizes. The dancing waters sprang into many varieties and patterns as multi-colored lights slowly and systematically played color upon the cascading, dancing waters as they continued through the many beautiful designs and effects. Along with this colorful display of color and water was an accompaniment of soft, healing music, so muted that it seemed to influence the waters in its cadence or rising and falling as the tone colors rhythmically imbued their beauty to both eye and ear, as well as the soul. Some of the musical instruments being heard were strange to my ears and not of the earth-world instruments and which, in itself, carried radiant, energy-healing frequencies. This soft music seemed to create the mood for the dancing waters, all a most soothing and relaxing sight to behold and to breathe into one's very soul; beauty indeed, beyond description. Also, I detected a delightfully faint fragrance being emitted, from where, I knew not.

"The only partitions noted, to separate the rooms, were those of the sleeping areas and which were walls of very full rainbow-colored, sheer, chiffon material which hung softly and gracefully about for any desired seclusion.

"Most vivid in my memory is the beautiful free-flowing staircase which seemed to have no supporting structures but rather, twisted gracefully in one complete turn and a half, then disappeared through the ceiling. I learned, when one stepped upon this most graceful stairway it simply, automatically motivated, or transported, the person right up to the roof where existed a lovely, formal, sculptured garden filled with many glorious flowers and plants. There was a viewing platform where huge telescopes and viewing instruments were located that the owner might scan the heavens and other planets, from this heavenly abode.

"The home was not cluttered as are most earth homes with many furnishings but was spacious and beautiful in its simplicity. About the sides of the circular room, were located here and there, long graceful lounges for sitting or reclining in relaxation. They seemed not to be placed upon the mosaic floor but were rather, suspended slightly in the air, and upon each such lounge were luxurious soft cushions of various soft, muted tones in pastel shades.

"Outstanding in my memory of this Erosean home, was a sort of television that filled one entire wall in color and was a three-dimensional project.

"When one wished to go from one area to another, there were no frustrating doorknobs or locks, but the slight wave of the hand quickly slid the particular section open silently and back out of sight. Other details are not so prominent in my mind but the very peculiar part of it all was, I had the definite feeling, and told my beloved, 'I'm going to build you a plastic house; I know just how!' And I described what I've just written here. Then he knew I had visited Eros. It made him very happy, of course, but do you know, the visitation still seems so real, as if it actually happened or will take place here in the physical! I know where I go when I leave this earth world, for I've just visited our spiritual home – one we have mentally and psychokinetically created on the inner and a delightful and elegant abode it is!

"And so, dear reader-friend, such experiences as these can be your personal realizations, too, and are in store for you each one, some time and place, as you travel your pathway – your bridge to Heaven.

"The Moderator today again expressed his great joy and feeling of fulfillment that I, too, was able to bring back these memories of the transportation to the spiritual planet. The many visions related before were of a different nature; often they were mental projections from the Brothers of Light – the Flame People, but this 'trip' was an actual visitation such as He wrote in his Pulse of Creation books, as he says:

371

'Now I can go when the time is right, knowing full well that the work will continue, that I shall be completely able to work through and with you as we travel on the Inner together in these Inner Mansions or dimensions! He feels as he has related, that this is the most vital part of his cause, for now he knows his mission shall be carried on, even though his cycle has been completed and that which he came to do, to express and to help prepare this one, has been achieved. As he says, 'My feeling of fulfillment is complete, I can now go on any time, knowing all things which I so set up to do have been accomplished in this present time on this, the earth plane,' and as he continued, 'Now this robot or android man can return to his people any time, for I can be satisfied that I can carry on from the Inner through you and with the compatible frequency which we have created as an oscillating polarity through eons of time in the future! So be it!"

All that which is in Heaven
has made my life complete.

* * *

Vaughn: Now in the past few days as the home of the da Vinci's was visited, and inspected, it was found it to be not only a home but

372

is a vast combined home and teaching center. However, upon further visitations and psychic viewing, that which seemed to be one large home was, in fact and essence, but one section of the seven large sections! Now these sections were constructed in the form of a concentric circle because of its immense dimension. I had been viewing but one of these great sections. The circle was divided into sections of seven, similar to cutting a pie, however, they did not meet at a point but had a very large, inner courtyard which was, in essence, a small parkland completely given over to shrubbery, flowers, plants, waterfalls and the familiar pools. Around the perimeter of the park area are seen beautiful flowing water fountains, placed periodically about the lovely grounds. These fountains are, of course, decorated with the most graceful crystal sculpturing.

Now, centermost in this courtyard stands a large conical-shaped building. This cone-shaped structure is of the familiar gold coloring. From the uppermost portion radiates seven varicolored crystal lenses; the purpose of these lenses is to pick up the frequencies from the students involved in study, who are furthering their evolution and come to these centers to study. These students are projecting their psychokinetical mind energies into these lenses. The lenses then act as a transformer by which means these energies are sorted into a particular frequency and then directed towards the earth world or astral dimension from which these students have come. Ioshanna: Is this all done directly or do you think these accumulated energies have to go to the lens or anything first? Vaughn: I believe that is the first step. The lens, of course, is the vast storehouse through which the frequencies are then sorted out and additional intelligence is added to that which the students have carried, then projected out through the lens atop the conical shaped temple.

Ioshanna: When you drew this little diagram of the large conical temple that is standing in the middle of this courtyard, and when you drew the small point at the top, I immediately thought, that is where the energies come out to go into the lens; and the lens is evidently right atop this conical building! They are projected into, and intensified or picked up, regenerated and from there, they are drawn or projected, and demodulated down. Of course, the crown and the wand steps them down still further into the earth's aura for the earthman's frequency. The very minute you drew the diagram, I thought: that peak is situated directly under the lens.

Now, this was true also when you talked about the great building where the conclave was held which is conical shaped. Of course, this is the very purpose for the building to be conical-shaped, that it not only collects the energies, but being in that shape itself, intensifies or regenerates. Vaughn: In other words it is a directive force itself, simply because of its shape, the purpose of a triangle being to intensify any energies that have been collected within its own structure. Ioshanna: Yes, there is something very interesting about that shape because all of the pyramids in the past were made that way, so it is a very fascinating thing to me, that shape. Vaughn: We are finding out now, this is the most scientific factor and important key — the conical cone and the lens in combination and conjunction with the higher mind energies that are always interplaying and adding to, so we really have a vast and fantastic electronic system, to be oscillated down into the earthman's mind!

Ioshanna: Can you tell us anything else about that wonderful cone-shaped building that centers these teaching areas? That fascinates me. Vaughn: The cone-shaped building serves as a focal point for the students when they, themselves, are ready for a certain progression in their evolutionary progress according to the section from which they are receiving their instructions; so, in a sense, the temple serves as a method through which they receive their promotions. They receive it in an unusual method, in that they have a change or stepup in their own psychic anatomies. This is their so-called reward. Ioshanna: I am glad you said that, because I got that today, too, and I think that is wonderful. In this home-academy arrangement, you say they actually have also the red-crystal quartz block and flame? Where would that be located in the cone-shaped building? Vaughn: It is always directly under the apex of a column, which is exactly equidistant from the four corners of the outside perimeter of the building and which is, of course, circular.

Vaughn: Maybe this would be a good time to explain the mechanics of the red quartz crystal cube upon which the pillar of flame rests. Now, what is the relationship between the quartz block and the flame? Ioshanna: Well, of course, crystal is always a regenerator itself, and a great intensifier. Now, if I understand it right, these flames have to be built up with the other mind energies, but it is indicated too, that is an eternal flame; that it never dies; that it is also called the unfed flame, as they used to term it in Atlantis, and/or Lemuria. Vaughn: Now in this teaching center, the da Vinci academy, this flame also exists. It has already been created from the mind energies of the higher intelligences; that is, from your own and Leonardo's mind energies, and other masters there, but it is existent for these students, for their progression. They, themselves, have nothing to do with its creation. They only partake. Ioshanna: Now isn't that interesting that they can create these energies as a great pillar of fire and there it remains! Isn't that an interesting thing? Because they so created it in that particular manner, there it remains; it oscillates and scintillates, is very glittering. Sparks dart out from it. Those flames, I am sure, have fascinated many people, and one doesn't make a great deal of progress unless one has passed through those flames many times. Vaughn: The whole concept here is electronics. There is a purpose or relationship between one frequency and another, so the crystal block, in itself, is sort of a prism and the crystals have been formed through psychokinetical means so that there is a regeneration of the mind energies which are focused upon the crystal block and which, in turn, act as a catalyst, plus the prisms of the red, blue and yellow frequencies placed around the conical structure on the inside of the top portion, all of which act as a pulsating generating station, we might say. Once set in motion it is eternal, it is a perpetual motion machine, if you want to call it a machine, which it isn't. It holds the key to all of life.

Ioshanna: When the hierarchy said they were going to divulge the very secrets of heaven and life, they weren't fooling. I just don't know how much deeper one can get than this. It is creation! Vaughn: This might be going off the subject, but one of the great wall scenes (in the conclave temple) depicts this living flame as being created on the earth plane at the time of Zoroaster. When it was formed it was done out in the open, in a forest amongst very tall trees, a big, open space and the Higher Ones would visit the eartheans. They would actually come and visit them through the flame, because they could materialize thusly. This was many thousands of years after Atlantis. Ioshanna: Now, what about the colored lens? You say the lenses were on the outside of this conically shaped building that pick up the mind energies from those on the inner? Are they on the outside or

the inside? Vaughn: They are on both the outside and inside. It is very interesting about
these lenses. They act as sort of both a receiving and sending station! The energies are received from the inside (they are from the accu-
mulations) and projected outwardly to the outside, but before they are projected out, there is
another arrangement by which the great crystal
lens, which is in a parabolic effect, a convex
shape, that is over, above and outside the building where there then is an additional regeneration
of other frequencies that come from the great
crystal lens outside, then redirected back into
the seven lenses, which again are redirected to
the various earth dimensions. It is a two-way
situation. The wonderful part of it is, this is a
very special projector because these frequencies, projected through these lenses, are being
projected to certain people. I mean it is a very
selective situation; these are the people who
are related to this particular expression, which
is philosophy, science, art, teaching and the
directive aspects. Ioshanna: I am sure in every instance, these frequencies or electronics
that are projected from these higher minds to the
earth individual is all done strictly and purely
on an individual basis. It isn't that they just
gather a whole bunch of frequencies and say,
'pow, there you are', and toss them out into the
ethers. It is very different because every instance has a particular and specific individual
need, and only specific kinds of frequencies
are directed for each one's particular need.

That is what this wand has to do; it is a computer and locates and designates the specific need of the individual for whatever type of healing that is needed. It calculates and directs this particular, specific frequency into the individual so it is a very complicated and exacting science that is being related here. Now I think we pretty well understand that and perhaps the artist's drawings will relate this further, as it is rather difficult to convey this type of picture in words. These lenses about which you were speaking, Vaughn, certain circles, we shall say, were cut out of the cone building and the lenses inserted so that one can see through them and they emit the color through the lens. In other words, one sees them both from within and without the building? Vaughn: Yes, that's right. Ioshanna: You know, Vaughn, at one time I bought a bed lamp for the Moderator. It was a conical shaped blue glass lamp, and around it were impregnated colored glass beads. That fascinated me, and when I took it home, he said, "I once wore a hat like that, many thousands of years ago!" This now all adds up and makes so much sense. The whole picture is falling into place. To think of all that vast assemblage, of all these countless thousands of souls, of higher beings who were collected in that temple before at the assemblage and all wore those conical hats. This was the way of collecting their mind energies. Now you say this temple at our home was also shaped like that, so if we think on that, it gives us a wonderfully expanded consciousness. Vaughn: We can understand that the major purpose and the basis for life are the psycho-kinetical energies, all purposeful in their shapes, and which have baffled men for countless ages! They never could understand why the pyramids were shaped as they were. Ioshanna: Yes, I think the pyramids had some kind of pearloid covering; of course, there was gold on top, with some kind of pearloid covering. Vaughn: Yes, the pyramids were mostly a representation of the actual electronic generating station from Lemuria and Atlantis. These newer pyramids didn't really operate; they were merely stone replicas of the originals in the truly ancient times. Ioshanna: You know, Vaughn, there are many, many people who would like to know about the pyramids, about this vital and all-important function, this electronic plan, that you have described. My, it is a mind expanding situation!

Vaughn: If one wanted to, one could describe the electronic nature of these broadcasting stations and how they supply every known concept of power, which would completely eliminate all the varieties and means by which the lower planes accumulate their power sources. They have a variety of means, gas, electric, the chemicals such as coal. They have steam generating stations, and all of these are obsolete because the Infinite Creator abounds with energies. It is just a matter of drawing from it, and this can be done if one understands the mechanics by which the Infinite Itself oscillates. So here we have a perpetual motion generating station which supplies all the needs for man and which gives them the opportunity to give themselves over to the higher understanding of the finite individuals so that they, themselves, will find their own hookup with their higher selves or inner nature. Ioshanna: That information is wonderful and is a fine addition to the former revelations. It was said, wasn't it, that each one of these seven sections represented or designated or was specifically created for the different expressions. Vaughn: I don't believe we divulged the expressions. These teachings are in the area of science and include or cover all of the scientific fields of present-day knowledge, and of course. beyond – the biological sciences, the physical sciences, physics, astronomy, astrology, etc. The expression of philosophy, the esthetic sense of the relationship of man to the Infinite. the expression of art through the forms of dance. of painting, sculpturing, and the various art forms, such as jewelry, goldsmithing, carvings. the innumerable methods by which man relates himself in a graphical way, to nature.

Then we have the expression of teaching: the ways in which the clear understanding of man can be taught through the various mediums – either in writing and in directorship to the lower levels of expression. In the expression of art we have also the literary arts, the creation of poetry and literature.

So it must be realized that each of the seven great sections of this, we've termed 'academy', serve as one specific dimension or phase of learning; philosophy in one building, music in another of the seven, art, etc., so that no one study group interferes with the other. Yet, there is integration in all individual departments, but the vast differences in all these incredible centers of teaching is that the student enters into the subject himself in various ways, other than simply reading. If he is studying, for instance, acting and projection, he actually starts with the factual stage presentations and likewise, on into all seven sections. Yes, it can be factually said, of those so studying painting, they are visited periodically by the one whose great construction this is — Leonardo da Vinci himself — and he is very apt to take the brush of the student and personally give suggestions, adding a few strokes himself. Likewise, Iona (or Uriel) visits the various sections and lends her own wisdom in dance, drama, music, poetry, sculpturing etc. Ioshanna especially favors the operettas and often bedecks herself out in the regalia of some beautiful role, joining the great choruses. Oh, yes, she has expressed on the earth plane in such lead roles as Donato, for it was she who lived the life of one called Lurietta. She was then a coloratura soprano (1817).

Among the various and numerous interesting innovations seen in this great and lovely academy, (as well as a unit within the home of the da Vinci's) is what the earthman would term a television. The so-called screen covers a good portion of one entire wall. One views, not a small square box, but sees the entire area. One can tune in to any planet within its vast radius and zaps in unto the city or town, or he obtains any news on just about anything desired.

Now this incredible equipment shows not merely some flat surface screen or viewing, but one sees the scenes in third, fourth, and fifth dimensions; all people thereon seem most life-like. The details as to how it functions are not presently related, but it is indicated that such equipment shall, in time, be made known on earth. When one has come to the end of that which he cares to view, a pass of the hand causes the entire screen to slip back between the walls of the room, out of the way. This television viewing is quite advanced to that of the earth plane, as are all things on these inner worlds of Light.

Both Vaughn and myself were fascinated as we saw the great size of the screen, which could easily be compared with your movie screens but the realism was most incredible. We are fascinated with this sighting and thought how wonderful when the earth people can enjoy such viewing. Of course, none of the usual advertising was existent there, nor were any of the decadent pictures of violence so common on earth but rather, all programs, if one can term them such, were of an uplifting or educational nature. Even those made for pure enjoyment, all carried the continuity or continued life in the stories. The enjoyment level was raised greatly as we were introduced to these unique television systems.

* * *

Vaughn: It seems our great pleasure, Iona, has been in reminiscing, reliving, thinking upon and reattuning to various parts, scenes, activities and all of the procession of this great Conclave has been as interesting and exciting as the first time we viewed it! I could not count the many times that I have passed the entire procedure through my mind and each time greater understanding, or more vivid description, or display is made evident in my consciousness. Especially was the most exquisite crystal floor, which you described just after you had entered the great Hall of Learning, which we have called by so many different names. We have termed it a museum, a temple, an enclosure, a structure, a building; and yet there is no one name that would properly define this great and magnificent enclosure! Its purpose, as was mentioned, is mainly for educational purposes. For, what with these great, live scenics throughout the entire many miles of walls, both interior and on the outside, as well as the various artistic portrayals of the paintings and art work, throughout the entire thoroughfare upon the great golden crystal floor, the beautiful floor with the rosy hue. All these things, I keep returning to, in consciousness and it seems almost sacriligious to just view them once and forget about them; it could not be done. It just couldn't be done, because it is so mind-expanding and creates such a beautiful feeling within one to reattune. We again sense the warmth, the beautiful radiation and the love that exists everywhere there;

the peace profound; the beautiful serenity which each Being there possesses or expresses; that it is a most delightful experience to again return in consciousness. As we do so, we can again view this great elaborate display of beautiful art, the art work which we have not been able to factually relate, as yet. We have talked little about it; but surely, earth words do not convey the great reality of it all. For instance, the elegant and exquisite work that is portrayed in the crystal structures of the floors themselves, exhibited these paintings and art which seems luminous from within or behind. Each art work, painting or whatever it may have been, seems lighted from within and we view it as a fourth or fifth dimensional reality which has depth, breadth and height. The texture of the face in the portraits just seems to take on life, a radiance, as one looks into the eyes of these beautiful old portraits. One actually tunes into the psychic anatomy or creation of this great art work and is transcended with the viewing. For he tunes into the psychic anatomy of the artist or painter, who is, in many instances, a very advanced spiritual Being himself. Thus we can, through this means and by this measure, attune to the whole or entire infinite dimensions.

Ioshanna: As you have so related, Vaughn, of the floor, and as we again think upon these things, we can see it is literally covered with these great art works of the past, such as the beautiful paintings of Michelangelo, of Leonardo da Vinci, of Van Gogh and many of the others

385

who have been spiritually quickened and portray in their art work, the energies from these higher dimensions which will relate the viewer unto this higher frequency and attunement to the spiritual worlds. This is the great difference and importance between an ordinary painting and one from a truly developed genius or artist. And what a wonderful thing it was that you viewed as you call her, your Madonna of the past, as you tuned into the great portrait on the floor which da Vinci had painted of her and that it opened up something within you that you could, at that moment, remember that this was the great painting of the (what you call) your Madonna, in your consciousness, in a time of your life when you needed love and to have some direction. It has served, as you so aptly put it, as a pivot point, or a turning point in your entire evolution to that of one of a more upwards direction. At the same moment there, you came into the vivid realization of who da Vinci was; that this one here in the third dimension, called Ioshanna, was actually the biocentric of Leonardo, who painted the portrait; and this meant a great deal to you. I remember well, when that happened in our living room, that it was indeed a quickening or revelation to you. I saw the illumination come over your face and your eyes and, for the moment, you got a bit wobbly, or jelly-kneed, so to speak; for I knew that something wonderful was happening to you! Says Vaughn: That was indeed a most memorable and never-to-be-forgotten moment in my entire evolution! Ioshanna: I know too, Vaughn, that you will be able to tune into other scenes on the wall and the floors, as they are so numerous and one could, frankly, never come to the end of this great educational center! Ioshanna: But, do you know the most interesting, I believe and shall we say, most surprising of all, and yet there should really be no surprises with me, for I have worked with these things on the inner for countless thousands of years, to help in the preparation of it all; and yet, my higher self has evidently blocked certain things from my conscious mind to reserve, in a sense, a bit of the surprise element. So it was, as was said, a bit of a surprise to me, when upon these great walls were viewed the entire procession of this great pageant from start to finish, in the many, many points of interest!

As one enters on the left side of the wall, begins this procession and there, in full life color (and the pictures are much more than life-size), they do take up a great portion of the wall; each one portraying a part of the procession. The picture, which portrays the great and sharp-looking group of trumpeters as it actually took place, there they are lined up in such a precise way, their toes all seemingly on some invisible line, with their shiny white boots that reach over their knees, half up to their hips. The great colorful frock coats that hang down from their shoulders in a most beautiful blue, contrast between the rest of their suit, which is gold. Then, on the right shoulder of each, is this great red drape, or scarf, with many folds that drape down over the arm, which holds the trumpet and which is most graceful in its fullness as it nearly touches the ground. Their heads, topped with the conical gold helmets upon which rests the two beautiful ostrich plumes, one of red and one of blue and their trumpets all at attention similar to some tall swords at their sides – what a striking picture they make!

Then, it was just after these trumpeters sounded off that the tiny ring bearer stepped forth in her sprightly little steps, bearing her pillow with the precious load – the two rings. Behind her came the great group of the tiny flower tots, bedecked in their little dresses, each portraying some individual flower, each of the color of the particular flower they represented. On the tops of their heads were tiny hats with the stamen of the particular flower. Oh, they did make such a glorious picture there with the many, many beautiful white doves overhead, where, you remember, the various colored birds had just made their exit that the doves could have full possession of the entire upper area; and how the doves were attached together with the colored ribbons. Wasn't that a beautiful sight to behold? He replied, Oh, indeed so! And now, directly underneath the doves, the beautiful Queen has made her entrance with the great train that stretches out over several blocks in length. At each side of this great beautiful billowing train, we see the elegant ladies, each holding one side; they who carried the great sheaths of flowers in the other arm, and that were tied with the great bows that hung to the floor. Yes, Ioshanna, remember how these beautiful ladies were all specially picked and were noted for being both of beautiful face and form, and how elegant they looked in their gowns, all of a different shade, representing the dimension from which they came, and upon their heads, each wore the beautiful tiara. Oh, this was an unforgettable, beautiful picture. Now, all I need to do is tune into these beautiful portrayals on the wall that show each and every section and, as was said, these depictions seem to actually come to life as we slowly pass in front of them. They seem to actually create the motion and I can tune in now to these depictions as the lovely flower ladies, the bridesmaids, with their elegant long, flowing golden hair which hangs down near to their waistline. And upon looking at the portrayals again, it is noted that they all have beautiful blue eyes. Then we see the procession moves forward and on through the several blocks into the distance, in order that the great and vast assemblage, which number many, many thousands, may have their view and attunement with the beautiful entourage. Again, the next scene shows her continuing on around the great circle as she moves forward with this great throng. It is noted, that about in the center area and up about midway towards the ceiling, there is a large, seemingly pink, cloud upon which rests seven little groups of the tiniest Angels, all dressed in their sheer little nighties; each wearing a little halo of gold, carrying the tiny instruments – the flute, the violin, the triangle. One, I noticed in each group, had a big base viol. The very interesting part of these darling tiny Angels, (the littlest Angels) is that instead of having individual auras, each little group of seven is engulfed and encompassed in one large aura, as though it was one person and each little group of seven is encircled with a little golden band around the edge of this great circle as though they always travel together. What a beautiful sound comes from these little groups of seven. They seem to hover just over the entourage over the Queen herself, as they move along with the procession. That is the next scene that is shown upon the walls here. I know Ioshanna, you are seeing and enjoying it with me, even though you are more quiet about it, but remember the scene now in view, how it is at this point that we draw nigh to the great and vast chorus of these beautiful opera singers! I don't believe that we have yet been made aware of the number, but it now seems they are thirty three thousand in number. The great chorus here is very large and the music coming from that section is most magnificent. Never was there anything quite like it; for I am sure they have such an accumulation of beautiful voices, never before assembled. These personages have come from places other than the earth world; from other spiritual planets as well, and they all have an especial affinity with the honored guest – the Queen. For, as was told, she was, at one time, one of these vocalists.

The next point of interest that is shown upon the walls, after the entourage has encircled to a good extent, the entire circumference of the conical temple, is that where the Queen meets the Moderator (the One who was, on the earth plane called, the Moderator). As you told, the wall scenes do show his light is so brilliant, that one can scarce see anything other than a great white circular light. But as He met this Queen, Ioshanna, and she took his arm, he was, at that time with his biune and they took her to meet her biocentric, Leonardo, who was but a few steps beyond.

Again the portrayals on the wall here show, first the Moderator and his biocentric, Erza, (who are now named Raphiel and Muriel), the other two Archangels; however, the two new Archangel names – Michiel and Uriel – were not bestowed upon the newly-crowned and ascended biocentrics until after the crowning took place. Thus as it shows, in the next great and glorious color, real-life depiction or, as you have termed it and more factually so, the reenactments of the next action that took place, was the ascension of the two, Raphiel and Muriel, who are the Moderator and his polarity, as they ascended the three crystal-colored tiers and walked through the three great pillars of fire. There they awaited atop the throne platform until the two at the base of the throne made their ascent. The scene I like most is the one of the tall Angel of the Night, as he is called Love who held and read from the Book of Life, the cere-

391

mony that joined the two as one. He is such a soulful one, and tall! The comparison in his size and the tiny tot of three, who is shown reaching to him, high above her head with both hands, the tiny pillow of rings — he, being almost gigantic, had to stoop low to reach. It made such a jolly sight. Then the two are seen within this unique depiction upon the wall as they follow up the three colored tiers and through the flames of gold, until they arrived at the top where the other biocentrics (the Overlords) stood in await.

Then, in the next depiction, we see as we move along the wall, the two great Angels that suddenly appeared on either side of the great throne; and it was just after the great Overlord was placing the crown upon the head of Ioshanna, they suddenly and silently made their beautiful appearance, each with his very long wand of gold with a brilliant star at the end. And after the Moderator had touched Ioshanna on the shoulder with his golden wand, which was the electronic computer, almost simultaneously did the beautifully tall Angels dip down in unison and together, they touched one shoulder of the Queen with their wands, then they were gone. These were especially beautiful in their luminescence. They had such a warmth about them, and within, such a glow. The love they emitted was indefinable, for they were very, very advanced Beings and had come from a very distant galaxy. They just made the great trip for this one moment's appearance; they dare not stay long in this very ascended consciousness. Then the Queen placed her hand, momentarily, upon the beautiful great Book of Life, in a new dedication as the pair of biocentrics each expressed the symbolic gesture, common to all those in the assemblage. The assemblage, all joined and in unison, the two forefingers of the right hand touched the forehead, the heart, the lips; then the hand was raised in front and above the face. Each and every one of the many, many thousands of illumined persons in this entire great assemblage, joined in that instant rededication of Love to the all-creative Infinite; a rededication of each to his own forward and regenerative, progressive evolution.

This is a beautiful depiction upon the wall- one I love and treasure most of all. It was at that very moment, as likewise shown, that the great and wondrous One, called Serapis, appeared – remember, the One who just never appears in anything other than this great golden flame. He must be twenty feet tall and seven or eight feet in diameter, this great golden flame, who so swiftly and unobtrusively dropped so lightly upon the water and there oscillated, giving his mental message of Love to all who were present and, especially directed to those atop the great crystal throne platform. This was a momentous experience and time – a moment long to be remembered by all present. Ioshanna: I might say, Vaughn, that I have always had a great affinity and feeling of love for this One called Serapis. He has often entered my con-

consciousness and I have a great feeling for the very advanced Being that he is. Although his stay was no longer than perhaps sixty seconds, then he was gone. It was a most impressive experience to all! Great Love then generated, most Infinite in nature.

Then, as we travel down the wall very slowly, we see the next depiction and, a most impressive one, for the moment has arrived where the great Overlord Leader and his biune take the throne. They, as one, take the seat. As he sits, his hands touch the great golden arms; this, then sets all electronics in action! And, as has been related, all Heaven opens up. Doubtless has there ever been, or will there ever be again such an electronic explosion! So much electricity was generated in that flash second, that it seemed to illuminate the entire Heavens above and all about. And I'm sure many wondered whether they would regain their sight; yet, full protection had been installed for everyone present, and no harm was felt. Yet it was quite a shocking experience by all, and only portrayed, perhaps not to a full extent, but related regarding the vast powers that now have been made available for the earth worlds below. It is interesting to note as we view this scene upon the wall, how almost everything is blotted out by this great white circle of Light. It seems to fill the entire temple area; but if we look closely, we can see all the people below.

Then, moving into the next area of the elegant wall, is shown the couple have moved down another tier of crystal steps that are simply of a rosy hue! They are confronted with their great golden coach – a princess coach if you will, or perhaps more correctly, a queenly one; and a more exquisite golden coach there has never been. It is beautiful beyond any description; exquisitely carved and embedded in the carvings are pressed gems of emeralds of green and blue, similar to the coloring of the peacock. Over the oval circular crystal doors of the coach of gold, is the insignia to the da Vinci's ray. Their scientific symbol is inlaid with diamonds. As we look closely, it is plain to see that the decoration on this gold coach is matched by the reins and bridle of the horses, which is likewise embedded with gems – all precious; and this is a most beautiful display! As we look to the depiction, here we see the whole thing come into action; we see the beautiful, prancing horses, rearing their arched heads back; they appear to be nodding as they step so highly with their golden hoofs, their graceful and narrow ankles making a very beautiful picture indeed, as the very sedate coachmen sit erect atop the coach, with their costumes so brilliant.

Then we see in the next depiction, the inside of the coach which is all lined with downy soft cushions of gold, upon the floor of which is a tiny square cushion upon which her slippers of crystal will rest. There is a package she is seen opening, with a large golden bow. As the top is popped off the box, there is seen lying in the pink cotton below, an indescrib-

able, great seven-pointed star, made purely from
diamonds; it is a very large and an elegant star!
As her biune related, it was a resemblance of
her, star-ship to him, that she reminded him of
a big, beautiful, shining star — his guiding star.
Of course, this, she treasured most highly; a
most loved gift. Then is shown the coach moving
forward, as again the doves make their entrance
to usher the beautiful coach. This scene shows
the countless assemblage, all tossing their beautiful flower blossoms from the crowd toward the
coach, and they use their mind energies to lift
the blossoms so that they do not drop to the
floor, but they are actually raised more to the
ceiling. The result is an actual raining of flower
petals. This scene is most beautiful! These
flowers continue to be tossed and rained upon
them throughout the entire exit which, of course,
continues on for several miles. Before the coach
had proceeded far, the tiny door was seen to pop
open and, as is depicted here in the next scene,
the tiny glass-slippered foot is shown outside
the door; the slipper has been slipped off and
raised high in the air; about it has been formed
a tiny golden rainbow! This, of course, simply
symbolic of the high radiations from this queenly
one.

Of course, no one chose to have this great
celebration terminate, and the wonderful part of
it all, as we have been told, is that it shall continue for an entire year — this projection program! All one need to do to again return, to feel
and to see, and to express this beautiful proces-

396

sion, is to think upon these things, and there we can again be present. This is the greatest gift of all!

These three gifts were assembled here in one large portrayal; the beautiful star of diamonds, the elegant peacock of blue, and the beautiful rose which (the one she calls the Moderator), the great Overlord of all who is now ascended to another planetary system so presented unto her; the rose that shall never wilt or die, and serves as an attunement 'tween the two.

When we look further along the wall, it is shown that the great Caruso, himself, is presenting to the Queen, a special vocalization in her honor. Then we see a portrayal of the most exquisite and elegant and again indescribable painting, which the beloved Raphael has so created for her. It is actually a great crystal dome, which will serve as her ceiling over her bed; for she has long treasured this beautiful drawing, one only Raphael could do, in his special manner and way that has always meant so much to her. She has long been in love with his work. So he has extended his love in this great and unforgettable painting for her, the group of angels and, of course, this great host of angels were those represented which did gather at one time during the pageant – those who projected their thoughts and their energies, through the hum of their voices. They were especially Illumined Ones. It was they who each held one long-stemmed, beautiful red rose; and at the same time, the flower girls were dropping their petals upon the thoroughfare. This great angelic group all dropped their roses, one each, toward our Queen as she passed under the gathering. It is all so beautifully portrayed here and, yet, it is true. Ioshanna says – I could scarcely make these attunements without being so transcended, that it is most difficult to speak; my jaw seems to get rather disconnected in the upliftment.

Although the entire assemblage did not attend, we do see here upon the walls, the great and beautiful home which Leonardo and Ioshanna (now Uriel and Michiel), have been creating for themselves throughout the centuries past, all made of the crystal structures and as she so viewed it in 1964, as she, herself, had the very vivid vision and realization.

Then, as we attune further, we see the other scenes showing the coach winding through the many beautiful and glorious parkways, that surround this great temple for miles in each direction; parkways that are filled with beauty everywhere; the various and numerous sculptured gardens, all things in perfect order, all things numbered accurately and harmoniously related. All these things have been grown and formed with the mind energies of those living in these Higher Worlds. The countless number of trees, plants and flowers grow so luxuriantly and abundantly, and the varieties of green are of countless shades; most of which seem to be of the paler greens, and many of the leaves one can see through, as they are of the crystalline structure – all soft as velvet to the touch. Everywhere and about all things, there is this radiation and feeling of love, of warmth, of oneness, of pacifism and joy, and of the actual infinite nature of all things that exist. Yes, all these things and many more, I have seen. Says Vaughn: Yes, Ioshanna, I have shared with you many of these visions, especially the many beautiful portrayals upon the wall; and I plan to make many more contacts, or to recontact the wall areas and the floor areas to obtain for you more of these magnificent and incredible reenactments. This will be my gift to you that you may include these in our book. We now know the true meaning of Heaven – it is no illusion, but quite different than the religionists portray it. Most wonderful of all – it's all only a thought away!

In thinking back and reiterating, through my psychic visions during most of these entire two weeks, both Ioshanna and I, together did "see" many additional scenes of different parts of the ceremony. As I focused attention more particularly pointed, greater detail was conceived. The temple was viewed as pyramidal in shape, except the sides were curved or rounded, or cone-shaped. In viewing from this above vantage point, I saw that approximately a hundred feet below, the roof spans out and down into pillars. In other words, instead of being solid all the way down, it separated itself and descended as fine pillars. Moreover, the pillars weren't vertical but were slanted at a ninety-degree angle. The building appeared to be standing on spider legs, except, of course, as we came close, we could see that they were not spidery. They were at least twenty-five feet thick, but the construction gave the spidery or dainty appearance.

One sees throughout the entire circumference of the building, the columns at a ninety-degree angle; and separated by at least seventy-five feet. Each of these "legs" (or props) gave the appearance of a colonnade. One could walk under and around the periphery of this gigantic building and the effect was quite startling. Moreover, the closest parallel I can come to, in any comparison of this great Temple, is by having viewed the Eiffel Tower in Paris, France. The architectural style of the lower portion is similar, but that is the only similarity. The temple is built something like a pyramid so that one may walk through and under the columns. There is a peculiar and very beautiful coloration that one "feels". As one walks around the periphery of the building, the frequencies in the crystals which form the columns are different for each column, and as one passes through, it is like walking through bands of rainbow-hued lights. It is as moving through the energies which one passes in certain ceremonies in these higher dimensions for cleansing.

So, if one were just to walk around the building, it would be quite a distance, at least about twenty-five miles. One would be refreshed simply by walking around any colonnade. These columns or pillars — thirty-three in number — form the foundation of the building. This huge temple — actually a living museum — has been built with such perfection, there is nothing in it that doesn't have a particular reason and an educational benefit to the visiting guest. One must pass through the doorways for which he is conditioned, and be of that particular frequency. One feels it — the archways emit the delicate fragrance which is the frequency itself of that particular dimension or realm; so one is directed or guided by that and the person's psychic antenna oscillates one toward the particular entrance which will be harmonious for that person's purpose or need.

After the ceremony, or Conclave of the Light Beings, the great cathedral is not closed because of the completion of the ceremony, for it is open to all who come in sleep state or from other astral or spiritual dimensions. One can come and enjoy a "holiday". One can view the extensive historical pageantry extending throughout all the walls and within the great crystal thoroughfares (we've termed floors) and for which one is conditioned.

The pageantry is such, that as one walks through the doorway, one sees life-like depictions of many thousands and thousands of years of the histories of the worlds and planes of the particular dimension of the administration of that Logos or Archangel. One can receive a great deal of instruction. In effect, it is all most educational; for when one views the scenes, the information is impregnated in the psychic, and whatever was necessary for the particular purpose to include in one's intelligence, is provided for that particular person!

The great cathedral or ceremony-temple was built especially for these spiritual energy projections, as well as to serve in this educational way, as the historical museum to the earths. Thus, the conical-shaped structure, similar to a pyramid but much, much larger in size, was built so that the energies could be directed upward and out through the specially-prepared conical opening, which added, due to the particular shape, a great thrust or boost, similar in effect to the booster of the lift-off in your moon ship.

Speaking of the all-important shape of this great structure, which we have so limitedly called a building or temple – a cathedral or museum would be a closer descriptive word – yet that, too, is far too limiting. Yes, the cone or conical or pyramidal shape is most vital for the energy purposes, even to the extent that all persons living in this great City of Light, wear the tall, conical hats of gold. Various gems are impregnated therein, according to the individual's particular frequency or dimension. All expressions on this great plateau are purely scientific and exemplify an extreme state of perfection.

The glorious temple or museum itself, was created, as was said, from all the collected Minds, the psychokinetical energies and the spiritual energies of all the great Beings, the spiritual Beings who live in this great city! They are all scientific, Spiritual Beings, and at least of the degree of Master before they

402

can (due to frequency relationship) even live in the great crystalline city of Parhelion or on the planet Eros, itself. Everything that is created, everything that is manifest, is done in no way with the hands but is formed with psychokinetical and mind energies, regenerative in nature; all in radiant crystalline beauty beyond compare. One experiences the feeling of wanting never to leave there — that is, those who visit in astral state, or as our physical mind sleeps and we become separated in consciousness, that we can so traverse to this great colorful world of beauty — at least in consciousness or astrally. It is truly a most unforgettable experience, and life-changing!

It is indeed realized by myself, that I shall never again be the same as before entering (even psychically) this vast array of color, of intense high frequencies, and a love never before sensed; the Infinite love by which all persons live in these inner worlds of Light. Yes, I've had a wondrous visit to "Heaven"; moreover, when e'er another attunement is made, or thought is directed toward any particular part of the great pageantry, it can again be regenerated or viewed and greater details conceived; details which were far too vast and numerous to ever conceive in one single viewing. Thus, the entire Conclave of Light Beings is an eternal creation existing infinitely! And it is but a matter of attuning to it!

And it's quite true as Ioshanna says, "This, the most frustrating experience of my life; to try to bring all this, almost inconceivable heaven of light, beauty and the very Infinite, and put it all in mere third dimensional words! But we make the attempt and depend upon the reader to tune into the frequency beam and thereby view, in part (perhaps) from time to time, and likewise experience his own Parhelion visitation in astral attunement. At this time, of but a few days after the heavenly visit, several students have, themselves, obtained glimpses of one part or another." Thus we say, "A most enlightening attunement!"

Yes, every scene which had been enacted was here on the walls all displayed in living reality. Oh, this was quite startling and mind-expanding, an inconceivable concept to the earth mind. And now we know from whence came the beautiful story of Cinderella. Someone had had a peek in this beautiful city of crystal and had tuned in to this future event, now taking place. So it is little wonder that Iona, herself, even as an adult woman and mature, enjoyed watching the movie, Cinderella, whenever there was the opportune time. She literally loved the story! And so is she possibly now, back into her physical earth world, again one who but had a beautiful dream? No, indeed! Iona continues to live and relive these beautiful memories of all this and much, much more; for it is not in the past with her, but remains ever with her in the present.

And, indeed, there is a happy ending, although there frankly is no ending to anything;

for now she knows how joyous the earth man shall be when he comes to the realization of these beautiful worlds, cities and experiences.

Now, if this all sounds like some fairytale, just try tuning in, to attempt if you will, to place within your mind these pictures. You may be surprised how you, too, may be transported or transcended, and that these glorious realities, these energy configurations which are living now in the present and shall, throughout eternity, become a reality within each one. Yes, dear ones, this is the world of Creation; this is the world of love, beauty and joy. This is that which the earth man has called Heaven, which he has so sadly distorted in so many ways. First, he must get straight with himself. He must eliminate his fears and his guilts. He must begin to discharge the many hatreds, the lusts, and begin to live the life as the Creator has so intended it to be lived. Then he, too, shall thus come unto the Kingdom of Heaven, as our dear Sister Iona has thus seen and experienced.

Yes, these scenes, these activities, all that which has been going on here is not strange to you, beloved Channel, Iona, for you have, in your sleep state, or ascended or separated states, been active in all these creations as well for the many years now, not only as you have lived this earth life but of the countless thousands of years of the past that you have so taken part in all these glorious and colorful energy crystalline creations.

It must be said that I, myself, in these mental

and psychic attunements do often become quite overcome and can scarce eject the words through the vocal cords.

Ioshanna: The entire history of all the numerous historical epochs in which both Leonardo and myself have been so involved throughout these five hundred thousand years is most interesting. Vaughn: There is no doubt that you and Leonardo have graced the earth planes with many noteworthy lifetimes and the records that have been left have yet, in many cases, to be unearthed by the archaeologists in their diggings. Going along further in my viewing of the temple wall, I see a scene depicting a civilization called Atlantis. There is shown here a city called Poseid, and that there is a king by the same name, Poseid. This king is the self-same person as yourself. Ioshanna: That is so familiar to me. I have delved into everything that I could find about Poseid. Vaughn: The Poseids, as the inhabitants were called, because of their pride of living under the influence of their king, Poseid, were a peaceful happy race. A great city is shown built on terraces. These terraces have been so designed that each house has a separation from the other and is beautifully landscaped with all manners of flowers, shrubs and trees. Many colors are predominant. Ioshanna: The Moderator and I have looked for that particular thing for many years, that you are describing — that type of a place on a hill, with complete seclusion! Vaughn: That is proof, isn't it? Now there is a system of transportation. On the top of each home is a flat roof, and one can navigate his own airship. They had individual air travel, as well as a public form of transportation. They dock their airships on top of their house. Also these terraces were quite wide and embraced a distance of a mile or more. The houses were quite some distance from the central city. In the city itself, there was a public transportation system which carried people without any cost to them. This system was an automated tube which slipped or slid over the ground on a special track, about ten feet from the ground. At further distances from the city the airship or tubes or trams increased in their height from the ground to about fifty feet. These tubes looked like pencil-shaped cigars resembling the spaceships that are referred to as flying saucer mother ships. They had many-sized spaceships that operated on the mechanics of the magnetic lines of force. They were completely organized small cities in some cases, and could rise to great heights. The scenes are shown of the overhead tram system and the tree-lined thoroughfares. There is a grace and beauty and abundant growth all about. No scenes of industrialization can be seen. The factories were all centralized in a separate area and did not intrude upon the central city. Ioshanna: These people had not learned the art of creating things with the mind yet, at that age had they? Vaughn: No, they did not as yet learn of the use of psychokinetics, like the spiritual Beings on the great spiritual planets. This was not known to the people at that time, but it was a beautiful era and epoch, and time and community. It was much closer to the way and manner in which the Beings lived on the higher planets, but they did have to form the buildings, etc., from the atomic substance of the earth. There was the harmony and the love, as the people had not degenerated to internecine and racial hostility.

Ioshanna: Isn't it interesting, that in viewing these pictures on the wall, you can get all this information from it? Vaughn: Yes, it is very interesting that one doesn't just see an engraving or a sculpture, but one sees the whole history; and this is what I have stated before; it is similar to viewing a movie. Ioshanna: It actually portrays its intelligence to the viewer! Vaughn: Impinged in the scenes are all the events and action. In other words we are tuning into the akashic of the artifact there and it is reenacted.

This is the most wonderful concept that I have ever come across. Ioshanna: How long ago did this culture of Poseid exist? Vaughn: This civilization existed long after the appearance of Amon Ra in Lemuria. This epoch was a period when the morality of the people was closer to the Life Force, the Infinite, and they lived their lives with this concept in mind; in other words they were a family. Ioshanna: Did they have a religion or did they really know the true concept of energy. Vaughn: They did have an understanding of energy, because this was what they based their civilization upon. The use of their mechanism indicated that they understood energy as the Creative Force. There was no religion, but there was a oneness that they expressed to each other and in this sense they lived much closer to the manner in which the spiritual beings lived, who had brought this understanding to them. Their ruler, King Poseid, was one such person who had introduced this spiritual expression. This personage, Poseid, lived a very, very long time and was able in this way to develop this educational attainment of the people. It is known that you, Ioshanna, lived this life, as these depictions so reveal your identity in the akashic of this scene.

Ioshanna: Would you have any idea how many of these souls or Ascended Ones went out in the beginning for this great plan? Vaughn: There were not many. There were only thirty-three hundred; however, they made up in numbers with their knowledge and the power that they could use with their understanding of energy. Each one of these Beings would come to a particular dimension or earth plane and stay for a certain period of time to so set in motion the plan they had envisioned for the salvation of the lower planes. The kings in these times, such as King Poseid, were spiritual rulers and not to be misconstrued with the kings that followed at a much later date, who were known as despoilers of the land and made a slavery of their people, either religious, political or economic. Teaching was done in the manner of mental transmission, rather than in direct personal relationship. There was person-to-person contact also; in such a way that the individual was given the feeling of inspiration for fulfilling a great project.

Ioshanna: How far back do these wall depictions go? Vaughn: Here is a very interesting thing I see here — a civilization on the coast of Northern China, called Yu. This culture precedes the Lemurian period by at least three hundred and fifty thousand years. The people who lived here were very unusual in appearance, in that they did not resemble those native to this earth plane. They had no hair, very large heads — almost egg-shaped; they were all intellect. There was no facial expression common to the earth people; they projected a feeling of calmness, poise, serenity, inner peace. Their city had an appearance from afar of many shapes, spires, minarets, ovals, etc. The buildings and the people had a crystalline appearance. They were tall people, at least ten feet in many cases. They floated as they walked and there was a translucent appearance to their features. Ioshanna: Now this is very interesting to me. The Moderator once said, "I could even tell you about places where the people looked like crystal or almost like jello, yet there was great intelligence." What part of the world was this culture? Vaughn: It was on the coast of China near the region of Japan.

Ioshanna: Could you mentally contact the psychic of the one called Yada? I feel he lived in that period. Vaughn: Yada did live in this civilization of Yu, as he was one of the original spiritual beings, along with yourself, Ioshanna, who initiated the great plan to rescue the earth worlds from their tailspin of degeneration. He was a great spiritual teacher and much of our earth history originated from this long-ago civilization. Yada was later to become known to the earthman as one of the great spiritual beings who is aiding mankind. Yada could not very well give any indication before, as to his identity, but he was the great spiritual leader of the civilization of Yu. This ancient civilization of Yu far outshone any former civilization known to mankind, including Lemuria and Atlantis. He and his polarity have worked in opposite dimensions as it was purposeful. There was always the possibility that a danger could exist with the two polarities to be on the same lower plane together. Ioshanna: Yes, any two highly-developed biunes work in two different dimensions, and there are greatly added powers in this manner. Vaughn: This would explain then, the success that has now been made with the completion of the Conclave of the Light Beings on Parhelion, Ioshanna: At one point in the teachings, the Moderator related about the quadrocentricity, or the double biocentric, functioning as one unit; instead of just two – the four. I have just come into the realization that this was a quadrocentric situation that started with we four Aryans. Vaughn: Here is a beautiful artifact depicting the culture of the Etruscan civilization. They had beautiful ways of living, interior decoration, styles and furnishings of pastel coloration. Their walls were entire paintings in themselves. The diggings of the archaeologists has shown only a small portion of what really existed in this highly advanced culture. The Etruscans were a peace-loving people; they had no wars but it was a replica of the culture that flourished in Atlantis at the time of King Poseid. This was one of the times that the results of yourself, Ioshanna, had its earmarks in the spiritual teachings you brought to them, especially in the fine arts, painting, the arts of the dance, sculpturing, etc.

A natural occurrence, a volcanic eruption, accompanied with tidal waves, ended this civilation. However, up until this time, this great and beautiful civilization, called the center of the world, the center of Light, was the rallying point for many people, as it was the center to which the philosophers and scientists would come for teachings in a temple; a building that resembled a huge coliseum, opened to the sky. The roof was transparent; one could see right through it. There were no supports seen and it was very expansive indeed, in size. In the center of the floor is a very large crystal cube, and upon it, a throne structure where a person sat while giving the teachings. There are pillars all around in a circular fashion, about ten feet tall, with beauteous figures of both male and female in various poses. The sculptures had the appearance of being lighted from within and were luminous – most beautiful. These people knew how to create the materials for the sculpture so that the very clay gave out its own frequency in color projections. These people had greater knowledge of science than exists in the earth world today. The decorative arts, however, seemed to have been predominant; yet, there were all of the uses of mechanization such as air conditioning, locomotion, water irrigation, air travel, etc. These people did not have atomic power, yet they had the knowledge of electronics. Ioshanna: It must have been a wonderful civilization and time. Vaughn: People lived as sisters and brothers; they lived as a large family. The feelings I experience as I continue to view these ancient civilizations causes me to wish to be there – so elegant in many ways.

Perhaps side-stepping for a moment, the topic at hand, but I've been thinking about and I shall never forget the great electrical charge I had received which had a special significance to me. I understand now, that since the psychic anatomy is a configuration of millions of wave forms which are oscillating in either a positive to negative or negative to positive direction, it indicates the bias which any individual would have; that is, if he had accumulated numerous negative experiences, his psychic anatomy would actually have a negative bias. The only way this bias could be changed, is to change the actual shape and direction of the wave forms within the force fields so that an additional positive charge had to be projected into the psychic anatomy in a certain specific frequency or base plane rate to bring about cancellation. This would be so intricate because it had to be a combination of thousands of different frequencies of these various wave forms; yet, they had to be all mixed together and then projected through what we now call the integrator, the wand which is connected to the crystal lens. Never before has such a projection been used on these earth planes. Ioshanna: Exactly! And this is all done to put one in an out-of-phase relationship with all one's past. Vaughn: Heretofore, the only way this could be done was little by little. There was no power other than the power projected from different cycles. But here, with the great amassment of energies which has been developed over these many hundreds of thousands of years, the complete cancellation could be brought about! The important thing is that there is now the way and means for using the power, or of projecting the power to dimensions where, through the demodulation process from the higher frequencies, it could be brought down into lower dimensions and healing resulting. It was the compatibility, or harmonic relationship of the crystal lens which is, in essence, the consciousness with the demodulator, which is the Channel – you, Iona, yourself! In other words no one before, could receive these high frequencies without causing damage, or even a possible demise which is an indication of the high frequency in which you oscillate with the great and advanced intellects, and of which you are now one!

So it can now be understood what happened. The reason I felt I was being electrocuted was that this great electrical charge was of such great intensity, and it need be so to correct the great negative bias that existed in my psychic anatomy.

Ioshanna: Yes, it had to be; if the change in your bias was to take place, it was to be done quickly. Of course, were it to be that you were going to take many years or lifetimes doing it the slow, hard way, you could perhaps have eventually done it yourself. But perhaps, too, the negative oscillations at that time in the future might have taken over and it would have become a degeneration and no change of bias could be instituted, so great could have become this negative bias within your own psychic. So this was the reason for that intense jolt and we are just so happy that it could be brought about.

Vaughn: Well, my present feeling now, just several days after the electrocuting jolt is a very peaceful feeling and this is a feeling I have been trying for whichever way I could, to attain. Now I don't have to do anything about it. It is just there! I don't have the fear; I don't have the feeling of fingers being pointed at me. I don't have the feeling of being found out or the fear, really of the negative forces which I was also concerned about. Ioshanna: What's more, it will never so exist again, because they were completely and totally changed within you. They can never again regain their former intensity and strength in a negative way, because the energies from all that inner power were used to create the positive bias. It is very, very wonderful. I am sure I could never express my true joy for you. It is the greatest and most rapid change I have ever experienced or encountered in any one individual. So glory be! Vaughn: I can also add another note because, while dwelling on the change, there is a great feeling of being at peace and being related in a higher way; of a feeling of compassion and a feeling of belonging. As I was dwelling on this and looking out into the skies, I saw many, many darting white and gold lights of the Higher Selves of the Brothers and I heard them say to me: "Congratulations, Vaughn! We are very happy for you, for we have worked with you for two thousand years. We have been those individuals with whom you had such a strong rapport through these many years: Ming-Tse, Kung Fu, Lao-Tse, Einstein, William James, Charles Peirce and, last but not least, Leonardo da Vinci and his biune, Iona!" Ioshanna: Yes, I can say, "Amen", to this! Yes, indeed so. And now it is Vaughn tearing! Beautiful! Vaughn: Last night I couldn't sleep. I was going around and around with everything that had been transpiring, the revelations and what had occurred and I had a wonderful experience. I realized when I awoke I had been walking down a hill on the inner with you, Ioshanna; we were going toward a crystal appearing lake. I saw two great, bright golden lights, one on either side of you and I knew it was taking place up in the celestial dimensions because of the glowing and radiating appearance of everything about. Those large lights were very huge and out from the light shot deep, golden rays. It was impossible to sleep because I seemed to be picked up with all of the immensity that was taking place. I was sort of between the physical and spiritual consciousness. I tossed and rolled, but the reason I couldn't sleep was that I was really sort of separated, in a sense. I was there, yet my body was here, trying to sleep but there was so much going on in the new consciousness that I wasn't tired physically. Ioshanna: That was a beautiful revelation, Vaughn. That meant a great deal to you. I am sure, in time, that will build up and you will realize more and more the significance there. Vaughn: The two golden lights, one on either side, were the higher selves of both you and Leonardo. Ioshanna: Vaughn, in the very beginning you said of our relating in this book, "I saw no human form or physical appearing bodies, and that the entire area seemed empty." Vaughn: Of course, now since consciousness is more pointed or focused and I have become more familiar with this frequency, and deeper vision has been extended, all things which have been described have become more apparent. Now, oscillation with them is compatible and complete. It is now understandable to us how, in the very beginning with the first visions or sights into the temple area, or within it, I was so blinded with the Light and luminosity that filled the entire area that it took a great deal of adjusting of the psychic eye or consciousness in order that all things could come into view in consciousness as they actually or factually exist. This psychic conditioning, an important factor in true clairvoyant vision, especially in such extremely high frequency contacts.

During the time that I have been working, helping with the book, the Conclave of the Light Beings, and when listening to the taped transmissions that Ioshanna would give at the different times, I have become aware of the duality that exists with her; it is becoming so that I can view her as she is in her higher self. That is, I am more and more appreciative of the fact that what is coming through the channel of her mind is from her higher self, and that I see Ioshanna, not as a physical person any more. Yes, I am aware of the physical person, but it is as a background scene; when I hear the infinite words of wisdom being spoken by her, then I view the true personage that she is in her higher self, and I have been very fortunate indeed to so view her in this inner infinite oneness. But the importance here is that the physical is but a mask or a costume to so don, that the wisdom from these higher realms not intimidate the eartheans, and so make them fearful; such is its power. When one is bathed in the true Spiritual Love as I have been for the past ten years, and more recently in the full viewing of the Conclave of the Light Beings, then can I say, my cup runneth over! Ioshanna: It should be

noted too, insomuch as mention was made regarding the beautiful gift of the white peacock,
and again the same great being whom I have
termed (and who many esoteric sensitives know)
as the one Serapis, sometimes called Prince
Serapis, that he was one and the same being
called, in the early Lemuria and even before
the early Lemuria, Amon Ra, the great sun being termed Amon Ra due to the great powers
he projects and the light which he is, which
is of great intensity.

This brings to mind, when I see this great
circle or ball of Light or even the pillars of fire,
my very first experience with these great, luminous ones and although it has been related
in my book "Bridge to Heaven" it should not
be slighted here. It has been, in the past, even
a mission of many great endeavors, and various
types of missions have been started and evolved
due to but one of these such visions; I refer to
the one as Moses, who saw the burning bush.
From that, his complete and total mission was
built upon; and of course, the burning bush he
saw was one of those luminous ones who had
built up the flame there to come to him thusly.

And so it was many years ago, some seven
or eight years before I heard of the wondrous
Moderator, the great Overlord of Unarius. As
I lie asleep one night, a great and golden sun
shone into my face. It was such a brilliant light,
I instantly awoke and sat up erect and thought,
"My goodness, I really overslept; that is the
midday sun streaming into my face," but after

419

I had become oriented, I realized it was two o'clock in the morning and, of course, pitch dark. When I felt and saw it to be the great luminous orb of gold, it then became evident the light was a great being who had come to me with the words which were very strongly impressed upon my consciousness: "Thou seekest the Holy Grail and thou shalt find. Go and tell no one." Now since the beloved and great Serapis, making the contact again as he has, and with the realization that he was the one Amon Ra, now I also realize it was he, the one who came to me in this two a.m. visitation, who appeared to be a great, round orange golden sun! It was very intense and very brilliant and I became so quickened that no further sleep was possible. All I could do was walk the floor and think about this magnificent, tremendous vision! And yet it was more than a vision, it was a factual, one could almost say 'materialization' in this world.

Then another time, I guess it would be about six months ago, around the latter part of September it was, that this great golden ball of fire, actually looking just like the sun, was seen on my window sill! This was also in the middle of the night, and the radiance and brilliance was most penetrating and startling. I was just so sure it was the bright sun shining in on me. But not at a distance; it seemed right before me. It appeared as though the sun was right there behind the glass or within the glass window, and again I suddenly sat up in bed and

420

peered out at the direction from where this great, luminous ball had appeared; but of course, by then it was gone. It was not just a flash, it remained there. I didn't count the seconds that it remained but it was there sufficiently long that I obtained more than just a passing glance. I was able to view it thoroughly within my consciousness, I would say perhaps six to seven seconds duration.

This was, of course, a most magnificent and wonderful experience and I knew that something wonderful would take place due to this great visitation; a visitor I knew to be far beyond the advancement and progression of any of these Shamballa or Unariun Overlords, and who are, in themselves, very, very advanced Beings. Yet, this is an outer-world being. He has, however, taken on various physical forms throughout the ages. So now, I recognize that here again, this great one (and he would not choose to be called great) from far in the very distant eons of time, who had been the one Amon Ra, and is now the Prince Serapis, appeared there on my window sill in the dark night, in my bedroom, and I am sure that was a preliminary or sort of a pronouncement of all this great spiritual conclave that is now taking place! And, as was said, many persons have built an entire mission on some one glimpse of some higher being; yet they are viewed, seen, sensed and experienced quite frequently, but it is never a commonplace thing; it is always a most wonderful and glorious revelation. So little wonder that I felt so appreciative of this green and blue, beautifully gemmed and jeweled peacock.

Ioshanna: I can't help returning in thoughts, Vaughn, reminiscing about the almost incredible historical scenes of the walls and floors of this temple, we witnessed, and of especial interest to me, are the very most ancient ones. Mention of such periods of time in the past as three, four, or five hundred thousand years, has always fascinated me. I recall too, of a time when, but a very few days after the Moderator and I came to San Diego, nineteen years ago to start the Mission, that I experienced a sudden urge to go to a used book shop here. I found myself psychically prompted to walk quickly into the basement and reach high up onto a shelf — one where I was unable to see what was there. Immediately my hand brought down a small paper magazine titled, "Search". On the cover was a colored picture of a very beautiful man's face; a man called Yada. He was very unique, very tall in stature with a rather oval head, eloquent eyes most expressive with a spiritual glow. On the forehead was an odd symbol of the rising sun. This picture intrigued me.

The contact of that picture brought about a very peculiar and strong reaction within me. I began to quiver and shake, and a strong feeling that somehow I must contact this person! After reading the article within the pages, it was soon learned he was a spirit being or an entity who had left the physical body and spoke, along with four or five other "controls" as they were termed, through the vocal cords of a certain psychic or medium in this city.

The tremendous inner shaking I experienced as I gazed at the photo became gradually stronger. No matter what I did, I couldn't shake or lose these strong vibrations that had been set up within me, due to this picture contact. After more than even forty hours time, this quivering continued on, and the following day was the time of Mark's meeting. I could think of nothing else 'til I had sat in the circle of Mark Probert, who in trance state, permitted this very unusual-appearing, Yada, to speak through him.. This quivering was a drive I've never before or since experienced. (I've written this all up in my "Bridge to Heaven" book in 1969.)

The Moderator and I went to Mark's home to learn what we would hear regarding this very ancient Being who, as the article stated – and he agreed, when he spoke (through Mark), that he lived in a civilization five hundred thousand years ago, called Yu, on the coast of China. Vaughn said: Yes, I recall you telling of that which interested me as well as reading your recording of it, but do go ahead. Ioshanna: It was he, the Being called Yada, with the penetrating eyes, (yet we saw only the sketched drawing) who told at that meeting, to the group, along with his relating to us there, regarding his own distant civilization, which was, as did the magazine relate, one of five hundred thousand years ago that he had resided there. He said also of the Moderator (through the medium, Mark), "There is one

Brother here amongst you who bears the marks of the crucifixion two thousand years ago, and who was also the Pharaoh Akhenaton. Is that not right, Brother?" The Moderator was forced to show the deep nail scars on his palms. So here we knew this Yada was truly "in the know" for no one present knew of this. That was the last I ever heard (consciously) from this Being who set my psychic shaking for the entire two days!

Now, Vaughn, I know that must have been a very large civilization and five hundred thousand years is quite a span of time, and Yada, perhaps may not have been too uncommon a name, but do you suppose you could get any further information from the akashics on the historical walls, with other attempts? I would be most interested! Vaughn: Yes, Ioshanna, I can and am doing just that at the moment. Your mention of him has reattuned me to these vast depictions, and, I'm viewing again the great area upon which this very ancient civilization was started. It's a most glorious era and time, and as I make the attunement you quest, it is no wonder you are so interested. Can you believe this Being called Yada was actually the spiritual leader of that era and civilization for some one thousand years time? It was this Yada of Yu who later became (only five hundred years ago) the artist and your own biocentric, Leonardo da Vinci! You were not on earth at the time but worked with him from the Inner. Now the tables are turned — he's there, you're here!

Ioshanna: Well, I can't really feel too surprised, for I know these things from the inner self, but it answers many questions. Isn't that food for thought — you had to go out to such a distant spiritual planet to learn for me the answers to this age-old question? It's so similar to your own vision of the Mona Lisa, or as you term her, your Madonna. You had to go to planet Eros to find out who she was — or is. Vaughn replies: Well, it's the factual and only way — psychic attunement or so-called astral flight — to learn the true answers. But we can get any necessary answers in this way when we work from inner or higher consciousness.

Ioshanna: You know, Vaughn, I was in a slightly transcended state when you related that my beloved biune, da Vinci had been the one, the Yada. I wasn't necessarily actually shocked or surprised, but after we return to physical consciousness and mull it all over, it's really quite incredible; that is, it would be if we didn't have the Science to conceive this attunement principle and how each thing or person has its or his own particular frequency. One needs only to tune in to the specific frequency, (similar in principle as with the television), and there it is! Yes, all the same, it's still quite a fantastic truth — one I'm sure many persons will long go around with. Vaughn: Indeed so; even myself too, when I think from the conscious mind viewpoint, these findings seem stupendous and really incredible; yet it answers all queries.

Ioshanna: Are you sure, Vaughn, there could be no mistaking of this individual? Although I know full well, as you tune in to these wall depictions, you tune into the akashic of the country, era, civilization, individual, or whatever may be the topic of expression. Vaughn replies: In this particular instance, I not only can see, feel, hear that which is taking place in this long ago (five hundred thousand years), but that Yada's countenance and personality appears to me as if he were living in the present, and his features are exactly as you showed me on that magazine cover! It's as if he is in the physical here now! So without a doubt, he is the one who has since become Leonardo. In fact, we could go a bit further and say he is nodding his approval, "That's right, Vaughn." Vaughn: And so this strong vibration you sensed, Ioshanna, nearly twenty years ago, was a time when your biocentric, Leonardo da Vinci, now called Yada, was making psychic contact with you and wished to impress within you strongly, the memory. It is, in a way, a similar situation to my own psychism with my vision of the Mona Lisa, when her true spiritual self came to me, except that in your case, it was a five hundred thousand year old contact and memory, or attunement.

* * *

426

Chapter 26

Amongst one of the very first wall depictions was a scene relating to the following: It is the year 158,000 B.C., the place, a peaceful island called Lemuria. The natural beauty of the country has not yet been spoiled by man, for only the aborigines have lived here and the numbers still but few.

The silence was broken by a crash-landing of a huge spacecraft that came from out the distant sky, unheard and unannounced. The men who climbed from out the wreckage of the craft were exceedingly tall and were eleven in number. They were perfect specimens of men, fair-skinned and all at least nine to ten feet in height. Some wore a sharply trimmed beard on the chin, and all eleven were of a very highly intelligent nature, coming, as they told the inhabitants, from a distant spiritual planet called Lemuria. Thus, they named the area where they landed on earth, Lemuria.

Due to the suspended state of animation in which they were existing for the trip, no one was hurt for, at the time, they were not of atomic form but assumed this form after the crash landing. The craft was unable to be repaired momentarily, but over long periods of time and with their great wisdom, they were able to put it in functioning order.

The eleven were under the command of one they called their captain – This Being became, in 1904, the individual named Ernest L. Norman. The tall men who dropped from the sky immediately set to work teaching the aborigines many of the ways and customs, shared with them much knowledge they had and taught them the universal language of thought transference. In other words, they communed mentally. This was the way of the tall sky-men.

The features of these sky visitors were as if chiseled from some rare marble, so handsome were they of face and form. This body perfection was due to the fact they had learned the art of Creation and so self-created themselves through the evolvement of time. Their wisdom was not limited to that of the present earthman for they were wise in the ways of Spirit and knew many things unheard of and undreamed by these earth dwellers. Thus, the tall Ones taught the aborigines many things, including the secrets of the atom. Many principles pertaining to the cosmic forces were related to these eager ones until they became quite adept in their expression.

Because the landing on earth by these eleven was not intentional but due to some faulty mechanism, they constantly looked forward to the time when they could get their craft in repair to return to their space brothers, so many thousands of miles distant. Meanwhile, they took pleasure in informing the short ones and sharing with them from their book of knowledge – which they kept within their minds. The scholars were eager for this learning and did learn rapidly; so much so that soon they began experimenting with the secrets related – pertaining to the cosmic forces – and they blew up their huge island. The cataclysms that followed were disastrous and far-reaching, drowning and killing most of the inhabitants. Fortunately, the tall Ones had, before this time, completed the repair of their huge silver craft and were seen as a flash, shooting out into the sky, becoming invisible momentarily, so rapid was their speed of departure.

The knowledge these tall Ones had given these earth dwellers was priceless and for the most part, was used to build a heavenly country – the beauty of which has never been equalled on earth – yet some thousands of years later, these same short ones reincarnated through evolution to the area now known as Atlantis – and again a heavenly place was built through many hundreds of years. The architecture and civilization of this era and epoch could scarce be described in words – so beautiful were all things. These people had learned well during their times spent on the in-between earth lives and builded a city of grandeur and luxury – excelled only by the former Lemuria.

The wealth of the land was shared by all, and these Atlanteans enjoyed the fruits of their knowledge and labor to the fullest. They had advanced in their understanding to the point where they experienced no ill, no sickness or pain did they know – so well had they learned of the creative principles given them long ago by the tall Ones. Atlantis knew not of prisons or hospitals, for life was lived in harmony by all; by all, until the day the dark-skinned ones who were less intelligent than most of the land, stole the secrets by which their generators were operated – machines that used cosmic forces to light the homes, operate their machines; yes, to run their vehicles, which were noiseless.

And again, due to the eagerness and ego structures of the few, the vast and beautiful island of Atlantis was again destroyed. This was due to man having been given too much knowledge when he was not intelligent enough to use it wisely. So the story has been and, so it goes even today in the 20th Century. Man's over-zealousness has been his downfall. He has not learned the balance of the spiritual with the material or physical!

Many have been the times that these wise Ones from the sky have returned to earth in one way or another, to try to teach man the ways of Spirit, but man becomes over-zealous, overly egotistical. But now, in the 20th Century, we know that things shall be different. The Spiritual Ones are again extending the hand.

* * *

Chapter 27

Vaughn: I was impressed with the fact that although the Louvre, the art museum in Paris which has all the great paintings from all over the world from ages past, yet, the paintings that I saw on these floors far surpass anything we have in any of the museums of this world. They surpass it, not so much in the quantity, but in the quality. These are the originals and what they had there in the museums were copies – replicas from these!

So, one walks into the temple and sees all these great art works. On the concourse, one sees all the great paintings – the Mona Lisa embedded within the crystal floor; and as we walk upon it, it lights up! If there are pictures about historical events, they move into motion and we see complete action pictures as we walk along. On the walls there are representations of all the historical pictures of each dimension. It is like going to the great museums and art galleries of all the earth worlds combined! Yet, they, there, are but third dimensional flat surfaces but here in Parhelion, it's living action – live art! Ioshanna: Now because this area, this plateau, this so-called city or temple is actually a representation of this gathering of countless other spiritual planets and dimensions, it would have to be enormous! Vaughn: I sense the circumference of the building itself to be at least 33,000 feet! Ioshanna: What I said in the beginning – the building seemed as a city – sounds incredulous; yet I know it was that large! There are many cities that are not five miles, so that would, doubtless, be a conservative estimate. But estimates or calculations of size on the inner planes are most difficult, for they do not have the limitations we do here on the earth world; the structures are not atomic. It is the world of reality. This, but a dim, dreary shadow of reality. But all this can be changed in time, too!

Relating further on the great wall depictions, referring in memory to the great festival of the Taurobolia (the slaying of the bull in Egypt), Vaughn, you mentioned you saw something more of interest that you'd not yet had opportunity to voice. Would you now try to again tune in? Vaughn: The Taurobolia festival in Egypt, during the reign of Queen Hatshepsut, was of great significance, because this was the time of the Spring equinox and indicated or was symbolic of the inpouring of the Infinite supply and here was the beginning of the growth of nature. The Springtime had come and everything had turned to green; the flowers, the trees – all took on their new-found splendor and life. And so, all of the country turned out for this celebration. Of particular significance was the fact that the Queen herself gave much of the information as to the costumes to be worn by the participants; what they should wear, the specific details of their dress and of the excessive flower decorations that she directed which were in abundance! A very wide and spacious boulevard can be seen. The people are gathered on both sides of the boulevard, and on either side are guardsmen who are very tall and ebony featured. They carry in their right hand a very tall staff. These men are not Egyptian, but rather, come from a part of the country known as lower Egypt, or Ethiopia, which is a colony of the mother country, Egypt. These Ethiopians in themselves, had a culture that predated Egypt. The natives of this country are fine and statuesque in appearance; they are wearing a headdress of feathers and flowers festooned and placed around their legs and torso. They are the honor guards for the Queen. Ioshanna: In this festival termed the Taurobolia which means the slaying of the bull, there was an abundance of flowers used; everything was bedecked with colorful flowers. Vaughn: Yes, the first thing that I saw were the flowers; that the entire boulevard was completely covered with the petals of many colored flowers. There were countless thousands of pastel-colored petals of many shades strewn on the pavement, forming a most pleasant covering for the parade ceremony.

Ioshanna: Yes, I could relate a very interesting story of a lifetime involving myself and my own little granddaughter who served as one of these little flower girls who used to scatter the flowers. As a matter of fact, the Moderator related to me many years ago, how I picked her out of the observers, or those who were watching the parade, as she seemed to be an especially beautiful young girl of about fifteen. The queen took her into the temple to raise as one of these flower dancing girls. Her mother didn't approve, of course, and she ran up to the temple steps where the queen was sitting, screaming, trying to draw the little girl back to her. One of the guards went out and took the mother away which left a psychic scar — a shock with the mother — who is now my daughter. So here, we three were brought together again; the little girl being my granddaughter and the mother came through my body as a daughter. Of course, there was great karmic working out there between the three of us, but it is all worked out now. To complete this little story even further, this little granddaughter was asked at one time to be my flower girl (at a second wedding) and because the preacher wanted her to hold the basket so that he could toss the flowers over us, she actually went into a depression because she was not allowed to scatter the petals! So there — it was a very definite reliving and proof of her life or expression at that time. Her memory was very vivid when I related it to her and she said, "I know!" And she had tears with it; so she worked it out. Vaughn: I can add a personal comment. Although I am viewing the fine depiction on the temple wall, I also have a personal memory of viewing this scene, as I was standing right beside Queen Hatshepsut, on the right side of the dais but on a lower level. I was looking down the length of the boulevard and was very proud to be standing beside her. Ioshanna: And you carried that pride that way with you today, and it is sweet and beautiful. Can you relate any reason why the ceremony is carried on at this time? Is this not a repeat or a symbology from other times? Aren't all of these parades such as the Rose Bowl parade, taken from people's psychic memories of these happenings on the spiritual planes, which we have been undergoing during the past two or three weeks? Vaughn: Yes. All of the parades and ceremonies of the earth worlds have all originated from the psychic memories of the people who are reenacting them now. The Taurobolia festival goes back to a time as far back as Lemuria. The first great ceremony that took place and which originated in Lemuria, was the commemoration of the visit of Amon Ra to earth. He had visited this civilization to give the great Book of Life to the people. He remained for a period of three hundred and sixty-five days and upon his departure he left a most beautiful white peacock to the high priestess, Ioshanna. So great was her love for Amon Ra, meaning the Sun God, that she swooned upon his departure. This very symbolic white peacock was Amon Ra's gift to you, Ioshanna, as you originated the ceremony or the festival of the peacock dance, a yearly commemoration that was held from that time on. No doubt the festivals of the future cultures and civilizations were drawn from this most memorable occasion. They all had their antecedants from this one commemoration in Lemuria. In the Taurobolia festival, there are many similarities to that of the Amon Ra time. And in this festival

435

of the Taurobolia, we can see the Birds of Paradise, the peacocks, strutting down the wide thoroughfare with their fantails erect. They make a striking appearance with the green-blue coloration and their many vortexes embedded in their feathers, shimmering in the sun as they lead the parade.

Ioshanna: This one called Amon Ra, I know came from a very distant planet. Do you think there is any tie, any contact, any relationship with this Serapis? I have always had a warmth, a tremendous feeling with this Serapis. I go right out to him when I hear that name, so beautifully, I could almost cry at the thought of him. He is pure flame, pure golden flame. Now what do you see? Was he not a golden disc, a golden sun? He was never in the physical form in Lemuria, was he? Vaughn: Yes, I have always been interested in the identity of Amon Ra. I have always been interested in the symbology of the sun, and we know that 'Ra' means, the 'rays of the sun'. After viewing the coronation ceremony and reading about the honor given to you by Prince Serapis, and that he did not appear other than as a great golden flame – as he has been depicted in the Unariun teachings – I became aware that this was the basis for the symbology of the Egyptian and the Atlantean civilizations. They worshipped the sun because of the psychic memory of the visit of Serapis, in that long ago epoch in Lemuria, or possibly before this time. He had inspired them in all of the higher things of the spirit. So there is no doubt in my mind as to the identity of Amon Ra being Serapis in the present time.

Ioshanna: I had a flash that this Serapis and the great Amon Ra were one and the same. Amon Ra appeared on the crystal block in the temple of Lemuria or Atlantis. This is the way that history portrays him, materializing on the top of the red quartz crystal as a great pillar of fire and who left the Book of Life, telling the people that if they took away or added to this knowledge, they could not progress. They would be destroyed. And so this is the way Serapis appeared there by the crystal throne. What thrilled me so was, when I realized that he, too, came and brought his presence, brought his golden radiating self as a symbol to me. There is no thing in the heavens above that I know of that could have thrilled my soul and quickened my heart so, as the knowing that this great and advanced Being would extend himself in that beautiful way. I can't think about him without being overwhelmed and being taken nearly out of the physical consciousness. It is beyond my ability to even think upon it now. It seems I draw him right to me. Vaughn: This would explain why you have had this especial feeling of love for Amon Ra, and that you were the person responsible for the commemorative festival of the peacock, even to the origination of the dance that the priestesses in the temple carried out each year. There is no doubt that the many civilizations on the earth planes have brought a continuity from the past. Ioshanna: If I don't get any other picture from this dear artist who was a friend of da Vinci's, of all things, I want him to make me a beautiful picture of this exquisite golden flame standing in the middle of the lake and oscillating his message of Truth, his lecture to the many people; his silent lecture through his mentality; the lecture that he gives in but a few seconds time, that the average earth person would take many years to learn and to give. The great love that pours out is just tremendous because he has such a direct contact. In fact, the way I feel about it now, is that he is as close to the direct "Source" as can be for now, yet we know there are no limitations. But believe me friends, he is the most (and I don't even like to call him a 'he') Advanced Intelligence that we have ever touched in this world or any other world. Isn't it tremendous! And I know you feel a tremendous frequency to even think upon it, Vaughn. Vaughn: Yes, I do. I find it most transcending. Ioshanna: The first I ever heard in my conscious mind was in Flower's books. There was a picture of this great flame sitting upon a rock in the middle of a lake; that is all it was, a great, beautiful golden flame, large at the bottom and it came more to a point than the tall pillar. It was more round at the bottom. There it was, and Flower sees psychically very, very well. I know my heart skipped a beat; I was just so thrilled to see that. Of all the few books that I have ever read, I was always looking to read more about the one she called Serapis. Then, lo and behold, in the Pulse of Creation books, there he made the contact! It was a glorious time for me. And now, here he comes to my wedding! So isn't it marvelous! But it is all so much more than any mere wedding. This is but a small example of the great Infinite Love of those great Spiritual Beings, the Saints and Angels, who have traversed far beyond any of these earth worlds; how we feel and love, and love all of nature, all things that are relative,. and see within each man, a part of this great Infinity which man calls God.

Do you see any further of the pictorials? Vaughn: There are so many scenes, but I shall pick one particular one of a beautiful Grecian scene which is familiar to all. It is the time of an annual event in which the Flame of Life is carried by an especially chosen young man — tall, blonde and handsome in form and feature. This young athlete carries a torch which is lit, and he has the honor and purpose to run to the top of the great temple of Apollo. With the torch, he will light the urn which will be kept continuously lit for the entire year. This is symbolic of the eternal life! Ioshanna: Yes, I just recently saw this scene portrayed on television, just as you described. So here they are repeating; but they don't know what they are repeating. All of these parades, many of the things that they do are handed down and they know not why they repeat them. Vaughn: They had other festivities which touched off sporting events in this era of the Golden Age of Greece.

There are many chariot races. Each chariot is formed of gold with two horses leading the chariot. A scene shows two chariots colliding; and it can be seen that there is a sharp blade or knife protruding from the spokes of the wheel. These athletes wished to prove to themselves and others that they could overcome dangerous situations and so mounted these long, very sharp knives on the wheel. The slightest contact severed the spokes of the wheel of the rival charioteer which would inevitably result in his overturning. Well, these games were not nearly so drastic in nature as were many of their so-called sports and fun games of that long ago era. Sadly too, to observe, man has progressed so little – if any – since these more ancient times. Thus we look to the immediate future to learn better!

The question was asked by Iona: Do you feel that possibly the scenes upon the walls and floors of the great temple go back beyond the time in which you saw the wall depiction of the culture or civilization of Yu five hundred thousand years ago? Vaughn said: Yes, as we continue our journey around the perimeter of the wall, here is a scene showing man in his natural habitat one million years ago! On a hill is shown the opening of a large cave and men and women coming and going dressed in the skin of animals, the fur outside, or showing. The surrounding area is lush and green and is completely open to nature. Another scene shows the inside of a very large cave and within, about a hundred yards or so, one sees a stone mound which is built in a circle, raised from the floor a distance of about three feet. In the center of this stone mound, one sees red-hot stones which are kept burning by the addition of wood or other forms of burning substances, tar pitch from trees, etc. The people who live in these caves, live around the perimeter of this fire. In this way they keep warm; they do all their cooking and their whole family life is congregated about this central heating arrangement.

This particular group of people are light skinned; they are fair, fairly tall — about five feet ten or maybe six feet tall. Ioshanna: Did they live free and uninhibited outdoors, and obtain their food the best way they could? Vaughn: Yes, the men and the women procured the food. They lived on the flesh of animals rather than on fruit, and they used the animal for every particular purpose. The skin was used for their warmth in the wintertime and the flesh was eaten; other portions were used to make artifacts, the bones being used for tables or for spears.

These people had a very happy disposition; they showed in their faces the lack of stress and strain, yet they lived as a monogamous group. They had their own polarity. Ioshanna: Was that a very large cave or did it accommodate a few people, or a large number? Vaughn: These caves were the homes of large families; you might call it a village of about a hundred people. It was an unusual sort of cave because the ceiling was at least fifty to seventy-five feet high. There was a great deal of light which was furnished by the fire and the cave was a natural one. The sun would reflect in, in such a way that the light would be within almost three-quarters of the day. The sun passed around it in a semicircle and they bored holes through the top of the cave, or the side of a hill, which was a very high one. They were able to bore these holes so that these fumes from the fire would not suffocate them. Ioshanna: And that, you say, was at least a million years ago? Vaughn: Yes, it was an idealistic atmosphere in which they lived.

I come upon another wall scene which is resplendent in its similarity to a portion of the ceremony we saw in the temple itself. This scene shows the creation of the pillar of flame in the open spaces of the forest. A group of white-robed people are standing in a circle and projecting their mind energies toward the center, upon which is a quartz crystal block. Ioshanna: about how big would you say this was? Could you tell by looking, Vaughn, at this quartz block of crystal? Vaughn: It was at least six feet high and twenty-four feet in circumference. One sees first a crystal block — that is one scene. As we view the next scene, we see the beginning of a flame; there is a very small, slender thread of golden energy. This is the culmination of the mind energies which are psychokinetically projected towards the center of the crystal quartz block, which itself is a generating element, and the mind energies of the Higher Being who will materialize atop the block is assisting in the creation of what is shown to be developing into a tall pillar of golden, lambent flame which seems to be about ten feet high and about three to four feet wide! Now the flame is completed and the individuals standing about are seen to raise their heads up and to greet the personage who has materialized in the flame. He is seen in this particular depiction to be dressed similar to the white-robed men. Ioshanna: How many people are there around this creation helping him? Vaughn: There seems to be about thirty-three people especially selected, of course, advanced — either adepts or masters. Ioshanna: Now, would you say that these people who are responsible for helping to create this new energy body — and that's what it amounts to — are always more advanced than the incoming soul? Would it be necessarily so? Vaughn: No, it would not be. The incoming soul is the more advanced and is of a much higher development in terms of his soul. Ioshanna: And yet these beings who were helping him to come into this dimension could be of a lower frequency and still be of help to him? Vaughn: But it took that many more of them to do so. Ioshanna: So long as these individuals are really the higher beings, at least to have reached mastership degree, then they would be in a position to oscillate the Infinite energies direct from the source, and would not necessarily need be a more advanced being than the incoming soul. Now you are there and you have the crystal quartz and the flame started to be built up and

443

now you were telling about the depiction on the wall that shows the very beginning of the flame. Vaughn: Then it shows the progressive light-ness and increased intensity. It actually shows the flame growing; then it reaches its largest size or dimension. The next scene shows the emergence from the flame by one of the higher beings who materialized. Ioshanna: In my opin-ion, that would be the most beautiful thing any-one could ever see, wouldn't it? Vaughn: One sees every one in the group — the thirty-three — lined up in concentric circles, so there are three rows of eleven. They all raise their hands, and as the one emerges, they have their right hand and palm extended.

Ioshanna: Yes, Vaughn, what you say is so true and I can scarce listen to your voice relat-ing these things without becoming thoroughly attuned to what you are pointing up, from even the portrayals on the walls! It factually attunes me to the actual happenings of these flames, many of which I have helped create, gone through and have seen so many thousands of younger students pass through. It is a very important part of our way of life out here on Parhelion. And every time I become attuned, I notice I say "out here". I actually feel like I'm out there! But the most wonderful part of it all is the beau-tiful transcending, ethereal feeling of love, of radiation and radiance that comes when one is in this transcended state or in those areas. Well, one just sort of falls apart!

It has been told that these pillars of fire (or

golden flames) serve to "step up" the individual into his next step in his promotional climb, however, it should not be felt that all these great pillars of flame in these inner worlds are identical, for there are almost an infinite variety of kinds, shapes and most of all, the differences lie in the frequencies from which they are constructed.

Now the plebeian, or the one just starting out from being an earthean, who has not yet entered into his conscious, spiritual development, or one who is just barely starting, would not need the great intensity nor could he take this great intensity of power, such as can, say, an Archangel or Overlord. These are all especially built or formed for each particular need; moreover, these great and all-important pillars of fire or electronic flames exist in many areas of this great plateau. In fact, many of the homes which have been included as a teaching center have these pillars installed for a particular purpose and need. Were such an advanced being as a Logos to enter into a pillar designated for the Plebeian, it would mean absolutely nothing to him for his frequency is so far beyond it, it would not lift, change or transcend. He would be scarcely conscious of doing so. The opposite would be true were an early, or first initiate, or the plebeian (one just entering his more progressive evolution) to endeavor to walk through one of the great flames, the oscillating, scintillating, golden flames that had been so set up and created for one to enter and emerge, such as an Archangel or Logos – he would indeed suffer great consequence, the difference in frequency would thus be so vast.

However, we here on this great crystal city permit no such accidents, for always is such individual so directed to his proper place according to his own particular frequency through the archways of whatever it is he is studying, or in whatever temple, building or academy that he has so entered, by the frequencies impinged in the archway overhead. As he enters, his entire electronic self is either compatible or incompatible to that frequency designation which is signified in this archway overhead. If he is incompatible, he could not go in. There would be the disharmony which does not exist on this plane.

All things are indeed so planned and ordered to great perfection, symmetry, harmony and, above all, thoroughly scientific in nature and the student or initiate likewise cooperates. It must be said too, such initiations are not something which the individual enters into every few days or every few weeks time. These changes are very time-consuming and involve great work, preparation, conditioning, study, and service on the part of the individual. He never takes on the next step or initiation unless he is thoroughly prepared and conditioned for it and that he has well-earned this next level of expression. Always when he is ready to take the next step, his own frequency will bring him into that position and place where it can be so attained.

Perhaps here, too, may be a good opportunity to bring out the fact that these initiations and steps up in one's position on his scale of evolution – whatever it is that the plebeian, initiate or adept is so endeavoring, he must master that particular thing or experience before he can pass his mentioned degree or move up in status quo, whether it be of any one of the arts of painting, sculpturing, metallurgy, of artistry or the field of cooking, whatever the interest is that the person is so involved in, that interest or that field of endeavor must be mastered before he can hope to step up onto another level. That does not mean that one may go out and learn to cook and thus he becomes a master. This is not the meaning, for as was said, each one of these particular levels has, within itself, thirty-three dimensions, tiers or levels of development. To become a master, he must go through the first degree of mastership, second, third, fourth, fifth – on up to the thirty-third degree of mastership. Even your Masonic Orders on the earth plane have been aware of this and they carry this out in their masonry – that is the principle to a degree, including their thirty-three degrees.

And so a person must become learned, aware and conscious or studious of having accomplished not only one field, but several or many fields of his endeavor. The point that is being made here, is that one must master and overcome any odds which seem to oppose or that may have given him concern in whatever field of endeavor it is or has been, in which he may have been involved with, in the many lifetimes. Now in many instances, some individual who has at least put his foot upon the path of truth and light, and he enters into some such field as philosophy and starts to study, say, he does gain some small measure of understanding, and he loses interest and lets the subject matter drift from him and pays no more heed to it. Of course, this only sets up an incomplete cycle with him which will, in some later time or lifetime, call him back to complete that cycle. One cannot just start a cycle or take up some study or interest, then let it go by the wayside and it will cease to exist, that he can go off onto something else and it will concern him not. The cycle that he has begun will some time, some place, meet up with him and he will need to carry it out to its conclusion whether it be that of religion, philosophy, astronomy, astrology, some particular field of science, or any one of the many fields of the art, etc. So any individual can save himself much karma and reworking out or reliving if he will begin at the early stage of his development and force himself to conclude all cycles, regardless of how small or how seemingly unimportant. He will be wise to conclude these seemingly unimportant cycles, for they are important to him; otherwise he will end up having a lot of loose ends or portions of cycles to oscillate with nothing and get him nowhere — but fast. This, too, is an important facet of this great development program which has been almost erroneously labled reincarnation. It is more correctly, regeneration. It should be said too, that it is not that one can climb or move into many different positions, such as moving from a plebeian, through an initiate, on to a first degree mastership in any one lifetime. Usually, if any individual makes such a change, one such change in any one lifetime is indeed a vast step made. We do not say this to discourage, but only to relate the truth. We would not have it so, that the individual believed he could just take a hop, skip and jump through these great and numerous, and almost infinite number of dimensions or plateaus, of levels of development and experience, education, overcoming, and serving, above all things, in any few months, years or lifetimes — not so! It is, as was said, one could relate it to approximately one million years of development, and yet one could take two, three, or ten million years to attain this same development were he not aware or alert, or that he regressed more than he progressed.

Yes, he may be able to do this same accomplishment in a good deal less than such time. This is all dependent on concept; upon the individual; his ability to conceive, to grow, to progress, to serve — and we do stress this word, service.

May we further view upon one of the floor areas where the arts are designated, which is the floor area of the temple itself? I know a time or two you said, ''Oh, there's so very much related on the floor, but I haven't had an opportunity to mention."

Vaughn: It is very interesting that the art work was placed on the floors and the pageant itself was placed on the wall, inside the temple. The separation is to give a greater perspective – so when one views the parade, he sees the pageant in detail and, of course, it comes to life as you walk around the wall but the art work is embedded in the actual floor. There is an interesting thing that happens. As you walk, you don't walk with your head down because, as you walk over the particular section where there is a painting or work of art (and this seems incredible), it is right in front of you. In some way, it is projected so that it is directly in front of you, as if it were hanging on a perpendicular wall! In other words, you see the view on the floor first, lit up; then while you are standing on that painting, it comes up in front of you! Ioshanna: Yes, I thought while one viewed the floor area, he would be conceiving a peculiar perspective – looking down. So they have a way to actually project the picture so it is perpendicular and you look straight ahead, and you are looking at it. Isn't that remarkable? Vaughn: Not only that, but each painting has a frame which is not seen when you view it on the floor but when it is projected to you, you view it in its actual state – the way it was painted with the frame, which of course, is a very important adjunct to the painting.

Ioshanna: So what would you say then –

that these depictions are actually, in a way, some means of television; that when one contacts it, the television screen appears in front of you? Vaughn: It is another expression of the great advancement and understanding of energy by these personages who live on this high dimension, which these celestial dimensions have and that it is simply a matter of attunement. Ioshanna: Now these are just flat surfaces, the paintings? Vaughn: We must go into that. The painting itself is not a flat surface. One is viewing a four-dimensional scene. You see around it, you see beyond it and it's alive! You're viewing similarly to the viewing of a television screen or a movie screen. You have all the senses brought into focus, and in addition to the visual sense, one also enjoys the contact in another way as well – that of smell. Ioshanna: So if the picture was about flowers, you would smell the flowers! Vaughn: if the picture indicated some domestic scene, you would smell the food cooking. This unique manner of displaying or exhibiting art is entirely new to the earthean. Of course, energy surrounds us all and it is just a matter of focusing and projecting it in such a way that the frequencies necessary to reassemble this picture are simply focused at a particular point where one can see it. Ioshanna: It is fantastic – absolutely fantastic! It seems incredible and yet I am sure when we really get out there and live, we will understand completely, all about it.

Vaughn: Now these pictures on the floor

aren't just completely disorganized – like you see one picture here and one picture there – one after another; they are all beautifully organized in such a way that they seem to be fittingly put in an assemblage; for instance, all of the pictures of a particular master are positioned in one area. All of Leonardo da Vinci's pictures are immediately in the middle of the temple. They are the focal point, and the centermost of his works is the heavenly Mona Lisa. Then one sees around it his major works of art; then you see Raphael's magnificent pictures. Now his elegant statuary is on the outside of the building on the brilliant, white fountains. His particularly great works are shown – the beautiful David, the Pieta, Moses – all placed in an appropriate locale.

I was explaining that the paintings of each master were placed in an especial focal point. They were in a designed fashion; for instance, all of the paintings of the Master, Leonardo da Vinci, are placed in a concentric fashion which is directly in the center of a great concourse or esplanade. Then in a star-shaped fashion is the work of another great master Raphael, and his works are shown so that they produce a most interesting pattern of color. They are all purposely done in all the geometric shapes known, then shown on the floor, each shape having a particular purpose – a rectangle, triangle, and continues in the hundreds of geometrical shapes that exist. So you see, these pictures are all purposefully put together. It is an amazing display, particularly when we see the colors shown. It gives it the atmosphere, simply because of the colors. If a close view is needed, we simply stand where the picture is.

Ioshanna: Now how is it, Vaughn, you were just talking about seeing something that is out in space, heaven only knows how many millions or billions of miles; you sit right here in your living room chair and actually view, see, and can describe pictures on the floor and walls that are actually out there, that far in space; you can actually see them sufficiently to describe them in detail, see things that you had never known of or seen before! Now how can that be? Vaughn: It is very simple when we understand the energy concepts; for each and every item, place, thing, has its own particular frequency, so it is but a matter of tuning in to that particular frequency of where you want to go or what object it is. So, for instance, when I want to again look at the depictions on this great, seemingly never-ending wall on Parhelion, I just turn my consciousness to the pictures and there they are! It is but a matter of following through or tuning in to the frequency, and because energy is not affected by space, distance or time; thus by becoming conscious of the objective one is instantly in attunement. One is there and yet one never moves; it is purely a matter of attunement — a psychic attunement.

Many people talk about astral travel, but it is rather a matter of inner attunement or attunement with the inner self, and in such times of attunement, one can view very minute and specific details in color and design. The only thing that is very difficult to define or describe is the actual size because size is not at all relative in those dimensions; size and space are factually nonexistent. Yet, to define them for this third dimensional earth world, some manner of measurement must be made; so we enter into the feet, yards, inches, etc., but which on the inner, are truly nonexistent. All things exist on the inner in cycular manner and fashion. It may be helpful if we added, as so many people are asking this question about building some kind of a machine that would tune them back to the past, to say, some particular historical event, if they could understand that there are constantly oscillating, countless numbers of frequencies which have already had impounded in them a particular intelligence or happening, and if it is this particular earth world they are concerned with, then this happening already exists. So it is no different than hooking up their television set to the broadcasting station and then selecting the particular frequency, to bring in the desired channel.

In the same manner, the person who is knowledgeable and has an understanding of energy and the frequency inherent in the energy forms, can himself tune and select that particular station or the scene which he wants to view. Ioshanna: But here's the joker; a person must be pretty well freed of his own past karmic, reactionary ties; I doubt very much whether a person could really tune in to such frequencies, such as the akashic readings which you are, in a sense, doing unless one has worked out the most of his karma. You tune in to the actual force fields of these creations, and where an akashic reading exists. But I doubt very much whether a person who was quite bound up in his reactionary, emotional self, that these readings could be brought about, because it does take the cooperation of a developed being on the inner worlds; the higher self of an individual living on the inner planes. Moreover, it is quite a wonderful and very significant function and proves the electronic principle.

I can hardly maintain conscious mind continuity when you describe these scenes. I am transcended out into these inner or higher dimensions of consciousness and feel I get pulled or slip right out into these higher states of consciousness and feel like I am falling asleep the minute we start in this attunement situation. As such, one is suspended, and more out of the body than in. The minute it is disconnected, we cease in the endeavor, we are wide awake. It is not a sleep state. It is very pleasant, yet when one gets so deep, it is rather difficult to hang on. Previously it has thoroughly and adequately been related in detail in the Unariun texts about the thirty-three dimensions on the higher Spiritual Planes, and the seven centers of these various dimensions, the thirty-three Logoi, thus the numbers thirty-three and seven are very important. We note with closer scrutiny and further

455

complete observation of all appurtenances concerned with the Conclave that the number seven (or its multiples) and thirty-three, play a vital and important part in order that all things are maintained in compatible frequencies, on these higher worlds called Unarius.

As we were hearing one of the conclave tapes, I was impressed with the importance of the various combined energies necessary to create one of these higher beings, passing through the pillar of fire. As was mentioned, not only are the mind energies of the one passing through the flames important, but also the frequencies from the projected colored lenses, the crystal steps, as well as the pillar of fire itself.

Now, there are always personages present. If there is no great assemblage such as was during this Conclave of Light Beings, there is a circle of a certain number of these higher beings present, at least twelve, usually in circular form. There are always higher beings to add their energies, to help the individuals taking the initiation to consummate this new spiritual or inner state.

I personally remember in the books which the Moderator dictated, that this was also related. Moreover, overhead and above the crystal tiers or the pillar of fire — whichever it is that the person is passing through — there are also three crystal lenses; one blue, one yellow, one red, which also project other energies down upon the initiate as was related of the conclave. I became conscious of the fact that now the most important aspect of this principle is that of the higher personages who had already made their ascensions and are higher in their frequencies and development, who add their frequencies to the incoming, shall we say, soul.

It would appear to me that this would be the main ingredient, including the other energies mentioned for the new soul. This help from the higher ones seems the most important factor of all other involvements, and so it has just slipped into my consciousness, or I have become aware that this being is actually a part of all these participants. Thus, little wonder then, that there is such perfect compatibility, or such harmony and love expressed between all, for this new incoming individual; he actually becomes a part of each one of these beings (or Higher Ones) so helping to progress or change her (or him) in his position or development. So, in other words, all the other souls who are higher in their development or progression, share their infinity – this love. They are, in essence, loving a part of themselves or it may be said: what they see in the other is an infinite part of themselves, or the all-creative Infinite, or the Father Within. Or, we could say, they are regenerating the Infinite, and this indeed is a mind-expanding concept. One could actually spend much time thinking upon this principle.

Thus, it is, we can now observe how no person could actually spiritually develop himself without the help of others and, very likely, many other beings who have, themselves, progressed to greater and higher states of consciousness. Thus it is evident how important it is to constantly reach down to the one who has not reached the plateau we may have attained, regardless of what point that may be.

Vaughn: My first feeling was that this explains a question that I have always had about the characteristics of the Infinite — just what it was. I had always had the notion that the Infinite was a generalization; that it had no specific content — individualized. I have often wondered about the concept of love; just what were the ingredients of love; how it could take in thousands or hundreds of thousands or millions of people or even hundreds of millions of individual intelligences. Now I can understand just how, on the higher planes, a whole planet can be a polarity, one to the other! Now, I can understand why for they are actually a part of each other — all one unit. They have helped each other in their own individual progression.

So thus, one does not actually have to think about loving; he just does it because it is he who is regenerating it — the love oscillation within the other individual. This has certainly added another dimension to my consciousness! I am so appreciative of this new knowledge and how the Conclave of Light Beings has added more and more of a dimension of awareness to the meaning of Infinite Mindedness. Most importantly, I am beginning to understand you, Ioshanna, who are an example of an infinitely-minded individual. Ioshanna: If you can understand me, that means that you can understand yourself; and if you can understand yourself, then you can understand all men. That is very wonderful, and I am glad that there is some one person who can understand me. It is important that someone does so, for thus, the principle can be related to the world. This is all part of the principle now being proven.

Now, regarding this element called love, this is more or less a compatible oscillation between two or more relative individuals — beings or groups who have Infinite Consciousness. What it amounts to is a compatible relationship in a positive stance or degree when it comes from the inner or higher, which has had its continuity in the abstract or in connection with the God Force Itself or the Central Fountainhead — the source of all. Our conscious mind cannot go too much beyond that; the abstract is so very abstract and the conscious mind cannot conceive abstractions beyond certain heights. Vaughn: I'm sure this is true. It is very broadening in the conscious state to be aware of the method or to conceive the components of love. Ioshanna: Man believes were he to find love, all his insecurities would be solved. What earthman calls love is not really love at all; they huddle together like the chicks under the mother hen to keep warm, and the mother keeps them under her for security, comfort and warmth. That's about all it amounts to with the earthman because the average earth person is so filled with his guilts, fears and insecurities, and all of the negations that he has incurred from his countless thousands of past lifetimes, that it is almost impossible for these people to find, or to experience what true infinite love is, or what is taught in the texts. That which you experienced and what I now too, feel coming from you is a beautiful feeling of infinite love radiation from the Infinite Itself. It is far more than a personal thing that the earthman calls love, which is only a feeling or need of security, one to another.

Vaughn: Yes, this is a selfish thing as it goes no further than the two persons involved. It is self-inclusive and I can see now why anyone holding on to such a concept has closed himself off from the very Infinite Source. Ioshanna: Indeed! For instance, with married couples, there exists with the greater majority much jealousy and fear of losing each other. That is certainly not what one would term true love. You see, it is all built upon negative aspects from the past. There aren't many couples that you can see that one would not be jealous of the other if they were seen with another individual for any length of time, without taking on this feeling of envy and jealousy. They are so insecure in losing that which they want to possess. Infinite love is not possessive; it is the direct opposite — it is a sharing of what one has, if one is in contact with the Infinite! The earthman's concept of love is misnamed; he doesn't know the meaning of it. Vaughn: In other words, what the earthman has done, he has turned himself inwards instead of projecting outwards. Of course, this is an entirely opposite direction from the Infinite and is degenerating in effect.

* * *

Most evident, above all things, were the great love emanations being projected from all those present. As was said, each and every one present (other than those filling the great galleries, who were separated in a certain energy shield) were at least of the degree of a Master. Thus, the auric emanations from this tremendous concentrated and consecrated gathering were far above and beyond any words to define.

It should be said, this love ever-present is a transcending sensation; a oneness with the All-Infinite Minds. Love, in these dimensions, is a most common thing. There are no strangers here in this beautiful spiritual world. Each one is our brother or sister, for we have learned to recognize this oneness of Spirit – the one great source of all, and which we have learned to use in our mind creations. Thus it is, all things being a part of us and we of them, there is no separation. The one infinite source flows through all things and we recognize this Infinite Oneness, the Father of all. Thus, the beautiful feeling of love is ever-present at all times, and if it could be said, especially so on this rare and wondrous occasion that we have, all, for these countless thousands of years been lovingly

461

preparing the way for this, the great day. And from our consciousness, our infinite mind energies, combined with the cosmic powers, do we create all things, we have grown and stored our energy supply to use later in the need, such as we have in the building of this enormous crystalline structure. And as all things within this crystalline city glisten with a colorful crystalline hue, all things regenerate at our will or desire. (A word from the Hierarchy:)

"Thus, it did happen to the one for whom we are holding this great celebration, this glorious day, whom we now call our Queen of this great plateau — that in her visit here to this planet and city nearly twenty years ago, she had viewed the great crystal walls surrounding this city — as she so rightfully described this many-miled, long wall and many yards high, crystallized pearl — which she felt was alabaster. As she related, it seemed opalescent and although for these things it would be most difficult to find adequate words in your third dimensional world; yet, we here on Parhelion know that even her word forms carry the power, that the reader may likewise view as he tunes in to that which she saw and has related.

Yes, the gates of Heaven have literally been thrown open to our dear sister, Iona, for well it has been, her crown well-earned; the Light shall now shineth onto the dark planet called Earth and there shall remaineth naught no unillumined corners. This is the promise that has been foretold. And were it not so, I would not have told ye, so sayeth the Lord.

But the Lord is not some savior to be worshipped. The Lord, as ye may have termed the all-creative source, is the radiant energies, the power with each living thing; yea, and that which ye call animate and inanimate as well. For there could not be, no, not one atom, lest it had so stemmed from this great Central Fountainhead; and indirectly, all things in your third dimensional earth plane have likewise so stemmed through the irrevocable principle, the vortexal concept and harmonic relationship, of which ye have been taught. Yes, the Infinite likewise extends and includes the entire finite; for the Infinite would not be infinite were it not thus inclusive.

Heed ye well and guard ye the word which ye hath been taught, for these words are the golden key which shall open the golden temple doors, that will lead you up the steps to the golden throne. Many have been those who have falsely believed that this crystalline city, all covered with gold, has been some wild dream or the religionists' paradise. No, dear one, all this is no dream, and the key placed within your hand shall open wide the great golden doors that you, too, may enter herein. The Father within, the Lord that we know, or from whom we all share of his Light, needs not your worship nor supplication; needs not the bended knee nor of your offerings burnt; needs not the flesh so tortured in pain as you may still practice in your world. For these false prophecies,

463

the false teachers of old, gaineth man naught but despair and these attitudes but tie man the more closely to his bed of nails and revealeth not nor releaseth from within, the true spirit; the true way to the center of Light. The golden key that shall unlock the seven great doors is contained in the great Book of Life. (The Unariun Library)."

Einstein once said to Ioshanna many years ago, through the vocal cords of the great Moderator: "Who else holds within his hands the key to Heaven and Hell for the earth worlds?" But at that time (1956), it carried not the great impact as now. Doubtless she knew within but now, the meaning is redoubled. Thus, we go forth in Light!

* * *

These seemingly endless walls and the countless depictions are without number, for the numerous reenactments and depictions entirely cover the complete concourse (or floor) extending throughout the entire museum (or temple) and are indeed most incredible, wondrous and beautiful. One could spend endless days viewing this great educational center, the entire floor of which was of crystalline structure of the warm, radiant, rosy hue. I was completely absorbed and amazed as I viewed the countless colorful portrayals or, more correctly, reenactments throughout the entire length of the crystal floor area of the concourse, which is quite different in structure or composition from these portrayals seen throughout the wall area. For these reenactments appear to be embedded in the very crystalline structure of the very beautiful floor itself. For the most part, these portrayals were depicting the art work as can be seen in the many art galleries and museums of the earth worlds. Outstanding amongst these scenes, were those of the artists such as Raphael, Michelangelo and Leonardo da Vinci.

The structure of the elegant floor itself was composed of crystalline substance which gave off a luminescense of a warm rosy-hued coloration, giving the appearance that each work of art was lighted from within – most magnificent to view. In addition to the feeling of admiration, one experiences a oneness as he attunes his consciousness into the art expression. No work of art on earth could begin to compare and, as one views these most elegant floor compositions, he seems to become at one with them! One sees no atomic structure; for, as was related in various places throughout this book, all things here, regardless of the type, have been and must always be created or formed from the crystalline structures, otherwise it would not be compatible to this entire planet. This, the reason and how it is; one actually becomes at one with, or attuned to, whatever it may be he is viewing.

Ioshanna: I am sure, Vaughn, that many people will treasure and value a great deal, all that you are finding; that you are actually tuning into the akashic of these recorded enactments of the walls there in Parhelion, conceiving civilizations, countries that existed long before man knew anything about them. It is very wonderful and mind expanding, to say the least. You have taken us back to a beautiful time in Atlantis and I know that Poseid was an exquisite, elegant place, back as far as five hundred thousand years and you find the spiritual ruler of the country of Yu was the beloved da Vinci! Isn't that interesting? That is what caused my great excitement, enthusiasm and rapport with the picture on the front of that old "Search" magazine, that started the whole thing here, nineteen years ago!

It is wonderful that you could get the contact and the information about the continent Yu, that far back. Vaughn: Yes, five hundred thousand years seems like a long time but, really, it isn't; not in the mind of the Infinite. Ioshanna: Only compared to the earth time is it long. Of course, on the inner, we are not conscious of time because there is no time concept. Vaughn: It is very apparent that the continent of Yu, the city in which these spiritual beings lived, was very similar to the beautiful crystalline cities on Eros of the Shamballas, that was brought two-hundred-fifty-thousand years later and which was very close to the same area but was further inland. They had all of the great means of travel, the Yu's. They travelled to all parts of the earth and brought back with them, in a dematerialized state, the various leaders of the earth countries.

They brought these people back with them and they remained in the spiritual city for a course of teaching for a period of six months to a year. When the course of study was completed, they were returned to their people in a conscious state and they made it their project to raise the consciousness of their people. In this way they could teach the whole world! After a period of time, certain individuals from the spiritual city would make their appearance in these various countries on earth, as they had been prepared to view the Yu's, and so would not be shocked by their appearance, those who, to them, seemed as gods. Ioshanna: That is a very wonderful plan. Vaughn: There seems to be a very beautiful light that emanates from the city of Yu! It is as one great sun and in very great contrast to other portions of the planet.

It was a great achievement for one hundred thousand years or more; there was a great emancipation. Ioshanna: What you are speaking about could very well be the same place, era and time, that this man who visited us here and sat in this very place, gave me a reading from my past. He was so fascinated with this particular city and he described much of what you are saying. Vaughn: Yes, this city was of Light. The people were crystal people; they were transparent. Ioshanna: That is very wonderful. But I do remember him saying that and, you know, I will have to admit that I was just a little bit dubious. I said to myself: what are you doing, making all this up? But now that you see it too, I know he was seeing true! This reader said that he just wanted to stay there in the city of Light, it was so wonderful. Vaughn: The spiritual beings who brought this city into being, created it from the spiritual realms from the inner. These beings could extend their lives to any period of time they wished — a thousand years or more. They lived in a body that was not made of the atomic forms of the earth. Ioshanna: I can believe that; these are factual portrayals of the akashic past history. These depictions are all from people who have been sent out from Parhelion, on a mission. Vaughn: Yes, they came from Parhelion on a mission; and they actually remained here on the earth plane for thousands of years. Ioshanna: So, this is where I get the idea that I can remain here as long as I want to, or need to! Of course, our bodies then were not of these physical atomic structures that deteriorate with time. It's all very interesting! We'll look further another time.

And now, almost three weeks since the start of this great conclave, comes another definite proof of this inviolate principle of evolution, of reincarnation; of how man continues on, life after life. This finding held an especial meaning for me, for it was just near twenty years ago when the Moderator and I came to this city of El Cajon near San Diego, in California, from our home in Los Angeles, to start the mission and work. As I have related in my book, "Bridge to Heaven", that my first psychic experience almost immediately after we arrived here was

468

to dash to a nearby book store, and although I was not conscious of what I was seeking, I walked directly into the back of the store and into the basement and there, upon a top shelf, I reached high and pulled down this little booklet called "Search". Upon the front of the magazine was a picture that stimulated me tremendously. It was the face of a man; a very beautiful person – beautiful in his spiritual way. His large head was very oval; his eyes were most eloquent and his features were exquisitely formed. He seemed slightly tanned; the eyes were most penetrating and I am sure that had it been anything more than a drawing, the twin beams would have been visible.

The rapport which I experienced with the contact of this picture was most unusual. It caused me to start to tremble within. I shook as if I were standing upon a great vibrator, and this great power that I seem to have contacted was tremendously strong. From findings inside the book, I located the person who had to do with that picture who happened to be a medium, sensitive or psychic, living in this area. I soon learned through a few telephone calls, that he lived nearby. Just as quickly as I could, I would get to the Moderator to tell him – and which was not until the next day – of my great urgency, my inner shaking; of this great power that had welled up within me and now, had finally subsided. But it was one of the most tremendous twenty-four hours that I ever encountered. I never did thoroughly understand it until this very day.

Now it was, when Vaughn was doing some of his very wonderful psychosometric readings, and we had discussed some of these elegant portrayals or, as he has so called them, reenactments, upon the great walls of this temple, both inside and out, that he had located some of these portrayals that were scenes from temples and civilizations of as long ago as five-hundred-thousand years; history of the worlds from a spiritual standpoint were hereon portrayed.

Thus, as he contacted one particular cycle of five-hundred-thousand years ago, he began to describe the spiritual leader of that time and that civilization. The exact words fail me, for we did not have a tape running at the time but it turned out that he realized, after I had mentioned Yada and who, by the way, was the individual in the picture of the magazine — and of the civilization of Yu, these countless thousands of years ago! He realized and knew that this was the beloved biune, the Leonardo da Vinci who had been (even at that time), the great spiritual being, leader and teacher!

So, again my cup runneth over. The inner feeling of peace and joy that I experienced with this finding can never be put into words. Suffice to say, that it has brought many things into a new frequency relationship, more harmony within me. When there have been unsolved things within one's past and they become resolved within the conscious mind, a new oscillation is set up within, and one is made even more whole. So it is with great joy and happiness that I have found this true love, even as far back as five hundred thousand years ago! But even this is not the beginning, dear ones, not at all.

And now, just a few moments past, and as my tiny mike hangs by my pillow, just as I lay my head down, there came into my vision a most magnificent, glorious, golden radiance. Before the gold appeared, there was a great blue aura, a brilliant, vivid blue, oscillating and vibrating which first drew my attention. Then, out from the center of that, came this great golden, whirling configuration. It appeared as a galaxy, spinning and whirling. The centermost area was the deeper of gold — almost of deep orange yet it was all the colors of the sun. This great Being swooped down into my consciousness, just as he has done so many times. This time, and with this visit, I had a great satisfaction and knowing that his beloved (who was my dear earth sister, Esther), was there with him. They have been joined in this great union termed biocentric. Then, it was just a few moments later, that I was inspired to speak the few words of love, and I felt her particular frequency and knew it was she. It was the first time she could come in that particular way. And again, I am more than overjoyed. It is the most wonderful feeling of peace, satisfaction and love that one could ever know.

Thus it was, that within a few moments after the appearance of the great luminosity, (the biocentrics) that the following message was received — thus proving further, her identity.

471

The following was received from Orda, the polarity of the Moderator, (also Ioshanna's former sister), in regard to the conclave:

"Hello, sister. This is Orda, and I was so happy that we could all meet together last night. It was indeed a most joyous occasion, and one which we have all worked hard toward. I just wanted to tell you how lovely you looked; the Light shone so brightly, it made a beautiful spectacle. I want you to know how very proud I am, rather, that we all here are of you and of your great accomplishments to your own earth world. For so it is, as has been told to you in years gone by, that it is not many who would set aside their own pleasures and desires to give themselves to the work for mankind, such as you and dear Ernest have done. You have earned well, all that has been bestowed upon you, and your Light shineth ever the more brightly, adding more brilliance each day.

And I know that you can scarcely contain yourself until the time when you have completed these earthly endeavors, and can then lay aside the physical body and return to us here in these Higher Worlds, in full consciousness, and as the Moderator, himself, has said, 'to return no more' – that you will need go out no more. It is soon you shall see over the horizon and begin to see expressed all that which you have so striven and endeavored so diligently toward. For many shall be the hearts that you have made lighter and their loads easier to bear. Yes, it is true, as has been spoke, the great power from this glorious city shall continue to shine upon all your earth worlds, for the very Light of Heaven has been shed into areas and places from which it can be drawn for eons ahead.

So it is, and so it shall be throughout this entire year, we here shall be in a totally compatible position and frequency with your earth world. And I do not mean your earth world, dear sister, Iona, for it has never really been your world. Many have been the worlds that you have endeavored to enlighten and great has been the success! But the greatest success of all is the one which you are presently approaching, and gladdened shall be your hearts.

So live ye well each day, dear one, live in the oneness of the spirit you have attained and of which we are all a part. My love, and the love of all we Unariuns shall be ever forthcoming unto you, into all of your earth endeavors.

May I add a p.s.? For I see this is the way you always write a letter. It is so good to see that you have three such avid and willing helpers who are sharing in this great episode with you, to help you with the many pieces of placing together the seeming jig-saw puzzle. They are all doing very well. Kisses, your sister, Erza, (or Orda), (Esther). Yes, you saw correctly the Beloved One, (whom you call) the Moderator's Light which you viewed and which you doubted within your inner consciousness, that He would come from such a distance – from another galaxy; yet we did so for your book. Goodnight, dear."

Ioshanna: To further help the student realize
that he continues to have the inner, higher help
of the beloved Unariun Moderator, although he
has left the physical body, it should be told
how, with my every thought toward him or of
him, immediately flows into me, great waves of
electrical power! His frequent Presence and
higher energies are often made known. Also, he
is seen in my consciousness as the great oscillating luminosity appearing similar to the photographs of the universes taken of the night sky!
He often descends into my aura, there to oscillate and remain for several moments time, always leaving, in his stead or path, a great luminous cloudlike formation – healing energies
for the earth world.

So be not concerned, dear student, that the
one who returned to deliver the Unarius Mission
and Message, the Unariun Moderator, has left the
earth. He is, in fact, equally as interested and
concerned with this, his mission and you, as one
upon the path of Truth, as when on earth, now
that he is freed of the limiting fleshly body.
Ours is an eternal and infinite Cause – a labor
of love. I am, at this time, strongly impressed
by him that you must, each one, be made aware
of his ever-existing Presence, his help and love
unto you, which is but a thought away. This,
his wish and Infinite Love to you, each one.

474

The following letter was written by the Unarius Moderator during the early years of the Unarius Mission, to a young lady who was having an inner struggle with herself. As much earth history is involved, it was believed the letter could serve well to be included here. This information could well be applicable to any one individual:

"Let us start back in the ancient civilization of Atlantis some 15,000 years ago. There is a great pyramid-like temple in the center plain of this continent of Atlantis which looks very much like the pyramid of Cheops in Egypt, except that it is constructed of beautiful, glowing, crystal-like alabaster. In this center, there are different observances and ceremonies, one of which is connected with white peacocks. At that time, Ioshanna was the head priestess in that temple which observed the ceremonies.

Now, of course, worship, in any sense of the word, is repugnant in the Unarius concept and the Atlanteans at that time had degenerated or corrupted to the point wherein they were observing rituals and ceremonies which were quite contrary to those originally founded in the Atlantean concept from the Unariun Brotherhood. This was more or less the same situation in Lemuria. And so to prevent further corruption, one of the Lemurian teachers, who was called by the Atlanteans, Amon Ra or the Sun God, came to Atlantis from another world or another distant planet. He lived among the Atlanteans and knew you (and Ioshanna), just as he did the others. You sat at his feet, as did the others and listened to his teachings.

Amon Ra constructed for them, or materialized, shall I say, a huge block of pure crystal substance, much like quartz, in the center of the great temple, and upon this, he placed the Flame of Life which burned eternally and without moving, day and night, unattended. Beneath this flame, he placed the Book of Life. The books which you now have in your possession are written of concepts very similar to those which were written in that Book of Life. Amon Ra admonished the Atlanteans that so long as they would take nothing from or add nothing to the Book and live according to the principles, so would they prosper. Yet, hundreds of years later, they digressed or degenerated more and more away from these teachings, and eventually, the dark-skinned serpent worshipers from the East overpowered them and destroyed the civilization in a great holocaust of atomic power which they unleashed when they stole the different spaceships and other scientific apparatus and they penetrated into the subterranean caverns where the huge cosmic generators had been throbbing endlessly for thousands of years.

The shock of this great cataclysm caused the earth to change and the Rocky Mountains from Alaska to the Peninsula of Yucatan, rose up as a wrinkle in the crust of the earth's surface, as did the Swiss Alps and the Himalayan

476

mountains. It also partially destroyed another civilization, one which had been started by the Aryans in the long-ago. Now the Aryans had migrated from the great sister planet of Aries; that is, it was a sister planet to Lemuria. The Aryans were very much like the Lemurians; they were very tall, very beautifully formed, but much lighter in complexion, with pure white skin, blue-eyed and golden blonde hair, rather than copper gold, as were the Lemurians. The Aryans were very esthetic people, loved dancing of the highest order and other different cultural assets which they practiced very extensively. The Lemurians, on the other hand, were more scientifically bent, but otherwise, through space travel, they merged, in a sense, the advantages of their two cultures.

So it was no small happenstance that on a great plain in the area which is now West Pakistan, or a small portion of that area which is called Shalimar, we find the great civilization of Aries. These things are important to remember as we come down through the pages of history to trace your course of evolution. So now we will leave the Temple of Atlantis and turn the pages of this book of history up to the time of Akhenaton IV, in a civilization of Ancient Egypt which flourished at the time of Akhenaton at 1300 years B.C. Akhenaton was very much like Amon Ra, in a sense, that first he destroyed the Egyptian pantheology of false gods such as the Incubus, or fox, and other animal-like god forms which were worshipped by the Egyptians.

Stone carvers cut off these images from the temple walls and defaced the names. Priests were sent into banishment. In other words, Akhenaton tried to do a very thorough job of eliminating this pagan worship from the Egyptian culture. He even moved, with his loving wife, his own headquarters to a place farther down the Nile river where he constructed a new palace, out of sight of the great Temple of Karnak.

Akhenaton had five daughters. The eldest was named Nefertiti after her mother, and it was this daughter who married Rameses I., who followed after the grandson of Akhenaton. Now as we come down from Egypt, let us turn the pages of our book to about 500 B.C., nearly a thousand years later – about 800, to be more exact. This was the beginning or epoch of Grecian culture, and the king or emperor of Greece at that time, was Pericles. He was a statesman and a politician, and behind Pericles stood a very tall man with copper-colored curls and a red beard. His name was Anaxagoras. It was this man Anaxagoras who really started this era of Grecian culture. It was he who gave the first atomic theory to the world, the infinite subdivision or the solid appearances of mass. It was he who placed the astronomical bodies and planets in their proper orbits and gave the Grecians their first true glimpse into the firmament. It was Anaxagoras who was architect and designer of the Acropolis and the Parthenon; he instructed the Greek craftsmen how to build the temple, the columns of this temple each slightly thicker in the center and leaning slightly inward at the top, to destroy a certain optical angle of incidence – an illusionary form of incidence which would have given the wrong perspective to anyone who looked at this temple.

Anaxagoras gave much more to Greece: poetry, arts and sciences of different kinds. Later on, Socrates took up the teachings of Anaxagoras, and Socrates became a famous figure in history, perpetuated in his martyrdom by the poisoned cup, just as it was administered to Akhenaton in the long ago, by the priesthood; the resurgent priesthood, who had rebelled against Akhenaton, and came back to claim Egypt into its paganism. Socrates taught Plato, and Plato, in turn, taught Ancient Greece much of the concepts of Anaxagoras. Two hundred years later, Archimedes gave to Greece and to the posterity of mankind, certain scientific principles, such as the hydrostatics which are presently used in modern-day shipbuilding, all of which were expressed first by Anaxagoras. And again we find the Lemurian influence, the science, as it is now taught in the books and lesson courses of Unarius.

Anaxagoras was born in Asia Minor, very close to what was once the Aryan civilization and as a young man had journeyed into the different provinces or towns where the Aryans lived at that time. These tall, beautifully-formed blonde people were a strange contrast to the more native people – the dark-skinned people who lived in that area – and as Anaxagoras lived among them, he met a very beautiful Aryan princess named Nada, and married this woman. Later on, they journeyed to Athens and began to build the Grecian culture, as it has been immortalized in Grecian history. Through the union of Anaxagoras and Nada (and as you should guess by now, Nada is now the one, Ioshanna) there was born into the world, a lovely little girl who wrapped her tiny pink fingers around my heart strings so completely that they have been entangled ever since. Yet, she was not new to us, nor to myself, for I had known her in Atlantis, and I was again to know her when she knelt at the foot of the cross 2000 years ago at Golgotha, at the crucifixion. With the other women, she sobbed her prayers as this tragic event took place. Now you, dear sister, were this young lady whose mother was Nada, the father, Anaxagoras!

Anaxagoras, in about his sixtieth year, was brought to trial by the rhetoricians of his time, the religious fanatics who worshipped the pantheology of Ancient Greece. Anaxagoras did not believe in these false gods, no more than he does today, nor did he in the time of Atlantis, and it was only through the great oratory of Pericles, that Anaxagoras was saved from execution. Yet, he fled because he knew it would not be long before these people would find a way or a means to kill him, and he was forced to flee back into the security of a little island where he lived in hiding in some limestone caves 'til death released him.

However, before this time, as his young daughter grew up to a beautiful young lady, to her estate as an adult in a Grecian culture, she started along with her mother, the Aryan princess Nada, or Ioshanna, a certain culture which is known today in history as the Dionysian Culture. The young ladies of wealth and position at that time were sent to this school and there they were taught in all the arts and graces which were becoming to a woman of stature and dignity. Just as she could dance so beautifully in those sheer chiffon gowns — those light diaphanous materials which the Grecian women used so gracefully and which is pictured as part of the classical Grecian culture, so it was at that time that she taught these young ladies how to walk, how to speak and how to conduct themselves. Yes, her mother had taught her well.

No, she really didn't have to be taught or learn the Unariun concepts; she had listened to them in that long ago many, many times at the feet of some Lemurian who had come, time and again, to this planet to establish an equilibrium of thought, mind and consciousness within the hearts and minds of people. Some of these were more successful than others, but nevertheless, these have been stabilizing periods of histories of the world wherein some great climax, some great transmission of human endeavor has been successfully overcome, or that it is being more fully realized, just as it was in the Grecian era, in the Grecian culture.

This too, could well be a part you, Freda,

may play in your future – to be a shining light in the Center of the Unariun Brotherhood, to help guide those less able along this thorny pathway, to project to them the necessary courage and inspiration. Yes, there will be many who will come along in this united effort, and we do trust that you will meet all needs and all demands, for you have trained long for this. Do not be as Lot's wife, or your convictions and all that you have worked so hard for will be turned to salt. Like Peter and Simon, when you hear this call, cast down your nets and follow without looking back, for this is indeed your hour of decision. I can only add as I would, my own strength, my own courage, just as Ioshanna extends here. Just as we have met and travelled upon the pathway of life in this long ago, so will all these things be well served and brought together in the future. And if I may add, all of this is very strong evidence of the great and wonderful magnitude of the Unariun Brotherhood which is coming into existence and expression upon the earth today – a great movement in which you can play a most historical part as one of those people who helped and assisted in founding this great brotherhood of man which is to flourish upon the earth in the future, a time known as the Aquarian Brotherhood. I and the others here will remain with you in spirit. Our constant and never-ending love will flow to you, and we will abide by whatever comes to pass in the future which I feel sure will be replete; will be a complete justification and a fulfillment of our hopes and aspirations; for these are indeed more than hopes and aspirations.

This is a great plan – a plan that has been in the making for many thousands of years – a plan which will eventually develop, at least for many people on this earth, into the Aquarian Age, the Aquarian Brotherhood or the Unariun Brotherhood.''

Signed, (Ernest L. Norman)

Chapter 29

As an added measure and proof positive, another individual or "seer" has, in months gone by, not only viewed and predicted this great lens so related on the inner, but of the great work Ioshanna would be expressing; of the many added Angels and of her vast healing powers, which have, throughout this book, been related. This was given in a personal psychic analysis or life reading for the Moderator (E.L.N.) and Ioshanna (R.E.N.), on August 22, 1972, written as follows. These readings were sent, at the time, to many students to help give them faith and hope:

"This (Ernest Norman) is a man who was exceptionally gifted; who not only possessed an analytical mind, a mind of a thinker, the mind of a scientist, but also possessed tremendous powers of insight into the minds and spirits, and even into the souls of people. Here was a man who was a student of life; who saw through the eyes of people, the book of life of each person's soul and was able to learn by penetrating into the souls of these people more about his own soul and his own purpose in life. This man is on a very high plane of spiritual evolvement; a man who has been a spiritual teacher in many past lives and who was brought to this plane — to this earth life — in order to establish a certain foundation so that work could be continued on a higher plane, a higher plateau of spiritual evolvement. And yet, the foundation, the hard pioneering work, the difficult setting up of a church, of a foundation, of a school, of a way of life, had to be done by this man because of his need to be a spiritual leader, a teacher and a counselor.

Ruth, you knew this man, Ernest, in Tibet when you were taught as a Tibetan priest, and a Shaman and a lama. Your teacher was Ernest. He was the head of your lamasery where you were taught; he was the head teacher, the head instructor. He taught you Tibetan mystery school teachings and esoteric wisdoms which have never been written in books and which were passed mouth-to-mouth by the esoteric teachers of wisdom of Tibet, by the holy men, the Shamans of Tibet. Ernest was one of those holy men; was a teacher of other holy men; was a teacher of Shamans.

Ernest's mind is capable of reaching the highest possible level of high teachings in the Eastern world; He is capable of reaching the level of a Babaji and of holding communion and contact with Babaji. Babaji, as was given to me in my own teachings (and yet I am not a yoga, I have no interest in India, have no interest in oriental teachings) yet, Babaji's name was given to me and his purpose explained – his title and his rank. Babaji was told to me to be the "Being in charge" of a whole phase of teachings which were given to this planet. Babaji, in addition to being the guru who led his host of students across the Himalaya mountains and who was responsible for the souls of students who attended Him, is also responsible for a great deal of the occult and psychic teaching which has been given to the world at the present time. He is a Golden Age teacher, a Master; an ascended Master who is involved in the wisdom that is being given to the earth world now from the highest possible worlds in the universe.

What is fascinating to me is the teaching which I have been given which indicates that Christ is not a person but a Principle. This is one of the key tenets of the New Age teachings, or the Space Age teaching. As has been taught to me, and must be promulgated to other space age teachers, which includes you, Ruth, that Christ is a Universal Principle and the reason that it is universal is because of its meaning. Christ means the crystallization of energy into form and into structure. Therefore, in the beginning, there is energy or the Creator. The Creator, in its original form, is pure energy. When the Creator wishes to structure itself, or to create parts of itself, to manifest itself or to learn lessons about itself, it then invokes the Universal Principle of Christ, which is crystallization. It then converts its energy body into a crystallized or a structured form, into a denser frequency which is then a lower frequency than energy, and is thereby made material, or concrete, or having dimension. This is the Principle, the Universal Principle which is obeyed in all parts of the universe. This is the Principle of the Universal Christ of the Universal Principle of crystallization.

Ernest was also in Atlantis. He was one of the men, one of the Beings who was raised to a very high level by outer space Beings, by flying saucer Beings so that he could be the medium, be the conductor between their worlds of the ethereal and the earth. He was the teacher and the leader who taught the priests and the priestesses, including yourself, Ruth, how to work with the crystals and with the rays; with the resonators and with the devices, and with the machines of Atlantis in order to create psychic and magnetic fields for purification or for wisdom, or for increasing the magnetism of the aura. He was the go-between, the middle man, the medium, the conductor, the communicator – the Messenger.

It is also interesting, and yet beautiful, that Ernest, before he came to Atlantis, before he started his earth cycle of lives, was already experienced as an Angel. In other words, in the world that he had come from originally, before his earth venture, he was trained in the study of Light. Therefore, Ernest had earned a title in the world from where he came, so that when he was ready for an earth body, he had already acquired the title of "Master of Light", because he could control Light. He was enlightened, he was illuminated, and he could work with the forces of Light and use Light as his aid and his communicator – his bridge between worlds. So Ernest, in addition to many other titles and many other degrees, earned not only in this world but in other worlds, and achieved the title of "Master of Light".

Ernest is in a position now where he has volunteered to stabilize himself as a medium, using himself as a clear crystal lens where he can focus the Light of the higher worlds — this Light, a great crystal focusing lens — so that the Earth may have the purest Light; may have the most direct and the most accurate, and the most pure wisdom transmitted to the Earth and to the minds of the psychics on the earth through the bridge and the communication of Light.

So Ernest, right now is working with Light as his conductor of wisdom, as his communicator, his telephone between many worlds.

It is interesting, and again I am tracing now past lives in the life, Ruth, in which you were a Hungarian pianist. Ernest was your son, his role in that life was to be a doctor. He became a doctor at that time. You were a pianist and, in that life, you paid him back with love and with affection, with comfort and with shelter, with insulation and with giving him the love of a mother — the love of emotional support. You paid him back for the lives before that, when he had been your teacher and your mentor, your advisor and your medium between yourself and higher worlds. So this was a recompense, a payment back for lives that Ernest had given to you — of himself.

It is interesting, here my whole reading was made as if Ernest has ascended to a higher plateau — almost as if he has passed over to another world, and yet I feel inspired in this reading, as if Ernest has been taken over and is being used by Beings from a higher world to act and to perform the functions that I mentioned in this tape; so that a part of his mind has been separated from him and is being used as the crystal ray, as the crystal-clear lens, so that the higher teachings can be focused through him and through his vibrations. This is the part of him that is stabilized and is acting as the lens.

In order for Ernest to be one with himself, he must allow himself to be used as the medium, as the conductor of Light. It is fantastic that Ernest, who had earned a degree as "Master of Light" in another world, now is being asked to prove this degree; being put to the test, being told, "As you have been given the degree of Master of Light, now is the time that you must demonstrate by stabilizing yourself and making yourself a clear lens so that Light may pass through you and that wisdom may be channeled through you as pure, as bright, and as full of Light and wisdom as possible." So this is what is being asked of Ernest – to perform as a stabilized lens, as a clear glass, as a pure water so that the teachings which are given as being Light can be conducted through him without resistance, without interpretation and without distortion.

So he must be a lens that is clear and pure in order to avoid distortion, interpretation, and incorrect channeling. This is the function that

Ernest is involved with now; this is the Space Age teaching; the teaching which is upon this earth and which will be upon this earth until the Space Age is fully with us.

So your function, Ruth (Ioshanna), in addition to working out your own personal karma, is to use your influence, your power and the foundation that you have established over the many years that you have been a spiritual leader, in order to set up a chain of communication — a series of Space Centers where information may be channeled through higher awareness, to psychics who are capable of receiving the teachings of other worlds; higher worlds than have ever reached this earth and who can interpret and translate and teach certain people the teachings of the Space Age. It is fascinating that we are now at a time where discoveries will be made, such as the Dead Sea scrolls and other artifacts discovered, especially regarding Christ. This is part of the work that you and I are being asked to participate in.

It is also interesting that in order to do this work, it was necessary for your husband to go into a freer state to act as a medium and a channel between you and the higher worlds. So a higher, clear channel was necessary. In order to accomplish this, your husband is being used as a crystal lens to focus the highest possible teachings, through his presence, into your atmosphere of your mind. So you see, the work goes on, whether it be in life or in death. The same work, the same continuity, the same Master

Plan, the same program of teachings goes on.It-self — it changes; but the same program goes on.

You are entering, Ruth, a new phase of your life. Within the next four months, you will be given a new directive, a new chain of command, a new band of Angels. This will be the signal for you to be given, through a clear channel, using your husband as a conductor, as a medium, newer teachings than you have ever been given before — newer concepts. You will be taught how the soul comes to be; what happens to it from the time of its inception; what, or how, or where it travels through the universe in its journey through eternity. You will be taught the plan of life, the plan of the soul from its beginning until it reaches the earth — to be given some understanding of a new concept.

Ruth, for many years I had believed karma was earth-life karma and records of past lives on earth. And then, when I had analyzed in the many hundreds of people I have analyzed, certain people were revealed to me in analysis to have space karma that did not come from earth lives but that came from outer space lives, and it was taught to me that karma is the total cause and effect and the total learning of the soul which involves outer space lives, interdimensional lives, out-of-the body lives, spirit, mind, body, as well as earth lives. So to really search the history of a soul, you would have to be able to read the karma of that soul from the beginning of that soul or from the start of its evolution, when it was first separated and made individualized

491

from the body of the Creator. This is the new teaching, Ruth, this is the teaching on a soul level, not on a mind level, not on a body level, not on an emotional level, but this is soul teaching, taught on a soul level.

More power will be added to you, Ruth, within the next four months than you have ever had in your entire life. The presence of your husband as a magnetic field will be made apparent to you. You will realize that new Angels, a new band of Angels have been added to the Angels which you have already. You will be doing a work, Ruth, that will require the constant attendance and the constant attention and supervision of you by eleven Angels. So your work is supported by a cast of eleven Angels. This is the extent and the magnitude and the importance of the work that lies before you. This is as if you have been reborn, as if you have a second life, as if you must finish this piece of higher teaching and higher participation in the greater plan which is of things to come, and yet, is of things that are.

In another one of your lives, which I find fascinating, you were a man who was a goldsmith who worked with gold and who did carving and designing and intricate scroll work on gold in a Florentine pattern. This was in Florence, Italy, and you were a disciple and apprentice to one of the greatest goldmakers of the Renaissance period. This would be about the 1500's. So you were, among other things, also a jeweler and a designer of jewelry and a craftsman of fine Florentine-type gold design and gold jewelry. In your

492

vibration, Ruth, the most favored metal for you, the best metal for you to work through and receive power is gold, which has the value and purity of not less than 18 karat or 24 karat gold. Gold has the power to raise you to a higher strata; it has the power to tune you up. When you wear gold, Ruth, you are involved in an auric type ascension where the vibration of the gold acts as if it is a subliminal sound like an aum-m-m-m-m and vibrates your auric field and raises you to a higher ascended awareness. So for you, gold is a vibrator; it is a stimulator to your auric field."

Sincerely, Irwyn Greif.

* * *

Vaughn: It was told earlier, Ioshanna, how each and every person of the many thousands present at the conclave were all relative or acquaintances of the Queen. With a moment's thought, it can be realized how she has lived literally many thousands of lifetimes, during which time countless thousands were contacted and helped; for in such consciousness or development, to contact one is to help in some measure and way; then such persons become the charge of the Higher One.

A great number were, of course, repeatedly contacted, as was the, shall we say, villain of our story — and we must repeat — the true life story. Thus, it can be factually said, our Queen

Uriel (Ioshanna) has been responsible for the up-liftment of each soul present, to some measure or degree! Those who have been more respon-sive, create for themselves a relative or harmoni-ous frequency with her and have remained in her consciousness or oscillation over various or many lifetimes.

Keeping in mind one such being functions not as an earthean with the single track mind oscil-lation, but rather such a one oscillates similar in principle to the broadcasting station upon the hill which radiates to or reaches numerous tele-vision receivers. The number of souls or individ-uals the developed being works with is not limited but there can be many thousand – even at one time in any one second!

Thus, in such analyzing, it is plain to see how and why this advanced Being we have called Ioshanna – now Iona – was so greatly honored, for we could well say she was, in great part, re-sponsible for these countless persons who are also making a step up or are experiencing an in-itiation which leaves one with much to think upon in one's own personal development.

Little wonder it was then, these days were of especial joy and happiness for her; for it was for each one that she expressed her joy, pride and gratitude to see the progress with each one – a success story of the millennium! – yes, of all time!

Vaughn continues: Several places in the text of this book, mention was made how I was able to view the higher self of Ioshanna (or Iona). The

494

first experience of twenty-four years ago was, of course, most exciting as the picture, or should I say, portrait, of the person (now known to me as the Mona Lisa) was projected to me as I worked the night shift in the Los Angeles post office. Then in 1972, I viewed the higher self of Ioshanna and knew then that this was the self-same person whom I had seen in my psychism twenty-four years previously, which had caused me such great wonderment as to her identity.

But it has not been told about the great golden Light that is projected outward from Ioshanna which has been seen by myself on many occasions. Frequently while talking with her or listening to her (while relating about some principle), I would notice the radiant energies oscillating and darting out about her. The wall behind her would light up, regardless of the light texture and paint material, for the light that shone from Ioshanna would cause the wall to appear dark. This radiance takes the form of many changing colorations, of golden white light, that seemingly swirls about and oscillates in and out of each other. At the same time, there is present a transcendency to the viewer. My eyes, in these instances, would begin to flutter and I would become drowsy as I would listen to her discourse.

On one of these instances when I viewed the aura from her higher self, it was so magnificent and yet so natural and normal as I sat viewing it that I had, in retrospect, to think about it for some days before I realized what a tremendous happening I had had the privilege to view.

It was a time that I was living in a mobile home, and as Ioshanna and I were sitting in the large clubhouse lounge room relaxing, she sitting on a sofa opposite me, that I saw her physical form become noticeably darker, so that it was rather difficult to make out her features although I was only about six feet from her. Then I glanced at the wall behind her, which was at a distance of about twenty feet and saw that the entire wall, stretching for fifteen feet, was as if a kaleidoscope had been projected upon it. Many colors were being played on the wall, weaving in and out of each other. White and gold radiations were scintillating in their radiance as they oscillated. This pattern seemed to be in the very wall itself, and to change the structure and composition of the very paint. It was a magnificent and awe-inspiring sight to see the great distance that the aura emanated from Ioshanna's higher self, and the radiance of the gold light that took on the appearance of almost a solidity, such was its intensity.

This viewing meant a great deal to me, as I now realized that Ioshanna was indeed a personage of the highest spiritual rank, and inwardly I knew that here was one from the higher worlds, now on the earth plane, extending to all eartheans the great power that would change the negative bias of this plane to a more positive one. Yet there was more, as I realized that here, wherever Ioshanna would be physically, the power that was projected from her higher self would be a catalyst and would oscillate eternally to regenerate and so help any one individual or even thousands of souls who would associate in the area where this power was so expressed. This was a significant revelation – one long to be remembered!

Chapter 30

A word from the leaders of Shamballa (Unarius): Thus it is now, as the cycles swing, Ioshanna and Leonardo da Vince have finally, for the first time, (when freed of her present and last earth life), concluded the million-year spiritual endeavor. They shall live in the higher spiritual worlds to go out no more; to live in the harmony and love only such beings can know. They function as one, or they can move about and work as individuals, and we could sense the great joy they now know! One would not be far removed from the other, for this joining and uniting has required the entire millennium! Each one has traveled up through the ranks over the eons of time, up to the state of an Initiate, through the thirty-three degrees of Mastership, each in between step requiring at least a thousand years to complete; on to the degree of Logos, and another thirty-three steps of a thousand years each; then to the position of Angelship, then to Lordship and again requiring the same countless years to complete each of the thirty-three degrees, to attain the title of either the Logos or Archangel. Here, too, there are numerous steps in this level to attain and to prove one's self.

When the Unariun Moderator (Ernest) stepped from the flesh in 1971, after his great victory over the forces of evil, and brought to earth the great Book of Life called the Unarius Library, he and his biocentric, Erza or Orda, made their final ascension from all the Shamballas and into another galaxy, freed from all these countless past lives. He was Overlord over all during the two thousand years time, or since the Jerusalem episode, having taken the position Gamaliel previously occupied as Overlord of all. And now it is, this great God Force, the Moderator and his biocentric, function in their new exalted position on a higher dimension and galaxy. However, mental or psychic communication is easily established or maintained where e'er they may be.

Now, dear sister, we are pleased that we have so successfully and thoroughly surprised you; that, as you have been expecting for these near twenty years, as was so promised and prophesied, the Greatest Love Story ever told, and that you had quite naturally expected as we thus so intimated it to be, that the true life story would be of Ernest and Esther. Now you find, after having been so lavishly honored, that the story is actually your own life — yes, of your many lives (as well as that of these other two). Although your Higher Self is in very close touch with the conscious mind, the separation is almost nil, we are all most happy that we could retain some semblance of the surprise element, which we here, on the inner worlds, take great pleasure in expressing.

Now it can be said, as you have heard it prophesied, the story of your sister, Esther and Ernest is now a replica of your own life in the past. The unity you have thus earned, of your-self and your biocentric (or the biune), the one whom you have called Leonardo da Vinci, awaits in these higher dimensions. He and you now occupy the second to the high seat in this great world of crystal and light, and upon completion of this, your earth cycle, this topmost position awaits you and he, as one. So it is, as was promised, you now have the greatest love story ever told — the story of your own life, as well!

You and your biune have been building well the beautiful home that you shall occupy, and as you well remember, you wrote in your own book, "Bridge to Heaven", a few years ago, describing the crystalline floors; the manner in which the sounds of your beautiful organ rolled in great clouds of colorful radiations over-head to the ceiling, and of the great crystal staircase. Oft' you have wondered why you have such a love for a wide, winding stairway. The one you have created is indeed a most magnificent, free-standing crystal one, fully fifteen feet wide, all created from the beautiful crystalline structures, made with your own loving mind energies and the great Source of all. The walls are bedecked, just as you would have them, embedded with gold. Yes, dear sister, it is a magnificent home you have builded here in this city (of Paradise) Parhelion, where you shall long remain.

No, we shall not tempt you, for you are living it each day and your love for that which you are presently endeavoring to so express, far supersedes anything else which you could desire, and if necessary, you would remain in your present position for another thousand years or even a million years, for such is your unwavering dedication.

As it was also related at this same time when Mal Var was transmitting from these higher worlds about Orda and Ernest, it was Esther, herself, who said: "You know, we have all come from one far-distant planet, we were the Aryans, and we were all one great family." Thus it was that Ernest and Esther had preceded you and your biune, as you watched, up these three crystal tiers and through the beautiful golden flames, where they took their seat on the great golden throne. Thus it is, the story of Ernest and Orda is an almost exact duplicate which you, too, have attained – or vice versa. They are one step ahead in their progression; yet, you shall always compatible be and commune as you choose, just as he (the Unarius Moderator) so delivered to you this very morning through your mind, the verse you so loved. And although you did not, at the time, remember or bring it down to conscious memory, it was the Moderator who took you upon his arm, ushered you, or gave you over to your biune, Leonardo.

The all-knowing, all-creative, Perfected Ones, ruling, helping and keeping the earth worlds evolving, are infinitely wise in all their knowledge and expression. Only the future will prove what is herein written, for it was thus foretold and prophesied two thousand years ago, all that which is now, in these very days, taking place and to you being revealed. The biblical prophecies are indeed being fulfilled!

And again we predict into the future, that the world shall see a renaissance of spiritual expression as it has never before known. Man shall come to know of the help he can receive when he will thus attune himself to the Inner. The young shall learn of these truths and the future generations shall be of a different breed. This is the promise of man's freedom on earth — freedom from his self-created bonds of the past.

Heed ye well and wisely the warning and promise. The Light shall, even more than ever in the earth's history before, shine the more brightly! The forces of evil shall be overcome. They shall slink from the great God Power and Light and even in their shrinking, they too shall find help. The Light shall be shed upon one and all; the earth world shall again evolve to the point where it shall occupy a more progressive position in the great infinite scheme of eternal evolution and man shall again learn the true meaning of living in the House of the Lord Forever. (The presence of Hilarion was sensed, along with others of the Hierarchy.)

Although the following verse has been printed in the poetry book, "The Anthenium", because the Moderator spoke it to Ioshanna and prompted her to do so, this favorite poem of these two is being herewith included:

502

An Angel's Way

How oft it is that high above, in some bright
    lighted sky
An Angel's caught by planets rushing by
An earthly place that spins a web of prayers
    that reaches out and holds Him fast
And there within its earthly coils
    He's born again, and lives within
    a body made of flesh
And comes and goes as all men do, and
    called by all of them as such as they;
Yet, there remains within His heart
    and mind an Angel's way
And in His hand an Angel's touch.

And so He comes and goes among all men
    who see Him not, nor of the Angel's
    ways or touch
Yet as He comes He brings a smile
    a warmer place, a better way;
And as He goes, He leaves behind a part
    of all these Angel's things
That lead these men from out their murk
    and mire.

A magic Light that's seen by none, yet
    changes all that's dark to Light.
For such is this, an Angel's way —
    and as He finds His way back there
    among the stars,
And in the brightened realms so far
    removed from earth —
His face will linger long in memory.

His blessing thus bestowed, to those
    create an effigy of Him
    that lives with Light.
And breathes the scented breath from Heaven.
And so He thus remains, in hearts and minds
    as Angels must, until it is the time
The earth will then ensnare within its web —
    another Angel.

(The Moderator, Ernest L. Norman)

Vaughn: As we were speaking of other former lives which our channel, Ioshanna, has lived, came to mind her reference to the sincere student, Richard Broughton, who was at one time, Richard, the Lion-hearted, in a past cycle. She called him "without thinking", or more correctly, from her higher self, "Edward". When she dwelled upon her revelation a moment, she experienced the give-away signal of the flashback — the transcended state and a tear. So we knew that here was truth.

As I shifted consciousness, it was made apparent that this young man, Richard, had been the one, King Edward IV, and Ioshanna, his wife, Queen Elizabeth, during the 15th Century. It was impressed within me that he called her, not Elizabeth, but rather, Bess. When Richard was told of our finding, he said, "Oh, yes, I'd be relative there, and I would feel right at home, calling her Bess; that's quite natural."

So another uncovering, and which, too, only serves to prove the countless times one returns to these similar expressions, once they are set in motion.

By the way, Richard was telling how he was feeling negative, walking up the street until he spied in a store window a full suit of armor. He had the strongest compulsion to go in and get it; he said he had to fight hard to keep from bringing home that heavy metal suit. However, after it was realized why he wanted it, that he was reliving some past life, cancellation occurred and he quickly lost interest, as well as the negative physical feeling.

So no wonder Ioshanna feels so at home in the elegant palaces that are bedecked with glittering crystal chandeliers and gleaming floors, etc. She came by it all quite naturally. Here would be a good opportunity to make mention of a time when a group of Unarius students were enjoying a holiday dinner at the elegant Westgate Plaza hotel in San Diego. The musicians were standing beside Ioshanna playing a favorite melody of hers, which the Moderator (from the inner) had inspired them to so play for her; she, of course, loving it and feeling so relative, as she attuned to the inner, where all things are so lovely and radiant. Soon we all noted she was especially transcended and tearful. When asked why, she told how the Moderator had mentally projected to her the few words, "My Princess should never be surrounded with anything less!" Of course, she was moved!

The following few lines were inspired to Ioshanna from the Moderator:

And the Angel spoke to me
    thusly and said,
I bringeth thee a New
    Heaven and a New Earth
And that it rotteth not
    with the time
Nor doeth it deteriorate
    with the mold of the earth
But that it endureth forever.

For it hath thus been created
    of the pure Rays of Heaven
And that the Love of thy God
    shall sustaineth thee
In all the days of thy life.

Thus it hath been spoke.

Chapter 31

Ioshanna: I was just going through some of these former dissertations of the times when we were in a higher attunement, Vaughn, and it seems necessary that we relate further about this all-important concept of the initiations or the progressions the individual soul makes in these initiation ceremonies, and all that is entailed in these various states of progression. For instance, first is the plebeian state; the initiate, the adept, then the mastership degree, etc., on up to all the other succeeding levels, such as the angels, archangels, logoi and Overlord of the Shamballas. It is very doubtful that any individual can actually conceive the great and vast involvements necessary to so attain, or the length of time so involved; yet, this word "time" is a misnomer. When mention of the conclave was first related, and as I was first realizing the vastness of it all, it seemed as though the length of time to attain such an archangel degree was about one hundred thousand years. However, now it is more thoroughly and completely realized that what I felt to be possibly the assumed hundred thousand years, has now developed to become even five hundred thousand years, as we have previously stated. Now our consciousness has expanded to the point that we can conceive such advanced development of two God Forces would actually require something nearer a million years time. We can say that one can develop to this particular point where he can become some oscillating pole or polarity whereby he can function and mentally oscillate through hundreds or thousands of individuals simultaneously! This Principle or expression is similar to the television broadcasting station atop the hill, which functions or directs signal to the many instruments that will receive the signal. This is the manner by which any one of these developed God Forces can so express after such great length of endeavor and attainment, as was suggested, a millennium.

There are thirty-three degrees in each particular step or position. In other words, it would mean thirty-three thousand years for one to attain or to develop into his mastership degree. There would be the first degree on up to the thirty-three degrees of mastership in the mastership degree, in itself. Now this would hold true with the subsequent positions, such as becoming an angel, the logoi, the archangel level, then on to the Overlord of all the Shamballas, and that of Prince. Now each of those plateaus require at least a thousand years on each of the thirty-three plateaus or levels. This may sound rather complicated but when one thinks about it for a moment, it will become very clear.

The length of time or what we call a thousand years, this time element is not actually the factor that brings about the progression, but rather, it is the way the individual conceives, becomes aware of truth, his growth, overcoming, the amount of involvement he enters and expresses in teaching, or in relating the understanding he has gained to others. Now if he is very wise, observant and positive, he can accomplish this in a shorter length of time, because the time factor is not the major ingredient. But generally speaking, we could say that it would require an average individual around one million years to so attain. If one were truly on his toes and knew principle, he could do it in a far less span of time because, again, time is only a third dimensional element. What is developed is the actual being who lives on the inner and higher planes, where time is nonexistent, so the determining factor is one's ability to conceive, rather than any length of time. Now does that help clear it up a little, Vaughn? You see it is always concept. Vaughn: Yes, indeed. Then, if one expressed and accomplished in one lifetime, always the complete positive bias, he could actually, in terms of third dimensional time, have traversed a thousand years. Ioshanna: He could. Like you said yesterday, compared to your previous few years, you have progressed yourself possibly a thousand years into the future! Remember, spiritual progress is not measured in the concept of years, it is purely relative to development in serving the Infinite. You have seen these inner worlds, which usually take man many, many thousands of years to so arrive at the point where he can conceive these things. You see, this is what progresses one forward – the new understanding gained!

510

Another thing that is very important: Man must prove himself on all levels in whatever he endeavors or takes up; whether it is some facet of art, science, music or sculpturing, painting or teaching, goldsmithing, astronomy, metaphysics, etc., regardless, he has to master whatever it is he takes up. So you can see how this thing of time is not the prime factor, but it is completely concept and proving one's self. You see, we are building or creating, as it were, this higher self. We ascend spiritually through understanding, in awareness and realizations of principle in action — whether it is due to the creation of a new gown or the forming of a garden — whatever it is we are involved with, all the positive energies of all the expressions into which we enter, the energies of a more positive nature are added to our higher self, and we are thus, therefore, creating the higher self. However, these expressions must needs have the infinite continuity to be creative. Vaughn: I'm thinking of your own particular point in your great advanced position, Ioshanna, and of the infinite time you have spent during your great climb and involvements. Ioshanna: Yes, but this particular level is still one step below the next one above — which we must ever strive toward; each of which may require anywhere from one hundred to ten thousand or more years to accomplish. According to the effort, the expression, so does one merit new levels. Because the earthman relates everything via this time concept, we have to give him some sort

511

of a time element viewpoint. But we must re-member that we are not actually aware of the great length of time involved in evolution. Man, and I speak for myself as well, is not aware of all of the eons that have been passed. There are many memories of things with which we have been involved, but one is not concerned, nor does he remember the great time involved. We live in today; always we live in the present moment − that is, we should do so. So perhaps these few remarks may help enlighten all that is entailed to actually achieve, acquire, and even more important, to create or to become such a being as a Lord, Overlord or Logoi, or even an Archangel − one who can oscillate and func-tion through or with, countless thousands of other persons simultaneously. There would be no limitation; there usually would be the con-tacts which the higher Being has formerly made, and this is very important too.

By the time, we will say, an Archangel has contacted countless thousands of individuals through these many countless eons of time in the past, as a result, this has created a thread-like oscillation with each of these individuals. She (or he) is connected, through frequency rela-tionship and harmonic structures, with all these individuals and can work with each (and all) of those persons simultaneously. They are in her frequency and thus, thereafter, whether they, who are on some one of the earth planes who would desire to express, say, in the literary arts or the field of music, the dance, etc., the developed one can work with them in a psycho-kinetical manner from the inner worlds.

Now, bear in mind, the higher being does not live in the physical body. The physical body is merely the means and conveyance whereby the wisdom can be related or oscillated through the physical body to the eartheans. But such a higher being never can, never has, and never will, live in this earth plane dimension due to the great difference in frequency. However, do let it be said that the oneness can be very, very close. At the moment, I can say there is no sharp borderline of separation. It is but a matter of attunement and the conscious mind and the superconscious mind become almost, we could say, as one! Yet, the higher being does not incarnate itself in the physical body. The inner work must be done through the body of an earthman. In other words, we build up the psychic body and come through in an infant's body.

Vaughn: When you are conversing and in contact with your own higher self, Uriel, the power is most beautifully felt and I receive a great teaching on the basis of listening. Ioshanna: And yes, this becomes a part of you. Then, in time, you will oscillate it out to others. As you are now writing the letters to the students, you will be able to draw on this energy because I am making myself a very part of you! I have done so, not only for the past ten years, during which time I have been in correspondence through the mail with you, but you can rest assured, I have been in contact with you many other times and years in the past, to help bring you up to this point where you can likewise serve. Vaughn: I have very definite proof of that in so many different ways, which has been objectified and proven to me, that you have always been as close as my thoughts or awareness. That has been a great help.

Ioshanna: I am not at all conscious of any time involvement. The great and wise Infinite, shall we say, has been most wise in this blocking off or screening out of the past. However, when we arrive at some semblance or state of dedication to higher attainment, we then glimpse or have very vivid memories of the past. In fact, these flashbacks can be very vividly oscillated into consciousness little by little; yet, they, too, are never brought into consciousness at any great length or many at one time, because these were impinged in cycles and thus they must be cancelled out and worked out in an identically similar cycle which is relative to the past, making all things compatible where it can be objectified and cancelled out. So the mind does not remember this great length of time involved. It is due to the great, wonderful plan and intelligence that has gone into this great expression which man terms evolution or regeneration, and which is a more correct definition.

For all things are regenerating, whether it be the rock, the stone, the tree, man, the animal, regardless, everything is regenerating; the atoms in the tree, stone, rocks, dirt – everything is regenerating. That brings us up to the point of creation – and which is nonexistent! Yes, some will revolt at this statement. When we arrive at some semblance or state of the abstract, we can see how no thing was ever created. It always did exist and always will, and it is but a matter of taking on a different state, a different frequency. This regeneration is a slow evolvement, such as some of these stones and rocks, and which the Moderator has so aptly described in his dissertations called "Of Atoms and Astronauts", in the book which will be published soon, called "Interdimensional Solar Mechanics", in which he has stated about the rocks, and that "creation" is a misnomer, a misconcept. For there is no beginning, no end; only regeneration. When man can thus conceive, he will have eliminated numerous frustrations and questions; for frankly, there are no unanswered questions when man begins to conceive these vital and all-important energy principles. When one begins to function with or from the Father within, he can receive, from this inner, the answers.

* * *

Vaughn: Much of our time of late is spent in delightful reminiscing, and with each such time of remembering, again do we become transcended and attuned to that glorious Conclave of Light. Comes to mind momentarily how it was that especially the Madame Blavatsky brought as her great gift to the Queen, her philosophical library; for now she is, in her present state of consciousness on the inner, able to see just how it was, the voluminous works poured forth through her pen. She now views the entire situation and sees how it was that you, Ioshanna, along with others from the inner and higher dimensions and realms did so oscillate to her mentally, these works, which could be left for mankind on earth. This, one of the many reasons these various and countless personages brought to you – to your home with Leonardo da Vinci, which you and he have created, as the great academy – these countless gifts.

Yes, so it was, the various gifts were most often representations of your own efforts, Ioshanna, with these countless persons as they expressed on some earth world, you working mentally with them via psychokinetics or mind forces! They were returning to you that which you helped them manifest!

Your very own story of the princess coach and the beautiful white horses, of the vast procession, of the many serving in the entourage, the countless angelic forms, etc., have all found their way in story form – most often believed to be fairy stories or tall tales from someone's imagination. Yet, they all took their basic concept from this incomparable pageant – which you, yourself, projected into their minds for the writings; for you, along with countless other Higher Ones have, as was stated, worked countless years, yes, eons of time to bring it all about and to make this the most glorious and

516

memorable occasion and gathering that has, at any time, anywhere, taken place. So it was, and it is being now so expressed, and many shall there be the stories written and movies made, due to the reading and the attunement with these words. If one obtains the "live recordings" on tapes, he will likewise experience another dimension – that of sound or music. Added healing energies are impinged with the voice recordings, and it should be told that we students find it most difficult, and sometimes impossible, to remain awake during the listening! Of course, at such times we always experience healing power and the inner help as we are thus "pulled out" of conscious oscillation and into what seems to be a sound sleep, but which is, in essence, quite different than sleep. One always feels so cleansed and refreshed thereafter. Of course, the more we maintain our attunement with this occasion and dimension, the greater becomes our buildup and attunement, and the ability to likewise attune unto or view these grandeurs – the many glorious sights.

It should be told also how, even after several readings or viewings, this great love story – and we could easily say, the sequel to the story, "A Dweller On Two Planets" – will never seem old. It is, and shall ever remain, a stimulating and uplifting relating. This, due to its source – it is an infinite creation and will regenerate on ad infinitum. We shall find that our great, great grandchildren will also be hearing and loving this, their fondest love epic – one that never ends.

None the least of interest and intrigue, the fact that the one, a lead actor in the play of life, the so-called villain (in our story) is not, as is true in most of your earth stories, punished or imprisoned. Quite the reverse! He is helped with our undying and never-ending help; he is nursed back to a more healthy mental state where even he could take an active and positive part in acting as the reporter, recalling from the first arrival in the great and never-to-be-matched cathedral — better named museum (an educational museum) – yes, about seven miles in circumference! And a goodly report he gave!

Yes, this true-life love story which was, to Ioshanna, quite a surprise sprung upon her, will live through the ages and shall become the true forerunner of the great new Golden Age — the age and time when the lion lies down with the lamb. Ioshanna: Thus, we could compare the life of you, Vaughn, with this lion-lamb symbology, for that was the true significance of the parable of Jesus. The lion becomes compatible to the lamb! Vaughn has felt so strongly about the book of Philos, "The Dweller On Two Planets", and relived the lives of Mainin right with him as he read of his downfall and effort to climb up; yet, the many lives Mainin, (the Incaliz), spent in his climb were actually trivia compared to the time involved in, shall we term it, Vaughn's resurrection from the past. It could easily be said, his has been a five-hundred-thousand year struggle to come back! — this, a small example of what is entailed when one really

518

topples after any measurable attainment. Most often one does not make it; so for Vaughn, we are more than glad, and I've welcomed him aboard – I don't recall how many times!

Vaughn: Although much has been told in my book "The Victorious Search for the Soul – or The Return of Pontius Pilate", of my continuous struggle, yet it should, by all means, be mentioned herein of the very great and lengthy negative life that has been mine to relive in this, the present life, in my efforts to extricate myself from especially the bonds and oscillations lived and expressed as Pontius Pilate, (or again, as Nero).

It was even several years after it became known to me that I had lived the life of this individual, yet I still could not free myself of the oscillation with that past. Proper cycles had not come into conjunction, and on and on I oscillated and met various persons who had likewise been in contact at that time, such as my former wife or personages who came into the Governor's mansion or palace. So this endeavor to completely free myself of this great guilt incurred as Pilate was a very lengthy and long-enduring, involved endeavor; it often seemed as though there was no end in sight. Yet, struggle on I must – and did. Due to the strong and negative past which has been mine to relive, I appreciate more thoroughly now, in the present, the complete opposite and positive stance I have now been able to move into, and from which to so express.

Thus it is, to say that I am a renewed person, reborn, or that I have been reborn of the spirit is understating. For one to have actually freed himself of so many and great negative pasts is, indeed, a tremendous thing, which causes a great upheaval within the psychic anatomy. The great infinite and spiritual help extended by, not only Ioshanna, but others of the inner realms have made it possible to now have my chin above water, and it is a most glorious feeling.

Now again, just last evening, I experienced a wondrous vision during my sleep. I saw myself in a classroom; it seemed as though I was teaching other personages — perhaps plebeians — but I was now in this more positive and ascended state, able to be a help to others. In my vision and sleep state, I was impressed with the fact that here I was in a classroom, helping others of a less positive or less developed position than even myself. Surprisingly enough, Ioshanna quickly made appearance into this classroom, gave me her blessings and praise, and it was felt she quickly placed a kiss upon my cheek, which I vividly remembered on awakening this morning.

So thus it is, I do indeed feel that I am now truly on my way to a far more positive and regenerative future. It is doubtful that we students can fully appreciate the word "regenerative". This word, in itself, entails much, much food for thought.

Speaking of the constant help of Ioshanna, it

should be related, too, how at one time, only about eighteen months ago at one of my very low and bad times, it was just after I had made a visit to California from Massachusetts to see Ioshanna, (then returned home), I had been overtaken by the negative forces. My mind was simply not my own. I was unable to do, go, or express as I wished; the lower or negative powers were in full control.

Although it was not consciously realized at the time, later on it came to me that I was actually reliving the time and cycle when I had committed suicide. The urge and compulsion was so strong and all persons, supposedly my friends, were pulling against my efforts toward Unarius and my going to help in its mission. So strong was the opposition, along with the negative past cycle of Pontius Pilate, of which I had not yet completely freed myself, I actually became frightened of myself and committed myself to a hospital in that city. It was a most horrible experience; it can truly be said, the worst I have ever encountered! Thus, I entered into the proper procedures to enter the hospital and was put to bed. To enter sleep was most difficult, but I finally wore myself out to the point where I did go to sleep. Then it happened!

At two a.m., loud and clear, came Ioshanna's voice into my mind, "Louis, get up and get out of there! You must fight for your very life!" It shocked me to arousing, and quickly I slipped into my clothes. Although the attendants gave me opposition — they didn't approve of my leav-

521

ing – yet, because I had entered of my own free will, could do so. It was soon afterwards I heard Ioshanna's voice on the phone and things quickly began to become normal, the rough seas calmed and once more I found sanity.

This is an example of how closely an advanced Being works with her proteges. Of course, my appreciation to her knows no bounds and she takes it all in as part of her normal day's functioning – yes, and the nights as well!

* * *

Our symbolic crowning, wedding and reception that took place May 28, 1973, was truly more than a mere mock ceremony. It signifies in this dimension that one can climb from the very lowest of depths when persistence is demonstrated. Thus, this little celebration in the third or physical dimension is, in a way, celebrating too, Vaughn's victory over self – and that's what the Science is all about anyway. He is indeed most sincere in his efforts to aid in the mission and is truly being a great help.

Again, we find ourselves recalling the wondrous and exquisite gifts the Beings existing in the even higher positions had created for Ioshanna. Referring to the elegant green-blue crystal peacock by Prince Serapis (formerly known as Amon Ra), of this significant gift, one student, Carl Wallenborn has written, just one week after hearing the recording about it, "I shall endeavor to put into words my psychic viewing of the peacock. First, I noticed the head in outline. However, the colored picture was quite dark at first and I mentally thought,"If only it were brighter!" Just as I completed this thought, each individual jewel stone commenced to brighten and sparkle with bright pencil-ray beams or shafts extending right into my psychic eye, almost blinding out the form of the peacock. It seemed to evolve as though I had watched the Being Serapis, psychokinetically construct this most beautiful artistry! And as I write this, I'm still fully conscious of this fantastic event; also, the brightness has not faded one particle of intensity or color!

"An equally fantastic psychic viewing of the Moderator's eternal red rose was my pleasure to behold. This was my first experience to see a rose with an aura of shimmering brightness extending outward with pencil-like gold streamers of light, mixed with the red brilliance. I consciously exclaimed, "This must be the Moderator's red rose to Ioshanna," and behold, there instantly appeared just above the pulsating rose, the face of our beloved Moderator! My cup surely runneth over for having the privilege to view such beauty. My conscious mind keeps reviewing the unforgettable manifestations of the rose and peacock scenes."

Sanosun (Dorothy Ellerman) also experienced a wonderful time during the Conclave, as she relates:

"Tonight was truly the beginning of my resurrection. The great power channeled by our Unarius Channel, Ioshanna, now Uriel, the Archangel, was tremendous, and as the tape began to play and the words of Light began to flow, my body began to shake with such intensity, I felt as though I would burst right out of my skin, but grateful in the knowing that a strong entity or negative vortex from this long ago life in Poseid was being removed. My throat burned like fire with the intense ray projected in my electronic body and my face was wet with the flow from my eyes. This done, I heard clearly Ioshanna's voice on tape and was taken to the great temple of Light and the Conclave of the most High. I viewed her and the radiant, dancing waters; saw the great electronic chandeliers, the thirty-three triangles of Higher Beings over which the chandeliers swing, then the beautiful blue, gold and rose tiers, the pillars of fire and the magnificent throne itself. I saw the Book of Life and her great and magnificent crown.

"Then another scene I shall never forget was projected. Ioshanna took me by the hand; as I saw her in radiant chiffon, she glided up some golden stairs, and I felt the help and the love existent to one who had denied the Light. I was overwhelmed with gratitude. Then her arms were around me and we continued up those golden stairs.

"Then I saw her great computer wand that dispenses the powerful energies from the world of the great lens. It was pointed at me and I saw the great square Light projected, computing exactly the necessary energy ray to the frequency of my psychic body.

"Yes this is truly the millennium, the beginning of the great Golden Age, and the geodesic lens and Ioshanna's computer wand is the means whereby the tide has turned for such as I. Instead of psychic suicide, I now turn to the Light and begin my climb from out the recesses dark. I have arisen this Easter time through the everlasting love of the Unarius Brotherhood and the Infinite Eternal Light that is our Ioshanna – now Queen of Archangels, Uriel. My cup runneth over."

Vaughn relates: It was revealed to me from the inner that although these two – the biocentric polarity for whom this great affair is honoring (Ioshanna and Leonardo da Vinci) – have never met on any earth plane, even though they have, each one expressed many missions on earth since this great and infinite plan was so set in motion – yes, a millennium ago – their only time spent together was done in the higher dimensions. Never did either one know of the love of the other or share of it during their numerous sojourns to the many earth worlds – this, the mark too, of the selfless ones; their missions and teachings to the eartheans always came first, and further proof of the great inner development and infinite love each one ever carried for the other as they labored through the countless centuries, alone – one might say!

The Unarius Moderator did likewise labor with, or more correctly, without his biune, yet in the cases of such a Being as a Logos, another of somewhat similar development would,

525

of course, be quite compatible. Thus, it was most important that the Moderator had such a one to aid in this, his mission on earth. It was Ioshanna too, who was with him to share her more compatible oscillation during his other five trips and missions to the earth world. She incarnated to appear as his mother in Egypt, his betrothed in Jerusalem, his wife in Greece, the wife in the present, etc. Such an advanced Being as the Unarius Moderator would, by necessity, require one of at least a similar frequency in order to maintain proper stability or oscillation in this earth dimension. This is of ultimate importance, otherwise, the one bringing the mission would be constantly drained and discharged of his powers. Thus, the pole or polarity was supplied in the person of Ioshanna.

This may not have been true with all persons so endeavoring but must needs be so where one had, or expressed such great powers as were related with Anaxagoras, Akhenaton, Spinoza, Jesus and the Moderator.

This same situation was likewise true with the Moderator and his biune. Never did they two know the love, the solace and company of the other polarity on earth but rather, each worked and functioned in completely opposite planets or planetary systems. Surely, greater love hath no man than to completely sublimate one's own desires, wishes, and likes for service to mankind!

Among the numerous love sonnets written by the Moderator during his lifetime on earth, to Ioshanna, the following is one of her favorites:

How Do I Love Thee?

How do I love thee?
May I never count the ways,
But let the moments of each day
Each bring a new way,
A different meaning to my love.

Why do I love Thee?
May I never find the reason
For as God created all things
    in beauty and in purpose,
Let my love too find beauty
    and purpose in all you are.

When do I love thee?
Let there be a time for creation
And a time to realize all things
But let my love for thee
Be a realization of creation
    in all things
With time but a wistful memory.

Chapter 32

Now another, to cap the climax! Both Vaughn and I have wondered and wondered just where it was that he fell after he started out on his more positive mission – his spiritual climb. As we were driving through the peaceful "Singing Valley" yesterday, I rather jokingly said to Vaughn, "Who are you, anyway? Where did you come from? Where did you start upon this trek of yours and when was it that you became so sadly detoured and fell so far back?"

The peculiar part of it all has been that Vaughn has a somewhat compatible frequency with me; I can relate to him – that is, when he is positive – and which he is most of the time – whereas there is no one else that I know of, who can oscillate in this particular positive way. For the most part, he is a strong, positive pole. So it has remained a bit of a paradox with me, for I have seen both extreme ends of his bias and expression, and when he becomes negative, it is unusually or extremely so. Neither he nor I, up to this point, had been able to figure it out but were aware that all things take place in their proper cycles. As we were discussing it, Vaughn said, "The fact that I can oscillate with you at all in a more positive way, perhaps comes from the fact that I spent twenty-five years with Leonardo da Vinci in his household; for he was as positive an advanced Being as has ever stepped foot upon the earth. Then I was with the scientist Johannes Kepler (who was yourself, Ioshanna), another past master; for, as you know, I spent a lifetime with Kepler as his own son.

Then we know of my life as Emperor Nero; however, Nero wasn't necessarily a positive or spiritual soul. Of course, we all know of my lifetime as Pilate and of his actions." But we were interested in locating the more positive lives he had lived with persons of a higher frequency which may have aided in a positive bias.

As I quested of him further as to where else we had been acquainted, from his inner conscious attunement, he saw how I had been his wife, Jasmine. Then I sensed him to have been the husband, King Darius. I felt there were three such kings and sensed him to be the eldest, then to return as his own grandson. Our encyclopedia served to fill us in there. So here were other more positive lives in which I have been working with Vaughn, helping to pull him up and along the way, that he could be ready to join here, to take a positive part and expression in this, the "Affair of the Millennium" and the Unarius Mission.

The beautiful part about that day was, we started out just for a ride in the morning as everything was so beautiful and peaceful; the sun was exceptionally warm and it was one of those rare, first new days in Spring! We both felt the stimulation of a beautiful, warm, most compatible cycle. It was this very same day (when we two became aware of our lives lived as King Darius and Jasmine), that Larry, the lovely ten-year old son of Vaughn, sent to his father (from Massachusetts) his photo. As Vaughn, read from the picture the akashic reading of Larry, he was found to have been King Xerxes, the son of Darius I. Thus, he had been my son, too, which explained my strong love oscillation sensed as I viewed the boy's photo. So here was another life that we had spent together, whereby he could oscillate with the higher power. This was a very interesting and wonderful finding, for all that day, we felt a beautiful closeness and love vibration. Later on, I was again questing him because I had not been satisfied we had reached far enough back in the past. "Just how far back do you think you go with me? When do you start making these contacts with me as a student?" Then he reminded me of the time when he was giving the readings from the walls on Parhelion that he found he had been in the beautiful city of Poseid with me! That was many thousands of years ago, but even still farther back was when he read that this being with whom I had such a rapport, called Yada, (who later became the one Leonardo da Vinci), who lived in the country called Yu, that Vaughn also had a tie or relationship there; he had the reaction and cry, and felt sure he had been there. Now that was at least five hundred thousand years ago! So there were some positive lives as well as many of the opposite. Vaughn replied, "I couldn't serve as a polarity with you if it hadn't been that I had quite a few positive lives with you and others of like frequency and compatibility." Well, this was what caused further questions within me, because I knew this was true, yet so often some slight negation would throw him and he would remain in a low negative state which caused me to wonder.

Then during the early evening hours as we were listening to a teaching tape, as I glanced over to Vaughn, sitting on another divan, it suddenly flashed to me that he had been the so-called "Fallen Angel"! I said, "Now I know who you are!" Of course, his concern was really aroused. Some writers have referred to this Fallen Angel as Lucifer and have stated that God kicked him out of Heaven and he descended to earth to rule the world. When this mention of my realization was made, dear Vaughn experienced the tell-tale trembles, or reaction; the rubbery-leg acknowledgement, and he knew this was the ugly truth! May it be emphasized that this story of the "Fallen Angel" or Lucifer could well be true of many an individual; it has been – countless thousands of times! Thus, the warning. The way the story goes, the being had attained awareness and illumination; he had climbed to the point where he could oscillate with the Infinite and become a channel for the healing powers. Then it went to his head; he became egotistical and began to believe he was the source of the power. He felt he was all-powerful. Right there is when he started his decline in subsequent lifetimes, as the power was used negatively to bolster the ego and for selfish purposes. He continued to regenerate the negative bias.

Now we don't know how many lifetimes it has been that Vaughn has oscillated in a destructive way, but from the soul-reading that Irwyn Greif gave him, there were quite a few. We will quote it below just to show how far one can digress and then, if he has the strength, can pick himself up. We will quote Irwyn Greif's reading (for Vaughn), although it is not a pretty story; but frankly, this information is one important thing that has helped Vaughn more than any other! I noted the change from the moment that he read it and accepted it; his change started immediately and then he began his climb and change. I am adding this purposely, for it certainly does prove the principle which the great Moderator has so often taught.

Following is a psychic analysis of one Vaughn Spaegel (formerly Louis), dated October 12, 1972, as quoted by I. Greif:

"This is a man who is working out past lives in his karma in which he was very egoistic, very self-righteous, and very intolerant of human life and human suffering. Therefore, this man is being channeled toward spiritual and therapeutic work in order to help compensate and to help melt his strongly crystallized memories of being self-worshipping and an insensitive person. The best employance of his karma in this life would be in the field where he would be able to be a therapist to work directly with people; to heal or to activate or to soften their physical and emotional aspects where he can work with people as a physio or a neurological therapist.

"Karma has taken great pains with this man to subject him, and introduce him, and keep him in contact with people who are spiritual, who are attempting to guide and direct him towards spiritual ends, but I feel that this man is very stubborn and insulated and his hard core of inhumanity and his self-worship is still intact. Therefore, the angels of karma will allow this man a certain amount of rope by which to hang himself, and then they will increase his teaching to such a degree and in such an unexpected manner, that this man will literally be the victim of karmic shock treatments and traumatic happenings, designed to give him the necessary shocks to penetrate his heavy shielding in order to reach the inner core of this man's stubborn, inhuman, and self-worshipful center.

This man is not capable at this time of any measurable happiness; neither is he capable of self-love; neither is he capable of the reward of feeling total reality. I have seen so many of these people who are insulated to such a degree that they are unreachable except by very traumatic shocks. This man does not realize that what he is setting up for himself is a prescription which he is writing with his own hand, and because of his own stubbornness, to effect his own necessary shock treatment therapy. This man has a history of bloodshed and a history of inhumanity in several of his past lives, which are standing out almost in bare relief because they are so strikingly dramatic.

This man was present at the time of Christ. This man was a Roman and was involved in the persecution and destruction of many Christians.

In that period of his life, he distinguished himself by being such a ruthless and efficient leader of soldiers that he could effectively accomplish a victory without taking any prisoners! So he has areas of conscience; he has areas of murder which do stand out in his records and his book of life, and for which he is designed, in this life, to make at least a partial karmic payment. His account is overdue. The shielding this man has, and the insulation he is hiding behind and has been hiding behind for many lives, effectively screens off and blocks himself from facing and realizing his own conscience. The angels, in order to penetrate this man, must rip away his shielding; must penetrate, must dramatize, must shock his insulation, his shielding so that this man will come face to face with himself which, in this case, is his own conscience in order to perform the purpose for which he is born in this life — to be a healer and a therapist; a humanitarian and a spiritually motivated worker of God. But the angels have a very heavy hand; if they wish someone to be reached, they have the power to move heaven and earth; they have the power over life and death to accomplish a therapy for a soul. Therefore, this man is being circled; his name is circled as someone who is in the process now of being prepared for a karmic therapy on a shock treatment level.

The same forces that he persecuted and attempted to eradicate, which were the Christ vibrations in the religion which had its beginning in Jesus, these same forces, through the mercy of the Creator, are being lent to him to guide him, to help him; the same forces that he tried to destroy are being used in the personages of people near him to help him; to aid him, to give him direction; to help him restore his own soul; to help him see clearly the image of his own self. So the very forces he sought to destroy are helping him now to help himself!

Louis is a medium and is a channel for negative forces, forces of the devil because they allow him his shielding; they allow him his ego structure; they cater to his need for self-destruction. And this is the design and motive his angels wish to convey to him at this time; at the time when he is being faced with the most difficult crisis of his life. If he chooses to align himself with the forces of darkness, then he will reap the whirlwind of karmic retribution. If he is able to cleanse himself and purify himself and establish a new point of reference, a new humanitarian motivation, a new need and desire — the main word is desire — to help himself and to work with the forces of Light and of Love, then he will be allowed to work out his karma through service to others which also means a service to himself.

It is interesting how Louis assumes he is a teacher level and that he is capable of great intelligence and great understanding whereas, when I look at his picture at the present time, what he shows is such a dry intellectual rot; as if I am looking at a mind that is a dead branch; that has no sap, that has no vitality, that has no life fluid; that has no soul nourishment. Therefore, it is up to Louis which way he goes, which will directly determine his emotional, mental and spiritual, and physical reward for this life. This is a time of conflict for him. This is the moment of truth for Louis. It is being set up within the next year that this is the crisis point and that he must make his decision to either identify himself with darkness or with the Light, to establish the future of his life at this time.

It is hoped that Louis will respond to Light and, like a flower, turn toward the life force of his soul and receive the nourishment from the Christ vibration and from the source of all life."

Vaughn listened repeatedly to the tape; each time he would try to accept more and cry a little, which was a discharge, and as was said, that realization helped him a great deal.

April 30, 1973 — Thus now, less than six months later, we find Louis (now Vaughn) having faced the harsh, cutting reading and, having worked it out, has taken firm steps up that progressive side of life; yes even so much so, he is capable of giving akashic readings for others, to aid them! Vaughn's dedication is truly concrete and his progress more than steady. He is going forward by leaps and bounds! Thus, this vast and direct turn-about direction Vaughn has been so successful in attaining and expressing, should indeed serve as a vital lesson in hope, faith and aspiration to others in similar situations. That Vaughn has overcome and is now expressing a fine, strong, positive bias, serves to further prove the karmic principle of Unarius.

So, this last evening, as it had come to me, "He is the Fallen Angel," I told him, you are the one who was called the Fallen Angel or Lucifer! Well Vaughn experienced quite a reaction. His solar plexus spun about; he told he became a bit nauseous, and heaven only knows what went on within his consciousness but he knew it was fact. I said: You have been with these Higher Beings in these various lifetimes to try to help you make the comeback and now you are being successful! Now you have become more positive in this expression with us here in helping and you must permit nothing to deter your regenerative, progressive ongoing! Vaughn said: Well, that answers so many questions and I know that is correct. Ioshanna: I have been calling him recently, "my guardian angel", because he seems to take special pride in doing little things that will help me in the work. Because in this peaked point of serving as the channel, as I do, I have become quite a bit less physical and am quite supersensitive and, of course, I would have it no other way. It is a joy, a pleasure and a wonderful thing to serve in this capacity – being a channel for the healing powers. Thus, the need for a strong, positive polarity is great. The "Fallen Angel" experience can happen to any individual and does happen to many which only indicates and emphasizes the fact of how very important it is after one does arrive on the path of truth, that he maintain the more progressive and positive bias. This is the all-importance. Although we could say that Vaughn has been the

Fallen Angel, after he had once aspired, having attained ability to channel the powers of Light, yet we repeat very sincerely and factually, there have been countless numbers of fallen angels. Now, to what degree they have fallen, of course, would be dependent on what position or point to which they had first aspired. So it was felt by myself that this was a good opportunity to include the warning. As a matter of fact, it is a tremendous climax for Vaughn, but it all seems so very natural — just a natural sequence of events. After it was placed properly with Vaughn, which is his new spiritual name, he had a very warm and wonderful glow; one of warmness and gratitude and he is now at peace with himself. It was but a few minutes after it was related to him that he went out into the beautiful spiritual worlds, psychically, and had what we term a lengthy "stepout". Now he really has something to masticate, so to speak, that will enable him to refrain from any further slipping into negation or falling off this high pinnacle — and which is not the easiest thing to maintain — at least until he has cancelled out most of his past negation. I now feel his past has been quite well discharged.

It should be related, too, that the decision which Louis (as Pilate) made, (he being the one who made the definite decision about Jesus as to whether or not Jesus should be condemned), of course left a great guilt within him because he has known better. With one who has not so attained or who does not really know right from wrong, his guilt is not so great, but once one has aspired to some appreciable level or degree, his guilt is much greater. So, because he had at one time aspired and gained access to the powers of Light, and to Channel them, then, as he fell off this higher plateau or state of consciousness and committed these negative expressions such as in Jerusalem, etc., it would, of course, cause a far greater guilt and fear; so much so, that, as has been told and as history has it of Pilate in Jerusalem, he committed suicide. Of course, this suicide didn't help things — not one iota; he piled up even greater karma and has, ever since Jerusalem, been trying to work out the suicide effects. Such an act against creation actually destroys a certain amount of the person's intelligence. It shatters (so to say) one's very psychic anatomy. So, as has been said previously, it is doubtful there is anyone who has had greater karma than Vaughn to overcome and yet, overcoming, he is!

The important point herein is to note the great and lengthy time it actually takes one to get back upon some particular positive higher level which he had once obtained — once he slips. This pointing up and relating re Vaughn should serve as a warning to any sincere devotee, for if the reader will analyze, as you carry the principles and theme of this true story throughout, it can be discerned that Vaughn has actually been countless thousands of years in his effort to get back up to where he once was! Yes, indeed, this realization of the Fallen Angel has great significance to him and means much. Surely, in viewing it in full consciousness, as he is now thus able, doubtless he shall never again slip one step below his present fine and positive manner and expression; but rather, shall he move ever forward.

Ioshanna continues: Let it be said, dear reader, that Vaughn's example should be a great lesson to each and every one, regardless of how far behind he has slipped in his path toward illumination. There is always hope, there is always that possibility, if one will maintain his steadfastness; maintain his positive endeavor and carry on in that forward thrust to gain, to conceive, to learn, to understand and, after some measure of understanding, to work with principle. This is the key! This is the key to your more positive future. Vaughn's favorite saying has been: "Seek and ye shall find; knock and the door shall be opened," and this he has done repeatedly.

Now it is understandable how and why he can work with me in his akashic readings; of tuning in and seeing these pictures that were portrayed upon the walls and floor in the great museum of the crystal city; and why it was that his Madonna, twenty-four years ago, came to him from the spiritual planes in his time of need, to help create a pivot point with him and move forward and maintain the more positive expression. "Now," as he says, "all things have been fitted into place and I know that my future shall be one of a continued, forward, progressive and regenerative motion." I must say that the gratitude Vaughn expresses is unlimited. His is a most appreciative state and, as he says, "I never had so much love poured upon me. I have never known what it is to experience this beautiful, spiritual love that you, Ioshanna, the students and the Brotherhood radiate to me." This is undoubtedly true, for this is the element that has ever helped to lift him upward and forward. So it can be with each and every one. It should be told too, how Vaughn had a strong desire, ever since he read the book "A Dweller On Two Planets" by Philos, to write his own story, so similar. Yet, this is being done in this book, as well as his biography titled "The Return of Pontius Pilate". He felt the story by Philos was factually paralleled by his own life, as it relates the great difficulty Mainin (the hero of the story) experienced as he tried to make a comeback, life after life.

* * *

*The Encyclopedia Britannica re Lucifer: "It is used in Isaiah XIV. 12, to translate the Hebrew epithet 'shining one', applied to the King of Babylon, fallen from his high estate to Sheol. The Fathers interpreted the words of Jesus (Luke 18) 'I beheld Satan fallen as lightning from heaven,' as a reference to this passage from Isaiah, so that Lucifer came to be regarded as the name of Satan before his fall. It is so used by Milton in Paradise Lost, and the idea underlies the proverbial phrase, 'Proud as Lucifer'."

It has been nearly twenty-four hours since

541

the shocking news was related to Vaughn – word that could have, had he not accepted it in the true light of understanding – brought about so great a deflation that he could easily have reverted to an even greater depth than at any time previously. I refer, of course, to my findings and the flash regarding his having been the "Fallen Angel" (or Lucifer).

To say this information bothered him not, would be untrue, for it did place him into a peculiar and depressed state – not pleasant. Regardless, he carried on in obtaining some life readings that had accumulated. Later he asked if he might take me for a drive in the warm sunshine, through the valley area I like so well. Vaughn looked sad and forlorn, although he did not become extremely negative, nor did he oppose the presentment; yet his eye had lost the luster, nor did the light shine through as I had, in the past, so seen it. I knew he had been deeply hurt; a great deflation had set in, yet, it was the only way out – or up.

I was pleased to get out and to set up a new small cycle. We found two outdoor lounge chairs on the lovely greens at a nearby golf course and sat, to drink in the inspiring Spring growth about. Soon we, each one, had fallen to sleep as we watched the golfers on their putting greens. Upon awakening and (by my wrist watch) I had dozed for an hour, just as I was coming to, I viewed the beautiful ending to Vaughn's most difficult experiences!

I saw myself with Vaughn in tow, holding on

to his hand – I, slightly ahead. Held high in my right hand was a great lighted torch – the Light of the world. It appeared similar to the Statue of Liberty torch or light but much larger! We were (in my vision) climbing together up three certain red quartz steps and into a golden flame! He was taking his initiation! His public confessions and acknowledgments throughout this book have earned for him a large step forward! That is the importance. He was most happy to learn of this flame experience, yet he had actually foreseen this a few weeks earlier. It should be related too, how, the following two days after Vaughn's great facing of self, then having been suffused with the purifying fires, he seemed quite discombobulated with the physical, so great the change. He says he feels much less physical – and a great change for the better is noted!

As it is conceived that this fascinating, true love story shall become a great motion picture, I shall give here the closing scene as I psychically viewed it: Vaughn is seen holding the hand of Iona as she leads him up the crystal steps and into the flame; as she passes on unto higher plateaus, she places within his hand, the hand of another. He is seen meeting and grasping the hands of his own polarity who happens to be Vaughn's own (physical) son – one who had progressed a bit beyond or farther than had Vaughn. This was his first glimpse of his son on the inner. Now, with the great help and his accomplishments in this book, the help he is now able to extend to others, he has advanced to the point where he can pass through the flame pillar with Larry — his true polarity or biune! Earlier in this life, Larry had been Vaughn's twin brother but he was killed in an air battle in the war when young, to return to him again as his own son! But here now comes full cycle for the two, and they are seen entering the third flame together. Larry had been prepared to await his arrival. As they (Larry and Vaughn) emerge, they are entwined, arms about each other in love — exuberant and happy. The joy they express is beautiful, indeed.

Iona (or Ioshanna) is seen moving into a distant area, approaching the higher plateau, where awaits her polarity, Leonardo da Vinci, (Archangel Michiel). In the lovely garden by the distant fountains are seen the two polarities, the Moderator and his biune (Archangels Raphiel and Muriel), also awaiting her arrival.

Although we do not see the two Archangels actually meet, they are rapidly approaching each other, almost floating along, as the heavenly scene fades away. (The movies term this a fade-out.)

* * *

Ioshanna: It seems like there is nothing of so great an interest as to again revert to and reattune to these wonderful scenics on the wall that convey so much — the entire earth history! After the last scenic you reviewed, Vaughn, you

544

said there were so many more to observe. Have you been doing any peeking lately? Vaughn: Yes, I have. I again viewed psychically and saw a large scenic depiction on one of the great wall panels on the left side, interior wall. This scene shows an initiation of one particular individual. As was said, the initiations through the flames are created for any individual who has arrived at some specific point of his (or her) ascension into a higher dimension. This scene shows a depiction of three red-quartz cubes. It should be mentioned, too, one part of the ceremony includes three large crystal lenses which are shown as red, blue and yellow which are radiating specific energies from the ceiling of the temple where the ceremony is taking place.

These three quartz cubes are ascended by three crystal steps. The flames atop the crystal cubes are about ten feet high and about four feet wide. They are golden in color and are scintillating. The wall depiction scene shows two individuals approaching the first flame. On the right hand side, we see a Being who has a great aura of pure white about her and who is holding in her right hand a large torch. A light of very high intensity is coming out of the torch.

This Being is holding to the right hand of another individual who is slightly in the rear; she is guiding or leading the other person up the steps into the flame. They pass through the first flame and we see, in the wall portrayal, a change in the aura of the person on the left hand side; as he passes through the second flame, another change occurs.

There has been a circle of thirty-three persons standing around these flame pillars, mentally projecting into the flames. The next scene shows one of these persons stepping up into the second flame to greet the incoming soul. The higher soul who had brought in the other, then placed together the hands of these two — her protege and the one awaiting. She then moved quickly out of the scene and seemed to vanish straight upward. Now as we view further along the wall scenes, we see the two persons step into the third flame together and upon emerging, they are seen to grasp each other, entwined in a loving greeting of joy and recognition!

They are biocentrics. The person who had undergone this ceremony has been raised to a certain level so that he could then meet his own biocentric who was awaiting, and thereby ascend together. Ioshanna: Now, Vaughn, just in case you haven't recognized in these scenic depictions these two beings, they are yourself and your own dear son, Larry! Did you know that! Vaughn: Yes, I did. This is a great wonderment and surprise. I'm filled with excitement and joy! In fact, I am quite overwhelmed.

Ioshanna: The story of that particular person (Vaughn) of course, has a great deal to do with the conclave and I believe that is the reason why this scene is on the panel, not only because of the celebration and the ceremony of the millennium but also, of the victory over the self, having been accomplished here by this

546

one particular individual — which is also an achievement for the conclave. It is the epitome and the object of the entire evolution of life. It is an example of the overcoming of the self, the sole purpose of the thirty-three hundred beings who had ascended from Aries to so accomplish and change the bias of the lower worlds. So, in this scene we see an example of one particular person who had been a part of the lowest of these lower orders and who had, especially with the help of one of the personages of these thirty-three hundred beings, so changed in his bias that he could now reenter the Light!

The fact that you see yourself going through and emerging from these flames shows that you have overcome very great obstacles and odds. You have achieved the good for which you have been striving, lo these — no, not one thousand, ten thousand or twenty-five thousand but at least — five hundred thousand years! And this number could well be conceived to a likewise similar length of time! However, as you, yourself, have so indicated and proven, Vaughn, it is not the length of time; it is the overcoming and achievement and, above all things, the good expressed toward mankind. These are the accomplishments; the forward thrusts that move man forward in his progressive evolution. So it took quite a bit of space to depict all that upon the wall but it was most impressive and it means a great deal to you, Vaughn, as well as to many others who shall so view these depictions in the eons of the future, and the countless persons who shall visit this planet and city from many distant worlds!

Vaughn: It has been related in many parts of this Book of Life that the very person who has guided me through the flames, then to join me with my own biocentric, is the self-same person who has been my teacher as far back as one can go; that is, five hundred thousand years ago, and in a sense, I am sure she has accomplished one of the greatest triumphs: bringing back, you might say a lost soul, from much more than physical death — back to the light! Ioshanna: So a victory for you is a victory for our entire Brotherhood as well for now we have a soul, rather than opposing, who is capable of serving the powers that be — the Light of the Infinite. Now, you are yourself, a messenger of the Light! So we have here, a real success story! The villain has become the hero! Vaughn: I am sure it will always remain so as an example of achievement for any one person. I am sure the Brothers won't have as difficult a time with me in the future. Ioshanna: This fall and climb (and we must emphasize the fall), applies to countless persons. The regression that individuals encounter, in which they become entrapped, is devastating. This is the situation that requires such a great length of time to climb back up to the level where they were, previous to the reverting because, as a rule, man does not have the wherewith, the know-how, to climb back. Only through the help of one who is in a higher position upon the path can this help be so extended; can he accomplish, and victorious become. Yet, each single life is but a mote in the eye of the Infinite. It could be compared with one grain of sand upon the entire oceans' floors.

The Hierarchy must have evaluated quite highly your successful climb-up to have had the details and story depicted upon the great walls in the crystal temple; for so great was this victory, not only over self but representing as well the victory of light over evil, or over the negative forces.

And so Vaughn, this wonderful closing scene that you have viewed upon the walls is most impressive; where you see the one who has guided you, leading you through the pillars of fire; where you meet your biune and then go through the third flame together as she ascends to higher plateaus — most impressive! Thus we could indeed say this is a happy ending beyond compare for all concerned!

Vaughn: In conclusion, I would like to add some lines written by the Unarius Channel, (Ioshanna), to me which are most meaningful for they relate how it is now with me, and of my great victory over self:

And now the sands of time
    go trickling down dim
    corridors of the past
The shadows of the darkened
    regions of the mind
Become illumined with pure shafts
    from Eternal's door.

Where once was filled with
    hollow mockery
    of deeds long gone
Now echoes lilting laughter
    of a new-born day and time.

The shrouds of gray that once
    did hold me bound and taut
I've loosed and severed each
    with spears of Light
    and promises — fulfilled!

The splendor of a new eternal sun
    is glimpsed, whilst the past
    I've so dismissed.
New courage now — unto the future
    do I stand.

My shield and buckler
    becomes the Truth – and Light
    of which I've gained,
And, step by step, will climb
    this golden stair.

So surely doth our past
    the future to become
Thus stark we stand,
    in radiance and in love
To face another morrow –
    another future, another
    lesson to so conceive
As we thus become the Infinite,
    and It becomes the man.

* * *

Mother's Day, May 13, 1973

As has been our custom during the past several weeks, since the beginning of the conclave affair, the three of us working here at the Center have extended our work time to the wee small hours in the a.m. Often two or three a.m. finds us still happily involved in working, on both the book and tapes. Thus, it sometimes becomes necessary to sleep later in the morning.

This morn, Mother's day, was one such day. As I came downstairs about ten a.m., the other two already busily at work, Vaughn said, "My, you slept so late; that's good!" I replied casually and felt I was joking, "They wouldn't let me leave from the inner!" I continued, "After all, they hold Mother's Day there, too."

Vaughn had set at my place at the table a lovely Mother's Day card and a dear jewel case with my favorite, a "rose", done in gold plate. He had found a gold plated rose and it is most beautiful, with a rosy tint. As I was admiring it and saying, "Did someone push?" he said, "No, that was just me and my idea."

This rose evidently attuned me into the inner and he, as well, for I became transcended and teary. I said, "After all, doubtless I've had many children and grandchildren during the many past lives, as well as helping care for others." At those words, I was attuned and saw psychically; the tears again were the "give-away", of fact.

Vaughn described what he was viewing at that moment. He said, "Oh, how lovely! I see you, Ioshanna, sitting in a huge golden throne. You are surrounded with literally thousands of little ones, each one dressed in a different pastel shade. They have each brought to you, one lovely mind-created red bud. These countless roses have been formed in a huge heart-shaped wreath all about you as you sit. The great wreath seems about twenty feet high. The children are all so happy and bubbly to have you there, and a tremendous feeling of love exists. It all makes such a beautiful picture — you in the huge, golden throne, surrounded with the great heart of red roses, the many children gathered about, sitting at your feet. I do wish I could photograph it all, yet the inner memory shall never fade.

I blame you not, for not wanting to return to the physical world this morn, for who would want to leave such beauty and love!"

As he related his viewing, I, too, saw the lovely sight!

Chapter 33

A Word From the Hierarchy

Never has there been given, not ever before during the entire history of the earth worlds up to the present, any lengthy description or detailed analysis of these higher spiritual worlds; nor has there been conceived or brought into consciousness of the earth world, or related to the earth world dimensions, such information as is herein related. There have been, on a few rare and isolated occasions, individuals such as Swedenborg or those who have obtained, through psychic or mental projection, brief glimpses of what we are here on parhelion; how we live or how all things are created via our mind energies, using the very substance of the Infinite Source — the radiating, radiant energies· as the means. But never (other than the Unarius Moderator), has man previously been given these true facts and realizations such as has been brought to your earth via the visitations to our spiritual planet by the one, Ioshanna, in the present time.

Thus, it is indeed a most monumental achievement for your earth world, by which one of your denizens has thus attained, not via any mere mental or psychokinetical projections from we here unto her mind, but that she actually made the astral or psychic visitation into this world, and so extended herself throughout the entire twenty days time in visitation or attunement. She was, indeed, living in the two worlds at the time! Then, has she recorded her findings and experiences first-hand.

It must be said that this expression is far removed from that manner in which many of your eartheans have and are relating their findings of the astral worlds and which are, in essence, mental projections or oscillations from those astral forces living there; thus, the reason and cause that your earth people are receiving such varied accounts, so many countless types, kinds and descriptions, even when the individual is attempting to describe the same situation.

These findings of your Channel are the things that have, in the past, only been whispered about amongst those few who have, in their transcended states, been projected in consciousness into these higher dimensions and a few have been given a glimpse. But none, other than the great Overlord Himself, the one you call the Unariun Moderator, has been given, up to this point, the full access, the full knowledge and the information, these vast secrets and concepts which have, in the past eons of time, been kept secret.

Now we know that no harm can come due to the earthman being aware; for, as was said, this light is all-powerful and no thing negative can remain in its path. Lest ye not be aware at this point, it was you, yourself, Sister Io-shanna, along with the one whom you call the Moderator (and Leonardo da Vinci, your bio-centric) and others, who so set this great infinite plan in motion upon the earth so many eons ago! Thus it was, you see the fruit of your labors from these countless evolutions of life through which you have so traveled and endeavored in this, the great master plan.

This is indeed the first time in the Earth's history this has been achieved (along with the vast work which the Unarius Moderator, Ernest L. Norman brought to earth, and where he underwent similar experiences). Thus it is, we here are most pleased that our sister has related and defined her findings thus, with but the limited use of the earth words, which far lack proper description; we are conscious of the great limitations she encounters in this, her dedicated effort so presently being expressed. Needless to say, the most dedicated Unariun student, Vaughn, has added greatly and supplied much in the way of detailed description in this great project.

We here have been most desirous for eons of time that the earth people become familiar with our way of life; this information could help enable man to extend greater effort in his striving to overcome the bonds and ties of the earth world whereby he, too, can so manifest a greater degree of spiritual oneness and move forward toward the Light in this, the great Infinite Plan. Thus, go ye now forth with a full measure of Light, power and understanding, with our blessing! You have, in your immediate aura added angels, added messengers and all the spiritual help that could possibly be needed; for with you, it is, at the moment, impossible to conceive all that shall, in the future, take place through this your channelship.

Needless to say that we here in this great city of Light which you have just been visiting with us for the past few weeks, share our undying love and remain in constant attunement; that we shall ever henceforth, be an integrated part of your very being; that as you walk forth, we, in our consciousness and your inner attunements, shall be with you, yea, even beyond the ends of time.

It can now be related, dear sister, in your present position and promotions or ascendencies, that you now occupy the second most high position of this great Shamballa (Unarius) Organization. And that as you so accomplish this entire mission, the topmost chair you shall fill! Thus, we shall disconnect in our conscious attunement with the most radiant rays and blessings of light and love.

We know, at this point, you need not the individual names for we are in no way separated and are all of one consciousness. But for the sake of the readers not so aware, let us say we are those with whom you have been working and who have been helping you throughout these many, yes countless, thousands of years. Call us Faraday, Manu, Gabriel, Gamaliel, Copernicus, Hilarion, Galileo, Einstein, Ming-Tse, and many others.

Thus we come to the happy conclusion to the story we all wish would never end; yet we have found with repeat reading, greater awareness is experienced; the vast power within the word is regenerated. In reminiscing, we conceive what a tremendous and wonderful success this great celebration has been; the high honors paid to the queen (Ioshanna) and the Moderator, in their most successful mission on earth.

Then of utmost importance: the revelation of the quadrocentric polarity concept into which the four have evolved, creating a double love story; the unification of not only two Spiritual Beings but of four — a love story lived through one million years duration, in service! To reiterate: it is now, these four God Forces or Archangels — the Moderator, Raphiel, his biocentric Muriel; Leonardo da Vince (and/or) Nikola Tesla — Archangel Michiel; and Ioshanna is the other; Uriel, forming the quadrocentric Archangel polarity.

Then, the happy conclusion: The two biune forces being joined in their spiritual marriage as one — an inspiring achievement extending over eons of time and endeavor . . . How it was that Vaughn found the true identity of the Mona Lisa. Then last but indeed not least, the celebration of the victory after the successful climb up from great depths by the one who has, in the past, been the villain of our true life story and who has now actually become the hero — one who now works in and with the Light! Surely, no greater success story has ever been lived!

May your repeat readings be equally as inspiring as has been the first!

Ioshanna, Vaughn and the entire Hierarchy extend to you, each one, Infinite Love.

Addendum

September 19, 1973 –

    And now it is about four months since our beautiful experience of "The Conclave of Light Beings" has been concluded. We are well on the way of the "Tesla Speaks" books and tapes; in fact, we have just concluded tapes for Volume III, of the "Tesla Speaks" books. And what books they are!!! During these many, many dissertations and recordings of the countless hours of receiving and recording word from the Brothers on the Inner, and even the contacts with the various polarities on the thirty-three earth planets, we have kept necessarily in touch with the one in charge of these contacts, and so-called switchboard and the lens. Of course, I refer to the great master scientist of all times, the wonderful and beloved Nikola Tesla. He has been most gracious and a loyal, wonderful friend and brother, and there has been built up between him and myself, Ioshanna, the most beautiful rapport and feeling of oneness and infinite love, far beyond word description.

    As I queried within myself, "How come and how could it be that this infinite feeling could so exist when Leonardo da Vinci was the polarity to this one?" – it caused not a consternation but a question within my mind. One of my dear sub-channels here, who was acting in this capacity in this great work with the "Tesla Speaks" book,

559

popped out one day, "Tesla lived the life of Leonardo! He was da Vinci!" Of course, the sudden thought of it was a bit of a shock to me, and I said, "Oh, no!" I could not conceive that such a one as either of those mental and spiritually advanced and wondrous spiritual Beings, could possibly love one such as myself. And yet, after but a few moments of analyzing, I knew this to be true — and how perfectly natural that this should be; for when we look into the historical records and writings about the one Leonardo, we can see a great similarity in his extensive and infinite number of drawings of mechanisms of all varieties and nature, of the infinite nature of both Beings that could have become, shall we say, mental giant of all giants, as is known of the one, Tesla — and which has been likewise true of the beloved Leonardo.

As this question was posed to him just last evening, no reply was given. He maintained a silence. Such great souls and Beings would not pronounce themselves. They are so far beyond this type of concern or ego consciousness that they would step behind such a concept. Of course, he knew that within myself I knew this answer. Well, it became profoundly known within me that such a wonderful consciousness of both of these entities or lives were now indeed one great God Being, and it was truly too vast in my conscious mind to absorb or conceive. So this wonderful concept has grown within me, and it is still a bit much, to feel that such a wondrous Infinite Source of Creation could be the polarity or other half of this Being. It is an overwhelming concept and causes me great humility and wonderment — for my intellect seems far less.

Immediately afterwards, my mind was filled with the concept of the beautiful white dove story, which I remember Nikola had related in some of his writings, so this morning as I came down to the Center, Vaughn located here a book which he had purchased for me some time ago, called "Prodigal Genius — the Life of Nikola Tesla". From its pages I will ask Vaughn to read for you this beautiful story of Nikola and his dove. So, Vaughn, if you will please read from this book what this man wrote of Nikola. Vaughn: Yes, I shall read from the biography of Nikola Tesla, called the "Prodigal Genius", written by John J. O'Neill: (Last few paragraphs)

"The manifestation of these united forces of love and spirituality resulted in a fantastic situation, probably without parallel in human annals. Tesla told me the story; but if I did not have a witness who assured me that he heard exactly what I heard, I would have convinced myself that I had had nothing more tangible than a dream experience. It was the love story of Tesla's life. In the story of his strange romance, I saw instantly the reason for those unremitting daily journeys to feed the pigeons, and those midnight pilgrimages when he wished to be alone I recalled those occasions when I had happened to meet him on deserted Fifth Avenue and, when I spoke to him, he replied, 'You will now leave me.' He told his story simply, briefly and without embel-

561

lishments, but there was still a surging of emotion in his voice.

'I have been feeding pigeons, thousands of them, for years; thousands of them, for who can tell – but there was one pigeon, a beautiful bird, pure white with light gray tips on its wings. That one was different; it was a female. I would know that pigeon anywhere. No matter where I was that pigeon would find me; when I wanted her I had only to wish and call her and she would come flying to me. She understood me and I understood her. I loved that pigeon.' 'Yes,' he replied to an unasked question, 'Yes, I loved that pigeon! I loved her as a man loves a woman, and she loved me. When she was ill I knew, and understood; she came to my room and I stayed beside her for days. I nursed her back to health. That pigeon was the joy of my life. If she needed me, nothing else mattered. As long as I had her, there was a purpose in my life.'

'Then one night as I was lying in my bed in the dark, solving problems as usual, she flew in through the open window and stood on my desk. I new she wanted me; she wanted to tell me something important so I got up and went to her. As I looked at her, I knew she wanted to tell me she was dying. And then, as I got her message, there came a light from her eyes – powerful beams of light.'

'Yes,' he continued again, answering an unasked question, 'It was a real light, a powerful, dazzling, blinding light – a light more intense than I had ever produced by the most powerful lamps in my laboratory. When that pigeon died, something went out of my life. Up to that time I knew with a certainty that I would complete my work, no matter how ambitious my program, but when that something went out of my life, I knew my life's work was finished. Yes, I had fed pigeons for years; I continued to feed them, thousands of them, for after all, who can tell?'

''It is out of phenomena such as Tesla experienced when the dove flew out of the midnight darkness and into the blackness of his room and flooded it with blinding light, and the revelation that came to him out of the dazzling sun in the park at Budapest that proved the continuity of life and the oneness of all creation.''

Ioshanna: Although this added information was not related at the time of this Conclave book, I felt it helpful and needful to be added, for after all, is not this story the greatest love story ever told? It must be said my infinite love has grown the more infinite toward and with this wondrous and beautiful soul, whether we term him Leonardo, Tesla, or any one of the hundreds of thousands of names he has used and carried during the eons of past millenniums – and even before, is of no importance; the importance that exists is beyond relating. It is of course also this relationship, oscillation and the oneness of not only the duality between these two but also between the other quadrocentric – the Archangels of the Hierarchy. The Infinite Creative Oneness between these four as one polarity or an individual could never be related in words. Suffice to say, any one of the four of these Archangels, Raphiel, Muriel, Michiel or Uriel, is a source of creation or an intense God Force in himself. Yet when combined, the four, functioning as one, do indeed create a most incomprehensible and moving force of the Infinite. They are, of course, a creative source of the Infinite, expressing into all worlds.

As you will read in the "Tesla Speaks" books, Volume III, how these combined polarities, along with the assistance of the entire Logoi, the Hierarchy, and the entire Beings of the dwellers on the planet Eros and its sub-planets, have polarized, healed, lifted and changed the very total or complete frequencies of the entire thirty-three worlds momentarily, or in some instances, instantaneously. Need we say more?!!

Thus, the foregoing is simply related to show how man can, when he steps up on a more progressive evolution, when he gains understanding of this vast and wonderful interdimensional science we term Unarius, that he can move himself forward in a progressive and regenerative manner; that the inner spark and glow within each one can be fanned to become a luminous flame of light where he will become a greater part of this Infinite Itself, whereby he too, can oscillate these radiating powers, light and love to all mankind.

Ernest and Ruth Norman
at their marriage in 1954

Note

Now it may be wondered by the reader as to just why – since there are four of the Archangels of the first degree – so little mention is made of the others. Upon our inquiry it was learned that the great honors are being paid to the Channel on earth due, in great part, to the deliverance of the great Unarius library, the universal science of life – which the Moderator wrote, and which Ioshanna is now distributing to not only this Earth world but to fifty surrounding planets as well and who, in turn, will relate to other worlds.

So it is a stupendous and magnanimous plan and expression; one well deserving of any or all praise possible. Moreover, Ioshanna has evolved in countless lifetimes past, from one cycle to another in this endeavor, in preparation – yes, many thousands of lifetimes always was her biune or biocentric on the Inner as she so expressed in the outer, and vice versa – she aiding from the inner as he so expressed from the physical worlds.

You will remember, of course, their lives – he as the Master artist of all times, Leonardo da Vinci, and she as his model, Mona Lisa (from the inner). Then in a subsequent life he, as Nikola Tesla and she came to him as the dove to keep him company and share of her spiritual love.

In order to conceive of this great Intellect, one must needs read the vast and extensive works expressed by da Vinci as well as Tesla – when he extended himself in these earth bodies – to factually begin to conceive the unlimited qualities and abilities of this great Being – the giant of all geniuses and inventors – (working hand in hand with the Moderator from other dimensions). Many of the countless writings and creations Nikola Tesla evolved and brought to earth were rejected or prohibited by the U. S. Government. Now happily, and through his own inspiration and guidance, we have obtained a most invaluable copy of a most isolated and out-of-print book of this Master Mind Scientist. Even greater the news it shall be reprinted and published by Unarius – if for no other reason than to show the earthean what had been given these years past – and refused! These mechanisms, equipment and devices are as valid today as then.

Within Volume 3 of the Tesla Speaks books, will be described and illustrated some of these invaluable creations. Look forward to subsequent Tesla Speaks books and reproductions of his own writings when on Earth – in three volumes titled Nikola Tesla (1) Lectures, (2) Patents, (3) Articles.

Moreover, the beautiful and informative story, The Return of the Dove, shall likewise become a republication by Unarius – just as soon as funds permit.

It is realized of the other two biocentrics of the quadrocentric polarity that the Moderator Himself entered the Earth world but six times in this preparatory expression; namely, in the long ago Egyptian cycle, as Osiris and she Isis. (Thomas Miller was their son, Horus); then as

the first, great scientist Anaxagoras — she his
wife in Greece; as Akhenaton, the great Pharaoh,
Ioshanna then his mother — and the other important cycle as Jesus, and she with Him as his
beloved and betrothed Mary of Magdela. Now, the
pinnacle and concluding cycle for all the present
20th Century, which will be the final time any of
the four will needs return to an earth plane, but
they shall go on to greater heights, greater and
higher dimensions and galaxies to extend and
express in their creative ways, the Truth and
Light.

It is felt that the one Archangel Muriel, the
Moderator's biune, has not expressed extensively
on the earth planes. She too has not lived on any
earth world with her biocentric for they realize
the greater benefits derived by so extending
themselves and oscillating between the two
worlds — one from the inner, the other from the
outer or physical world. It is realized that other
than her life lived as Joan of Arc, Muriel has,
for the most part, spent the countless thousands
of years on far higher worlds and dimensions;
yet always has the inner connection been maintained with the Twin Ray.

It is indeed a great time of acclaim and celebration for all, yet the Brotherhood is extending
this vast acclaim, honor and homage toward,
especially, Ioshanna, as she still exists on the
Earth world; the other three being received in
their own manner and expression — yet these
celebrations were mainly for the one remaining
on Earth.

Yet too her time is short, and soon she shall join them in these three higher worlds. Although this word and prediction is a bit in advance, it is now foretold as to her – no not demise, but that her ascension shall be one of a demonstration that shall strike joy within the hearts of the earthean!

The earthean shall view this Being of Light make her departure from the Earth in a full blaze of glory! This shall be in full view of the many! Then man shall come to know that he is, indeed, much more than he now conceives himself to be – but a physical person.

Yes, then the four shall proceed to travel the skyways from not only planet to planet; for these are but footstools to the galaxies which shall be visited by this great quadrocentric of Infinite Light.

And now that four of the Tesla Speaks books have been received and one already published, (the others being printed), we learn that there shall be a greatest of all celebrations on the Higher Worlds upon the return of Ioshanna to these Inner Spheres of Light – a celebration that shall be carried on for one thousand years! We learn that countless thousands shall attend from all surrounding planets of a spiritual nature.

It has been inspired that although the Conclave Celebration was the largest and greatest gathering or celebration to take place on these Higher Worlds, that this event which will take place within the next few years, immediately upon her arrival there, will far surpass the former event many times! Countless millions shall in attendance be. It has been told that all have received their golden engraved invitations already!

Doubtless, many eartheans too, shall attend in their astral states. Of course one's frequency would thus make these astral flights possible, and the means to create the higher frequency is, of course, through conceiving the great Unarius texts. Yes, your study and conceiving will earn for you, your personal invitation to this, the greatest of all spiritual events ever staged.

And all men shall come to know
   that the bell has struck
And the reverberation shall bring
   the pure shafts of Light
   to the lightened hearts — all of life
To focus upon the greatest of all things,
   that is each and every point
   which can be conceived.

The inconceivable is only a step away,
   never stop thy seeking and you will
   find the way —
Each and every one unto that brightened day.

Search the width and breadth —
   the high and low of it
And you too will come unto that temple
   to sit and be bombarded by love's endeavor
Never ceasing in its compassionate love —
   yes, caress.

Tenderness does not decay nor fade away
   but only grows stronger
And in some future hour, you will be
   within the arms of Eternity

So be it unto all, each and every one
    who will open their eyes and look about
To visualize and see that it is Thee.

And I who have found no resting place,
    do exist in all existing space,
    which I love
And in thine arms will we all surround
    and be in touch with this soft and
    radiant smile on each face.

So there is no existing space —
When we come from every place.

A SONG OF FREEDOM

The Promise Fulfilled

(Additional Verse which the Moderator inspired
to and through Ioshanna three days after His
transition)

Not bound am I by any man
    No prisoner am I of flesh and bone
For I have loosed these bonds of mortal man
    And to my home among the stars I've flown.

Yea, free as the soaring eaglet who builds
    his nest atop the craggy mountain tops
That none may find his hideaway.
    Free as the snow-white swan
    that silently glides the waterways
And yet, he too is bound and bidden.

And only we of Spirit — free
For we who are of Spirit
Knoweth not of the limitations of the
    physical worlds
But dwelleth in the House of the Infinite Forever.

Now breaks a new resplendent Dawn
    uncluttered by the fears and woes of man
I've sung my Song — and I've told it well
    for you, my children, upon which to dwell.

Let your hearts be light and gay —
Love ye one another, as I have loved you all.
My Message of Infinite Intelligence is renewed

to you each — this day.
The Infinite in all its Creation
    must grow within your minds
Until you too shall be joined with Me —
    in spirit.

For you, dear ones, have found the true path —
    way that leads unto the Inner Kingdom
I come to prepare a place for you, that where I
    am, ye may be also.
Be joyful in the knowing this, the way for
    all mankind.
For man is truly of spirit
    and each man but awaits his time
When he too, shall break his bonds.

His self-created chains will fall
And he shall find his world was but
    a shadow of all that is to be —
A never-ending panoply of birth and rebirth
And the starry Heavens, to which you often gaze
    shall likewise become your new abode
When your song of freedom has thus been sung.

Only when man learns the Way of Spirit — of
    the Infinite
Can he loose these chains — yea, stronger
    yet than steel, are these ties
    which man creates and recreates for himself
To live and to live again
Yea, so long as he does thus remain
    in ignorance and in fear.

Let the Light of Unarius blossom forth

in all its Radiant Truth
For we, the Flame People of the Inner worlds
of Light
Come to you in full Consciousness —
and love.

The Infinite in all its Creative Intelligence
must grow within your minds
Until you too shall be thusly joined with Me
in Spirit
And live in the House of the Infinite Eternally.

So mote it be.

* * *

(To Ioshanna)

You'll see my face among the fleecy clouds
Not bound nor bidden by earth world ties
I'll come to you as the Summer Sun
And in the Winter's new fallen Snow
In the moonlit nite my Light will shine
within each sparkling Star.

I will come to you as a vagrant Breeze
to kiss the evening dew
My Voice will be the Voice of the Meadowlark
who'll sing the Song of Eternity
unto your waiting ears
Until the time I'll hold you once again
into my longing arms.

* * *

SEEK YE WITHIN

Through you, in Me, all things are made whole
The halt shall walk - the blind shall see
And man who hear-eth nought shall hear

For in Infinite Creation is the sum
      and substance of all things
The regenerative process is applicable
      to one and all
Beyond all space and time.

For man but binds himself
      in his ways and limitations
So self erected in his mind
He knoweth not of his true worth

He stumbles blindly in his groping ways
Thinking this, his world is all
      and that, in death, becomes his termination.

For he knoweth not the ways of spirit
And that each man was so created of spirit
For he seeks the ways and the answers to life
      in the most unlikely places -
In the synagogues and temples - where truth is not.
For have I not, in that long, long ago,
      dear brethren,

Taught you, upon that Galilean hillside bare
That the kingdom of Heaven is within each one

And that ye needeth but to so look Within.
Seek and ye shall find,
          yea, knock and the door shall be opened
          unto you
And ye shall dwell in the House of the Lord
          forever.

———————

SONG OF CREATION

I'll come to you as the baby's wail
          as he cries defiance strong
And in the turquoise-crested wave,
          as it scatters its foam to the shore
You'll see my face in each man's face,
          For I am the Infinite.

The tortoise, the fish, the ocean wide,
          all speak my name and sing my song.
I'll come to you in the warm sun's rays -
          in the fragrance of the unfolding rose
I'll come in the young child's laughter
          as he romps in childish glee

As the raindrops patter upon your roof
          playing a rapid tattoo
They too, will carry my message of love

Yes, there is no thing where I am nought
    for I am the Infinite

The birds will sing of my love to you
    as they flit from twig to twig
Carrying with them my message of cheer
    for you alone to hear

For man must be of the Infinite
    so minded in ways and thought,
That only you and I can know
Yet, this too, is each man's way -
    his future to so become
As he travels from life to life -
    and learns to sing the song
    of Creation
The song of Immortal destiny.

——————

So wear my rose, my love,
And wear it well for me
And in its delicate effulgence rare
    my breath of life is shared.
And as we live in beauty and in grace
    and travel from place to place
The Light that we share,
    the love that we know
Shall brighten every corner
Where now, no light doth shine.

——————

REQUIEM

Long were the nights whilst from my Heavenly home
    I strayed
The Days Eternal did become
Those long years lived upon your earth -
    your hot and rocky plains
Didst parch my soul and rob it well

    of all its Heavenly attributes.

My swan song sung - return I have
    unto my home amongst the stars.
And with these stars I shall forever more
    remain
I'll await the day when you, my love,
Shall take my hand outstretched
    and climb this golden stair
Ne'er to part no more -   to part no more.

NEW DAWN

Now breaks a new resplendent day
Not cluttered by the cares and woes
of yesteryear
My heart doth sing the melody of love -
    the song of creation
So carried by every breeze
    across the meadow green.

To touch the heart of man
    where 'ere that he may be
To light the flame of life
Within the chalice of his soul.

MESSAGE FROM TESLA

This is Nikola: Good evening to you all! My Beloved One who walks the Earth now, to her I wish to say that she is most precious to we here, and that you ones who are near her must realize what you have in your midst. She has taken on, through sacrifice, a fleshly body to extricate the souls who wish to progress out of your Earth world. So heed her words which are our words combined. Each and every one of you, and those who are to come, must be as the Light bearers for the future world.

She will not be among you much longer, even if you call it years; yet on the scale of the Infinite Mind, there is no time. So as she expresses that part of her you call Ioshanna, yet she is traveling worlds beyond your conception into new vistas, into new creations. So believest thou this and be proud, yet ever humble in the knowledge that you have the opportunity to express by her side.

We here, of the Higher Worlds never cease our appreciation and love to this One, for without her expression, there would be no new age.

The beloved Moderator has so expressed his love to us; He has left behind that which can only be carried on by the One such as Uriel. There is no other — and never will be! Keep this in mind always. Man, in the future, will see the fruits of this Beloved One's labor, and he will wish to eulogize these words and deeds, but this cannot be so, nor will it be allowed. You today, who have come unto your time and place to bear up this Light, must go forth and express these desires of the Hierarchy. And as she came to me many years ago, now I come to her!

The Archangel Uriel
Healing Angel of Light